The Collected Columns Vol. I
Innocence & Intellect, 2001-2005

Books by Vox Day

Non fiction

The Irrational Atheist
Return of the Great Depression
SJWs Always Lie: Taking Down the Thought Police
Cuckservative: How "Conservatives" Betrayed America
(with John Red Eagle)
On the Existence of Gods (with Dominic Saltarelli)
On the Question of Free Trade (with James D. Miller)

Arts of Dark and Light

Summa Elvetica: A Casuistry of the Elvish Controversy
A Throne of Bones
A Sea of Skulls

Quantum Mortis

A Man Disrupted (with Steve Rzasa)
Gravity Kills (with Steve Rzasa)
A Mind Programmed (with Jeff and Jean Sutton)

Eternal Warriors

The War in Heaven
The World in Shadow
The Wrath of Angels

Collections

The Altar of Hate
Riding the Red Horse Vol. 1 (ed. with Tom Kratman)

VOX DAY

The Collected Columns Vol. I

Innocence & Intellect, 2001–2005

CASTALIA HOUSE

The Collected Columns Vol. I
Innocence & Intellect, 2001-2005

Vox Day

Published by Castalia House
Tampere, Finland
www.castaliahouse.com

Cover: Markku Koponen
Photography: John Wagner

ISBN: 978-952-7065-67-9

Contents

Foreword

I N 2001, the *Drudge Report* was still a fresh concept. Joe Sobran was still alive and his weekly opinions appeared alongside Pat Buchanan's. In those days, it seemed that most right-wing notions came from the AM radio stations, as we listened attentively to Limbaugh and Savage. At the bottom of the *Drudge Report* was a link to *WorldNetDaily*, and on that website there were a wide variety of syndicated conservative writers, many of whom were not carried by my local newspaper.

One particular writer had a unique presence at *WorldNetDaily*. The black-and-white photograph of him showed a young man in his prime, sporting a cutting-edge haircut and a look in his eyes of aged wisdom. This mysterious character called himself Vox Day.

Back then, Vox was known for being a Christian libertarian. Though I never fully ascribed to his line of political thinking, his writings went deeper than politics, delving into a philosophy of life with which I could identify. This man represented a younger generation. Reading his work back then, I thought to myself that after the other archons of the American Right passed away, this man would still be around, and he would be a successor to the twentieth-century conservative political fathers.

Vox appeared to be some sort of mutant. While the usual talking heads on the Right were repeating textbook conservative slogans, Vox's words were electronic, upgraded, and fresh. At the very bottom of his articles was a link to his blog, *Vox Popoli*. Once I jumped through that gateway, I found myself on Vox's own turf, where he shared whatever political or philosophical thoughts entered his mind. His approach to the issues, in his articles and his blog posts, seemed unconventional; yet his discussions cut through so many barriers the Right could not bear to breach. He went over, above, and beyond the minds of traditional right-wing pundits. His articles touched on many different topics, from digital media, to political philosophy, to the supernatural, to the culture of the Millennial generation.

One article that I will always remember was titled "Satan, Science, and the Supernatural." It was unusual to mix these three elements in a discussion the way he did. It was a new way to look at things. He produced a synthesis of different elements at play in the world. Elements of American society that were often overlooked were brought together in different amalgamations that I did not expect. Though the overall points Vox made in those days seemed to escape the older conservatives, younger readers—such as myself at the time— were able to grasp where he was coming from. His consistent readers came to share many of his sentiments.

Vox's most notable stance was visible shortly after the terrorist attacks of September 11, 2001. His opinion went against the grain of much of the country—which seemed completely ready for all-out war. He recognized that America would have to be master of its own culture before it could successfully defeat an external enemy. The axioms of his arguments differed from those of many talking heads. In fact, most conservative commentators were emotional about the War on Terror. America had suddenly been transformed into a nation of warhawks. However, Vox was steady and consistent, to the point that he was at the forefront of a cultural change that most did not foresee. Readers would discover that Vox was at odds with many Americans who felt justified to send our military off to war in Iraq.

> *War corrodes a society by allowing centralist forces within government to excuse actions they would never be allowed to take in more peaceful times, by encouraging the dehumanization of the enemy population, and by providing an easy means of stifling reasonable dissent.*

It was 2002 when he wrote this, and his sentiment would not be manifested by Americans until the mid-term elections of 2006, when voters were fed up with the wars and turned their backs on a power-drunk Republican Party. By then, the electorate was well aware that their representatives had used the War on Terror to excuse their runaway abuses.

At first, I was not completely on board with his opposition to the war. For me, it took another year—and more of his convincing insight. Meanwhile, by the end of 2002, Vox was reflecting on democracy's failures. He boldly admitted he had no problems with discrimination, and he was openly calling out the flawed worship of diversity. Bear in mind that this was at a time when the word "cuckservative" did not even exist. The Right was still living in dread fear of being called racist, yet he stood by his principles in the face of renunciations.

Before Alex Jones' *Infowars* became an internet sensation, Vox Day was calmly challenging the encroachment of globalism, Big Brother, the IRS, and the loss of Americans' individual freedom. As the years passed, the headlines to his columns showed more contempt and dissatisfaction with a bankrupt culture, and one could see this frustration in titles like: "The Stink of America Rotting," and "The Wrinkled Whores of Wall Street." Vox never apologized for his firm opinions on the state of things. And though this negativity seemed discordant to the older archons of the Right, his headlines expressed precisely the sentiments of people my age.

You would look at a picture of Vox Day, reflect on the alien mohawk he sported, and you'd almost think he came from the future. It sure seemed as though he could predict it. This was not a blowhard emotional young narcissist with a flimsy opinion. He always knew what he was talking about. Nor was he a one-trick pony. By the time the tide was turning, and Americans were having second thoughts about what Vox called the "War on a Tactic," Vox was already discussing the state of America's failing economy. Comparing Keynesian and Austrian economics, reconsidering American policies on international trade, and exposing the lying financial media, his articles were some of the first to recommend caution in the expectation of a coming recession. He recommended people get out of debt and invest in metals. In mid-2003, Vox was already discussing an inevitable real estate crash that wouldn't happen for another five more years. His expression of America's disdain for crippling "free trade" would not be fully realized until President Donald Trump's election in 2016—almost a decade and a half later.

From the beginning of his time with *WorldNetDaily* in 2001, his writing seemed to surpass all of the typical right-leaning thinkers up until that point. And now, with the benefit of hindsight, we can see that almost every one of his positions from that early period have been vindicated by the recent events of 2016. I consider myself fortunate to have been able to discover such a writer from the beginning, and I truly feel as though I witnessed the embryonic stages of what would later become a great cultural change in America. Vox Day did not hesitate to call out the grinning jackals and betrayers of our nation from the very start. He was, and still remains to this day, ahead of the curve.

Laramie Hirsch
Tulsa, Oklahoma

Introduction

IN 1993, I began writing a game review column for the *St. Paul Pioneer Press*. The column was picked up by Chronicle Features for syndication, and appeared regularly in 13 newspapers around the country, including the *Atlanta Journal/Constitution*, the *Boston Globe*, the *San Jose Mercury News*, and the *North Bay Nugget*. After Universal Press Syndicate bought Chronicle Features, they dropped the column, but the *Atlanta Journal/Constitution* continued it for several years. In 2000, after seven years of weekly columns, I felt that I was beginning to phone them in, and therefore decided to retire the column.

I'd been reading *WorldNetDaily* for several years at that point. I even spoke to its founder, Joseph Farah, in 1998, and he had expressed interest in having me write for them. But I was busy developing *Traveller* for the Sega Katana with Julian LeFay, and so I passed on the opportunity, although my father did subsequently end up investing in WND. Over the years, some of my critics have claimed that Daddy secured the sinecure for me, a false narrative that not only has the nature of the relationship backwards, but is belied by the fact that I never accepted any money for writing columns from *WorldNetDaily*.

About a year after retiring my game review column, I started to miss all the games and various devices showing up at my house on a regular basis. I'd been reading *WorldNetDaily* regularly, so I knew their coverage of games and technology was virtually nonexistent. So, I called Joseph Farah and asked if he might still be interested in a weekly technology column, which turned out to be the case. I wrote about the humble USB port for reasons that are now unclear to me, and my WND column made its inauspicious debut on August 24, 2001. At no point had I ever given any thought to writing about politics or current events; in seven years of columns and feature writing, the only news-related article I'd ever written was an analysis of the Unabomber's manifesto in 1996, written at the request of the editor of the op/ed page.

As my editor described it, he'd said: "Give it to that kid with the mohawk, maybe he can make some sense of it."

Like most Americans, I was stunned by the events of September 11, 2001. My wife and I had moved to Italy two years before, and I can remember that it was a bright sunny afternoon. I was having an espresso with an American friend who had come to visit at the local bar when my wife called to tell me that a plane had flown into the World Trade Center. We were shocked, of course, and the reverberations of the attacks stretched across the globe, reaching even to our quiet little town, as my friend found his stay with us inadvertently extended due to the grounding of international flights over the following week.

I had a column due the next day, but I found it very difficult to think about anything besides the attacks and their probable ramifications. I was particularly concerned about what I saw as the likelihood that the Bush administration would use the attacks as an excuse to target and destroy American liberties. I asked Mr. Farah if he would mind if I wrote my column that week about the attacks, and after he agreed, I wrote what was published on September 14, 2001, as "Yield No More Freedom".

The response from the WND readership was exceedingly encouraging. It was one of the most-read columns on WND that week, and as a result, Mr. Farah encouraged me to branch out and start writing about current events in addition to my usual subjects. I was a little reluctant to do so, but as a long-time fan of Ann Coulter, I couldn't resist writing a column lauding her *WorldNetDaily* debut in November. I gradually became more comfortable writing about events, ideas, and people rather than technology and games, and by the time 2002 rolled around, I discovered, somewhat to my surprise, that I had rather more to say about the former than the latter.

After a second column, entitled "American public schools: Working just as designed" also generated an incredible amount of enthusiastic email, it became apparent that my column was rapidly becoming one of the more popular ones on the site. In fact, it wasn't long before it became the third-most-read weekly column on the site, trailing only those by Ann Coulter and Pat Buchanan. In order to make it difficult for the Left to dismiss the column as "stupid", their customary perjorative, I sent my PSAT scores into Mensa, ⑴⑴⑴ ⑴⑴ ⑴ ⑴⑴⑴ and joined the organization for a year. The Mensa membership was a useful addition to my column bio, which was still quite scanty when compared with all the various academic and political credentials brandished by my fellow columnists. It also enraged more than a few critics over the years, as the mere fact of my eligibility for the high-IQ society tended to weigh on the Left's intellectual insecurities.

The *WorldNetDaily* column had barely been running for a year when it was picked up for syndication in 2002 by Universal Press Syndicate, who were looking for a younger columnist to replace their longtime conservative headliner, William F. Buckley, who was preparing to retire his weekly column. Eighteen months later, having only managed to briefly sell the syndicated column to a single newspaper, the *Dallas Morning News*, Universal dropped the column with a note that explained why they felt their attempt at syndication failed.

> *After a survey of our salespeople and some reflection over the sales perfor-mance for past year-and-a-half, I've been given the mandate to tell you that Universal Press Syndicate has decided to terminate the active syndication of your column. The decision was based on the tightness of the text/column market, the immergence of Ann Coulter as a name brand and the sales division's inability to sell your column into newspapers.*

> *I think the strategy behind deciding to syndicate your column was the right one: a young, intelligent conservative to fill the void when/if some of our "old guard" stopped writing. Unfortunately, the market did not respond. I know we've talked about sales tactics, market truths and the realities of a modern-day newspaper editor, and I think all of these combined (along with Ms. Coulter's prominence) presented too much of an obstacle for us to overcome.*

Universal correctly viewed Ann Coulter—who they syndicated much more successfully—as the primary obstacle to the success of my syndicated column, since most newspapers only permitted a single right-wing writer to sully their editorial pages. And who can reasonably blame any editor who preferred to give that one slot to the woman who was already in the process of becoming the most influential voice of the Right over the next decade? But there was a more fundamental problem too. Universal had simply never understood that I was not, and had never been, a conservative, or that the Christian libertarianism I advocated was utterly alien to the secular liberals who guarded access to their opinion pages like miserly dragons sitting atop hoards of stolen gold.

Since I had warned Universal of that problem from the very start, I was neither surprised nor disappointed by the failure of the syndicated column. I never made any attempt to tailor my column for a broader audience, and indeed, I believe you will find it impossible to determine when the syndicated period began or ended from reading the columns collected in this volume.

I named this collection *Innocence & Intellect* because, when looking back at the columns from this period, those are the two significant features one tends to take away from them. While many of the columns contain a credible level of intellectual analysis, the effectiveness of that analysis is somewhat reduced by the undeniable naiveté of both the author and the times. Remember, 2001 was only eight years after Francis Fukuyama published *The End of History and the Last Man*, declaring the final and eternal triumph of secular liberal democracy over all other forms of government. It was the same year that Karl Rove spoke of Republican dominance that would last a generation, and three years before the Speaker of the House, Tom Delay, told Republicans to "start thinking like a permanent majority".

The period from 2001 through 2005 was a time when it was still possible to imagine the U.S.A. as the global policeman, bringing freedom and capitalism and liberal democracy to benighted nations everywhere from Moscow to the Middle East. It was a time when Hispanics were seen as "natural conservatives", the Euro was assumed to be an economic benefit to the European economies, and purple-fingered Iraqis were believed to be freedom-loving devotees of democracy. It was a time when serious economists declared the Dow would reach 36,000, economic growth would continue indefinitely, and housing prices would rise without limit.

It was an innocent and foolish time.

In discussing how to present the columns collected in these three volumes, we considered several options. Initially, I had favored sorting them by category, putting all the economics columns in one section, the columns devoted to presidential campaigns in another, and so on. I'd also considered annotating them. But upon further reflection, I decided that it is much more useful to read them in the order they were originally published, because doing so serves as an educational glimpse into a period of recent history that is now not only gone, but one that already appears almost unbelievable, even to those of us who lived through it and can still remember it clearly.

Vox Day
January 29, 2017

Yield no more freedom

September 14, 2001

I N RESPONSE to a number of questions inspired by last week's column, we were working on a piece related to PC security, specifically the sort offered to one's e-mail communications by various encryption technologies, when we were interrupted by the horrifying events of Tuesday. The fatal hijackings and subsequent media response has been difficult to dismiss from our mind, so we have tabled the usual technology review for a week in favor of some reflections on these recent events.

One of the many troubling aspects of the hijackings is the brutal demonstration that we, as a people, have received very little of the security we were promised in return for the many violations of personal freedom and civil liberties that have been enacted over the past decade. We would go so far as to raise the question if this had not been a fool's bargain, wherein we have given up something of precious value in return for… arguably, nothing. It is bad enough that we allow the FBI to filter our e-mails and record our keystrokes, that we permit the National Security Agency to intercept every electronic communication floating through the aether, but it is even worse that we have done so without realizing that which we hoped to gain.

Just as the drug war has not reduced the amount of illegal drugs used in this country, the sacrifice of our civil liberties on the altar of national security has not brought us security. Keep this in mind, as the inevitable drumbeat begins for more sacrifices, as the calls begin for Americans to give up even more of their hard-won freedoms. National security cannot seriously be cited any longer in the attempts to ban personal encryption technology, not when, as WorldNetDaily reported yesterday, far better forms of communications encryption have already been delivered to terrorist-sponsoring states like Syria with the full approval of the previous administration.

It is said that the price of freedom is eternal vigilance, but that vigilance must be applied within as well as without. A thousand suicide bombers could not destroy America, but America is quite capable of destroying itself in the pursuit of any number of false idols, among them wrongheaded and illusory notions of security at any price. Individual privacy, like private property, is one of the foundations of our freedom, and it must not be thrown away out of fear. Anonymous cell phones or encrypted e-mail missives could be used by a terrorist, true, but the same is also true of a razor blade or a flight simulator.

What our leaders must realize is that personal technology is not a foe, but a powerful ally. The enemy we face can be subdued and contained by soldiers, bombs and a strong national will, but it cannot be ultimately defeated through conventional war. But satellite transmissions and the Internet know no borders, nor does the concept of freedom. Our enemies recognize this, which is why they fearfully denounce every sign of American influence as decadence, because they well know that they cannot raise another generation of suicide warriors if that generation is allowed to partake of the dangerous and forbidden fruit of freedom.

Some have protested that America must not strike back, that doing so will only perpetuate the "cycle of violence", that others will only rise up to replace those we strike down. But this is demonstrably untrue, as no German ever rose up to replace Hitler, nor does a Japanese war party trouble us today. It is appropriate for a nation to fight a war in its own defense, especially when war has been openly declared upon it. But in doing so, we must resolutely resist the call to sacrifice that which makes the United States of America a country worth defending—our inalienable rights and our individual freedom.

QUESTION OF THE WEEK: Why not cover Mac, since they have innovated almost everything the windose world has adapted to their inferior technology?

THUS SPAKE VOX: Using this reasoning, we should be devoting space to Xerox, who invented, among other things, the graphical user interface, the mouse and the ethernet link, subsequently "innovated" by Apple. The candy-coated computer shells, OK, that we'll give you, although we confess to being utterly mystified by their unquestioned appeal to the masses. However, it is clear to us that there are a lot of Mac fans who read this column, and so we have, as promised, contacted Apple.

E-mail encryption made easy

September 21, 2001

I T IS OUR ASSERTION, concomitant with the Fourth Amendment right to the security of one's person, house, papers and effects, that no one should have the ability to snoop through your e-mail without your permission. We stand by this, even in light of last week's terrible hijacking attacks, which have led to calls for the concession of even more intrusive eavesdropping power to the various federal agencies. While we have no intention of revisiting last week's subject of liberty and the propriety of secure personal communications, we do hope to explain how you can make use of available encryption software to protect your own e-mail.

The most popular solution is PGP, otherwise known as Pretty Good Privacy. Based on the public key/private key concept introduced by Whitfield Diffie and Martin Hellman in 1976, PGP offers a quick and relatively easy way to encrypt your e-mail to ensure that it is not read by your employer, your ISP, packet data sniffers, the NSA's Echelon system, the FBI's Carnivore or anyone else with whom you'd rather not share your information. It is perhaps worth noting that while there was some discussion of pursuing PGP's creator, Paul Zimmerman, for the violation of U.S. export controls a few years ago, there is no law banning the personal use of encryption software. Nor, in our opinion, should there be.

The dual key approach is simpler than you might think upon first looking at the program. The concept is easiest to understand if you forget about the software for a moment. Imagine that you have a mailbox dedicated to your sole use. One key, called the public key, is required to put a letter addressed to you in the mailbox, but cannot be used to open the mailbox. Another key, the private key, is needed to open the mailbox and take the letter out. Without this second key, no one can open the mailbox and read the letter, not even the sender. This is why there is no harm in allowing your public key to be widely distributed, as it is essentially just a means of putting letters into your private mailbox.

Some of the older versions of PGP were a pain to use, but with the new version, 7.0.3, we are pleased to say that operation is almost shockingly smooth. For reasons we are still trying to understand, we are in the habit of using MS Outlook Express for our regular e-mail, and PGP works in such nice coordination with it that the only explanation is that Microsoft is too worried about upsetting the U.S. Department of Justice to directly incorporate PGP and screw it up by making it "more user-friendly."

Keeping out the NSA

September 28, 2001

A HEIGHTENED INTEREST in the subject of personal communications security is quite understandable in the light of some of the U.S. federal government's more unfortunate responses to the Sept. 11 attacks. And while we are more interested in discussing the technological implications than the political, we do question both the utility and motivation behind the attempts to violate Americans' Fourth Amendment rights while at the same time "building an anti-terror coalition" with noted anti-terrorists such as Arafat, Putin and Assad.

Many readers have indicated some level of concern about the security of PGP 7.0.3, so we have done some research and spent a few cycles cogitating upon the e-mail encryption system's various vulnerabilities. Last week, we specifically mentioned three problems: back doors, Van Eck freaking and brute force attacks. Of the three, it is back doors that are the most worrisome, primarily because NAI's refusal to release the program's source code to the public precludes the ability to verify that there are no back doors, PKZ's statement to the contrary notwithstanding.

A back door is an intentional security flaw designed directly into the software, allowing a third party to read messages encrypted by the first party intended only for the second party. We have tried to think about how a back door could be reasonably introduced into PGP, and have come up with three possibilities:

Generally speaking, we believe it would be very difficult for a reasonably sized, bureaucratic technology company to create a back door of the sort we have mentioned without word of it leaking out somehow. We are not too concerned about the possibility, especially considering that the alternative for most people is not to encrypt their e-mail at all, leaving it wide open for perusal by even the clumsiest hacker. On the other hand, we just don't like the fact that there is a reasonable basis for suspecting vulnerability, however unlikely.

There are at least two solutions to the problem of potential PGP vulnerability. One is to add another level of encryption. We logged on to Hushmail the other day, and while we applaud their embrace of the Open PGP program, we have some issues with the very concept of secure web-based e-mail, especially one that appears to require the use of ActiveX controls. But pasting an encrypted PGP message into Hushmail, thus encrypting it a second time with Hushmail's Open Source (independently verified free of back doors, etc.) system, should add an additional level of protection.

Another option is to bag Windows altogether and make use of an Open Source program like GnuPG, which requires the use of LINUX as an operating system. Despite the rapid improvements in the various forms of LINUX, this is not yet a serious alternative for most casual computer users, but we will be writing a future column on exactly how difficult one can expect the switch to be, as well as likely problems to be encountered. One big positive for LINUX, though, is that it does not have anywhere near the amount of security holes as the various Microsoft products, both accidental and otherwise. With the approach of Windows XP and its ominous Big Brother approach to ID'ing and tracking online users, we expect a lot of people are going to be looking for alternatives to the Evil Empire. (Note to Mac fans: We already e-mailed Apple. If they can't bother to reply, don't blame us.)

So we encourage the use of Hushmail and GnuPG, and we eagerly await the release of a solid Windows-based Open PGP solution that integrates seamlessly with the popular e-mail packages. But do keep in mind that it is far better to make use of encryption that has only potentially been penetrated, like PGP, than to make use of none at all.

ISSUE OF THE WEEK: Oracle Chairman Larry Ellison. National ID card for all Americans. What is up with that?

THUS SPAKE VOX: Larry Ellison is a Nazi rat bastard. He is the intellectual descendant of a long, ignominious line of industrialists like Gustav Krupp, who wrote to Adolf Hitler upon the occasion of the Fuhrer's ascension to power in 1933: "The turn of political events is in line with the wishes which I myself and the Board of Directors [of the Reich Association of German Industry] have cherished for a long time."

Unlike us, Larry "Your Papers, Please" Ellison doesn't care about the Fourth Amendment. "Well, this privacy you're concerned about is largely an illusion," he says. Which naturally brings to mind the Platonic notion that "no Being or reality can be ascribed to Not-being." And who could deny the wisdom of Aristotle when he wrote that "all men by nature desire to know"? On this philosophically sound basis, we are thus convinced that it would be impossible for Herr Ellison to object in any way to the public release of his social security, credit card and cellphone numbers. Had we a heart, it would surely be its fervent desire to see those lovely little bits of information floating wild and free across the great savanna that is the Internet.

High-tech hoops

October 5, 2001

G AME REVIEWS are always tough. Not because we find it difficult to pronounce judgment one way or the other, but because it is almost impossible to properly play through a modern game in the short window of opportunity that exists while a game is still hot. This is primarily because there are approximately three billion games being produced every year, most of them by obscure French companies intent on exploring the comedic possibilities inherent in hiring cheap translation services.

But we fear nothing, least of all the accusation of being untimely. Let others be the first on the market, the fastest; we, on the other hand, stake claim to being massively thorough. We have played this game, yea, we have played a lot of this game, which is why this review of NBA Live 2001 appears almost in time for the ritual anointing of the Los Angeles Lakers that is otherwise known as the 2002 NBA season. If the purple-and-gold clad Minneapolis expats didn't blow up for the Zen Master last year, there's no way they're going to fall apart now, not even if Paul Allen adds another pyschopathic malcontent to the seething mass of lithium deuterium that is the Portland Trail Blazers. Six championships in a row is the only way the Lakers can overshadow the fantastic achievements of the Zen Master's Bulls teams, and don't be thinking that thought hasn't crossed Kobe "Keyshawn" Bryant's mind.

NBA Live 2001 is not only the latest version of EA Sports' venerable basketball franchise, it is possibly the only way you will ever see Allen Iverson voluntarily passing up a shot. We know it is a cliche, but the graphics are truly fantastic. While the players' faces are only vaguely recognizable, and demonstrate about the same range of expression as Keanu Reeves, their movements are fluidly athletic, even graceful, much like their real-world counterparts.

Crossovers, stuttersteps, 360 jams and the awkward, double-foot stomping hopscotch dunk are all in there.

Unlike many sports games, though, the AI-controlled players are smart enough, at least on the two more advanced levels, to force you to play a team game. Unlike past NBA Lives, you can't simply drive into the lane and jam over and over again. In fact, this formerly successful tactic will likely see you quickly fouling out with six charging calls. An open shot is much easier to hit than one with a defender in your face, as it should be, although this doesn't necessarily hold true for Steve Smith of the Blazers, who is apparently possessed of supernatural powers from behind the three point line. He regularly dropped 30 or more points on us in one hard-fought series until we were forced to send Kevin Garnett out to double him, at which point Rasheed Wallace went postal on the low post and… we don't want to talk about it. Suffice it to say that the Timberpuppies went home in six with their tails between their legs.

So the graphics are very good. The gameplay action is great, with a few minor flaws, but nothing that seriously detracts from sucking casual bystanders into the game to the point that even the most disinterested viewer will be inspired to shout such things as: "Chauncy Billups's open on the wing… don't– don't– didn't you see Chauncy open on the wing?" To which, of course, the correct response is to say, "Yes, darling, I did indeed see that Mr. Billups was open on the wing, but what you don't understand is that Mr. Billups is more likely to hit the guy sitting in the fifth row behind the basket than the bottom of the freaking net!" Pssst… here's a hint if you're playing with the Timberwolves. Give the ball to KG.

Unfortunately, NBA Live lacks that certain something that would help it approach true legendary status. Two certain somethings. There's no franchise mode, which means that one season and out is all you've got. No team building, no skinny rookies with fake names and rabid hops, and, in the end, a lack of the endless, just-one-more-season appeal that makes the mere mention of John Madden's NFL game drive otherwise videogame-friendly women to physical violence. What may well have been Spacebunny's quote of the year was a hilarious, if unladylike, response to Pat Summerall's endlessly repetitive use of the phrase: "Right up the middle, can't find a hole." "Just find the d   hole already, will you!"

The other thing missing is a fantasy draft, which precludes the possibility of stacking a team with a collection of talent against which the other teams don't have a chance. Well, unless you're playing with the Lakers, that is. The classic all-star teams dating back to the '50s are cool. The one-on-one streetball stuff is fun. But the lack of fantasy and franchise options really does detract from the ability of the game to hold your attention for more than, maybe, three months solid. But it is a very well-produced game that is a lot of fun for the serious basketball fan as well as the more casual video gamer. We give NBA LIVE 2001 a solid 8 out of 10.

Mistake of the Week: Just wanted to let you know that GnuPG is available for Win32.

Thus Spake Vox: Yep, our bad. We abase ourselves. GnuPG does not, in fact, require LINUX, and we thank Andrew, Pierre and Michael, each of whom took the time to correct us. GnuPG for Windows is a reasonable alternative for those concerned with potential backdoors in PGP 7.0.3. Another reader wrote in to recommend an alternative web mail encryption site at MailVault. Unlike Hushmail, this program does not require any ActiveX or OCX programs, which are potential security risks.

Parlez-vous français?

October 12, 2001

I T'S NOT ALWAYS the most expensive software that works best for every-day use. For example, there's Microsoft's Picture-It, which runs high dollar for a massive box full of graphics applications that soak up a statistically significant percentage of your hard drive and isn't nearly as useful for viewing your digital pictures as a humble little shareware program like IRfan.

The same is true with language software. We have a certain interest in communicating with humans of the non-English speaking variety, and so we have tried a number of different language CDs, most of which boast various extraneous capabilities such as record and playback, video clips, and any number of features that turn out to be basically useless when trying to learn how to say much beyond the "hey, what's up?" level, or more precisely, the "good day, how art thou?" level, as most of this sort of language instruction seems to focus on how the nationalized broadcasting system wishes people would speak instead of the way they actually "parlay the fransay."

What has been an interesting discovery over the last few years is the process in which we have learned our various human tongues. Following the first stage, otherwise known as "I can't understand a word you are saying," is the heady second stage, the "Check this out—I can actually talk this smack!" phase. Unfortunately, the third stage is a long and frustrating one, namely, "OK, I know this one... hold on... wait... oh, forget it... sounds like..." This is the point at which you start to realize that while you may understand everything involving grammar, pronunciations and irregular forms, what is now holding you back is your vocabulary.

Enter WinFlash. We have the hots for this little program. Were she human, she would be that adorable 5'2" blonde for whom you have a total jones but you figure is probably just a bit on the young side when she unexpectedly walks over and reveals that she's not only already graduated from law school but has passed the bar and is now a junior partner at a downtown law firm and, by the way, is wondering if you might like to join her for a margarita over Happy Hour. At which point you suddenly lose your entire ability to speak English or any other language and are reduced to dumbly nodding your acceptance and praying that you don't say anything too blitheringly stupid when you're finally able to make use of your voice again.

So what, precisely, is this fair object of our infatuation? Essentially, Win-Flash is a computerized system of flash cards. You build a deck using one of four possible card styles, Standard, Fill-in-the-Blank, Multiple Choice or True/False. Standard is just a basic flash card, with two sides that can be filled with text, graphics or sound files. For language purposes, we tend to most frequently use the Fill-in-the-Blank style, with the English word on one side and the foreign word on the other. It's not necessary, of course, but we like the added challenge of not only knowing the word but spelling it properly, too.

We have been most impressed with the results of using the program. After downloading an Italian deck of 650 verbs, our average success rate went from less than 20 percent to over 65 percent in three weeks. This did not involve particularly a serious effort, as we have simply run through 100 random cards twice a day, which involves two six-minute sessions, for a total daily time commitment of around 12 minutes. This expanded vocabulary has translated into an improved speaking ability as well, as Italian-speakers of our acquaintance were left with the impression that we had begun taking language classes again. Not bad for a program that, at $25, is one-third the price of other, fancier language aids.

In addition to the vocabulary drill, we've also found that WinFlash works quite well as a workbook substitute. We took the liberty of copying one of our workbooks into the card format and have found that the ability to repeatedly run through an exercise on the computer is a lot easier than writing it out on paper. Not to mention the fact that we're a lot more likely to have our laptop handy at random moments than one of our language workbooks. WinFlash supports a variety of characters through customizable icon bars, so the various oddities in Italian, German and Spanish are easily accommodated for.

WinFlash also includes a fair amount of options, so if you want to set things up in categories, randomize your decks, run through reverse sides, set specific time-scales and keep track of your correct percentages, you can do all those things. It is a bit of a do-it-yourself program, despite the existence of various language decks (including Guarani! Yes, Guarani!), as well as other random decks such as those used for learning "common non-neoplastic conditions," "amino acids and their chemical structures," and of course, "Chemical, Biological and Radiological Warfare," contributed by Mr. S. Hussein. OK, the web site says that the CBR Warfare deck was actually contributed by somebody called Todd Fowler, but we all know that's just a nom de plume.

You can find all of these downloadable decks, as well as a 30-day trial version, at http://www.openwindow.com. Being a big fan of the software, we've pestered Mr. Bryant, the creator of WinFlash, and learned that he is currently working on a new version 7.0, which will reportedly offer, among other things, the ability to handle up to six fill-in-able blanks per card, which is just the thing for verb conjugations. For teachers, there's also a version of WinFlash which is designed to handle the production and management of tests—WinFlash Educator, which runs $34.95. If you're trying to learn pretty much anything requiring rote memorization, we highly recommend you check this out. Dude, Guarani! How can you not check it out?

QUESTION OF THE WEEK: Recently I read about a device that provides excellent telephone conversation privacy. It is also affordable by consumers. I just can't remember what it was called or how to get additional info about it. Would you be familiar with any such device?

THUS SPAKE VOX: We've never heard of it, but perhaps one of our readers has. So how about it... anyone... anyone... Bueller? E-mail us and we'll pass it on. We would also like to thank the reader who contributed the theory that Mr. Larry Ellison, Apple board member and Nazi rat bastard, is behind Apple's refusal to respond to our uncharacteristically polite request to review their Macintosh products. It's probably not true, but we'd sure like to think that it is.

Admiring Ann Coulter

November 6, 2001

THERE'S A LOT TO LIKE about Ann, WorldNetDaily's new columnist. Not only is she hot, slender and blonde, but she is possessed of wisdom and a wit sharper than a micro-surgeon's laser. She is always must-see TV, as there are few sit-coms to rival the good humor of seeing Ann verbally dissect some poor liberal sap who can't believe that this particular woman has dared to disdain the Talibanesque purdah of the infantile Gerberism that passes for feminist thought these days.

In fact, my admiration for Ann is such that she is one of two celebrities, (the other being David Spade), with whom I am forbidden to meet. Not because my wife is lacking in the hot, slender and blonde departments, but because, as she freely admits, she is weak on constitutional law. And, come to think of it, my love's lack of slashingly acidic wit isn't such a bad thing when I've forgotten to take out the trash for the third time that week.

But oh, that poise, and that elegant, swan-like neck. And that rat-tat-tat of irrefutable logic, suppressing the idiotic assertions of Democrats and the unsupportable protestations of left-wingers like a 50-caliber machine gun working over a poorly sandbagged hillside bunker. Those exquisite insults, at times slipped in almost imperceptibly like a Venetian assassin administering a silent coup de grace with a glass stiletto, at others delivered with the sledgehammer cruelty of a ninth-inning Yankee bat.

Where Ann is at her finest, where her thinking is most fundamentally sound, though, is on the question of the American liberal. She despises this odd creature, whose very appellation is a falsehood, who like the bastard offspring of Frankenstein's monster and a rabid cocker spaniel attempts to bite not only the hand of the very concepts that feed it, but those that gave it life in the first place. Has there ever been a creation so perverse in all the history of Man? To the question, are they evil or are they stupid, we can only answer: Yes!

So, Ann, I beg of you: Don't let your publisher steal from us the precious pearls of your outrageous scorn. Six hundred fifteen pages of obloquy and derision heaped on that most deserving of beasts—oh, that there were a thousand!

How eagerly I await this masterly tome, sure to be a classic in the line of Gibbon's "Decline and Fall," or at least P.J. O'Rourke's "All the Trouble in the World." Ann is not so much a treasure as a precious American resource, more graceful than the Golden Gate Bridge and more necessary than the *New York Times*, the *Washington Post* and *ABCBS/NBCNN* combined. Dulce et decorum est, how fitting and proper it is, that the finest conservative American columnist has finally made her stately way to WorldNetDaily.

Thinking the unthinkable

November 13, 2001

I LEARNED A BITTER LESSON in thinking about the unthinkable last winter. We had two dogs, one of which, a Rottweiler, had a distinct predisposition for roaming. We were living in a secluded area which didn't have much traffic, and where most of the dogs are allowed to run free. While I was concerned about the dog getting hit by a car, I felt reassured after being told by those more familiar with the area that I did not have anything to worry about. And after a few weeks, I relaxed my strict safety-first philosophy and was letting her run around off-leash like everyone else.

When she was hit and killed by a car five months later, it was cold comfort to hear that I was not to blame, that it wasn't really my fault because I was "just doing what everybody does." Because it was my fault, and the fatal accident would have been easily prevented had I only continued to do what I knew I should. What I learned from the incident is that what everybody does is to refuse to admit the possibility of the unpleasant, even when they have good reason to know better. It was both ironic and infuriating to learn later that several of the people who had assured me that nothing bad was likely to happen had lost more than one dog to cars themselves, some in that same area.

What is unthinkable about the current situation is not that al-Qaida might release biological agents into the water supply, or set off a nuclear device in a shipping port. If Islamic terrorists are indeed responsible for the Sept. 11 attacks, and there is every indication that they are, then it has already been made abundantly clear that there are no limits to their willingness to wreak death and devastation on the United States. Whatever weapons they have will be used. Furthermore, it defies logic to believe that with the terrorists' financial resources and their connections to states like Iraq and the Islamic republics of the former Soviet Union, they do not have access to both biological agents and some form of fissionable material. Indeed, the Israeli arrest of a terrorist in possession of a crude dirty bomb—a radiological dispersal device, a conventional weapon designed to disperse poisonous radioactive material—is almost certain proof that they have such weapons and intend to use them against us.

But as hideous as these thoughts are, they do not fall into the realm of the unthinkable. No, what is more troubling by far is the notion that the U.S. government is somehow complicit with these terrorists, or is permitting them relatively free reign in which to operate. This may sound ludicrously paranoid, of course, but the facts are such that the concept demands a fair hearing. It is not an impossibility, after all. We know beyond any shadow of a doubt that the federal government has been blatantly lying to the American people about many things ranging across a wide spectrum of events, from the ratification of the 16th Amendment to the 1983 bombing of the U.S. embassy in Beirut to TWA Flight 800 and Oklahoma City and many other, less significant events.

The question, as always, eventually comes down to the central issue of incompetence or evil. While I myself have tended toward the incompetence argument for many years, over time I have come to rethink my position. My reason is that history repeatedly shows that in every society, there are those who are not content with the wealth and power which they already possess, who ardently lust after the ability to exert power over their fellow men. The histories of Athens, Byzantium, and Rome are filled to the point of monotony with the repetitive accounts of one power-seeking scheme after another. Does it not seem ludicrous to assert that such a driving aspect of human nature has been somehow defanged by our republican form of democracy, especially when our current culture puts the lie to the myth of human progress in a thousand different ways? Abraham Lincoln, no innocent when it came to the art of power, warned about such men, and our founding fathers structured the Constitution in such a way as to defend against their ambitions.

There is not the space, in this single column, to explain the Socratic roots of the perverted Hegelian thinking that would justify the deaths of 5,000 innocents in order to establish order out of chaos. But two things should be made clear. First, there are elements both within and without the federal government that are at war with the U.S. Constitution. These elements have both motive and opportunity to, at the very least, make use of the current situation to further their insidious ambitions to become what they already believe themselves to be, what Plato once called the Guardians of the State.

Second, it is not only dangerous, but illogical to expect the federal government to protect you. Federal courts have determined that even the state police have no responsibility for you. Furthermore, it is insane to expect the same institution which provides inferior schools and many other inferior services to provide superior security. It is worth remembering that the only effective defense measures on Sept. 11 were those taken by the private citizens on United Flight 93. This will, I suspect, only become more and more clear over time, and I hope that freedom-loving Americans will respond by embracing their responsibilities and refrain from turning in fear toward the only entity that is capable, in the end, of destroying their liberty.

.

An ode to e-mail

November 14, 2001

IT'S EASY TO FORGET the benefits of new technology, especially those that are so nifty that we quickly integrate them into our daily lives. Let us, then, take a moment to reflect on the wonderful invention that is e-mail. This is an apt moment in which to do so, especially in light of the terrorist attacks and the harrowing reality of anthrax in the mail, two Very Bad Things which only serve to remind us of our blessings in having such a fantastic method of communication at our disposal.

E-mail is, first of all, an amazing testimonial to the power of the free market. The creative destruction of the market is such that not even two centuries of government monopoly on the mail could prevent the development of e-mail. A letter, after all, is basically just a string of text, and since text takes up such a miniscule amount of bandwidth, there is essentially no way to prevent people from sending a chunk of text from one computer to another. So e-mail is faster than a first-class letter, it is cheaper than a first-class letter and, best of all, the only viruses that can be attached to it are those of the electronic variety. Sure, it can be a pain to have to reformat your hard drive, assuming you fail the stupid test and actually run an executable file sent you by a stranger, but that sure beats fighting for your life in the intensive care unit.

Those of my generation are fortunate to have lived through very few disasters, (as of yet, anyhow), but it was interesting to note some of the differences between the terrible events of Sept. 11 this year, and the large earthquake that hit the Bay Area eleven years ago. Thanks to e-mail, I had received word that all of my friends, family and acquaintances in New York were safe less than three hours after the second tower collapsed. Contrast this with all of the frantic phone calls being made by friends from San Francisco, some of whom were not able to get in contact their families until the following day because the Bay Area phone system was overloaded.

Another great thing about e-mail is that you can send it from anywhere. It doesn't matter if you're in Prague or Sydney, as long as you can beg, borrow or rent an Internet connection, you're in business. On the afternoon of Sept. 11, it was clear from the e-mails we received that people were gathering together wherever someone had a solid online connection and were taking turns spamming all of their friends and relatives in order to let everyone know they were all right. The message below from one college friend was typical of those we received that day.

"I live not far from the former World Trade towers. I'm currently a little further north at my friend's house with quite a few people watching TV and using his connection. I'll give you a detailed one when things settle down here… I don't want to tie up the e-mail from others."

E-mail is so efficient that, thanks to an ancillary development—the mailing list—entire communities of people with shared interests are able to keep in contact on a daily basis. For the last three years, I have been a member of a mailing list which is a small group of around 700 people living around the world who play an obscure and complex game of World War II infantry combat. In all that time, I have only met 20 or so list-folk in person, but nevertheless, I have gotten to know many of them well as friendly acquaintances. We use our list mainly to discuss the game and its rules, but also to set up tournaments, congratulate each other on little things like marriages, children or winning the World Series co-MVP, and to recommend hotels and restaurants to list-folk visiting town.

Not that e-mail is perfect. While it's easier to trash spam than junk mail, it is nevertheless annoying. And who doesn't know someone with a terminal case of Forwarding Finger, that odious bane of humanity who simply can't resist passing on the many painful, cliché-ridden essays with their afternoon-school-special philosophies that infest the Internet like kudzu. Myself, I'm not sure which is worse, forwarded spam or the professional variety. Would you rather read something with the subject "re:re:re:Send This To 10 Strong Women You Know" or try to explain to your Significant Other why "Hot Nude Teens" keep showing up in your inbox? It's like having to decide whether Dan Rather or Peter Jennings is your favorite spawn of Satan… I mean, unbiased news anchor.

But isn't spam really a small price to pay for the ability to give the proverbial avian salute to the U.S. Postal Service, who—come rain, sleet, snow, Hell or high water—will tell you that they really, really, really need to raise the price of a first-class stamp again. I'm proud to say that I don't even know what that price is anymore, and that is thanks, of course, to e-mail. Let's face it, the art of written communication was dying out because of the telephone, and it is only back in style due to e-mail and its younger European cousin, the mobile-phone text message: 1 tht wud no dbt confuze shakespr n prbly outrite kill mr danl webster but still its riting, k?

Even before the onset of home delivered bio-warfare, there was no question that e-mail is a tremendous improvement over the traditional post office. More than just a convenience, it has also been a small step forward in the cause of human freedom. But here's a thought to ponder: Isn't the propaganda and shallow misinformation delivered to your door by newspapers like the *New York Times*, the *Washington Post* and many local rags like the *Minnesota Star & Sickle* all too similar to an anthrax for the mind? Just as e-mail has taken the place of the postal service, it is time for the online New Media to replace the ideological monolith of the mainstream news media.

Bias in your face

December 31, 2001

I CAN'T SAY I'M SURPRISED by much I've heard about Bernard Goldberg's new book, *Bias*, regarding left-wing bias in the mainstream news media. Well, the line about Dan Rather and his "jailhouse bitches" did catch me completely off-guard, but it just provided one more reason to read a book that promises some slashingly good humor as well as anecdotal support for what everyone with an understanding of the media and its ideological spectrum already knows.

I've had my own experience with mainstream media bias, you see. After four years of writing a weekly game review column for the *St. Paul Pioneer Press* during which time I'd been only the sixth columnist in the paper's 113-year history to become nationally syndicated, I decided to ask for a regular spot on the editorial page when I heard of two vacancies there.

I knew that my libertarian politics were a little unusual from the paper's perspective, but in a town where serious lunatics like Jesse Ventura and Barbara Carlson were the two leading radio commentators at the time, my ideologically-challenged views didn't seem like much of a problem in comparison.

I knew there wasn't any question about my ability to string words together in a coherent manner. My first novel had been published a few months before by a large New York publisher, and I'd even written a 750-word letter which had appeared on the editorial page of the rival *Minneapolis Star Tribune*. I was at least 10 years younger than any other editorial page columnist, and the clincher, I thought, was that by adding a second writer to the right of the paper's usual neo-Marxian slant, the *Pioneer Press* would be able to distinguish itself more clearly from its larger rival and ideological twin, which is known locally as the *Star and Sickle*.

The move only seemed to make sense, considering that Minnesota has a strong conservative minority which comprises perhaps 40 percent of the population, our shameful performance in presidential elections notwithstanding. Minnesota Republicans read the paper too, even if they haven't sent any votes to the Electoral College since Abe Lincoln was first starting to think about sporting the chops and whatnot.

So I fired in three sample columns, plus the letter which appeared as a Counterpoint in the *Red Star*, and confidently awaited a phone call from the gentleman responsible for running the editorial page. When it never came, I called up to see what was going on. I will say this for the man, he did his best to avoid any outright dishonesties, and even had the grace to sound somewhat embarrassed when he told me that I was "just not a good fit" for the paper. He conceded that my writing was of an acceptable standard, that my arguments were logical and reasonable, and even that my style was entertaining, but remained staunch in his insistence that the editorial page simply was not the place for me. Game reviews, sure, but editorial? Forget it!

Perhaps I should mention that the *Star Tribune* article was one supporting gun rights and advocating the passage of a carry law being debated at the time by the state legislature. One sample column was an attack on government-financed sports stadiums, based on free market principles and supported by a landmark study which exploded the myth of the economic benefits of such stadiums, benefits that were being assiduously promoted by the St. Paul paper. I don't recall the content of the other two, but WorldNetDaily readers familiar with my previous columns will have no doubt that they were more than a little offensive to left-wing sensibilities.

Now please understand, I'm not looking for sympathy here, or a shoulder to cry on. I'm delighted to be writing novels and now a regular Monday column for WorldNetDaily. But I believe it is important for everyone to know that the bias of which Mr. Goldberg writes is not accidental, and that the editors of the commentary pages across the United States see themselves as an elite group of guardians, vigilantly standing guard atop a sacred wall past which the un-illuminated shall not be allowed. Ideological soundness is all, and one's qualifications do not matter in the least if one cannot be trusted to bleat in the approved boot-licking manner.

It's worth mentioning that I am not the only one to notice the leftward tilt at this particular paper. About a year ago, I telephoned a business writer to discuss a four-part series on the decline of the Twin Cities as a technology leader to which he'd contributed. This was a major series, one that probably took up something on the order of 15,000 words, and not once was it mentioned that Minnesota suffers from one of the highest state income taxes in the country, 9.5 percent. Now, everyone in the local business community knows that the high taxes are the primary reason so many small business owners pull up and leave for friendlier climes—I once attended a party thrown by a $50 million corporation, and 12 of the 13 board members were former Minnesotans now living out-of-state—but the writer told me that the paper's editors "don't believe taxes are an issue."

I suppose they think the real reason businesses are leaving is that the voters still won't let the state pay for the Twins' new stadium. Yes, Virginia, the mainstream news is biased toward the left, and if you don't believe me, then read Mr. Goldberg's book. He was there, and he knows the truth about what goes on behind the scenes at *ABCNBCCBS*, the *Washington Post* and the *New York Times*. And now that you know the truth as well, understand that there is only one thing you can do about it. Turn them off and tune them out! Cancel your subscription and let them know why!

WorldNetDaily has shown the way; may a thousand WorldNetDailys spring up to fight the mainstream media and its poisonous message of slavish dependency!

QUESTION OF THE WEEK: In this world, does anything survive that has abandoned its reason for being? Can anything survive that has outlived its usefulness and core mission?

THUS SPAKE VOX: The answer, all too often, is yes. But we live in a fallen world, and so we should not be surprised when institutions eventually devolve into rotting parodies of what they were originally meant to be. Still, hope springs eternal and we are always free to roll up our sleeves and begin the process anew.

Fighting the Eurofascists

January 7, 2001

TWICE IN THE PREVIOUS CENTURY, misguided European political experiments have resulted in American soldiers shipping out and fighting Over There. On Jan. 1, 2002, the euro made its debut, the latest in a long chain of events which will, sometime in the next two or three decades, result in the citizen-soldiers of the New World being forced to administer yet another bloody lesson on the battlefield to the Old World's freedom-hating elitists.

While the attention of most Americans has been understandably focused on the continuing war on terror, the significance of the successful implementation of the 12-nation euro should not be ignored. This new currency is the latest and most important step in accomplishing what Hitler and his National Socialists failed to do, namely, establishing a single centralized and anti-democratic European state.

Unity, union—these words strike a harmonious chord in the ears of those of us who are so fortunate as to be born in these United States. But not all unions are the same, nor should the consummation of all unions be desired. To unite can also mean, "to bind together, to fasten together as one." Thus was derived the ancient symbol of Roman authority, the fasces (an axe, surrounded by a bundle of sticks), from which the epithet fascist evolved.

Fascist is an apt word to describe the true nature of the European Union, for like their Italian and German forebears, the state socialists, the fascists of the European Union are gaining power through an illusion of democratic approval. While not one European country contains a popular majority supporting the full integration and complete abandonment of national sovereignty sought by the Eurofascist elite, the long march towards the single central state continues. Indeed, in most referendums wherein the people of Europe have been given a voice, the euro and the EU have been defeated.

Do not be misled by the naive cheerleading from businessmen intrigued by the prospects of stable 4-percent growth in unionwide GNP. Fascists have always appealed to business leaders, as I pointed out in a previous column about Larry Ellison, Oracle, and the national ID card. The European Union has little to do with business and everything to do with the concentration of power. Indeed, the promise of free trade has been its stalking horse from the very beginning, taking in even the best and wisest of Europe's conservatives. In the memoirs of her Downing Street years, Margaret Thatcher writes:

> *The wisdom of hindsight, so useful to historians and indeed to authors of memoirs, is sadly denied to practicing politicians. Looking back, it is now possible to see the period of my second term as prime minister as that in which the European Community subtly but surely shifted its direction away from being a community of open trade, light regulation and freely co-operating sovereign nation-states towards statism and centralism.*

There is simply no question about the anti-democratic nature of the new regime. The European Union is like the Hotel California, a place from which you can check out, but never leave. As with Germany in 1933, one final vote takes place and then the wolf is within the door, and it is no longer considered necessary to revisit the issue ever again.

"The euro is forever," said Romano Prodi, President of the European Commission, giving fair warning to the Danish public on the eve of their vote on monetary union. The Danes, surprisingly, braved the disapproval of their Eurofascist leaders and voted no.

When Austria voted the anti-EU Freedom Party into power, the foreign ministers for the other EU countries immediately imposed diplomatic sanctions on Austria for daring to voice an opinion contrary to the will of the Union. And when Irish voters declined to ratify the Treaty of Nice, EU leaders ominously demanded another, and illegal, vote on it within months. But as an English Member of Parliament writes:

> *In practice, EU leaders have rarely allowed the letter of the law to stand in the way of deeper integration. After Denmark's 'no' to Maastricht in June*

1992, the Danes were told to think again. A second referendum was held in which they were told that they had been given concessions although these were described in the rest of the EU as 'explanations' of the previous text.

Every step along the way to the single central state has been marked with similar dishonesty and lies. Lady Thatcher adds:

We had to learn the hard way that by agreement to what were apparently empty generalizations or vague aspirations we were later held to have committed ourselves to political structures which were contrary to our interests.

We Americans have a strange reluctance to believe what is right in front of our eyes. It took eight years and thousands of lives being lost before we could bring ourselves to respond to the threat posed by radical Islamicists opposed to our government and our way of life. Perhaps it is because the mundane dishonesty of our political system encourages us to ignore all statements of purpose as meaningless, or maybe it is a fundamental sense of decency which prevents us from comprehending the reality of naked evil when it presents its face. Remember that Stalin, Mao, and even Lenin have all had their apologists here in our country, not in benighted backwaters, but in important places, in academia and the *New York Times*.

Americans want to believe well of even the worst of men, and we strive to do so until it becomes impossible to continue denying what is undeniably true.

And so it is still possible, at this time, for some to deny the fascism that beats at the heart of Brussels. It is possible to look past the violations of national sovereignty, the shattered promises, the raw hypocrisy and the outright lies. But deny it or not, the beast is nevertheless there. Sooner or later, it will be exposed so that none will be able to dispute the truth. The European Union has no legions, but an empire of stealth and wealth is an empire all the same, and its grip is no less iron for all that it does not wield a sword—yet.

European union is not inevitable. That lie is no more true today than it was in Hitler's time, or Napoleon's. But now, as then, the lie must be resisted or it will begin to become reality, and the world will once more rue that which was never supposed to happen again. My hope is that we'll fight the Eurofascists sooner rather than later, but either way, you know we're going to win.

Britons, Spaniards, Italians, Germans—we've already beaten everyone but the French, and if we can't beat the French, well, we might as well go ahead and surrender to Omar and Osama right now.

QUESTION OF THE WEEK: [Referring to the mainstream media] Why waste your time with them?

THUS SPAKE VOX: I don't think that anyone should waste their time with the mainstream media, indeed, I encourage every reader of this column to cancel their subscription to papers like the *Washington Post*, the *New York Times* and *USA Today*. I encourage everyone to turn off the *ABCNNBCBS* news, and *Fox News* too if they're going to continue collecting *CNN*'s excremental leavings such as Geraldo Rivera and Greta van Susteren instead of giving us more voices like Bill O'Reilly and Sean Hannity.

However, we cannot successfully oppose the enemy unless we know them, and so as long as the mainstream media can credibly claim to be America's "opinion leaders," I will continue to track the propaganda they attempt to pass off as truth and expose it for what it is. After all, you can't hit a target at which you're not looking. That being said, I look forward to the day when we can all safely ignore them with impunity.

Words and warfare

January 14, 2002

OVER THE CHRISTMAS SEASON, I happened to encounter two things which got me thinking about war, in general, and the recent performance of the U.S. armed forces, in particular.

Now understand that I am a libertarian, and I am fully cognizant of the way in which war is used by various elements within and without the government to strengthen the central state and to tempt individuals into sacrificing their liberties in the vain pursuit of security. History has certainly shown that the American government has not always been innocent in these matters.

But if war is not necessarily the battle between good and evil we would like it to be, it is often the case that one side is significantly worse than the other. FDR was a terrible president whose insidious legacy haunts us to this day, but there's no question that any sentient being would prefer to have lived under his stewardship than Mr. Hitler's. In the present circumstance, even most fundamentalist Muslims might prefer to see the United States defeat al-Qaida rather than have to live under the totalitarian rule of these particular co-religionists.

It was disturbing to listen to the translated videotape of Osama and his pet Saudi sheik as they discussed the Sept. 11 attacks. What was most interesting to me, though, was not any question of the tape's legitimacy, the ludicrous poetry or even the theological dichotomy between Osama's holy dreams and the Koran's position on noncombatants. No, what primarily caught my attention was the manner in which the two men went on and on and on and on, as if they hoped to bury the United States under the sheer mass of their verbiage.

I have a theory, you see, which is that any culture's ability and willingness to fight is inversely proportional to the tendency of its people to talk. Anyone who's ever witnessed an Italian soccer game will understand what I mean. The last five minutes of any game, at nearly any level, invariably involves all 22 players on the field shouting at each other, making it impossible for any of them to understand what the two coaches and all the players on both benches are yelling at them. The spectators are also in full voice at this point, but they're mostly occupied with threatening the referee with bodily harm.

Two or three brief spats always liven up the final minutes, usually forcing the referee to distribute three or four cards of various colors. But the altercations never amount to anything, and five minutes after the final whistle blows, everyone is happily lighting one another's cigarettes in a touching display of sporting unity, if not health consciousness. Contrast this with the English game, where the cheers could not be more verbally minimalistic, "England, England, England, England, England... England!" and even the highest-paid professionals aren't above punching an opponent in the face just because it's there.

Mussolini, of course, enjoyed a daily harangue, but his Six Million Bayonets barely managed to account for a weaponless Ethiopian empire before having their fascist backsides abused by the Greeks. And has anyone ever talked more smack before the big game than Saddam "The Mother of All Rhetoric" Hussein? I find it hard to believe that the Marines are shaking in their boots at the notion of a second round with the feared Republican Guard.

Speaking of the USMC, that finally leads me to the other thing I mentioned earlier, which was reading the biography of Chesty Puller, one of the Marine Corps' more popular generals. General Puller liked to speak his mind, and even managed to get himself into a little hot water with the press from time to time, but the book makes it very clear that this Marines' Marine knew when to talk, and when to fight. He had a few things to say about his experiences in Haiti, Nicaragua, Guadalcanal and the Chosin Reservoir, but he preferred to do his talking after first having had the opportunity to excel at his craft. That, by the way, is Chesty-speak for killing large numbers of enemy soldiers.

Osama and his ilk can prattle on about Allah, American decadence, and American weakness. But Americans, for all our latter-day ignorance about the world and its evil, still understand that a few simple words like "Let's Roll" and "Follow Me" mean far more in the end than a thousand flourishes of rhetoric. That is why we will win this war.

American public schools: Working just as designed

January 21, 2002

THE AMERICAN PUBLIC SCHOOLS are not failing. Quite the contrary, in fact; they are succeeding at doing exactly what they were designed to do. The problem that has inspired so much press and political action over the past 30 years is one of cognitive dissonance, not performance. Education, you see, in the eyes of the educational establishment, is not about reading, writing and arithmetic, as so many misguided parents believe, but about directing the development of children into the kind of adults the establishment and its supporters want them to become.

As William Torey Harris, one of the fathers of the public school system, once wrote:

> *This is not an accident but the result of substantial education, which, scientifically defined, is the subsumption of the individual.*

Subsumption of the individual to what? The State, of course. There is nothing more dangerous to the would-be Guardians of the State than individuals with a strong moral code who are capable of independent thought. This is why the destruction of the traditional one-room schoolhouse became necessary, and it is also why the homeschool movement is considered such a dangerous threat, not only by the educationalists, but also by those who favor a strong central government. Totalitarians have always placed great emphasis on maintaining tight control of the schools, as they know that children free to develop as independent thinkers will inevitably resist control of their minds, bodies and spirits.

Indeed, it may come as a surprise to most to learn that the concept of the classroom was first developed in India, where it was used by the Brahmin caste to handicap the mental development of the far more numerous lower castes to keep them more easily in check. This is why it should not have been a surprise when the *Washington Post* quoted a study reporting that nine years of homeschool was essentially equivalent to 12 years in a public school or 11 in a private school.

But what about socialization? Again, the dragon of cognitive dissonance raises its ugly head. The socialization provided by the public schools has nothing to do with learning how to function as an adult in a civil society. Indeed, it is designed to do exactly the opposite by hurling the child into a savage environment where they are literally demoralized in every sense of the word.

I still remember riding on the bus during my last year of public school, sixth grade, and listening to a ninth-grader attempt to talk his girlfriend into sexually servicing his best friend. "But I don't want to f— with him, I only want to f— you!" she protested weakly. It was rather eye-opening stuff, even for a kid who'd been through a year of Sex Ed only two years before. Although I switched over to a private school the following year, by that time I'd already been properly socialized.

And let me share something with you parents who think that while most schools are in bad shape, yours is OK, and your good little children are doing just fine. The vast majority of you are totally wrong. They're not OK, and I know it for a fact because I knew parents like you back when I was in high school, when I was out partying with your sons on the sports team and having sex with your daughters in the youth group. The fact that you live in a nice community where everyone goes to church and drives a German import means nothing, and the fact that a school might send a few academic high flyers off to Harvard doesn't indicate that the moral foundation of its students has not been destroyed.

It is important to understand that there is no fix for this, because it is not a problem with the system. The school system we have today is exactly what it was designed to be—a place to detach children from the values of their parents, destroy their moral foundations and degrade their ability to think independently. There is no excuse for any parent who would knowingly sacrifice his son or daughter to the fires of this Moloch, no excuse for wittingly allowing a child to remain within the system for one day longer than necessary!

I have heard it said that homeschool is not for everyone, but I say that the American public school system is for no one, especially not the children of Christian parents. What fellowship can light have with darkness? Get a clue, and get your children out of the schools!

The homeschool railroad

January 28, 2002

APPARENTLY LAST WEEK'S COLUMN struck a nerve with many of you, as I was not prepared for the deluge of e-mail that threatened to explode my inbox. However, one e-mail in particular caught my attention, from a lower-income father of two. He wondered if I was just another elite journalist insensitive to the challenges facing those for whom making the rent can be an issue, who do not have the time or the resources to even consider homeschooling as an option.

After I stopped laughing at the thought of Dan Rather, Tom Brokaw and Geraldo "The Lion of Tora Bora" Rivera choking in indignant fury at the suggestion of my inclusion in their midst, I realized the man had an excellent point. I also thought of a young woman with whom I've recently become acquainted, who lives near her work but drives 90 minutes every day to ensure that her young son is cared for by a family she trusts instead of spending his days in institutional daycare. She is a single mother, and as much as she'd love to stay home with him, it simply isn't an option. Since I do not wish to be numbered among the legion of commentators who can only criticize, I decided to devote some time to thinking about the problem.

The answer, I believe, can be found in history. The struggle against the public schools is not the first time Christians and like-minded individuals have battled against an entrenched institution. Indeed, there are many parallels between the continuing exodus from the public-school system and the fight to end slavery in America.

In the years from 1830 to 1865, more than 30,000 slaves traveled the underground railroad as they made their way from bondage in the south to freedom in the north. The travails of the journey might have been beyond many of them, but they were harbored along the way by brave individuals who were willing to risk much in order to help their fellow men find freedom.

These rescuers received no reward except the gratitude of those they did not know and would likely never see again. Still, they persevered, and most of us today would say their nameless efforts were well-justified.

I suggest, therefore, that it is time for the homeschooling movement to follow the example of our abolitionist forebears in adopting a conscious strategy of concerted opposition to the public school system, with the ultimate goal of abolishing the institution altogether. I believe the best way to begin this process is to reach out to the less-fortunate around us and give their children the benefit of the same homeschooling we provide our own children. Imagine the staggering impact of 500,000 homeschooling families all welcoming one additional child into their midst five days a week! Imagine the difference this would make in the lives of those children, in the lives of their parents and in the minds of those who are still allowing their children to remain within a mind-destroying, soul-deadening environment.

There is no question that bringing another child into the homeschool would be a major sacrifice, and represents a burden that many homeschooling families could not, or would not, be willing to assume. Nor can I imagine the educationists will take this sort of overt provocation as anything but a declaration of war. But Leviathan cannot be destroyed by purely defensive measures, and one cannot expect a war that has already spanned generations to be won without sacrifice.

And do not be deceived—because this is a long-running struggle for the hearts, minds and souls of America's children. It is not a war that most parents have sought, but it is one that has found them nevertheless. Right now, homeschoolers and their parents are fighting thousands of individual battles all around the country, and victory is declared whenever one wins the right to be left alone. But this is not enough!

Those of us who can see the fire have a responsibility—not only to help others see the danger, but also to take them by the hand and lead them to safety if they cannot make it on their own. Our president has said, "let no child be left behind." I suggest we take his words to heart and consider extending a hand to a child who, without us, will otherwise be left behind to steep in the poison of a pernicious system.

One world... one big, bloody problem

February 4, 2002

IT'S NOT HARD TO UNDERSTAND why globalism is so persistently seductive to people of genuinely good intent. Long a staple of hack science fiction writers and the producers of Saturday-morning cartoons, the notion of one central and benevolent government for all humanity appears like a light shining in the darkness of a world that is still wracked by warfare, terrorism, famine and disease despite the past century's incredible advances in technology.

Of course, it was pointed out several thousand years ago that the road to Hell is paved with good intentions.

In fact, if humanity's past record is a reasonable guide, globalism may represent the single deadliest threat to mankind in our long, murderous history. The Economist has reported that in the last century, more people died at the hands of their own governments than in all the wars and civil wars combined—170 million deaths vs. 37 million. However, the implications of this fact for global governance have not often been considered.

Supporters of globalism are optimistic that under the aegis of a single government, the world will experience peace, one way or another. But even if we put aside the questionable notion of an enforced peace, which the Balkan conflict demonstrated is merely a matter of putting off today's violence for tomorrow, it must be understood that an end to war is not synonymous with an end to violence and bloodshed.

Just as soldiers going into battle for the first time tend to think in terms of what they will do to the enemy instead of what the enemy will do to them, globalists envision one-world governance as an efficient means of imposing their views on others. This is why political activists of nearly every stripe tend to embrace globalist institutions even if they oppose a specific aspect of globalism. Thus the radical environmentalist who protests the World

Economic Forum nevertheless supports the Kyoto Treaty on global warming.

But there is no guarantee that a one-world government will respect the laws, customs, and institutions of the traditional freedom-loving West. Indeed, the institutions which are most deeply enmeshed in the globalist movement show strong signs that it will instead imitate the autocratic habits of its intellectual predecessors. For example, the U.N.'s Universal Declaration of Human Rights states in Article 29, section 3, that:

> *These rights and freedoms may in no case be exercised contrary to the purposes and principles of the United Nations.*

Jawohl, Reichsfuhrer Annan! Consider also the possibility that a coalition of Arab and African states might take control of the global government in the same way they've been able to exert undue influence over the U.N. General Assembly. Then everyone could enjoy the religious freedom enjoyed by Jews and Christians living in Saudi Arabia and the Sudan .

Unfortunately, that's far from the worst possibility. Two of the governments responsible for the worst civilian massacres in history, Russia and China, boasting 62 million and 37 million murders, respectively, hold permanent seats on the U.N. Security Council. And for those who argue that Russia isn't the same government as the Soviet Union, I have only one thing to say: If they're not, then what is Russia doing on the Security Council?

Even in medieval times, intelligent people understood that the fact that one king was a wise and benevolent ruler didn't mean the next one wouldn't be a complete psychopath. For those of you without historical reference, I'm talking about a situation like the one depicted in the movie "Gladiator," wherein Emperor Marcus Aurelius was succeeded by his son Commodus. The peril of central power is why America's founding fathers decided to ditch the whole concept and did their best to break it up, scattering it as far and as wide throughout the land as possible.

Regardless of how global governance is implemented, it is sure to attract every evil, power-seeking individual and organization like pedophiles to a public schoolyard. The intrigues and conspiracies will make Byzantium's internecine power struggles look like a student-council debate by comparison. Every would-be Hitler, Lenin, Mao and Mugabe will be converging on a single institution, and the most ruthless of them will be the winner.

The National Socialists had a saying that still sounds ominous now, 50 years later. "Ein Volk, ein Reich, ein Fuhrer!" One world, one government may not sound so scary yet, but it should. Because one thing is certain. Totalitarian government doesn't improve with size.

Fruitcakes, vegetables, and the icons of the left

February 11, 2002

I'M CURIOUS TO KNOW what Michael Kinsley might make of this column, in light of his article last month in the *Washington Post* wherein he expressed some surprise that anyone to the right of, well, himself, is capable of reading. Of course, considering that it seems like half the homeschoolers I've met are studying either Greek or Latin, I'm fully expecting some e-mails criticizing my translations.

Most people who've given the issue any thought understand that the primary conflict between the right and left revolves around the rights of the individual vs. the rights of the community. What is less often understood is that this is an age-old intellectual war which began long before FDR instituted his New Deal, before the Sons of Liberty were tearing up Boston, and even before the establishment of the Roman Empire. This war actually goes all the way back to the writings of two massively influential Hellenic philosophers, Plato and Aristotle.

Consider this passage from "Plato's Republic":

The guardians and auxiliaries, and all others equally with them, must be compelled or induced to do their own work in the best way. And thus the whole state will grow up in a noble order, and the several classes will receive the proportion of happiness which nature assigns to them.

This is a stellar example of pure leftist thought, which from its focus on mass identification to its wildly optimistic view of government compulsion could be easily mistaken for something said by Karl Marx, Benito Mussolini or Hilary Clinton. Indeed, many points of Plato's statist program live on today in policies championed by the American Democrats and their sycophants in the mainstream media.

Conversely, Aristotle, the champion of the individual, would have been most contemptuous of the American left. Indeed, he seemingly anticipated Dan Rather by approximately 2,350 years when he wrote in his "Metaphysics":

> It is absurd to seek to give an account of our views to one who cannot give an account of anything, in so far as he cannot do so. For such a man, as such, is from the start no better than a vegetable.

As Mr. Kinsley himself has noted and lamented, the intellectual state of the left is in tatters. Not only do their books fail to crack the bestseller lists, not only have their policies changed very little in the last 2,000 years, but the list of fundamental contradictions in their thinking is fast approaching encyclopedic status. Paging Mr. Diderot. Abortion supporters decry sex-based abortions in India. Affordable-housing advocates call for rent control. Women's organizations concerned about male violence want to ban handguns. Zimbabwe.

OK, I don't know if there's actually anything happening in Zimbabwe which I can reasonably blame on the left's obstinate folly, but considering the general state of African politics, I figure the odds are on my side. And it starts with Z, so there you go.

What is most ironic is that those who have assembled this massive compendium of irrationality consider themselves to be the intellectual descendants of the Age of Reason.

But despite its claims to truth and moral superiority, the left has always been profoundly dishonest and anti-intellectual. Its icons are not devotees of Truth—as they pretend—but pseudo-intellects who manage to parlay meaningless verbal gymnastics into reputations for deep thought and mental acuity. When Jean-Jacques Rousseau, who had long preached against the evils of the novel, was confronted with the contradiction involved in his authorship of La Nouvelle Héloïse, he denied that his novel was, in fact, a novel.

I suppose It Just depended upon what Monsieur Rousseau's definition of "was," was.

Shots in the dark

February 18, 2002

THE RECENT DECISION of Washington, D.C. officials to pursue parents who refuse to vaccinate their children with fines and even jail time makes sense in a twisted sort of way. After all, the old solution of banning the children from attending public school was beginning to look more and more like an incentive plan, considering the ignominious performance of the District's notorious schools.

But why are so many parents steadfastly refusing to inject their children? Perhaps because they've learned to be dubious of the official line that vaccines are A Good Thing. The official line rests on a few simple notions, most of which fall apart completely once they're closely examined. A particular favorite of doctors is to state that no scientific study has ever found a causal link between vaccinations and autism, or between vaccinations and a whole host of Bad Things which most parents would very much like their children to avoid.

What generally goes unsaid is that no serious studies have been done on these issues, since it is in the best interests of the pharmaceutical companies manufacturing the vaccines, the politicians requiring them, and the doctors administering the shot, to avoid delving into the subject. Even a much-ballyhooed report last year from the English Institute of Medicine rejecting the MMR vaccine-autism link was not a study proper, but a critical review of Dr. Andrew Wakefield's study of 170 English children who had "undergone regression after receiving the vaccine."

When pressed on this dearth of study, vaccine proponents fall back on insisting that it would be immoral to allow a control group of children to go unvaccinated, thus creating an impenetrable circle of illogic in defense of their assertion that vaccines are A Good Thing. The shotmeisters also make a habit of blaming various outbreaks of things like measles on the unvaccinated in our midst, which is simply not true since by even the rabidly pro-vaccination Center for Disease Control's reckoning, only 27.7 percent of the measles cases in 1987 could be considered preventable.

On television, you know that a child is doomed as soon as you learn that he's unvaccinated. I'm still curious to know if *NBC* and *ER* collected some of that Clinton administration propaganda money for the episode in which a misled mother's nice young unvaccinated boy dies of measles. But out here in the real world, in the unlikely event that a child does get measles, the chances that the disease will prove fatal are extremely low. The worst outbreak in the last 15 years was in 1990, when there were 27,786 cases and 89 deaths. That's a 0.32 percent chance of dying on top of a 0.0115 percent chance of coming down with the disease in the first place, compared to a child's 0.2 percent chance of coming down with autism by the age of 5.

Because the number of measles cases was 12 times greater than normal in 1990 and the fatalities occurred in people of all ages, a child under 5 is approximately 800 times more likely to develop autism than die of measles in an average year.

Other diseases for which vaccinations are provided are barely worth mentioning, since children almost never die from tetanus or rubella. Contrast this with the fact that the federal government has been forced to pay out more than $1 billion since the establishment of the National Childhood Vaccine Injury Act in 1986, and this despite the admission by a former head of the Food and Drug administration that "only about 1 percent of serious events are reported to the FDA."

It is true that there is not yet any absolute scientific proof that vaccines injure and kill thousands of children every year, but the money trail and anecdotal evidence continues to pile up in a manner that would suffice to convince a jury, if not a scientist. It is imperative that these matters be investigated thoroughly and completely, and if it is found that these mandated vaccines are indeed wreaking havoc on the children of America, those responsible for creating, mandating and administering them must be severely punished.

Satan, science and the supernatural

February 25, 2002

O NE OF THE MAIN REASONS for modern skepticism toward the supernatural world is it cannot be detected by the trusted methodology of science. There is no question that science has not, to the best of my knowledge, ever been able to perform reliably replicable experiments capable of proving the existence of the supernatural. But does this necessarily mean that the spiritual world does not exist? As the apostle Paul would say, by no means!

Many religious worldviews postulate the existence of intelligent, supernatural beings whose actions affect the physical world. The Christian view, in particular, puts forth the notion that our world is ruled by an evil supernatural being, one who long ago usurped humanity's God-given sovereignty. This being, Satan, is not only self-aware, but has been intelligent enough to fool the mind of man from the very start, beginning with the first temptation in the Garden of Eden.

There can be no doubt that Satan, if he exists, is a powerful being. When Satan showed Jesus all the kingdoms of the world and offered them to him, Jesus did not question that this was a meaningful offer, nor did he dispute that the world was Satan's to give. After all, if this had not been the case, it wouldn't have been much of a temptation. Jesus also indicated that Satan was skilled in the arts of deception and specifically referred to Satan as the Deceiver on several occasions. Significantly, the apostle Paul mentions how the "god of this age" has exerted himself to blind the minds of unbelievers.

So put yourself in the hypothetical position of this evil being ruling over all the earth. Is it in your interest to reveal yourself to humanity? Or is it better to lay in wait, hidden in the shadows, as the mortal world convinces itself that neither you nor your plane of existence are real? Given the disastrous results of this past century, as the world has increasingly turned away from belief in the God of the Bible and his truth in favor of Man and his scientific proofs, the evidence would seem to suggest that unbelief in the supernatural serves the interests of this evil being.

And if it can be argued that this is the case, the next question naturally follows: Does this Deceiver possess the power to hide the spiritual world from us? The logical answer, given his apparent power, would appear to be yes, but the Bible contradicts this conclusion to some degree. What it teaches is that although the Deceiver rules over the earth as the god of this age, he does not have the authority to prevent God from manifesting power on earth through the person of Jesus Christ. It is here, then, to Jesus and those who worship him as Lord and Savior, that science will have to turn if it is to glimpse behind the veil of the supernatural.

Following this logic, it becomes clear that scientists will find nothing if they continue to seek for evidence of the supernatural by examining occult phenomena such as ESP, telepathy, fortune-telling and witchcraft. Satan is the lord and master of such things, and he does not deign to be unmasked, at least, not yet.

What I find fascinating is that some scientists have actually found apparent evidence of the supernatural in an area which could bear fruit. In 1983, a study published in the *Journal of the American Medical Association* concluded that prayers by born-again Christians appeared to quantifiably aid the healing process of strangers. And it was not long ago that *NBC*'s Dateline reported on research indicating that people who attend church regularly live longer lives. In fact, the report stated that attending church was as beneficial to good health as not smoking. Thus it seems possible that continued research in this area could finally provide scientists with the conclusive evidence they require in order to confirm the existence of a world beyond the natural.

But, unfortunately, no amount of scientific fact will ever convince those who are determined not to believe. Science, for all of its tremendous accomplishments, is still merely the epitome of Man's knowledge, and is by itself incapable of seeing through the Deceiver or understanding the mind of God. The light shines in the darkness, but the darkness has not understood it, nor will it understand until the Son of Man comes again, in power and great glory.

You go, Joseph!

March 4, 2002

A CENTRAL HALLMARK OF TOTALITARIANISM is its need for control. Control of the military, control of the police, control of the courts, the laws and the legislatures. But before all of these things comes control of the media. This is because the common people are far more powerful than they realize, and as history has shown time and again, the independent minds in their midst must either be unleashed or exterminated—they cannot be controlled.

They can, however, be influenced, indoctrinated and deceived. In some ways, then, the media is more powerful than other institutions, because only the media has the ability to affect the way people think. While the media cannot directly dictate one's fundamental beliefs, it can subtly frame the manner in which an issue is contemplated by the selective distribution of information.

Over time, this can be an extremely effective tool for those wishing to guide the thinking of the populace. Indeed, besides the public-school system, it is the only effective tool. The results can be startling. For example, 76 percent of the Swiss people voted against joining the United Nations in 1986, but 13 years later, a government drive which barely collected enough signatures to qualify for a national referendum marked the beginning of an unobtrusive but extensive media campaign for Swiss membership in the global governing body.

Today, one day prior to the referendum, the latest reports indicate that 54 percent of the Swiss are planning to vote in favor of joining the United Nations, vs. 37 percent against. If these numbers are accurate, they indicate a staggering shift of 30 percent in only 15 years, which is extremely unusual in a matter so rife with national and emotional significance. Of course, one has no choice but to wonder about the accuracy of the Swiss media's polls when the same story claims that "two-thirds" of voters turned down the proposition last time around. Characterizing 76 percent as two-thirds is just one minor demonstration of how the media can delicately alter the way in which an issue is perceived.

The same thing happens in the United States. When only 40,000 people showed up for the anti-gun Million-Mom March a few years ago, the mainstream media deceitfully reported an estimated attendance of 750,000. Such reporting creates a false impression which over time can significantly affect not only a person's ability to think logically about an issue, but can even destroy their facility for recognizing facts when finally confronted with them. Unfortunately, this insidious intellectual direction manages to pass for objective reporting throughout the mainstream media—especially where the government is concerned.

But not at WorldNetDaily. This is why the denial of WorldNetDaily's press pass should not be regarded as a minor bureaucratic incident, but rather as a significant indication that the powers-that-be have recognized WorldNet-Daily as a real threat to their continued thought-policing. Al-Ahram and the Beijing Daily are no danger to the government-media cabal's mind games, which is why they are permitted to wander through the high halls of power with impunity.

WorldNetDaily, on the other hand, is dedicated to truth and freedom, two sacred ideals which stink like sewage in the nostrils of those who use lies to seek control. Evil not only cannot afford the truth, it cannot bear to see itself reflected in the harsh mirror of truth's condemning light. This is why William Roberts, chairman of the Standing Committee of Correspondents, was so enraged by Joseph Farah's refusal to tamely submit to his committee's illegitimate dictates.

Mr. Roberts is angry now, but it won't be long before he'll be a fearful shell of his formerly arrogant self, eating his foul words. His days and the days of his unconstitutional gatekeeping are numbered, and he will soon pass into history like the ideological dinosaur he is. The Soviets learned, as did the Romans before them, that truth will always win out in the end.

So I'm with Joseph on this new crusade… how about you? I don't know the best way to burn these News Nazis and their little Reichntag, but in the meantime, one thing I would suggest is to hit them where it hurts by shutting off *Bloomberg News* and *ABCNNBCBS* (except for Alan Keyes's show on

MSNBC, of course). Mr. Roberts and his ilk may not listen to reason or polite discourse, but I'll bet they pay plenty of attention to the sound of falling ratings.

The secret lust for power

March 11, 2002

O NE OF THE EASIEST WAYS to dismiss something out of hand is to label it conspiracy theory. Although the word "conspiracy" simply refers to the act of joining together in secret agreement to do a wrongful act, tacking it on as an adjective somehow evokes images of unfounded fears and even paranoia.

But is it reasonable to believe that there are truly none who wish to do wrong, or to think that if such men exist, they will always be foolish enough to declare their intentions openly?

History speaks eloquently on the subject. In the 1,129 years of the great Byzantine empire, the average reign of an emperor was 12 years. This is a bit longer than the eight years we now allow our president, but is rather short considering that the Byzantine position ostensibly offered supreme power and lifetime tenure. But if it wasn't unheard of for a ruler of Constantinople to die peacefully in his bed, it was also not the norm.

For example, in the 135 years following Maurice's peaceful succession of Tiberius Constantine, seven of the empire's 12 rulers saw their reigns end in assassination or execution. Of the five who were not slain outright, two were deposed, and one, Constantine IV, was only able to keep his throne by mutilating his two fraternal rivals.

Roman history is little different. While the violent period of the civil wars is familiar to most literate people, less is known about the 92 years of near-anarchy which began with the drowning of Commodus and ended with Diocletian's ascension to the purple. During that century of imperial crisis, Rome was under the caligae of 26 soldier-emperors, most of whom died—as they lived—by the sword.

Keep in mind that these murderous successions mark only the successful conspiracies, and in the case of the Byzantines, it was not unusual for an emperor to put down as many as three major plots against his throne in a single year. Nor is it an exaggeration to suggest that the highest circles in Constantinople, as in Rome, bubbled with almost constant intrigue fueled by the desire to claim power.

Has anything changed today? On the surface, the answer is certainly yes. But is it truly reasonable to think that human nature has changed much over the 549 years that separate us from the last days of Byzantium? I submit not, especially considering that we are closer to the 11th Constantine, Dragatses, than was the first Justinian to Julius Caesar. Nor can democracy be considered some kind of magic antidote, as the subsequent careers of successful politicians such as Alcibiades and Adolph Hitler inform us.

But where does that leave us, then, if the leopards have not changed their spots, but remain undetected despite stakes that would take Caesar's breath away? The Marxian theory of history has been thoroughly discredited. The Great Man theory cannot explain the dichotomy between the proven conspiracies of yore and their seeming absence today. The Accident theory is a vapid ontological argument. Only the much-belittled conspiracy theory of history, which stubbornly insists that events are not always as they appear on the surface, holds together in this light when examined in a historical and logical manner.

Consider the following words, spoken in 1838:

> *It is to deny, what the history of the world tells us is true, to suppose that men of ambition and talents will not continue to spring up amongst us. And, when they do, they will as naturally seek the gratification of their ruling passion, as others have so done before them. The question then, is, can that gratification be found in supporting and maintaining an edifice that has been erected by others? Most certainly it cannot.*

> *Many great and good men sufficiently qualified for any task they should undertake, may ever be found, whose ambition would inspire to nothing beyond a seat in Congress, a gubernatorial or a presidential chair; but such belong not to the family of the lion, or the tribe of the eagle. What! Think you these places would satisfy an Alexander, a Caesar, or a Napoleon?—Never!*

Abraham Lincoln, no stranger to the illegitimate seizure of power himself, understood the dangers posed by those who hide in the shadows to plot against the rights and liberties of the common man. Such men exist, the only questions that remain are: Who are they, where are they and what, exactly, do they hope to do?

1,000 eyes for an eye

March 18, 2002

I N THE YEAR 375, an assembly of Turko-Mongolian horse tribes invaded the lands of the Germanic Goths, setting off a great wave of tumultuous migrations which finally ended in 568.

The Visigoths ended in Spain, while their eastern neighbors headed south for Italy. The Burgundians, originally from northern Germany, settled in France, while the Vandals, from present-day Poland, sacked Rome on their way to establishing an African kingdom based in Carthage. The Angles retreated west to a large island which presently bears their name, while the Lombards finally ended the long process with their conquest of the Ostrogoths in the region of northern Italy now known as Lombardia.

This was not the last wave of great migrations, as anyone living in the United States should be able to attest. It is clear, then, that the current plight of the Palestinian people is nothing new, nor is it something that has not been experienced at one time or another by most cultures.

What is different in this situation is the Palestinian leadership's inability to recognize that they have been defeated in a war of territorial conquest, not once, but several times. Moreover, they were defeated by a people who have demonstrated an unprecedented determination in returning victoriously to the lands from which they were expelled 1,932 years ago. The Jews will not leave Israel again.

But it is not only the Palestinian leadership which has a problem recognizing reality. The Israeli peace camp, the European heads of state, the Bush administration, and now Israel's national unity government have all demonstrated that they do not know how to deal satisfactorily with Yasser Arafat. It is obvious to all but the most obstinately blind that Mr. Arafat is a murderer and a terrorist, but few seem to recognize that he is first and foremost a tireless warrior.

Give the man his due. Yasser Arafat has persisted despite setbacks that would have caused a lesser man to despair. Adolph Hitler committed suicide when his dreams of a pagan Teutonic empire began to collapse around him. Were Arafat made of such fiber he would have been buried long ago. He will never give up the fight, not of his own accord. Unfortunately, he is also incapable of understanding forbearance, or that a failure to wield power is anything but a failure of the will.

The Jewish people have long been cursed by the inability of their leaders to recognize men of implacable ill-will. One of the sadly ironic tragedies of the Holocaust is the participation of Jews such as Mordechai Rumkowski and Jacob Gens in the administration of the Nazi's murderous bureaucracy.

Like Shimon Peres and Binyamin Ben-Eliezer, "they believed in the bargaining process … in the vain hope of thereby protecting and saving those who remained." But both men—along with the vast majority of the hundreds of thousands of Jews in their charge—were murdered by the bureaucratic machine they so unwisely chose to serve.

Warriors such as Yasser Arafat recognize only power and violence. But the strident reactions of his spokesmen to the recent invasion of Ramallah demonstrate that he knows when he is in real danger. Because he is both rational and intelligent, I believe that the only way to force Arafat to end his war is to force him to choose between surrender and merciless brutality.

The Israeli government must announce to the world a unilateral cease-fire, balanced by the deadly promise that for every Israeli soldier killed, 25 Palestinian police will die. For every civilian, 100 non-combatant Palestinian adults will be slain, and for every child, 1000 adults.

Furthermore, if another Jewish child is murdered, Mr. Arafat will be the first to pay the price. Only Palestinian children will be considered off-limits for these terrible reprisals. Whereas the historic 10-to-1 fatality ratio maintained a cold peace, the current 3-to-1 ratio foments a hot war. A 1,000-to-1 ratio will bring a permanent peace, one way or another.

In a fallen world, violence does solve some problems, and at times extreme violence is required. I do not wish for a single Israeli or Palestinian death, but a savage blow to end Yasser Arafat's war is far, far better than allowing more innocents to die without an end in sight. The choice for peace or death is Mr. Arafat's alone. And if he elects to die as he has lived, then remember that even the hydra had only nine heads.

Prime-time wussies

March 25, 2002

D URING THE E-MAIL BOMBING by Muslims whipped into varying degrees of hysteria by the Council on American-Islamic Relations over last week's column, I couldn't help but notice a few things. First, there appear to be very few non-Arabs who disagreed with me, as exactly nine percent of the negative e-mail I received was from people without blatantly Arabic names. It was also interesting to note that of the many e-mails I received supporting my statements, only two were Jewish, either by name or self-identification.

Well, there was also one from a confused Jewish man who accused me of being a Nazi and demanded an apology "to the freaking Jews!"

But the occasional psychotic aside, I wasn't the least bit surprised by the vast gulf in opinions expressed by Arab and non-Arab Americans—since I'm not a Jew, a Zionist or a Nazi—and I reached my conclusion as a largely indifferent observer to the conflict. I do know my history, though, and I think it's worth pointing out that while Winston Churchill might have said that "jaw-jaw is better than war-war," he nevertheless worked hard at talking the U.S. into ending World War II by killing very large quantities of Italians, Germans and Japanese. Nor have we had to fight any of them since. Sad, but true.

Peace almost always comes through violence, and this has been so since the Chronicles of the Assyrian Kings were first chiseled onto tablets. Peace must either be chosen freely by both sides, or forcibly imposed upon one by the other.

I'm curious to know what CAIR and my new anti-fan club think of the latest developments in the Middle East. Not only have there been three successful and 20 unsuccessful suicide bombings in the three days since the latest purported ceasefire, but similar attacks are now being threatened against

Egypt and Jordan. Furthermore, it was Jordanian troops that killed two recent Palestinians infiltrators, so it seems a bit of a stretch to pin those deaths on Israeli-Zionist Nazi genocide.

If Islamic extremists are really planning attacks against this week's Arab League Summit as has been reported, who should bear the blame for if they take place, Ariel Sharon? Or would it somehow be America's fault? It wasn't the U.S. or Israel that assassinated Anwar Sadat, after all.

Now I'm not enthusiastic about being called a "Jew lover" or a tool of "the blood sucking scum that is Judaism," "an ugly and bad spot on the face of humanity," or worse, "David Horowitz," but I'm more troubled by the fact that aside from the Internet media and Charles Krauthammer, almost no one is discussing the Middle East conflict in realistic, rational terms.

What color is the sky in a world where Yasser Arafat's promises are reported as if anyone actually believes them? How is the $5.25 billion in annual U.S. aid to Israel rounded down to the $3 billion reported? Why did *Fox News* stop reporting on the Israeli art student spy ring? In what Arabic dictionary does Islam mean peace? And isn't peace process really just a synonym for not-peace—as in war?

This incomplete, and often dishonest, coverage serves no one well—not the Palestinians, not the Jews, and not Americans forced to watch the horror unfold. The result is that Mr. Arafat is falsely encouraged to force his people into another war they cannot win, the Israeli government is dissuaded from taking the only actions that can possibly lead to peace, and Americans risk sacrificing liberties while being dragged into a war wherein we have no legitimate national interests. And the blood of the innocent still flows...

I couldn't understand why the media coverage of the Middle East is so incomplete until reading a recent interview with Bernard Goldberg in the *New York Press*. Then I got it. The Dan Rathers, Peter Jennings and Ted Koppels of the world are afraid. They're afraid to make basic statements of fact or to say anything that would invite criticism of any kind, much less face a vicious electronic onslaught of the sort that writers like myself, Joseph Farah and Jonah Goldberg of *National Review* have endured.

In short, they're cowards, overpaid prime time wussies.

A number of those who've written me have saluted my courage and whatnot, but I'm not afraid to speak the truth. I am deeply concerned, however, about what happens when no one does.

The essence of Easter

April 1, 2002

W HEN VIEWED IN A HISTORICAL SENSE, the news that the Lavender Mafia has been buggering a host of teenage boys for decades is almost on the tame side for a Catholic scandal. As awful as these revelations have been, they nevertheless pale in comparison with Pope Alexander VI's murderously nepotist imperialism or the Church-sanctioned massacres of the Crusades, and they represent less of a complete institutional failure than the cynical sale of indulgences once did.

But there is no question that the abusive, hypocritical evil revealed by the sins of these gay fathers is going to taint the Catholic Church in the eyes of every American for a long, long time. I may not be a Papist myself—I happen to be a Christian of the Protestant variety—but the revolting behavior of these priestly predators nevertheless makes me feel a sickened sense of betrayal.

Still, the Catholic Church will survive this nightmare, as it has survived others. But even if it did not, what of that? We Christians—Catholic and Protestant alike—do not worship an institution, a tradition or a man. We worship a living God, the Son of Man, Who was crucified, died and rose again. And 2,000 years later, we eagerly anticipate His return, which, with every suicide bombing in Jerusalem, appears more imminent. That some of those who claim to serve Him should fall in such a deplorable manner changes nothing about our Lord and Savior or the truth of His Way.

I have not always been a Christian. Educated at an elite university, I was steeped in the amoral existentialism that is the ineluctable result of secular humanist logic. But like Saint Augustine, I eventually came to realize the double-minded futility of pretending to exalt Reason while spending my days in slavish service to Kundalini and the lizard brain.

Over time, I also came to discover that reason and faith are not contradictory. Indeed, one of the fascinating things about studying the history of the conflict between science and the Bible is discovering the many occasions when the ancient document has triumphed over the intellectual conceit of highly educated men. Keep this in mind when the next person asks how you, an otherwise intelligent and educated person, can possibly believe in the literal truth of the so-called Word of God in spite of what everyone knows to be true.

A favored technique of past scientific debunkers was to note something cited in the Bible, then point out that modern archeology had "proven" that it did not exist. The mythical Assyrian empire was often cited in this regard, as was that of the legendary Hittites. While both nations were frequently mentioned in the Old Testament, they remained undiscovered by archeologists until the late 19th century.

However, in 1906, excavations at Boğazkale led to the discovery of Hattusa, the capital city of an empire famously defeated by Pharaoh Ramses the Great at the battle of Kadesh. Hittites to the Jews, they were called Hattians by the Assyrians, whose own existence had been proven in 1842, when Paul-Emile Botta uncovered the first Assyrian monument at Kouyunjik.

Furthermore, the Chronicles of the Assyrian Kings reveal them to have very much been the bloodthirsty, warmongering psycho-killers described in the Bible. And while modern archeologists still deny the historical authenticity of the Old Testament account of the Jewish people's invasion of Canaan, the new chronology developed by David Rohl threatens to demolish the scientific assumptions of this generation's scientists as well.

With regards to Jesus Christ himself, it suffices to say that in addition to the biblical accounts, the Christian references appearing in Tacitus, Josephus, the younger Pliny and Lucian offer more support for His existence, if not His godhood, than exist for many accepted figures of antiquity. Unless one is prepared to also deny Alexander the Great, just to give one example, it would be wise not to rest too heavily on historical scholarship as a basis for one's unbelief.

Thus even in this time of war and ghastly bloodshed, in a time when nations battle over Jerusalem and a great Christian institution shows every sign of rotting from within, those of us who claim Jesus Christ as our Lord and Savior can still say with confidence and joy: "He is risen!" and "Come, Lord Jesus."

Is the IRS American?

April 8, 2002

T HE FEDERAL INCOME TAX is a hideously complicated structure, but it is actually much easier to understand than one might think. What is more difficult is putting aside one's misconceptions of how the system works based on years of surface exposure to it.

Just as time spent watching TV does not give even the most dedicated couch potato a comprehensive understanding of the hidden mechanics of his television, the fact that you have faithfully paid your taxes every April 15 does not mean that you, or your accountant for that matter, know anything about the realities of the federal income tax in all its sordid glory.

Because the status quo has existed for so long, it is extremely difficult for most honest taxpayers to fairly examine evidence which suggests that they have been victimized by one of the most impressive con games in history. I know this because I used to faithfully fill out 1040s and have the appropriate taxes withheld every year myself, until some bizarre behavior on the part of an IRS agent caused me to begin wondering if there just might be some truth behind what I had always considered to be aberrant and wishful thinking on the part of the anti-tax lunatic fringe.

Another aspect to this subject which makes it a difficult one to grasp is the bewildering amount of information and misinformation available. But if the wide variety of claims being made against the legitimacy of the federal income tax are troubling, perhaps it is worth remembering what happened the last time a powerful governmental figure lied under oath. That lie, as often happens, spawned more lies in turn, until the entire web of deceit was finally exposed by a piece of evidence which did not remain hidden.

Given that there is strong evidence suggesting that lies have surrounded the income tax for most of its 89 years, I would not be surprised if most of the extant anti-tax arguments should, over time, be proven true. There is not space in this column to list them all, nor to address even one in detail, but there are some points worth mentioning nevertheless.

The most important thing to mark, in my opinion, is the definition of the United States in the section of U.S. Code relating to taxable income, which deviates from the usual definition of the United States of America. This United States is better described as the federal United States, consisting only of territories like Puerto Rico and Guam which are governed by the federal government but are not part of the 50 states. This is where the con apparently enters the game, as the income-related law written specifically to address these territories is then falsely interpreted as applying to the fifty states as well.

While the IRS points to court cases such as Collins, Becraft, Barcroft and Ward in an attempt to refute this argument, it is very interesting to note that in each case, the agency relies solely on a court's unsupported statement instead of a proper legal reference, which, of course, is what the illegitimate jurisdiction argument is based upon.

Which naturally leads one to the question, do we live under a government of laws, or men?

The assertions of the IRS become particularly curious when one examines a document submitted by the U.S. Attorney in a 1993 civil case in Idaho, wherein the attorney "denies that the Internal Revenue Service is an agency of the United States government but admits that the United States of America would be a proper party to this action." This distinction becomes all the more intriguing when one considers that the IRS was first established as a Puerto Rican agency and supports the contention that there is a significant distinction in law between the federal United States and the constitutional United States of America.

There is no question that the truth is easier to ignore if you don't know what it is. But if you consider yourself a freedom-loving American, can you in good conscience refrain from examining the facts for yourself and considering the possibility that a portion of your freedom has been stolen from you through federal chicanery? Read the law. Read the facts about the 16th Amendment and about the 25 percent of non-filer cases the IRS loses every year. Then do what is right, not what is expedient, and refuse to be swayed by anyone who attempts to hide the truth through bluster, intimidation and lies.

Shut 'em down

April 15, 2002

What the judge said put me in the red
Got me thinkin' 'bout a trigger to the lead
No, no my education mind say suckers gonna pay
Anyway... there gonna be a day.

—Public Enemy

MAYBE IT WILL COME TO THAT ONE DAY. How much longer will we tolerate an illegal tax system supported by a corrupt judiciary and enforced by a foreign agency, especially when the elected officials who serve us do not even deign to answer our simplest questions? This April 15, it is time to remember that we are the descendants of honest men who did not fear to revolt after having one wrongful tax too many rammed down their unwilling throats.

I heard from a variety of people in response to last week's column about the IRS, ranging from well-educated folks who have decoded their IRS master files to the wholly ignorant, some of whom appeared a little shocked by my statements. A common complaint in both cases was the lack of Internet links to source information, so this column is an attempt to rectify that. Please note that I have no connection to any of these web sites or organizations.

The best place to start is the home of the organization sponsoring the Truth-in-Taxation hearings which took place last week in Washington, D.C. There is a mailing list, news updates and an excellent hour-long webcast of an April 8 press conference in which three former IRS agents took part.

For information on the IRS, formerly known as the Bureau of Internal Revenue, Puerto Rico, there is a nicely researched article on the agency, its history and jurisdiction. Its central thesis tends to be supported in page 2, No. 4 of this 1993 court case.

With regards to Puerto Rico, one reader wrote in to tell me that when his master file was decoded, he learned that his business was listed by the IRS as being registered in Puerto Rico. This was news to him, as he'd never been there in his life! It's also no surprise, as IRS agents regularly fill one's file with false information indicating tax liability under genuine constitutional law. Given that you may well be a victim of this fraud yourself, you might want to consider this CD which contains information on how to request and decode your own file.

Since the Supreme Court ruled that the 16th Amendment changed nothing regarding Congress's ability to enact a tax, it appears that the amendment was nothing more than another element of the great smoke scheme. Still, The Law That Never Was is an important education in the corruption of our government.

Of more practical application is the income source case presented by Larkin Rose. I definitely recommend reading the downloadable taxable income report, which is readable despite some unavoidable complexity. It's fascinating to see how income tax law has been changed over the years in order to continue misleading people while staying technically within the bounds of the Constitution.

Regarding tax convictions, I was working from memory last week and my numbers were off. In 1994, there were 2,447 prosecutions and 456 dismissals, which is an 18.6 percent rate of failure, not the 25 percent I mentioned. However, in 2001, the Department of Justice declined to prosecute 1,235 of the 2,511 cases referred by the IRS, and there were also an additional 155 dismissals for an effective 55 percent failure rate.

So perhaps that's something to keep in mind for those of you who know the truth but are afraid to act on it. The IRS itself says 35 million Americans don't file, and despite its elaborate architecture of lies and half-truths only manages to set up the conviction of .003 percent of that number.

But more important than playing the numbers game is personal integrity. Do you want to go to your grave saying, "Well, at least I did the expedient thing"? We have the honor of living in a time when our actions matter, even if one does nothing more than refuse to submit to tyranny by checking exempt or refusing to file.

Never forget that they fear us far more than we fear them. We the people own our government, not the judiciary and especially not a bunch of freaking Puerto Rican bureaucrats. The day is coming when we will shut them down!

What, me biased?

April 22, 2002

ONE OF THE BENEFITS of an addiction to pop history is that one finds oneself equipped with a formidable array of useless trivia. For instance, I have been assured by the renowned semioticist and medievalist, Umberto Eco, that the ancient Romans did not distinguish between the colors blue and green as we do, seeing them not as distinct colors but merely varying shades of cæruleus.

In like manner, the inestimable Mark Neuman has asserted that in the eyes of the ancient Greeks, the ideal penis size was rather smaller than the "9-inch tool" which features so prominently in the more sordid gentleman's publications. Were the Hellenes of yore less tormented by machismo than we Freudian-plagued moderns? Perhaps, but the main reason for this diminutive Greek ideal was the popular cult of the pederast, which placed a premium on the ability to sexually abuse boys of all ages.

I mention this not to explain the poor endowment of Athenian statues, but to underline the fact that systematic homosexual abuse of boys and young men is hardly new. Given that the Catholic Church was the only institution harboring men capable of reading the Greek classics when the West rediscovered them in the 12th century, it is safe to assume that the church hierarchy has not been unaware of the potential for this form of abuse to become institutionalized for at least 900 years.

Nevertheless, Andrew Sullivan, the most coherent and intelligent "gay" writer in the media today, feels that the long-overdue unearthing of his church's Lavender Mafia is an indication that the Vatican must overturn time-honored Catholic teachings on the evils of homosexuality, contraception, priestly celibacy and the designated hitter. This is questionable enough; what is worse is that he has unintentionally launched the argument against the existence of mainstream media bias to Himalayan new heights in insisting on a right to be considered bias-free in all circumstances, even when his personal interests are manifestly at stake.

Andrew Sullivan, you see, is not only a homosexual Catholic, but is unfortunately afflicted by one of the terrible consequences of homosexual behavior. He is HIV-positive. That is his personal problem, but where it concerns us is that he, like Parkinson's victim Michael Kinsley, has taken the astounding position that suffering from a life-threatening illness grants him the right to argue for political action of direct and vital benefit to him without considering it evidence of bias or a conflict of interest.

He even writes of Kinsley: "the right to privacy—especially about medical matters—would have and should have trumped that conflict of interest as a factor in ethical journalism."

But what is of greater benefit to an individual, making money or survival? Survival, obviously. So if calling for congressional action to inflate the value of a public stock one owns is a conflict of interest worthy of termination, how can one possibly justify calling for more government spending on subsidies for AIDS drugs or stem-cell research when one's own life is on the line?

Mr. Sullivan asks: "Does this mean that because I'm HIV-positive, my view should be airily dismissed as too biased?" Well, yeah! It is! Yet Mr. Kinsley insists that this would be a "bizarre inference."

Now, I suppose that if in your world, Yasser Arafat is a peacemaker and all conservatives, libertarians, Republicans, Christians, Nazis, Zionists and Chinese Politburo members are indistinguishable right-wing extremists, the notion that one's will to live could unduly influence one's opinion on a matter directly affecting one's chances for survival might seem just a little odd.

But at least Mr. Kinsley is honest enough to admit that his disease has trumped that famous "journalistic objectivity" which, until now, was more bulletproof than Kevlar. What happened, Michael, did you take one less 300-level journalism course than that famous bastion of journalistic objectivity and integrity, Dan Rather?

Of course, it's nonsense to insist that journalism school magically inoculates one against bias. What Messrs. Kinsley and Sullivan have inadvertently done is to demonstrate that even if media bias can be proven, it will be considered acceptable if one is singing in the left's Greek chorus. And so we see again that the mainstream media cannot be reformed, it can only be ignored and, eventually, replaced.

I wish both men well in their battles against their respective diseases. But I would also remind them that suffering does not give one a free pass on ethics, journalistic or otherwise.

Fight the real war!

April 29, 2002

D
ESPITE MY INTEREST IN MILITARY HISTORY, I am not a fan of war. War corrodes a society by allowing centralist forces within government to excuse actions they would never be allowed to take in more peaceful times, by encouraging the dehumanization of the enemy population and by providing an easy means of stifling reasonable dissent.

That being said, some wars are unavoidable, especially when a nation is under attack. And America is not only under assault now, but was even before Sept. 11. Americans not only have a right, but a responsibility to undertake the military struggle that is before us, unfortunately, the War on Terror is not that war.

The War on Terror is not, in fact, a war being fought by the American people. It is a federal military-police action being enacted without regard for the proper forms and procedures set out in the Constitution of the American people. American troops are spanning the globe on the orders of a single man, even as his employees attempt to ensnare our country into more of the entangling alliances against which our first President warned us.

Terror is a tactic, not an enemy, and the current phraseology only serves to obscure the fact that America has real enemies committed to her destruction. Who are these enemies? Those who have declared themselves at war with us. War, unlike dance, does not require two to tango, and thus we must be prepared for the possibility of a war not of our choosing.

It is not news that al-Qaida, Hamas, Iran, Iraq and other Islamic and/or Arabic organizations consider themselves at war with us. Recently, one Sheik Saad Al-Buraik, a Saudi television host and official government cleric, announced that America "is the root of all evils, and wickedness on earth" and ordered "Muslim Ummah don't take the Jews and Christians as allies." Understand that by Muslim Ummah, he means the entire Muslim community, not only in Saudi Arabia but throughout the world.

Furthermore, the sheik announces that "the battle that we are going through is not with Jews only, but also with those who believe that Allah is a third in a Trinity, and those who said that Jesus is the son of Allah, and Allah is Jesus, the son of Mary."

A sentiment to warm the hearts of Christians everywhere, I'm sure.

This is not a war that America has sought, but it is one that has found us nonetheless. We are being given no more choice about fighting violent expansionist Islam than were the Franks and Spaniards of the 8th century or the Hungarians and Moldavians of the 16th.

And like Charles Martel, America will win this coming war because, as Victor Davis Hanson explains in his excellent book "Carnage and Culture", we are the inheritors of the Greco-Roman way of war while our self-declared Islamic-Arabic enemies are not. Here's some ideas for getting things started:

Arm pilots and pass federal laws to permit the profiling of air travelers and incoming visa holders. Let the Supreme Court decide constitutionality, not the media.

Fire Secretary of State Colin Powell.

Announce that America has no further interest in interfering with Arab-Israeli relations.

Hold a congressional debate on a declaration of war against all Islamic or Arabic nations and organizations whose representatives have, explicitly or implicitly, declared war on America. If the measure passes, repatriate all non-American citizens with any ties to the above organizations or their host countries.

Inform the U.N. that any attempt to oppose the American war effort will result in immediate American withdrawal from that organization and termination of all funding. Convey a similar message to all foreign aid recipients.

Inform all oil-producing states that America's reaction to any oil embargo will be to commandeer their oil fields with an eventual return to the jurisdiction of their former British, French or Russian masters. What the West hath given, the West can take away.

Let the generals drive. Once the surrenders begin, President Bush can establish friendships and close personal bonds. But not until the white flags start waving.

Perhaps the American people aren't ready for this yet, but in time, they will be. America's enemies have underestimated her since the Redcoats fought her first defenders at Lexington. They do so because they do not understand the source of her strength, which stems from that which they hate most—the notion of freedom, liberty and justice for all.

.

Random ruminations

May 6, 2002

P RAGMATISM IN POLITICS always sounds like the reasonable position of a reasonable man. But if you're driving off a cliff, what
difference does it make if you are going 20 or 120 miles per hour?
Michael Bellesiles, the author of "Arming America," is a liar and an idiot.
I understand why he lied—because the anti-gun movement is almost completely devoid of facts in support of its policies. What I cannot understand
is how he thought he was ever going to get away with it. The Big Lie cannot
work wherever there is a press that is even remotely free.

Muslims who oppose America while living in it seem to have more faith in
the good nature of our government than I do. I seem to recall that the federals
didn't hesitate to incarcerate thousands of innocent Japanese-Americans during World War II, and I'm pretty sure we had the same Constitution then that
we do now. If jihad comes to America, I can't imagine the ATF and company
having major pangs of conscience about rounding up everyone named Ali,
Omar or Mohammed. I mean, look what they did to that mutant bunch of
wacked-out Baptists down in Waco.

Ann Coulter is hot.

Since socialism has never worked anywhere, why does it continue to hold
so much appeal to intellectuals everywhere? Have any of them ever even read
"Das Kapital"? And once it's conceded that the Labor Theory of Value is a
steaming pile of digestive detritus ejected from a steer's posterior, how does
the rest of the Marxian program hold together? Can someone even try to
explain this to me?

The terminology of the political spectrum is beyond repair. Extreme Left
and extreme Right do not meet, they are in fact the same. The fact that Nazis
and Communists battled for supremacy in 1920's Germany did not make
them ideological opposites; who was left and who was right when Bolsheviks

were exterminating Mensheviks? There is the collective and the individual and there is totalitarianism and libertarianism—that is the true spectrum.

Disturbed is more than a little disturbing. But oh, how they do rock!

It's not so hard to figure out why bad things happen to good people once you realize that the world is under the rule of a supernatural serial killer. As C.S. Lewis wrote:

> *All I am doing is to ask people to face the facts—to understand the questions which Christianity claims to answer. And they are very terrifying facts.*

Why do people who loathe monopoly in private enterprise believe that government monopolies are A Good Thing? How does adding the power to tax, jail and execute one's customers make for a more responsive or responsible monopoly?

Now that the European Union is on the verge of banning the Old Testament and has returned to the old sport of Jew-bashing, how long will it be before it begins openly persecuting Christians? I'm guessing 15 years. And 20 years will see the EU's first Civil War.

Do the opponents of homeschooling realize that the socialization which homeschooled children are missing largely consists of learning apathy, cruelty and sexual technique?

The institution of a bureaucracy inevitably leads to a divergence of interests between the bureaucratic class and those it purports to serve. Not enough work has been done on studying this phenomenon, which plagues institutions in and out of government.

I have seldom despised a literary character as I do Rand al'Thor, the central figure of Robert Jordan's, "The Wheel of Time". Has there ever been a whinier, more self-centered or less-appealing protagonist? I am now actively rooting for the bad guys.

The status quo always appears to be immutable, until change arrives, usually more suddenly and violently than anyone expects. Once the new status quo is established, it is quickly forgotten that things were ever different before.

Reading Plato quickly cures one of the notion that progressive thought will lead to any improvement in the human condition. "The Republic" is nothing but a nightmarish vision of a totalitarian society ruled by an oligarchical elite, devoid of all respect for individual rights and freedom.

I am beginning to worry that the Minnesota Vikings will not win the Super Bowl in my lifetime, despite being young, healthy and descended from long-lived stock. Then again, the Patriots won last year, which may be the most convincing argument for a random universe created by chance that I have ever encountered.

Death and the left

May 13, 2002

THE ASSASSINATION of Dutch politician Pim Fortuyn and the hysteria that surrounded the recent French elections are illuminating with regards to the current state of European politics. The myth of the EU's dedication to democracy has again been exploded, and the left has once more shown its ugly, murderous face—this time, interestingly enough, from one of its hitherto more innocuous aspects.

In Europe, as in America, the media has contorted the terms of the political spectrum and rendered them almost entirely useless. As in America, there is no hard left or extreme left in sight, although there are open communists, Trotskyites, Socialists and a panoply of other collectivists who would regard Sen. Ted Kennedy to be a reactionary of the same ideological stripe as Sen. Jesse Helms. Meanwhile, a homosexual man with generally moderate positions is demonized as being of the "far-right," as is Mr. LePen, whose ideology is actually more collectivist, more truly left-wing, than the majority of the American Democratic Party.

Of course, the entire dichotomy between both media's left and right is a false one. The difference separating a socialist and national socialist is no greater than the distinction between a Leninist communist and a Stalinist communist; in fact, the primary differences are precisely the same. Whereas the Leninist communist is focused on global revolution, the Stalinist, or national communist, believes that the world must be conquered one nation at a time, just as the national socialist attempts to build state socialism around nationalist forces instead of trusting in the blind hand of history and the enmity of the social classes.

This is why Benito Mussolini was not only able to leave the Italian communist party and form his fascist movement without seriously altering his philosophy, but also to bring a great number of "ex-communists" with him.

One cannot, on the other hand, think of a single anti-collectivist or champion of individual freedom who has embraced either communism or facism, because, far from being opposites, they are ideological brethren. They are parallel lanes on the road to serfdom.

The European situation is useful to us here in America because lacking our historical foundation in individual rights, Europe's ideological battles are delineated in stark outlines which make them easier to see clearly.

Whereas the American left is forced to lie about its intentions if it is to have any hope of winning elections, its European counterparts know no such restrictions. Thus American greens must conceal their inherent leftism (though what could be more collectivist than turning over huge tracts of land to the central government), while European environmentalists feel free to go so far as to extend the logic of leftism to its inevitable and ultimate conclusion—a bullet in the head for those who refuse to submit to the will of the collective.

Which makes sense; if the right of the collective always trumps that of the individual, then even one's life cannot be considered sacrosanct. After all, "political liberty is sham-liberty, the worst possible slavery," in the words of Friedrich Engels. And if Marxian criticism is a weapon, whose object it wishes "not to refute, but to destroy," then the correct response to an enemy's wrong-minded exercise of his presumed freedom of speech might well come out of the barrel of a gun.

Fortuyn's murder, and the despicable reaction of Europe's political elites to it, should cause the European people to rethink their willingness to be led by the nose into the EU's Fourth Reich, but that is unlikely. In Austria, France and now the Netherlands, it has been demonstrated that democracy and freedom of speech do not entail the right to speak out against the left and its union.

How greatly does the left fear freedom, that it attempts to tar even its feeblest advocates with the dread fascist brush? Not that there is a true "right wing" in power anywhere in the world; nowhere is there a nation dedicated to the supremacy of individual freedom and liberty that does not make major concessions to the collective. Sadly, the American Constitution is the closest thing to such a mythical beast, and it has been under assault from those sworn to defend it for most of its two centuries.

The recent events in Europe should remind us why our Constitution is worth defending, and why we cannot afford to be pragmatic, tolerant or less than vigilant in its defense.

Overfeed the world?

May 20, 2002

REMEMBER "Live Aid," "USA for Africa" and "Feed the world… let them know it's Christmastime"? According to the latest news from Geneva, they were not only effective, but too much so. Which makes one wonder, how long will it be before instead of being subjected to heart-rending pictures of starving young children with distended bellies and skeletal limbs, we'll be seeing Sally Struthers weeping tears of supplication on behalf of disadvantaged little fatties without Slim Fast, exercise bikes and the Atkins Diet. Can't you just feel the incoming Saturday Night Live skit?

Now I am no expert on the Third World, so I can't help but think that news of the study which was presented last week to the World Health Organization must have been some kind of joke. I mean, the idea that people in Africa are generally starving has been a base assumption of my entire life, right up there with Newton's Third Law of Motion and the notion that "the crust is the healthiest part of the bread." Then again, Mom wasn't entirely honest about that last one (shame, Mother, shame!), and so I suppose it shouldn't rock the foundations of my world to hear that in some parts of Africa, four times as many children are obese or overweight as malnourished.

Apparently Egypt leads the way, with 25 percent of its 4-year olds firmly on their way to tubbydom. Morocco and Zambia follow at 20 percent. This is big news—and not just for Lane Bryant executives salivating over the thought of expanding to what will apparently be, in more ways than one, a huge Chinese market.

The news, you see, demonstrates the truth of what P.J. O'Rourke pointed out in his brilliantly sardonic book, "All The Trouble in the World." Hunger and starvation have never been a problem of food production, they have always been a problem of evil central government. O'Rourke showed how Third World countries which did not wish to exterminate large portions of their populations were able to survive harsh famines and a disproportionately greater loss of their food-producing capacity without suffering the great loss of life typical in murderous regimes like Ethiopia, Sudan, Rwanda, Angola and Uganda—which routinely allowed hundreds of thousands of their citizens to starve. Mass starvation is never an accident.

Hunger has always been a weapon of collectivist elites, as Vladimir Lenin and Josef Stalin honed the technique in the massive Soviet famines of 1921 and 1932. Which makes me wonder, is there some sort of "Famine 101" course at Patrice Lumumba University in Moscow?

The WHO report is also delightful because it again explodes the myth of the modern Malthusians, who, despite more than 200 years of woefully inaccurate predictions, still insist that the Earth is overpopulated and cannot possibly feed 6 billion people. Indeed, Mr. Malthus and his intellectual descendants have been so consistently wrong that "Malthusian" should rightfully be considered an adjective which means "I have absolutely no idea what I'm saying," and should precede any mention of the following media creatures: Frank Rich, Julianne Malveaux, Molly Ivins and Eleanor Clift.

This good news of Third World obesity is likely only the first of many stories relating to corpulence and the human condition, although in this post-X-Files age it seems all too '90s to suggest that perhaps aliens are fattening us up for eventual consumption. No, instead we will soon be reading of the largest class-action suit of all time, as trial lawyers, fresh from their tobacco farming, will train their guns on the fast-food manufacturers who have forced their wares past the unwilling maws of millions of Americans.

But if WHO is seriously concerned about the terrible thought that great numbers of African children are not starving, perhaps they should forget scolding their naughty parents and get into the business of building gyms. Here's a little secret for those who want to get slim: Forget the exercise bikes, aerobics classes and treadmills, and hit the free weights instead. That goes for women, too—you won't start looking like Arnold or those powerlifting she-males without a dedicated high-caloric diet and a series of steroid cycles.

Muscle burns fat all the time, not just while you're working out, but even while you're sleeping. It's the easiest way to stay fit by far, so stay strong, my Third World brothers and sisters, and enjoy the fruits—not to mention pizzas—of 21st-century prosperity.

Massacre in America

May 27, 2002

I T IS RUMORED that Jedi Master Mace Windu has a certain acronym engraved upon his lightsaber. This is not due to any arcane minutiae from deep within the bowels of the Star Wars canon, but because the actor who plays the Jedi, Samuel L. Jackson, is a notoriously Bad individual with significant Oedipal issues. Although I, like many other red-blooded American males, would like to consider myself likewise Bad, I find that I cannot, despite six years in an egregiously violent martial arts dojo and a bench press of 325 pounds.

I cannot, because I spent most of those six years taking regular beatings at the hands of JD, a true Bad Dude who held a brown belt in jujitsu in addition to his black belt in our style. I can still remember my last belt test, when for one brief shining moment, I thought I could take the man. A kick that sent me flying 10 feet backward into a wall—which I struck so hard that it knocked the wind out of me—quickly illustrated the delusional aspects of that notion.

And I'll never forget going out clubbing with JD and some other Dragons, and being confronted by a drunken lout who seemed to take offense at the mere notion of the martial arts. When he demanded to know what use our training would be if he were to pull a gun, JD simply smiled, slid back his jacket to reveal a .40 caliber compact Glock, and explained that while he trusted in his ability to cope with those he could reach with his hands and feet, he felt it was also important to be prepared for those he could not.

Like I said, a Bad Dude. Now, what does this have to do with the situation currently facing America? Well, if even a deadly martial artist will freely admit that he is not capable of defending himself against an armed attack without a weapon, then what hope does the average American have?

None. Absolutely none. We are helpless.

And while I agree with the logic of Joseph Farah's recent argument that suicide bombings are unlikely in America, I am less sure that the next round of al-Qaida attacks will be the sort of shootings executed by the Japanese Red Army, Fatah Tanzim and Hamas Izz a-Din al Kassam. Whereas these groups have simply been trying to kill Jews, al-Qaida seeks to terrorize the most powerful nation on Earth, and mass shootings won't cut it in the country that invented Columbine.

This does not, of course, mean that Americans should not be prepared. Quite the opposite. I also don't expect any more hijacking attempts, since everyone in the world now knows that a hijacking no longer means a brief detour to Cuba, but that doesn't mean we should turn off the metal detectors. Indeed, our president has told us that we must all do our part in this war, and I say that we take him at his word.

Americans must remember We the People are sovereign. We have not only the right, but the responsibility to defend ourselves and our country. Therefore, I am calling for the establishment of an unofficial national holiday, Guns Against Terror Day. And to celebrate it, I have the following three suggestions:

Obtain a firearm, learn how to use it and begin to carry it at all times. Decent people do not find deadly power intoxicating, but sobering instead. This is why exactly zero of the bloodbaths predicted in the 31 states to pass carry laws have ever taken place.

Every commercial airline pilot must ignore the ridiculous announcement by the Transportation Security administration which continues the ban on firearms in the cockpit. If every single pilot in America shows up for work with a nine-millimeter on his belt, are the security bozos really going to shut down the country again? History shows that when faced by mass disobedience, governments always cave.

Teach your kids to shoot. Teach them safety, and to respect the power of a gun. If this war lasts as long as our leaders are telling us it will, they may need those skills someday.

I'm told that America will be under attack soon, so the time to act is now. I think July 4, 2002, would certainly be an appropriate day for We the People to flex our sovereign muscle and take responsibility for defending ourselves.

The ethics of revolution

June 3, 2002

I RECEIVED AN E-MAIL in response to last week's column which inspired me to think about the rights and wrongs of revolution. While the author agreed with my sentiments, he accused me and other freedom-loving writers of spending too much time on words and not enough on action. Considering that individual rights are now being violated in means more significant and systematic than they were in the time of our revolutionary forefathers, I concede he has a point.

And yet, it is worth considering what forms of action are appropriate for those who would see a return to a constitutional government respectful of individual rights and freedom. I agree that the American political system is irretrievably broken, indeed, the intricate design of checks-and-balances has mutated beyond recognition from what was originally intended to be a limited form of republican democracy, and I do not believe it is possible to effect positive change from within the bounds of the corrupt and monolithic "two-party" system.

Vote Republican, vote Democrat or don't vote at all—it makes absolutely no difference in matters of lasting significance to the nation.

Thomas Jefferson once praised the benefits of a little revolution now and then, but he may not have been entirely aware of its destructive potential. Indeed, a close look at the differences between three famous revolutions, the American, the French and the Russian, reveal that the manner in which a revolution is conducted has a tremendous effect on its aftermath. The morality, or lack thereof, demonstrated by a revolution's leaders is a matter of the utmost importance and inevitably shapes the form of the government which inherits the mantle of the old, illegitimized authority.

While the authors of the French and Russian revolutions felt that violence was quite justifiable and resorted to it as a matter of course, it is striking to see how long the Sons of Liberty waited, from the time of their formation in 1766 to "the shot heard round the world" in 1775, before shedding the blood of a single government agent. The Sons refrained from lethal violence even after the 1770 Boston Massacre, and it is worth noting that when the war finally began at Lexington and Concord, the revolutionary action was a defensive one against an armed invasion of government soldiers.

This is very different from the dialectic form of modern revolution, inspired by the French and Russian examples, wherein violent provocation is conceived in order to inspire a violent reaction that, in turn, hopes to inflame the common people to a state where they will rise up en masse to overthrow the government. The problem, of course, is that the people are usually repulsed by the revolutionaries' own violence, and so successful revolutions of this type usually require significant outside support. In fact, this form of revolution might be better characterized as a paramilitary coup, and it is no surprise that revolutions sown with such seeds of violence tend to reap the bloody harvest of the gulag and the guillotine.

In the case of the ethical revolution, the primary assault must not be on the power, but the confidence of those who rule.

There are few truly evil people in the world, and so it is of vital importance for those who wield illegitimate power to deceive themselves into believing they do so justly. There is no question that had King George and his Parliament chosen to exercise the power of the British military to its full extent, they could have crushed the rebellious movement. However, they did not have the will to do so, because Samuel Adams and his fellows had succeeded in creating serious doubts about the justice of the anti-revolutionary cause among their fellow subjects of the Crown.

The Second American Revolution, if it is to be successful, will depend on a resolute opposition to violence until the moment when the government, facing a crisis of confidence, betrays its true foundation in a manner so vicious that the scales will finally fall from the average American's eyes. Then, and only then, will it be time to raise the rattlesnake banner and remind our would-be masters of the lethal venom in the people's liberty teeth.

This does not, you understand, mean that there are not other ways to resist a lawless government that has overstepped its rightful bounds. But more on that next week…

The actions of restoration

June 10, 2002

A CALL FOR THE RETURN to constitutional government is perhaps not so much revolutionary as it is a demand for restoration. A restoration of the supremacy of the individual over the collective, of the state over the federal and, more generally, of the rule of law, not men. It is unfortunate that the current U.S. government has abandoned these principles to the point that such a restoration will require great sacrifices on the part of those who would bring it about.

Last week, I explained how violent acts of revolution would be self-defeating. This week, I have a few suggestions which are not only justifiable for men of conscience and good will, but also will help bring about the restoration of lawful constitutional government in America. The good news is that because the government's behavior is so often outside the law, the legalities are usually on our side. The bad news, of course, is that most officials prefer the status quo to enforcing the law as written.

A hallmark of totalitarian government is to co-opt those who passively oppose the enterprise by forcing them to participate in the process, which allows those in power to claim that their right to rule is legitimate. Striking at this pretense is paramount, therefore, it is imperative that patriotic American Restorationists refuse to take part in the corrupt fraud that is the federal election process. It will be very difficult to claim democratic legitimacy if the vast majority of the people refuse to take part.

Another related tactic is one I have mentioned before. The former Bureau of Internal Revenue, Puerto Rico, now known as the IRS, has successfully conned most Americans into believing that they have a responsibility to pay federal income taxes. Most do not, because very few Americans are residents of the federal United States, being instead residents of a sovereign state which is a member of the United States of America. The fact that a few corrupt judges disagree with this is of no account—look up the law and read it for yourself if you do not believe me. Then act accordingly, which for most of you means to claim exempt and stop filing.

A third step is to hammer those third parties who act as virtual agents for the federal government. Not only are you not required by law to provide your social security number in order to open a bank account or visit a doctor, but they are legally banned from asking for it. The tax reform act of 1976 and Title 42, chapter 7, subchapter II, sec. 408 (a)(8), make it a felony for any agency or instrumentality to require the disclosure of such a number, punishable with up to a one-million dollar fine, censorship, five years in prison, or a combination thereof. So, every time someone demands your SSN, call the cops on them.

Because the investment and banking systems have been inextricably tied to the IRS reporting systems, take your money out of them. Buy gold, physical gold. The government hates this, which is why FDR banned private owner-ship of it in 1933. It would be even better if individuals began accepting it as an alternate means of payment for goods and services. In any case, it's not a bad investment right now.

Read up on the laws regarding your local officials. In Oregon, more than half of the state's circuit court judges appear to be illegitimate since they've never taken the required oath of office. Check your state constitution to learn if one is required—if it is, see if the judges' oaths are on file with your secretary of state. This is a good and lawful way to eliminate the worst federalist whores. After all, your Honor, ignorance of the law is no excuse!

If you don't have a gun, buy one. If you've got one, buy one for someone else.

Now, these six suggestions may seem like petty pinpricks to the gargantuan colossus that is the federal government, but it's not as if dumping a shipload of tea into Boston Harbor shook King George's throne... at first. Government is a fragile beast, and I have no doubt that these actions, if acted upon by a dedicated few, will begin to bring about the freedom and lawful rule we seek.

If 700,000 pot smokers are willing to be arrested for their cause every year, then how much more should we, the sons of American liberty, be willing to risk for ours?

Repent and resign

June 17, 2002

And if anyone causes one of these little ones who believe in Me to sin, it would be better for him to be thrown into the sea with a large millstone tied around his neck.

—Mark 9:42

T HERE IS NO QUESTION that the Catholic Church has done humanity great service over the last 2,000 years. The Petrine rock upon which it was constructed has been a strong redoubt of light, truth and blessing throughout the centuries, and from its intellectual ramparts have sallied forth some of mankind's greatest thinkers and philosophers.

But the public unveiling of a church wherein seminaries are infested by homosexuals, bishops protect pedophiles and sin is not only embraced—but celebrated—may well come to be seen as the death of the Catholic Church in America. As with the leadership of other dying denominations such as the Episcopal and Presbyterian churches, the Catholic priesthood sold its collective soul in order to accommodate the world, in the name of tolerance and love.

And while tolerance and love may sound well enough, they have little to do with Christianity as taught by the Lord Jesus Christ. The commandment to "love others as oneself" should never be misconstrued as an instruction to tolerate sin against the Most High God, because it is primarily an order to place the same priority on others' needs as on one's own. And the needs of others, it must be said, may be for material things such as food and shelter, or for spiritual things such as correction.

For when Jesus offered his famous advice about not casting the first stone, he also went on to tell the woman, "Go now and leave your life of sin." Note that in his own words, he was not condemning her by saying this. Correction is not condemnation.

Now, sin is sin, in the eyes of God, and so it is no more fundamentally evil to be a homosexual than to be an adulterer, a murderer, a thief or a gossip. However, even a repentant sinner still bears responsibility for his actions, and if he is in a position of responsibility in the church, he must resign it because he has lost his spiritual authority. This is why James wrote that few should presume to be teachers, because those who teach "will be judged more strictly."

Indeed, the ongoing Catholic nightmare should come as no surprise to those who are familiar with the Bible. The following passage, written almost 2,000 years ago, could just as easily have been penned yesterday.

> For certain men whose condemnation was written about long ago have secretly slipped in among you. They are godless men, who change the grace of our God into a license for immorality and deny Jesus Christ our only Sovereign and Lord.

> —Jude 1:4

The infiltration and subversion of Catholic seminaries by godless men was predictable. In like manner, the Resurrection of Jesus Christ has been attacked in every mainline denomination and the same assault is currently under way in every Baptist, Southern Baptist, evangelical, Pentecostal and charismatic church as well. Although the means are often different, the aim is always the same: to subvert and ultimately deny the Gospel of the Lord Jesus Christ. And once a church makes the fatal decision to befriend the world and seek its approval instead of that of the God whom it is called to serve, its fate is sealed.

But Catholics can take heart in remembering that as Christians, they do not serve an earthly organization and they do not worship fallible men. A shattered church does not mean a shattered faith. I am a Southern Baptist, not a Catholic, but if my church should ever choose to elevate the dogma of men above the teachings of the Bible, I will leave it without shedding a single tear or ever looking back.

As for the fallen priests, it seems they already face a worse fate than burial at sea. With regards to the Catholic hierarchy, it is certain that every bishop or cardinal who has abused his position by protecting a predator must resign. It is equally important for those who then remain in authority to return to obedience by barring homosexuals and all other unrepentants from the seminary and the priesthood.

This is a battle for the soul of the American Catholic church. But far more importantly, it is a battle for the souls which that church serves.

Bear markets and bullfeathers

June 24, 2002

W HAT GOES UP MUST COME DOWN sounds better in song than in a stock market, and certainly it has not been true in America for quite some time. That being said, it is clear that the markets have finally noticed that something is awry with the structure of the American economy.

Unlike the professional analysts, I will not pretend to be able to say if this is primarily due to the loss of confidence in the system's integrity represented by the Enron-Arthur Andersen scandal, the continuing interference of government in the economy as represented by the Microsoft lawsuits, the statistical indicators, terrorism or the pending war.

Furthermore, being of the Austrian school of economics, my rejection of the entire field of macroeconomics means that if you would like a detailed statistical analysis, you will have to look elsewhere. If one is interested in fairy tales, then it should suffice to point out that an AFC team, the New England Patriots, won the Super Bowl this January and so a down market is inevitable.

But even if the statistical numbers are nothing more than frighteningly inaccurate estimates, this does not mean that they cannot be used to observe obvious trends. As has been said for years, foreign investors cannot be expected to finance the American trade deficit forever. A trade deficit normally creates a weaker currency—one that is worth less—although the U.S. has been largely immune to this in recent years because its currency has been, in effect, the global standard. As long as foreign investors were willing to keep their holdings denominated in dollars—either in the form of cash, stock, bonds or real estate—the trade deficit was not an immediate problem.

A weak dollar is not necessarily bad, because it makes investing in the U.S. a relative bargain. The problem arises when confidence is lost in both the dollar and U.S. assets. If the stock market is declining alongside the value of the dollar, this is an indication that foreign investors prefer to own non-U.S. stocks or keep their money in euros, francs or pounds. Since the historical P/E ratio of the S&P 500 is 15.5, the run up to 43.22 at the end of May was a strong indication that the U.S. stock market was very overpriced. While the dollar index is still reasonably strong, at 108, it does represent a fairly steep drop from over 120 at the beginning of the year.

And while it is anathema for most televised market analysts to discuss the probability of a serious downturn, the fact is that if these simultaneous declines in the dollar index and the stock market do indicate a newfound distaste for U.S. investment on the part of foreign investors, it is quite possible for the market to return to what would, historically speaking, be considered normal levels. Which would be, for most investors, A Very Unpleasant Thing.

Indeed, I suspect that the introduction of the Euro may have played a role in this new development—not so much because it is a competitor to the dollar, but because millions of Europeans saw their familiar currencies become worthless overnight by government dictate. They understand viscerally, in a way that we cannot, that a dollar is nothing but paper and an electronic bank account denominated in dollars is something even less.

I think that this may be a contributing factor in explaining why the price of gold, long the historical monetary standard, has risen from $260 in April, 2001, to $324 this week despite massive sales by central banks around the world. Metal investments look particularly interesting when you consider that the gold price was as high as $420 as recently as 1996, and up to $675 during the last major recession of 1982.

Now there are those who will point out that stocks always rise in the long run, and certainly if you look at charts tracking the Dow Jones average over time, this appears to be true. The problem, of course, is that of the companies which made up the Dow 100 years ago, exactly one company, General Electric, remains. So much for learning from history.

I am not, like the Marxists, predicting inevitable capitalist doom. However, I do suggest that this is a good time to pay closer attention to the markets, do some research and consider your investing alternatives.

The free market blasts off

July 1, 2002

We're going back to the Moon!
We're doing it as private enterprise!
You can come, too!

O NE OF THE MOST DEPRESSING THINGS about the state of the post-millennial American psyche is the readiness not only to accept, but actively seek out government involvement in nearly every aspect of life. From Head Start for toddlers to subsidized subscriptions for the elderly, not-so-disinterested parties continually prescribe more government aid to somebody, usually themselves.

I'm far more concerned about American addiction to government largess than any other form of dependence, since history has shown there are only two things which kill large quantities of humans in short periods of time: governments and infectious diseases. But just as it's hard for many Americans to pass up the chance to acquire some of the more social infectious diseases, it's also hard to forgo the siren song of a nice fat check from Uncle Sam.

This is why it was so refreshing to page through the strange, but weirdly compelling articles of *Artemis Magazine*. Named for the goddess of the Moon, *Artemis Magazine* is, in its own words, "science and fiction for a space-faring age" and is the house organ of the Artemis Project, a private venture to establish a permanent, self-supporting community on the Moon.

Nor are these people quite as reality-challenged as you might imagine at first. For one thing, they have a clear understanding of the primary difficulties facing them, which are not technical, but financial. Hence the presence of articles such as "Spacebiz: Sustaining the Enterprise" which analyzes the Low Earth Orbit market and examines how economies of scale will affect the financing of a hypothetical lunar station.

And for another, some of the companies involved in sponsoring project-related things like the third annual "Return to the Moon" conference don't bring to mind wild-eyed freaks who've seen "2001: A Space Odyssey" too many times so much as the Fortune 500. I really don't think Bechtel would be involved if they didn't smell the chance of making a lot of money building something somewhere, someday.

But speaking of sci-fi, there is also good bit of science fiction in the magazine, three short stories and a surprisingly good novelette by Roxanne Hutton in the issue I was reading. The novelette aside, the overall quality isn't quite up to par with *Asimov's Science Fiction Magazine*, but it's better than I expected.

The single-minded focus on all things lunar doesn't distract at all—in fact, it's quite entertaining in its own right and about halfway through the third technical article, I found myself mentioning to a potentially affected party that, come to think of it, it might be kind of cool to live on the Moon after all. Apparently, the skin-absorptive, mind-altering substance used to coat the pages of the magazine works pretty well.

I'm NOT going to live on the Moon!

—aforementioned party

Despite its commitment to the free market, the Artemis Project is not as rabidly anti-government as Adam Smith or my own bad self. Its members seem to have a very healthy respect for NASA and its past achievements, but simply aren't interested in entrusting their grandiose dream to the fumbling, bumbling hands of bureaucratic infighters. The Project rightly takes exception to NASA's notion that "human exploration is the responsibility of NASA" and, interestingly enough, also appears to disagree with NASA's current focus on Mars, since it is believed that establishing a base on the Moon is an important first step in the future exploration of Mars.

Myself, I don't particularly care about the Moon—and, to be honest, I wouldn't be shocked if we learned one day that the whole Eagle-has-landed thing was faked after all. But it does my skeptical heart good to see a group of determined people banding together and relying on their own resources to pursue their goal, however daunting or quixotic, instead of throwing their energy into trying to steal our money for the job.

I really hope they make it some day. And if they do, I think I just might tag along.

Muslim Murder

July 8, 2002

FIREWORKS ASIDE, it was a thankfully uneventful Independence Day. Not to trivialize the El Al shootings, but let's face it, our home-grown psychos usually rack up a bigger body count when they go off at the local post office, and what we were all worried about was something more on the order of another 9-11.

I didn't spend much time watching the tube, but what little I saw did manage to boil my blood. I am so very tired of hearing journalists and talking heads delicately dancing around the central issue of who these killers are and what they stand for. I am sick of talk about a war on method and I have no more patience for those who worry about offending the delicate blushes of people whose religious leaders chant "Death to America," burn American flags and threaten Christian, Jew and atheist alike.

It was downright painful to hear the *Fox News* reporters, and worse, the various poobahs at the scene, bending over backward to avoid what was immediately obvious to even the most casual observer. Come on! When someone goes into an airport and starts shooting Jews at El Al Israel Airlines, the chances that this is a random act of violence are lower than the odds of Barry Bonds passing a steroids test.

It is long past time to call a spade a freaking spade. On July 4, 2002, the Islamic Jihadist Hesham Mohamed Hadayet—like the Palestinian Islamikazes, like the 9-11 attackers, like Osama bin Laden, like the 1983 Beirut truck bombers, like the Lockerbie bombers, like Yasser Arafat, like his pal Gameel el-Batouty (the co-pilot who flew Egypt Air Flight 990 into the sea)—was committing Muslim Murder.

Muslim Murder. If we must have war on method, let us declare war on that. This is not rocket science.

And before CAIR gets its panties in a bunch again, I am not saying that all Muslims are murderers. Please note that the word "Muslim" serves as the adjective here, and not the noun. If you are not capable of understanding this distinction, don't write to me, go buy a dictionary and learn how to read the English language.

Every Muslim who kills innocent people in the name of jihad or fatwa or Allah is guilty of Muslim Murder, in exactly the same way that a Southern Baptist who blew up 3,000 people to imminentize the eschaton would be guilty of Christian Murder, or Baptist Murder... whatever.

Of course, outside of fiction and Hollywood's fevered dreams, no Christian has ever actually tried to intentionally bring about the Apocalypse. But if they ever do, I'll get on their case too. Just to be fair.

Now, I really don't care about Islam. It's not my religion. Nevertheless, I do not want to hear any more about Islam being a "religion of peace." It is not, nor has it ever been. In addition to engaging in aggressive wars that conquered reasonable chunks of the Middle East, Africa, India and Europe, Islam has a long history of internal violence dating back almost to its inception.

The second Caliph to succeed Muhammad, Umar ibn al-Khattab, was assassinated, as was the third Caliph, Uthman ibn Affan, as was the fourth Caliph, Ali ibn Abi Talib.

This history of violence was not inconsequential. The fifth Caliph and founder of the Ummayad dynasty, Muawiyyah, managed to survive long enough to pass the holy mantle of leadership to his son Yazid, who, when faced with a challenge to his rule by Muhammed's grandson, Husain, did not hesitate to massacre Husain and all his followers, including Husain's infant son.

The murders of Ali and Husain were the first great grievances of the Shiah i-Ali, better known to us in the West as the Shiite Muslims. And many centuries of similar "pacifism" followed, hence the Abbasid, Fatimid, Seljuk, Safavid, Moghul and Ottoman Empires.

Sadly, there is not the space to go into more detail regarding the serene history of this famously "peaceful" religion. Enough already. If Muslims don't want to hear about Muslim Murder, then perhaps they should consider not murdering people as an act of faith.

Fattened for the kill

July 15, 2002

I HAD AN ARGUMENT with my father a few years back. He had read Dr. Atkins book and, as is his custom, was preaching it as Holy Writ to anyone who was either A) willing to listen or B) too polite to flee. Naturally, I thought both he and Dr. Atkins were insane, since at the time, everyone knew that getting fat was a combination of eating too many calories and/or too much fat. Remember Snackwells? This was during the heyday of the no-fat cookie and ice cream sans fat. It sounds terrible now, but that Turtle Fudge Brownie was actually pretty good.

Anyhow, I felt my case was bolstered by the fact that, while Dad was carrying around some 40 extra pounds of lard, I was, literally, a lean, mean fighting machine. For two years, I ate nothing but coffee, cereal, yogurt, skim milk, tuna and protein shakes, and stacked on fifteen pounds of muscle while reducing my body fat to a level low enough to be immeasurable by the various methods available at the health club. This, I felt, was proof of my diet's superiority, never mind the fact that I was not only young, but also doing two hours of martial arts six days a week, plus lifting heavily at least five days a week.

Dad, meanwhile, was loading up on the steak and eggs for breakfast, eating salads consisting of equal parts greens and meat, and devouring so much cheese you would have been forgiven for thinking he harbored a personal grudge against Wisconsin. So no one was more surprised than my own bad self when 60 days later, Dad showed up at my brother's wedding absent 38 pounds. He claims he could have lost it faster, but he has this weakness for Cheerios, you see.

This was a bit of a blow, but I remained unconvinced until I went on a trip to Italy and Ireland. In Italy, the people were remarkably thinner than here in the U.S. despite a diet that, in the north, seems to revolve more around meats and cheese than pasta. Horse meat, elk meat, goat meat, rabbit meat, you name it, if it died a violent death it was on the menu, and the pasta dishes were approximately one-quarter the size of that to which I was accustomed. Contrast this with Ireland, where dinner consisted almost entirely of carbohydrates in one form or another. Another Guinness with that potato pie, sir? So I finally threw in the towel and conceded over a very nice steak, followed by a cheese course.

(Now diet isn't everything, of course, but let's face it, the world is divided into those who exercise and those who never will. I eat pretty much whatever I want, but I'm a gym rat and as one of my weight-lifting buddies once said, the primary benefit of stacking on muscle is the ability to burn more calories watching TV than most people do while running.)

Dad's a good winner, he didn't even say "I told you so" when the *New York Times* magazine reported last week that, well, Dr. Atkins and his high protein posse may have been right after all; he just e-mailed me the link.

So, what does this say about the official FDA recommendations, which declare that we should all be eating low-fat, high-carbohydrate diets if we want to stay in shape? For one thing, it says that the government's record of screwing up everything it gets its hands on remains intact—did we really expect anything different from the people who gave us the Department of Education, Title IX, agricultural subsidies and the New Deal?

Unless the FDA diet is doing exactly what it is supposed to do—fatten us for the kill!

I don't know if it's radical environmentalists who want to reduce the amount of land needed for producing food or aliens with a taste for human rump steak, but I have no doubt that someone is behind the charade. Dad says it's people who secretly want to reduce American life expectancy, perhaps because the pyramid scheme that is Social Security will collapse otherwise. It sounds insane, but he's probably right. Again.

But it's not all bad news. Red wine, check. Filet mignon, check. Maybe the market's tanking, but things really are looking up! Now all I need is for scientists to discover that watching NFL football makes you smarter, healthier and better-looking.

The big bad bear

July 22, 2002

I AM NO INVESTING PROFESSIONAL, but regular readers may recall that a month ago, I recommended looking into alternative investing options to the stock market, including my preferred safe haven, gold. Had you done so, you would have cleanly avoided the 15.52 percent decline that took place in the equity market in the last month, as the price of gold has remained at exactly $324.40.

While I was not as forcefully articulate then as I perhaps should have been—fly, fools, fly—it seems worthwhile to repeat the point. Why? Because if you look past the inane and self-interested declarations of *CNBC*'s analysts, you will see that nothing has changed since a month ago. Consider, if you will, a warning that was made some six years ago, and from the investor's point of view, about five years too soon.

Seldom have the unwanted words of a Cassandra been more ignored than Alan Greenspan's speech on "The Challenge of Central Banking in a Democratic Society." In that speech, given on Dec. 5, 1996, he coined the now-famous phrase "irrational exuberance" in reference to "unduly escalated asset values, which then become subject to unexpected and prolonged contractions as they have in Japan over the past decade."

It is worth noting that on that day of warning, the Dow opened at 6422.90, 19.38 percent lower than last Friday's catastrophic open of 7967.20. This is a clear indication that the market not only can continue to go down, but probably will. The mention of Japan is especially significant, because the American markets appear to be following in the Nikkei's footsteps, which hit its peak at 40,000 in early 1990 and steadily declined to below 10,000 in September 2001, where it currently languishes.

There are, of course, some major differences between the American and Japanese economies, but the most troubling aspect of the situation is the way in which the Federal Reserve has imitated the Bank of Japan's unsuccessful strategies. Injecting more liquidity into the money supply by lowering interest rates to stimulate investment in the economy certainly works, for a time, but eventually one runs out of bullets as the cost of money approaches zero. Since Japan has not been able to escape this liquidity trap for over a decade, it seems most illogical to suggest that a lengthy down market is an impossibility.

Now, one thing the American markets have going for them is the position of the dollar as the effective world standard. However, because of our past dependence on foreign investment, which comprises approximately 11 percent of the equity markets, foreigners face a veritable grizzly bear in comparison with our own hairy beast. The Dow has declined 14.79 percent since the introduction of the euro in 1999, but thanks to the euro-dollar exchange rates, European investors have suffered an additional 12.37 percent loss. Given this additional hammer to the portfolio, it is easy to understand that the average European investor is probably even less inclined to get back in the water than someone who has seen his 401k melt down to a 201k.

I could not possibly provide an exact number for a definitive bottom, and I must say that I view predictions of $1,254 gold with the same jaundiced eye with which I once regarded the 36,000 Dow. I have heard men whose financial acumen I respect greatly, tell of their expectations of a bottom in the neighborhood of 2,500 Dow and a 500 NASDAQ. If we are to finally take Mr. Greenspan at his word and recognize that a 6,400 Dow might have actually been irrationally exuberant, then it is important to realize that these dire prophecies are every bit as likely as the analysts' daily assurances that this time, we really, truly, certainly have hit rock bottom.

So what to do? It seems that many have elected to go into real estate, which doesn't appear to be the best idea since prices are already at all-time highs and may already be well into a bubble of their own. Gold, on the other hand, is still in the lower range of its historical pricing, and the increased volatility of gold mining stocks (which tends to run triple the percentage change in the spot gold price) offers some real upside if you, like me, expect the equity markets to continue their long march down the hill.

Caveat emptor: I hope you understand that this advice may not be worth more than you are paying for it, but given the last month, it seemed worth mentioning. After all, if you can keep your capital while all about you are losing theirs, then you're not doing so bad.

Christkillers

I AM NO PARAGON of secular virtue—and I enjoy a good racist/sexist/ ageist/dietist/sexual-orientationist/handicapable-ist joke poking fun at the foibles, insecurities and inadequacies of people who are not like me every bit as much as the next guy. Let's face it, life as a straight white male from a well-to-do family is pretty much a target-rich environment—I used to park my Porsche in a handicapped spot every now and then just to see people flip out.

Lecture me all you want, it was still pretty funny. Try it sometime... it's amazing how fast people who otherwise subscribe completely to a philosophy of moral relativism will do a complete 180 when faced with the Eighth Deadly Sin of someone parking in the blue space.

Growing up in the Midwest, in an area with approximately the same ethnic diversity as Heinrich Himmler's vision of Aryan paradise, I didn't know any Jews. What little I knew about Jewish culture and history was through Leon Uris and Chaim Potok, and it wasn't until attending college on the East Coast that I came into direct contact with any of the Chosen. I can't say that I noticed anything particularly different about the Jews on campus, except a lot of the girls going in for nose jobs sometime between matriculation and graduation.

As I delved into my studies of history, though, I was amazed to learn how much antipathy for the Jewish people was developed by so many different cultures. At this point in time, it's pretty much only the Chinese, Japanese and Eskimos who haven't harbored large numbers of Jew-haters in their midst, and you pretty much have to leave out the Japanese since they generally seem to hate everyone. (You can lecture me on the parking, but not this: Foreigner = gaijin = devil, wakarimasen-ka?)

I never understood why, from Haman to Hitler and Hamas, folks have had it in for the Jews in a very big way. Sure, it made sense for the average medieval king-in-debt to do away with his arrears by eliminating the lenders, but this hardly accounts for the murderous zeal of the common people. The Church ban on usury certainly must have created some envy of those who were not bound by such laws, but it's not as if the inability to legally run your own lottery often triggers the burning of Indian casinos today.

In fact, no explanation made much sense to me until later, when I became a Christian and began to twig to the spiritual element behind this human need to destroy. As with many things evil, it ultimately traces back to the fact that this world is ruled by a supernatural serial killer—who wishes destruction on everyone—but most of all upon those who belong to God. The problem is that whereas Christians have the benefit of what Paul describes in Ephesians as "the full armor of God" and are equipped to fight back against the super-psycho and his legions, Jews have little more than a promise that they will not be completely destroyed.

So, despite their differences on the Messiah's identity, Jews and Christians are on the same team. There is no great division between them, since God does not break His promises and He will keep those that He has made to both peoples. Any other division is man-made, and it is as stupidly nonsensical to blame Christians today for the wrongdoings of our medieval forebears as it was for those forebears to blame the Jews of their day for crucifying Jesus Christ. Who, by the way, was a Jew.

The *New York Times* may find it hard to understand why Southern Baptists in Texas and Evangelical Lutherans in Iowa firmly support Israeli Jews they've never met, don't know and with whom they have nothing in common, but I don't. Because when the fallen world in all its rage comes slavering after the chosen people of God, it is our job as Christians to stand in the gap and protect them. Corrie ten Boom understood this—so did Padre Ruffino Niccacci of Assisi, Rev. Dietrich Bonhoeffer and many others.

I still don't know many Jews. But I know that if the force which once inspired the Endeks, the Black Hundreds and the Waffen SS—and now inspires Hamas and the Islamic Jihad—ever comes for them here in the USA, it will have to get past me and millions of other like-minded evangelical Christians first.

Driving with a sledgehammer

August 5, 2002

Watching CNBC or reading the business section of the *Wall Street Journal* leaves one marveling at the wondrous ability of federal bureaucrats to scrutinize—down to the millionth decimal place—everything from the percentage change in the price of bread in Topeka to the number of durable pieces of machinery manufactured in July. Ah… if only the philosophers of an earlier time had known these marvelous techniques—they surely would have been able to accurately calculate the number of angels who could dance on the head of a pin!

Precision, you understand is important, because without it the Federal Reserve could not "fine-tune" the economy, trusting in the gargantuan brains of Chairman Alan Greenspan and his posse to wisely use the tools of monetary policy in order to outwit the Invisible Hand of the ostensibly free markets. And without such Keynesian fine-tuning, we would presumably otherwise be living in caves, or worse—never mind the centuries of economic growth and technological development that took place prior to the creation of the Federal Reserve in 1913.

Still, I know economics can seem boring—hence "the dismal science" appellation. So, if this column is putting you to sleep like an unwanted pound puppy, please feel free to depart for the esteemed and doubtless more interesting scribblings of Mr. Medved, Ms. Simpson or, ladies and gentlemen, Mr. Joseph Farah!

Still here? OK, let's rock. You may recall that one of the reasons the market gave up most of its 444-point gain from a week ago was the news that economic growth for the second quarter was worse than expected. Instead of continuing to hum along at the extraordinarily healthy rate of the 6.1 percent reported for the first three months of the year, the economy grew only 1.1

percent from April through June. Bad news and a big decline, but at least the economy is still moving forward right?

Wrong.

The problem is that the GDP numbers being reported are less accurate than Tony "INT" Banks. The Austrian economist F. A. von Hayek pointed out the impossibility of gathering the accurate economic data required for socialist calculation more than 50 years ago, and his contentions tend to be supported by a look at the numbers used by the Grand Masters of the Universe themselves. Here is a chart containing the official GDP numbers reported on July 31, 2002:

Quarter	GDP Growth	GDP Previous
2001 Q1	-0.6	1.3
2001 Q2	-1.6	0.3
2001 Q3	-0.3	-1.3
2001 Q4	2.7	1.7
2002 Q1	5.0	6.1
2002 Q2	???	1.1

As you can see, the difference between the previously reported "official" numbers and the new "revised" numbers averages 1.22, which, in light of the data for the current quarter, is a discrepancy of a mere 111 percent. This is as if *ESPN* reported that Babe Ruth hit 714 home runs… or, upon further review, 1,507. Or something.

This huge margin of error is actually lower than the Federal Reserve's historical standard, which is 1.4. Thus, the 1.1 percent growth reported last week may quite possibly turn out to be a .3 percent decline three months from now, and would mark the onset of the second phase of the double-dip recession that all the financial analysts were busily discounting as they announced their daily sightings of the bear-market bottom.

If the Q2 numbers are revised downward in such manner, then all of the decisions which are being made now—from Alan Greenspan considering new basis-point cuts to first-time homebuyers wondering how much of a mortgage to assume—will almost surely be incorrect. After all, what business wants to commit to new capital investments if the economy is entering a serious recession and its sales are about to drop? Decisions based on bad data are not necessarily wrong, but they are more likely to be wrong, and especially if one is under the false impression that the data is accurate.

Now, I am with the Austrian school of economics which asserts that this data is not only bad, but essentially fictitious, and attempting to use it to outsmart the Invisible Hand is both a threat to freedom and doomed to failure. But I hope you can see that even if one accepts the economy's statistical indicators at face value, using them to fine-tune the economy is like driving a car with a sledgehammer. Repeated blows on the steering wheel might allow you to keep the vehicle on the road for a while, if you're lucky, but eventually a crash will come.

So, in the immortal words of Public Enemy, "don't believe the hype." The double-dip is here, and I'm guessing the S&P 500 will see an eponymous 500 before it gets back to 1500 again.

It's on!

August 12, 2002

THIS IS NOT a column in support of the notion of invading Iraq—nor is it intended to criticize any such invasion. As any student of military history knows, the truth of what leads up to a military action is seldom wholly discernible by those who are not at the center of events. What seems obviously justifiable at the time may appear much less so in the future, and even the most apparently outrageous action may turn out to have been merited upon further review.

For the last month, the mainstream media has been buzzing with the news of a peace camp and a war camp within the Bush administration, senators have announced that they know nothing about any military plans, European leaders have washed their hands of any potential involvement, and any number of top-secret, mutually contradictory military plans have appeared in major newspapers.

You would think, in light of this heightened interest in all things Iraq-related, someone would bother to mention that the invasion has already begun.

In the image conveyed by Hollywood, wars start approximately eight hours after the president clenches his jaw and drops a few determined f-bombs in the direction of his well-starched Praetorian Guard. In reality, there are weeks, even months, between the time that the fatal decision is made and the shooting begins. For example, the tragic events of World War I became inevitable as soon the major players had set their grand mobilization plans into action.

Admittedly, the case of Iraq is a little harder to judge because our armed forces have been consistently bombing Iraq almost since the end of the original Desert Storm, but there is no question that the actions now under way are of a distinctly different nature than the cat-and-mouse game that's been played for the last decade in the No-Fly Zones.

Now, it is possible that the news reported by DEBKAfile is simply more of the misinformation and disinformation flowing so freely out of Washington these days, but given this particular website's past track record, I submit that this Internet information is much more accurate than that provided by any White House spokesman.

It is worth noting that the destruction of the Iraqi air command-and-control center at al-Nukhaib appears to have ensured that the U.S. forces will enjoy the same air supremacy which was wielded to such deadly effect in Gulf War I. The six air bases constructed and now ready to go active inside Iraqi territory, plus the giant new bases in Qatar and Afghanistan, will no doubt obviate any need for the dubious assistance of erstwhile allies such as Saudi Arabia and Egypt and allow the U.S. to blow off both these so-called Arab moderates as well as their European apologists.

But what is most interesting is the report that Turkish forces are now acting as American auxiliaries. If the Bamerni airport is truly in the hands of our newly active allies, then a significant portion of the Iraqi oil supplies are already under U.S. control. This will make any Iraqi strike against Saudi Arabia or Kuwait much less dangerous to world oil supplies and the American economy. Of course, this would also seem to increase the chances of a desperate Iraqi strike at Israel, which is no doubt why Israel has recently installed new Arrow-2 anti-missile batteries as well as demonstrating an uncharacteristic lack of concern for international opinion in recent weeks.

What is particularly significant in the long-term is that the new Israeli-Turkish-American alliance, which has also forged strong ties to India, hints at a major shift in the strategic balance of power. Turkey, India and Israel possess more military power than the entire European Union, and given the threat radical Islam poses each of these three nations, it is clear that the Bush administration has much more in mind than a mere sequel to Gulf War I.

Thus, it would not surprise me if before the end of what could be a Seventh Crusade, we see new governments come to power in Iraq, Iran, Saudi Arabia, the Palestinian Authority and perhaps Egypt. Deus le volt? I don't know.

None of this is news to Mr. Hussein, of course, nor to the man who claims he hasn't yet decided how or when Mr. Hussein will be removed from power.

But given that we live in a country where we the people are supposed to be sovereign, I thought you should know, too.

Of the banks, for the banks

August 19, 2002

I T'S HARD TO IMAGINE something more egregiously offensive than the upcoming baseball strike, which features billionaire owners and millionaire players competing for our sympathy, but the Bush administration has managed it nevertheless.

We like to think that we live in a free society, but the truth is that we do not. Just try buying a new car with that paper that says "this note is legal tender for all debts, public and private" and you'll soon find out how flexible the government's definition of private property has become. And as the recent bailout of Brazil quite clearly demonstrates, the idea that we live in a free market economy is another misconception. My Econ 101 days are a bit hazy, I confess, but I can't imagine Adam Smith describing banker's loan insurance as a proper function of laissez faire government.

In fact, even the description of the recent International Monetary Fund's action as a "bailout of Brazil" is a misnomer. The bailout is not for the benefit of the Brazilian government, much less its people, but for large American banks like Citigroup, J.P. Morgan Chase and FleetBoston which are faced with the prospect of writing off $25.6 billion in bad loans should Brazil default on its debts. This is why the IMF recently handed over $37 billion to Brazil with the approval of President Bush and Treasury Secretary Paul O'Neill despite candidate Bush's supposed opposition to such bailouts.

Nor is this the first time that American taxpayers have been forced to bail out Brazil, as the country of progress and order received $15 billion last year, in addition to $41 billion in 1998 under the Clinton regime. It makes no difference if there is a Republican or a Democrat in the White House—if the large international banks get themselves in trouble, the politicos of both parties come running to heed their masters' call.

The fact that this comes at a time when so many Americans were unwise enough to put their entire savings into the stock market on the advice of their financial advisers and *CNBC* gurus only makes the Bush administration's corrupt decision that much more despicable. One expects this sort of thing from an openly dishonest man like Bill Clinton, but I can understand if some of you hoped for more from his successor.

What is perhaps most ludicrous about the entire episode is that Citigroup and J.P. Morgan Chase bid fair to go down in flames anyhow. Morgan is the most likely casualty, as their derivatives exposure is $23.5 trillion according to the U.S. Office of the Comptroller of the Currency. To put this in perspective, the entire U.S. economy is considered to be about $10.4 trillion annually!

An important part of Morgan's exposure appears to be linked to the gold market (the bank owned 68 percent of all bank-owned gold derivatives earlier this year), so if the price of gold manages to puncture $330 sometime despite the best efforts of the central banks, shorting JPM would probably be a very, very good idea. One investment analyst who began researching Morgan's massive derivatives exposure about nine months ago claims to have already made almost 400 percent through a series of JPM shorts.

Unfortunately, J.P. Morgan Chase is not alone in its financial mismanagment. In fact, the 30 companies that make up the Dow Jones Industrial Average have only $728 billion in book value compared to $3.3 trillion in liabilities, according to their quarterly reports. So put that in your 401(k) and smoke it!

Though we obviously don't have an entirely free market, I suspect the Invisible Hand still packs enough punch to take down more than a few of these mishandled corporations. Unfortunately, in the process, many will have to suffer for the evil machinations of an egocentric few. Should that day come, I have no doubt that many impressive words will be spewed by Democrats and Republicans alike, but don't let the rhetoric blind you to the fact that it's those holding the leashes at Citigroup and J.P. Morgan Chase who created the disaster in the first place.

In the meantime, please keep in mind that a portfolio divided between large caps, small caps, growth funds and hedge funds is not a diversified portfolio. Money markets, real estate and gold are all integral parts of properly managing investment risk even in the best of times, much less in times of war and a rampaging bear market.

A lethal addiction

August 26, 2002

I LIKE JONAH GOLDBERG. Not that I've met him personally, you understand, but I've been reading his columns for National Review Online for quite a while now. He's funny, insightful and most sound on the French, or "cheese-eating surrender monkeys," as he prefers to call them.

I recently returned from Paris, and I must say that it is, indeed, good to hate the French. Mr. Goldberg not only understands the important difference between a democracy and a republic, but also correctly acknowledges the advantage of the latter over the former. And one can't help but admire a writer who devotes significant amounts of space to Cosmo, the Wonder Dog. If you don't read his stuff, you should.

Now, you can probably hear the "but" coming on like Jennifer Lopez in spandex. So here it is: Like most conservatives, Jonah appears to miss the most significant aspects of libertarian thought, and even flirts with intellectual dishonesty from time to time by deliberately reducing serious philosophical objections to silly straw men.

Conservatives seem to think of libertarians as a combination of pothead idealists and philosophy-mad sex addicts, while viewing themselves as hard-headed pragmatists firmly rooted in the grit and grind of the real world. And they are the salt of the earth, truly they are, but when it comes to libertarian thought, they simply do not understand it.

I'm not saying, of course, that I don't know any libertarians who smoke the devil ganja from time to time and there are surely a few who have personal inclinations to make Caligula blush but, by and large, most of the serious libertarians I know and read are nothing more than ex-conservatives. Just as a conservative has been described as a liberal who was mugged, a libertarian is a conservative who got wise to who is really doing the serious mugging in this formerly great nation of ours. So put that in your water pipe and smoke it… or Just Say No, as you like. That's the beauty of liberty.

The atomic foundation of libertarian thought is nothing more than this: Government is like fire. Fire can be useful, fire can be desirable on a cold winter day and it can even be desperately needed on occasion, especially when the alternative is eating raw dead pig. But fire is always—always—dangerous, and if you turn your back on it, it will burn your house down at the first opportunity, most likely with you in it. Government may occasionally be a necessary evil, but it is an EVIL! Government bad, freedom good. Aristotelian individual liberty trumps the Platonic public imperative.

Can you seriously argue with that? Remember, in the previous century, more people died at the hands of their own governments than died in every war and civil war combined. If people are given Nobel Prizes for trying to outlaw war, then shouldn't something be done for the individual who has contributed the most in attempting to outlaw government?

In the shadow of the 9-11 hijackings, leftist journalists have tried to argue that government is "making a comeback" and that "public trust in government has never been higher." How could that be? The one thing the federal government is supposed to do is to provide for the national defense, a responsibility for which it failed miserably, in a shockingly obvious way!

Yes, the firefighters and policemen who gave their lives doing their jobs were very brave, and we rightly honor them, but they were individuals and there is nothing inherently governmental about their occupations. Volunteer firefighters and private security guards not only provide very similar services as their publicly-funded counterparts, but they significantly outnumber them across the country as well—by a factor of more than 10 to one.

Indeed, many of those brave firefighters might well have survived had they been working for a private firm which did not use the labyrinthian procurement methods of the New York City government, thus allowing them to have state-of-the-art communications equipment.

Conservative proponents of government, unfortunately, have increasingly tended to mutate into the pale echoes of their socialist (liberal) counterparts. They support Social Security, but in a reformed manner. Ditto for subsidized health care. They support the unconstitutional federal income tax, but they want to see the rates reduced. On every issue of substance, from the Federal Reserve to the IRS, the IMF and the United Nations, their positions are identical to those of their supposed ideological enemies.

Which raises the question: If even the conservatives are progressives now, why do we bother with a Constitution?

False idols of ideology

September 2, 2002

WHILE MOST OF THE RESPONSES to last week's column on conservatism and libertarianism were favorable, there was also repetition of a few specific criticisms which, due to their general fogginess of logic, demand address.

First, libertarianism is not anarchy. If it was anarchy, or a total lack of governmental order, one would simply call it that. There would be no such thing as libertarians, only anarchists. The fact that the two parties identify themselves separately and are easily distinguished should serve as the first clue that perhaps libertarians are not, in fact, anarchists.

Second, to be libertarian is not necessarily to be a libertine. A libertine is a hedonist, a devotee of personal pleasure, whereas a libertarian is one who defends the libertine and his lifestyle against the heavy hand of government. This does not mean the two should ever be equated, as libertarians will just as readily defend the evangelical pro-life protester, the Jewish intellectual, the pagan pothead or the Catholic cigarette smoker.

However, it is the third criticism in which I am most interested, which is that a society run by a Libertarian government cannot possibly function as conceived. What puzzles me is the implied demand for the Libertarian Party to be judged by a standard which is never, ever applied to either the Democratic or the Republican parties.

Political ideologies represent the manifestation of intellectual ideals. Shall we not then examine the intellectual ideals of our two major parties? Democrats like to blather interminably about democracy, which presumably represents their ideal. But despite some whining about the Electoral College after the last presidential election, no Democrat ever talks seriously about using the power of eminently available technology to wholly replace the three branches of federal government with what would be the perfectly realized Will of the People.

Of course, it is not true democracy that interests Democrats as much as the expansion of central power at the expense of the states and the individual. In either case, one seldom hears critiques based on either of the party's ideologies, eponymous or hidden.

Republican ideology is based on republicanism, which conceives a government in which the sovereign authority is granted by the people, and which rules according to law. This ideal is rather closer to our constitutional form of government, but has not been in force in this country since 1865, which is when the first Republican president elected to use military force to end what was a legal and distinctly constitutional secession. Say what you will of slavery, but the South still surrendered at the point of a gun.

Indeed, Republicans in office show no more regard for the law than their Democratic counterparts, who at least have the theoretical excuse of being ideologically opposed to the notion of limited government. The Republican party, for all its small-government posturing, seems to more accurately represent the ideal of maintaining the status quo and using the power of central government on behalf of more traditional interests. And since history shows that the one thing that cannot ever be maintained is the status quo, here, too, the Republican ideals fall short.

Therefore, if you would judge the hypothetical failings of Libertarian ideology, how much more must you condemn the manifest flaws of the Democratic and Republican ideals?

The truth is, neither I nor any other Libertarian can say precisely what is the true and proper size of government that would maximize individual freedom and liberty. What I can say with complete assurance is that it is much smaller than the massively corrupt institutions that plague us at the local, state and federal levels.

By the way, I'll go so far as to assert that God, in addition to being a monarchist, also has strongly libertarian leanings. How else can you describe an all-powerful king who goes so far as to let his creation choose whether to obey him or not? Liberty is all about the individual freedom to choose, and those who try to deny it are not on the side of the angels no matter what they might think.

No, I'm not "pro-choice" in the sense of pro-abortion terminology—quite the opposite. This stays well within the framework of Libertarian logic because there are, quite obviously, at least two parties involved, possibly even three. The fact that one is incapable of consent only makes the Libertarian anti-abortion argument that much more clear.

Feeble-minded feminists

September 9, 2002

I LOATHE FEMINISTS. While there are elements of the left which I can respect, they are not one. I despise them wholeheartedly—not only for their murderous tendencies and the havoc their ideology has wreaked on America and its families, but also for their feebleness of philosophy and total disregard for logic, consistency or easily foreseeable consequences.

More dictatorial than Sulla, more two-faced than Janus, feminists are the poisoned dregs of American politics.

Rush Limbaugh once predicted that the fastest 180-degree spin on record would be the homosexual lobby's abandonment of its generally pro-abortion position, if and when the "gay gene" was scientifically proven. Of course, the Q-gene turned out to be a fictional thing, and so Rush's prophecy went untested.

But the chaotic genius of technological change is now delivering yet another ethical challenge to those who ponder the good, the right and the true of things, and promises to demonstrate once more that feminists speak with forked tongues even with regards to their most cherished "right."

A company called Microsort, in partnership with a Belgian laboratory, now offers a service wherein it separates the X- and Y-chromosome-bearing sperm, thus allowing prospective parents to choose the sex of their child with a 91 percent success rate in the case of a girl, 75 percent in the case of a boy. The procedure runs around $6,500, and the odds can even be improved in conjunction with a pre-implantation examination.

Now, it is no secret that for the last few millennia, people have generally shown a strong preference for sons over daughters. This has been for a variety of reasons, some relevant today and some less so, but the increasing gender imbalance in China under its "one-child" policy demonstrates that this preference persists into modern times.

Feminists, of course, purport to stand for "a woman's right to choose." And yet, the first women to speak out on the procedure, naturally, are against this unnatural form of sex selection. Dr. Francoise Shenfield, from the University College Medical School in London, says:

> *I simply do not feel it is right to be able to choose the sex of your child for no medical reason. What impact would it have on the other children, and what would it mean for women's position in society?*

It is quite possible that Dr. Shenfield is no feminist. But can anyone seriously doubt that her words will be echoed by American feminists as soon as this sex-selecting technique comes to the attention of the mainstream media? Then, Mr. Limbaugh's favorite punching bags will be in the undesirable position of arguing that (a) it's wrong for a woman to choose the sex of her baby, but (b) she has the unquestioned right to kill the baby if she feels like it.

Nevertheless, they'll argue this—you know they will—not just with straight faces, but with a self-righteous air of indignation.

I don't see anything morally wrong with sex selection myself, although I would sure hate to live in a society where men outnumbered women 1.44 to 1, as they already do in some parts of China. Freedom means that one has the right to make foolish decisions as well as smart ones, and this is just as true for a society as an individual.

Certainly, there's nothing in the Constitution which provides a basis for the federal government to pass laws about this, although if enough people are upset, they'll probably come up with some tortuous reasoning relating to how the shortage of street hookers is affecting interstate commerce.

Thus, I'm pro-choice. I believe that prospective parents have the right to complete freedom with regards to how many children they have, what they're called and whether they wear pink or blue hats in the nursery. They clearly don't, however, have the right to kill them, pre- or post-birth, given that part in the Declaration of Independence about the right to life endowed unalienably by one's Creator.

In answer to those who think it's so unthinkably unfair that one mistake should saddle a girl with the responsibility of a child, well, that's life, sometimes. There are plenty of smaller mistakes that carry far more terrible conse quences, like falling asleep at the wheel and crossing the highway divider, or diving into a pool without first checking the depth.

There is no justification for murdering babies and there never will be. I say calling a feminist a feminazi is an insult to National Socialism.

The NFL, Europe and Iraq

September 16, 2002

U NLIKE OTHER SPORTS FANS, I am not in the least perturbed by the defeat of the U.S. national team at the World Basketball Championships. While I do believe that sports can be a reasonable metaphor for war, I don't believe them to be so in the flag-waving, jingoistic sense that permeated the Cold War rivalry between the USA and USSR.

It may be embarrassing that our highly-paid professionals have finally been unmasked for the hopeless one-dimensional charlatans sans fundamentals that they are, but basketball is a simple, easily mastered sport at which any country can excel, given a little time, effort and a few overactive pituitary glands. Yugoslavia may be a basketball giant, but I wasn't too concerned about their imperial ambitions even when Slobodan Milosevic was constructing Greater Serbia.

I am, however, concerned about the fact that Johnnie Morton, the number three wide receiver on my fantasy football team, barely caught a pass as the Kansas City Chiefs racked up 40 points. I am even more concerned that those 40 points were racked up on my Cleveland defense. Even worse, I'm a lifelong Vikings fan—thus I knew that Dwayne Rudd is a hopeless yahoo, and I picked them anyhow. What was I thinking? If I were The Sports Guy, I would now set myself on fire. Fortunately, the New England D was still available on waivers.

Now, in addition to the American game, I also follow European football, generally known as soccer. On the club level, I follow Arsenal, and the fact that Manchester United has already dropped six points on the Gunners is like a balm to my wounded purple soul after the last-minute debacle in Chicago last week.

What does this have to do with anything, much less Iraq? Here's the point: Europeans understand American foreign policy about as well as they understand our game of football. Which is to say, not at all. Not only do they not understand either, but they are hopelessly confused as to the fundamental underpinnings of both.

Europeans focus almost exclusively on the physical side of football. They see it as an incredibly violent game that falls barely within the realm of civilization, a brutal, barbaric sport which appeals primarily to the lowest human instincts. What they do not see is the incredible amount of planning and strategizing which goes into every play, the powerful cerebral elements that define and shape the game. If football was only a game of physical talent, the St. Louis Rams could never have lost to the Patriots in last year's Super Bowl, but the NFL is 60 minutes of chess played with muscular humans in the place of pawns.

Soccer, on the other hand, involves almost no strategic thinking. I cannot exaggerate how hopeless Europeans can be when it comes to this sort of thing. I once played for an Italian team which was excellent defensively, but had a lot of trouble scoring. This was because our primary form of attack was to send the ball to the corners, then cross it in looking for headers. Not a bad tactic, in general, but a little sub-optimal when your two strikers are both less than 5 feet 4 inches tall.

Our manager's answer to our scoring problem, of course, was not to change strikers or strategies, but to practice our crosses more often. That worked almost as well as the sanctions on Iraq have so far.

This lack of strategic thinking is why the United States cannot expect any help or even reasonable discussion from our European allies. They are not capable of assessing the situation in a logical manner, nor are they able to formulate viable strategies—much less tactics.

As for me, I'm not sure of how I feel about the ongoing war on Iraq. I certainly don't like how the government uses war as an excuse to trample our rights, but considering that they've already accomplished quite a bit of that with the Patriot Act, then we might as well reap some of the benefits too, like a new model Middle East constructed on the Japan plan.

And if you don't mind me casting cold reason to the wind for once, I think I'd like to see not one, but six 9-11 monuments. One in New York City, the others in Baghdad, Riyadh, Kabul, Damascus and Tehran. They started it, so let's finish it.

My hero, Alan Greenspan

September 23, 2002

A S THE EQUITY MARKET BUBBLE continues to burst, corporations hemorrhage red ink and the average investor's net worth shrinks like a cotton t-shirt inside a dryer set on high, it is becoming increasingly popular to criticize the chairman of the Federal Reserve, also known as The Genius That is Greenspan.

TGTG, of course, insists that he is not to blame for the ongoing equity debacle. He argues that not only are the wild outbursts of speculation that characterize an investment bubble totally unpredictable, but unstoppable as well. Why? Because, in his own words earlier this month, "changes in margins (the amount an investor is required to deposit in his brokerage account) are not an effective tool for reducing stock market volatility."

This would, of course, seem to fly in the face of what TGTG said on Sept. 24, 1996, when he admitted "there is a stock market bubble at this point … We do have the possibility of raising major concerns by increasing margin requirements. I guarantee that if you want to get rid of the bubble, whatever it is, that will do it."

Some say that TGTG is incompetent. Others claim that while he was fully aware of the implications of feeding a high-octane money supply into the overheated engine of the stock markets, he was too frightened of the recession that would inevitably follow to turn the pump off. Others feel that TGTG simply reveled in the glory of presiding over what was thought to be the greatest period of prosperity in human history, which brought him a knighthood among other things.

Regardless, there can be little doubt that the implosion of the equity markets will soon be followed by the pricking of the credit and real estate bubbles. As great financial houses such as Citigroup and JP Morgan Chase teeter on the edge of bankruptcy, it is well within the realm of possibility that the triple whammy of the equity, credit and real estate implosions will lead to the collapse of the entire global financial system.

And all thanks to TGTG. My hero.

You see, I reject the notion that TGTG is incompetent, cowardly or vain. I contend that he is a superhero, an agent undercover, a mild-mannered chairman of the Federal Reserve Board by day and a freedom-fighting Randian titan by night. Consider the two following quotes:

> *In the absence of the gold standard, there is no way to protect savings from confiscation through inflation. There is no safe store of value…. The financial policy of the welfare state requires that there be no way for the owners of wealth to protect themselves. This is the shabby secret of the welfare statists' tirades against gold. Deficit spending is simply a scheme for the confiscation of wealth.*

> —Alan Greenspan, "Gold and Economic Freedom," 1967

> *The substantive financial powers of the world were in the hands of these investment bankers (also called "international" or "merchant" bankers) who remained largely behind the scenes in their own unincorporated private banks. These formed a system of international cooperation and national dominance which was more private, more powerful and more secret than that of their agents in the central banks… They could dominate governments by their control over current government loans and the play of the international exchanges.*

> —Carroll Quigley, *Tragedy and Hope,* 1966

It is clear that TGTG, from his humble beginnings as an acolyte of Ayn Rand, has been secretly determined to shoulder the weight of the financial world on his shoulders, then, like Samson in the temple of Dagon, bring it down upon himself and his fellow Masters of the Universe who are holding us captive in endless financial serfdom. Hard days may lie ahead, but soon the day will come when there will be no more Federal Reserve, no more confiscation through inflation, no more federal debt, and no more unconstitutional income tax.

America will be free again, all thanks to my hero, the genius that is Alan Greenspan

The war vote

September 30, 2002

T HE SENIOR DEMOCRATIC LEADERSHIP says that the Bush administration should not politicize the war on Iraq. Let me get this straight. They are saying that in what passes for a representative democracy, our elected politicians should not have to tell their constituents exactly what their position is on this war. This ridiculous position, in itself, should be enough reason for any reasonable human to vote against a cretin like Daschle.

Still, it seems to me that a vote authorizing force against Iraq might be just a little late. Since it is commonly understood that hijacking four passenger planes and flying them into three buildings and an empty field is an act of war, what would we call it, then, if hundreds of planes had bombed Air Force bases at Edwards, Thule and Wright-Patterson and enemy armored divisions were occupying Michigan, Minnesota, Iowa, Wisconsin and the Dakotas? Ragnarok? You see, that's the equivalent of what we've already done to Iraq in the past six weeks with the help of our Turkish allies. In other words, this war is well under way regardless of how one feels about it.

I don't think Israel has forgotten that the last time the United States asked them not to respond to an Iraqi missile attack, our intrepid commander in chief reneged on his promise to finish Saddam Hussein. I suspect that Ariel Sharon will be just a little bit more willing to drop the hammer than was Yitzhak Shamir back in 1991.

Anybody else wonder if there are a few Air Force cowboys who've got "Killing an Arab" or "Rock the Casbah" cranked up in the cockpit as they drop their bombs between the minarets and all that? Then again, that's probably way too '80s for our current generation of flyboys, and something more on the order of Disturbed is probably in order:

Someone is gonna die
When you listen to me
Let the living die,
Let the living die

I think I should probably order that Enigma-David Sylvian-Enya chill-out CD one of these days. I'm just feeling a little less tolerant of "the religion of peace" and its practitioners ever since reading about the killing of the seven Christian charity workers in Pakistan. Regardless of how you feel about Christian fundamentalists, you must admit that we seldom shoot anyone execution-style, especially not people whose only crime is to be helping the less fortunate.

Granted, I'm a little more open to the notion of all things conspiratorial than your average guy, but does anyone else think the timing of the announced discovery of that 33 pounds of enriched uranium is just a little suspicious? Personally, I won't be surprised if they eventually find a UPS receipt from Calvert Cliffs addressed to one Mr. Saddam Hussein, Baghdad.

Since we're doing this war anyhow, I sincerely hope we do it without the blessing of the U.N. and the hapless gang of Euroweenies. And if we need a few extra troops to occupy Iraq, Iran, Saudi Arabia and any other former colony we happen to scoop up in the process, let's pull them out of Germany. If nothing else, it would be worth it just for the look of horror on French faces when they realize that Uncle Sam won't be around to keep the Hun at their feet any longer.

Speaking of the Hun, I assume we can all agree that Doris Schroeder is far too spitze for her little dumpling, Gerhard. What does she see in him? Then again, I don't understand what the German electorate sees in the man either. The German chancellor makes Sen. Daschle look like a wise and fair-minded leader of the people by comparison.

Considering how many innocent Jews died at their hands, you would think that the Europeans would be at least a little circumspect in criticizing how Israel is handling its war against the Palestinians.

Regardless of when this war officially gets under way, I don't think there's any need for all this apocalyptic talk. Of course, if Heimdall blows his horn from the Rainbow Bridge, all bets are off.

Kissing an Arab

October 7, 2002

I MUST CONFESS that despite being a Southern Baptist Christian fundamentalist, I have a certain thing in common with the average multicul-
tural atheist. They do not share my faith in Jesus Christ, I do not share
their rejection of the notion of Western cultural superiority. I do, however,
have all the cultural disdain for them that they hold for me and my kind.

In addition to an inherent suspicion of dead, white European males, their
accomplishments and theories, a multiculto (noun, singular, masculine em-
braces feminine) is defined by his belief in the equivalency of all cultures. This
is, of course, utter nonsense, as P.J. O'Rourke demonstrated so colorfully in
his imperative and hilarious call for "cliterectomies for all the girls!"

I am not saying that there is absolutely nothing that the postmodern West
could stand to learn from a tribe of Stone Age cannibals who have somehow
managed to eke out a subsistence survival for some 3,000 years, but I imagine
that the list of desired cultural additions would prove rather small, at least
from the point of view of the average American.

But reason works about as well in stopping the semi-detached minds of the
multiculti in their collective tracks as an opossum a semi-detached tractor-
trailer. This is unfortunate, because while you might think that in the face
of the threat posed by expansionist Islam, the multiculti gaggle (a goose
metaphor seems somehow appropriate, don't you think?), would see fit to
come to terms with the Western Christian culture from which it sprang, it has
chosen instead to embrace a benighted culture which has even less sympathy
for it than I.

This is not only unfortunate, but staggeringly ironic, given that in the eyes
of the multiculti, the primary sin committed by Western Christian culture is
its noxious interference with the goddess-given right of every man, woman
or child to engage in sexual relations with the animal, plant or mineral of

his-her desire. After all, who would have invented the steam engine, much less the integrated circuit, were not the individuals responsible free to slake their desire in the most personally satisfactory means available?

Since cultural development apparently depends on who puts what where, it can be no mystery why those countries wherein Islamic culture reigns supreme haven't achieved a whole lot since their much-appreciated development of the zero and base-10 numerology. On Oct. 3, 2002, Reuters reported that a 50-year-old actress, one Gohar Kheirandish, violated Iran's Islamic law by kissing the forehead of her director, Ali Zamani, who happens to be young enough to be her son.

The horror, the horror!

The chief of the local department of justice did not delay in ordering the arrest of these two dangerous miscreants, even as a representative of the Ayatollah Ali Khamenei organized a protest against these enemies for targeting Islamic beliefs and trying to harm Islam. If this is the official Islamic reaction to a chaste public kiss, it really makes one look forward to the inevitable verbal histrionics when Baghdad gets flattened later this month.

So perhaps the multiculti operate by an Animal Farm dictum wherein all cultures are equal but some cultures are more equal than others—or perhaps they're simply a ridiculous band of knee-jerk, anti-Christian, anti-Western, anti-American pseudo-intellectuals. I don't really care, but I remain astounded by their sensitivity and concern for the Muslims in our midst and out there in the Dar-al-Islam.

Islam does not mean "peace". It means "submission", as in: "If you ever give us half a chance, you can forget about Britney Spears, coed dorms and the Dallas Cowboy Cheerleaders." Thus, it's quite easy to see that "multiculturalist" indisputably means "clueless, self-defeating idiot."

P.S.—Yes, of course I know that Iran isn't Arab, but Persian. But you can't seriously expect me to resist a play on words like that now, can you?

Two wars

October 14, 2002

I WAS SPEAKING with an Australian friend last week, an insightful and intelligent man whose opinion I highly respect. He contends, and I do not disagree, that America has developed an increasing tendency to behave in an imperialist manner which tends to inspire hatred in its enemies and suspicion in those who are otherwise friendly towards it.

Please understand that I am not advocating the suicidal sacrifice of U.S. sovereignty to the evil fraud that is the United Nations, like those who would leave our national security in the hands of the French, Chinese and Syrian governments. I am, however, skeptical of such things as the global dollar economy, the International Monetary Fund and stationing American troops around the world in the support of questionable governments whose only virtue is a willingness to offer the well-being of their people on the altar of the overvalued dollar.

But while the war on Iraq reflects aspects of this financial imperialism, its primary significance is the role it will play in the ongoing clash of civilizations between Islam and the West.

For although the United States is now regarded as the Great Satan in Islamic circles, this is a recent development which came about long after expansionist Islam had revealed its vicious, murderous nature in Kashmir, in Algeria and in the Philippines. If the United States is particularly hated, it is only because it is feared for its overwhelming power—the most dangerous threat that the Dar al-Islam has ever known.

Nevertheless, Islam is at war with all the world, not just the United States or even all the West, hence the appellation Dar al-Harb, or abode of war, for those countries where Islamic law does not rule. Of course, it is not called this because war is a natural state of the Dar al-Harb, but because Muslims are continually instigating war within it.

My friend learned this last night, I fear, as dozens of his countrymen died in the Bali bombing. They were not murdered because of any antipathy for America and its wrongdoings any more than were the Hindus slaughtered in last February's Godhra train burnings or the thousands of East Timorese butchered by Indonesian Muslims. They were murdered because they were not Muslims!

This is not the first time the West has been forced to confront expansionist Islam. Then, as now, the West was weakened by its own divisions and a lack of resolve. While the Crusades, for all their great lore, were little more than a minor sideshow on both sides, the incredible invasion of Islam into Spain, northern Africa and central Europe had ramifications that affect us even now.

The fate of Constantinople should be a lesson to today's American leaders, as the once-mighty empire declined to a state so decrepit that only 4,983 men remained capable of bearing arms within its walls at the time of its fall to Mehmet II. This was not because of the prowess of its Muslim enemies, but due to the pillaging by the treacherous Venetians and their puppet crusaders. Should America be foolish enough to forget the implacable nature of its enemy and listen to the carping voices of the U.N. and the cowardly European nations, it will deserve to suffer the same fate.

So it is vital to understand this is not a war between rich, decadent Christian America and Islam—it is a war that Islam has declared on the entire world. It is not a war that has been caused by American actions—it is a war that is fundamental to the core of Islam. There are surely many Muslims, especially westernized Muslims, who will deny this warlike imperative, just as one can find many Christians who will deny almost every teaching of Jesus Christ. But these objections are meaningless, even deceptive, and historically ignorant.

There is no War on Terror. The war in Afghanistan, the ongoing war in Iraq, the latest chapter in the Israeli-Arab war and the myriad of murderous assaults on non-combatants around the world are all part of this great clash of civilizations. The flare-up in terroristic violence which will surely occur as the Iraqi war continues should neither surprise us nor intimidate us, but provide us with this encouragement: Terror is the weapon the weak use against the strong.

Let all of us who value Western civilization pray that our leaders find the will and courage to use our strength judiciously and crush those who would destroy it.

Snipe hunt

October 21, 2002

A WIT HAS OPINED that in addition to calling for national ballistic registration, an extension on the "assault weapons" ban and expanded gun control in general, the mentally-challenged anti-gun forces now emboldened by the fatal D.C. snipings should also be calling for the outlawing of white delivery vans. After all, white vans also appear to be an integral part of the snipers' murderous activities.

A van ban would do about as much good, too. After all, several of the shootings took place in Maryland, which already has the totally useless ballistic registration law in place, (and I do mean totally—not a single criminal has ever been caught due to this ridiculous and easily circumvented procedure). And just in case this little fact hasn't completely escaped everyone's attention, shooting people in the head is already against the law!

There are two primary possibilities. Either the shooter is an American sociopath, a right-wing Christian devotee of the sniper subculture as the *New York Times* would have us believe, or it's yet another peaceful demonstration of "internal struggle" (aka jihad) by devout practitioners of the religion of peace. While I have no idea who's actually breaking the notoriously strict gun-control laws of both Maryland and the District of Columbia—and shooting people in the head—I tend to incline toward the probability of the latter.

I'm no sniper, but I am a reasonable marksman, and I am well-acquainted with both former military snipers as well as a few talented long-distance shooting enthusiasts. Although they don't serve to completely dismiss the possibility of a non-Islamic psychopath, there are some things that appear to make it pretty obvious that it's a shooter, not a true sniper, running amok in D.C.

First, the caliber is a bit on the small side. While there are some sniper rifles, such as the Sig Sauer 550 Sniper, which shoot a .223 cartridge, a .308

Winchester is the round preferred by the U.S. and other militaries. Serious amateur enthusiasts, unsurprisingly, tend to go for the glamour of the big .50 caliber guns, like the Barrett 82A1, which are also known to be used by the Israeli special forces as well as the U.S. Navy Seals.

Second, the "so-called sniper experts" whom gun-clueless journalists appear to enjoy casting in a negative light aren't just engaging in manly chest-beating when they express a degree of skepticism about the shooter's ability, assuming the ranges reported by the police are correct. A decent marksman would expect to keep his shots in the black at 100 yards with a scoped pistol, and teenage varmint hunters regularly take out squirrels and groundhogs at much greater distances. As for professional snipers, one would expect them to take their shots from five times the distance, and confirmed kills of over one mile have been recorded.

But beyond the nature of the snipers themselves, the current situation does do us the benefit of greatly clarifying the protective role of the police, or rather, the lack thereof. These shootings have shown, as did Columbine, that even an active police presence cannot hope to protect a helpless citizenry. Being armed would not have saved even one of these victims, of course, but an armed eyewitness would not only have a greater chance of surviving to tell his tale, but perhaps even of ending the attacks altogether.

This is important because laws will never prevent weapons from reaching the hands of those who desire them. Remember that 50 years of murderous repression and total gun control did not prevent 200,000 illegal guns from showing up in China in a single month! The power of greed is such that Israeli Jews have been convicted for selling M-16s to Palestinian terrorists... and you don't think a Saudi-financed team of Islamic jihadists couldn't find the money to bribe a National Guardsman making $20,000 a year to look the other way when he's guarding the local armory?

So while the D.C. police and the FBI run willy-nilly on their fruitless hunt for the sniper, the cretinous anti-gun crowd marches on an endless snipe hunt of their own. That which they pursue, the bird for which they hunt so energetically, is a thing that simply does not exist.

When wolves stalk the flock, best not to chain the dogs. And the flock is safer yet when the sheep grow fangs.

You must fight

October 28, 2002

THERE IS A MYTH of the policeman in modern America. From a very young age we are taught that the police are here to protect us, and "To serve and protect" is a motto common to many police forces across the country. Sadly, the reality is that the police are not in the protection business.

Despite the pretense, it has been confirmed in more than one court that not only do you not have a right to expect protection from the police, but they have no responsibility for your safety and security. Do you understand the significance of this? The police have no responsibility to protect you!

This is not to say that the police do not wish to protect everyone. I know a few policemen at the gym where I work out, and to a man they are fine and dedicated public servants, determined to do their best to protect society from the depredations of the criminal, the mad and the depraved. But they will be the first to tell you that they cannot be everywhere, that it is foolish to expect them to prevent anyone from committing whatever crime they desire.

The police are not there to protect. The police are there to pick up the pieces, to find the perpetrator and see that justice prevents him from doing it again.

Contrary to misleading media reports, self-defense has always been the optimal response, even for an unarmed, untrained woman. In a 1990 study, Kleck and Sayles found that when women were attacked by a would-be rapist, fighting back reduced the chance of the rape by 86 percent, and that most injuries occurred prior to any attempt at self-defense. Women armed with knives or guns were raped less than 1 percent of the time, and never ended up being made into a prisoner, or worse.

But unfortunately, the myth of the policeman—always a perilous foundation upon which to stand for those who accepted it—has become even more treacherous in this time of Islamic terror. Consider the difference between the responses of Flight 93, which was prepared to resist, and the other three flights hijacked on 9-11 which were not. The brave defenders of Flight 93 were not able to save their own lives, but their heroic sacrifice saved hundreds, perhaps thousands of others. They were not police, they were just everyday men and women, but they served and protected all the same.

Evil, you see, always depends upon the willingness of the good to suffer its existence. One of history's saddest lessons is how the ferocious, lion-hearted resistance shown in 1943 by the Jews of the Warsaw Ghetto demonstrates how even the staggering evil of the Holocaust could have been mitigated, if not averted, by the victims' refusal to meekly accept their fate.

The evil of Islamic terror now stalks the Western world. The war in Iraq will not end it, and so every American must accept the fact that one day, he or she may be faced with a choice: to resist in awareness of the likelihood of immediate death, or to meekly accede in the hopes that someone else will step up to the plate.

Osama bin Laden and the jihadists are counting on the latter, that we of the rich, fat and decadent West are so complacent that we cannot even bother to defend ourselves. Our Islamic enemies think this of us, we the inheritors of "We few, we happy band of brothers…", "Nuts" and "Don't Tread on Me!" They are wrong. They are so very wrong.

The 2nd Division of the United States Marine Corps has a motto: "Follow Me." This is deeply meaningful, in light of the statistic which showed that in World War II, units with the highest rate of junior-officer casualties tended to have the lowest overall casualty rates. The Marines already know what we must learn—risk brings the highest reward and only sacrifice provides safety.

When Ron Lantz phoned 911 to report a blue Chevy matching the description of the D.C. snipers' car, the police told him to stay where he was, to not get involved. Instead, he used his truck to park it in. In this least civilized of wars, men like Ron Lantz and Todd Beamer of Flight 93 must be our model.

No fear. Resist. Don't let them tread on you.

A tale of two children

November 4, 2002

I AM ACQUAINTED with two children of pre-school age. Both children are extremely fortunate to belong to their respective families, each of which is strong, loving and rather wealthy. The two fathers are well-educated, intelligent and successful, the two mothers are warm, caring and stay home to care for the children. The children themselves are both bright, happy and well-behaved.

There are two important differences, though. One child is six months older than the other. Also, one child will begin pre-school next year while the other is unlikely to ever set foot in an organized educational facility.

What I find incredibly interesting is to see how this apparently small divergence of intentions has already played a major role in the intellectual development of the two children.

Because they know their child will soon be heading off to school, the first parents are relatively lackadaisical about taking an active part in their child's education. They read to him, of course, but it is primarily for entertainment—certainly not a part of a methodical process. Education, in their view, is the responsibility of his teachers and the educational establishment, which, after all, did a reasonable job of teaching them.

They are not in the least concerned that their child can only recognize 10 or 12 letters of the alphabet, and I am quite sure that they are correct that he will learn the rest quite easily in kindergarten and be reading fluently by the time he reaches second or third grade.

The other parents have elected to take full responsibility for their child's education themselves. They began teaching him the alphabet using Power-point slides around the time of his second birthday. After he'd mastered both the lower-case and capital letters, they began introducing him to simple phonics, again using Powerpoint slides jazzed up with cartoon animals. A-aalligator… B-buh-bear… and so on. They weren't fascists about it, and they generally do a single daily session which lasts about five minutes, unless the child specifically asks to "play phonics" later in the day.

Once the simple phonics were mastered, the child began getting bored until his parents introduced a new set of phonics to him, and now he has worked up to a randomized set of 120, which includes more complicated, multi-letter phonics such as "ance", "tial", "iest" and "aught." He has also learned the Greek alphabet, capital and lowercase, and has begun to make the distinction between consonants and vowels.

About a month ago, the parents were delighted to see that the child had discovered that just as letters combine to make phonics, phonics combine to make words. They then introduced him to the phonics-based Bob books, which he has now begun reading. Nor is he merely sight-reading based on familiarity, as he was tested by writing down some simple phrases which he could not have known in advance. I was rather impressed, since the child is all of three! The disparity between the two children is especially marked in light of the fact that the second child is six months younger than the first.

It seems highly probable that by the time the first child is able to read, some three years from now, the second child will be a much more advanced reader than he is today, and indeed will likely have already started learning specific subjects rather than merely building the tools necessary for learning. Furthermore, the first child will be progressing at the rate of the slowest of the 20 or 30 children in his class, whereas the second child will be continuing to advance at his own rate, which, if he is normal, will be significantly faster.

Thus, it is not hard to see how it can be true, as studies have suggested, that the average homeschooled child is as much as three years in advance of his age-peers by the time they have finished high school. Education is not a race, of course, but if it were, then it would appear to be a spectacularly unfair one.

I have strongly supported homeschooling for some time now, but mostly from a theoretical position. Now, seeing it in action, I am more confident than ever in the supreme importance of encouraging parents to teach their children at home.

Is Tom Brokaw a 'gay' black Muslim?

November 11, 2002

IVEN THE LEFT'S BELIEF in the paramount nature of group identity and the information which is beginning to leak out about D.C. snipers John Muhammad and John Lee Malvo, I don't think it's too soon to begin speculating about why the media has been downplaying the nature of the relationship between the two snipers, as well as their religious affiliation. Is Tom Brokaw a closet member of the Nation of Islam? Does Peter Jennings regularly "work out" at the YMCA with his "step-son"? And does Dan Rather look saucy in a burkha, or what?

I find Nancy Pelosi rather attractive. This disturbs me, on several levels.

I can't think of a situation in which a Public Enemy quote is inappropriate. And is it possible to open an official-looking letter without saying "I got a letter from the government the other day…" in your best Chuck D voice?

I am no Republican. I think it's a party of shameless political whores who have shown time and time again that they have no intention of living up to their professed ideals. But, man, seeing the Democrats get spanked like that still puts a little spring in my step.

We finally have an official number on the percentage of complete and utter idiots in a given society—21.35 percent. That's the percentage of Oregon voters who supported Measure 23, an idea so ludicrous that I thought it was an advertisement for Bad Ideas Jeans. Yeah, we'll have the government pay for all health care, including massage and aromatherapy, jack the state income tax up to 17 percent to pay for it, and you only have to sign a piece of paper to qualify for it all. How many doctors would remain in Oregon—six, maybe seven? But, hey, free scented candles!

If an Islamic judge has declared a fatwa against Jerry Falwell and Franklin Graham, does that mean the reverends have an open season on Muslims now themselves? How does this work?

I don't have a cute and alliterative name for this column, but if I did, I think I'd call it Defending the Mike. Then again, considering how many times I get asked about being down with Madden, approximately seven people would recognize the reference. How is it that you all can correct me on the minutiae of U.S. Code sections and the proper numbering of the Crusades, but know so little about your own culture? Consider yourself assigned to five hours of SportCenter this week.

If you know enough Latin to have an opinion on my name, you should know enough Roman history to know that it is not blasphemous... unless, of course, you happen to worship Nike or Jove, in which case you have a point.

I think it's funny that people who dislike homeschooling will write in to tell me an anecdote about a dysfunctional homeschooler they once met. Like it would take more than five minutes to find 100 dysfunctional kids at a single public school. Fifteen minutes, max, to score some ganja or a girl ready to go.

On a related matter, lack of socialization is the bugaboo of the anti-homeschooler. Of course, socialization during my high-school years largely consisted of learning how to be cruel to others, valuing the judgment of one's peers in the place of one's elders and improving one's sexual technique. So, if you're really concerned that your homeschooled child lacks socialization, a rigorous schedule of Vivid films and Nietzsche should set them straight in no time.

I am extremely confused by the way that the media is reporting on the current war with Iraq. Over a month ago, I noted that Turkish armored divisions had invaded Northern Iraq and were holding some 15 percent of the country. This weekend, Debka has reported that U.S. Special Forces, in company with elite British and Iranian military units, are fighting Iraqi forces in Southern Iraq in an attempt to gain control over the Euphrates River crossings. Combined with the training exercises in Jordan, this means that Hussein's main forces will soon be completely surrounded... which is a very strange situation for a war that supposedly hasn't started yet.

Dirty-girl politics

November 18, 2002

C ALL IT the "Dirty Girl Theory Of Politics." Democrats are skanks—there's no need to buy them since their principles already revolve around the pursuit of raw power. I have zero sympathy for these sluts of the political spectrum, and it was sweet to see the electorate dismiss the banal fearmongering by the party of the evil and the stupid.

But one expects nothing from those who stand for naught but union interests, barely watered-down socialism and baby murder. It would be ludicrous to expect more, just as it would be absurd to think that the class 'ho will go to her wedding bed a virgin. One expects nothing but evil and stupidity from Democrats, and one gets... Nancy Pelosi, which is to say, evil and stupidity in Chanel.

Nevertheless, it is the Republican party which inspires me, a former Young Republican, to outrage. I still subscribe to exactly the same principles which caused me to become a Republican in the first place—namely: freedom, liberty and the American Constitution. Yet, were it not for the harsh lessons in reality which drove me to become a Libertarian, it would be sickening to see how George Bush and his brothel of unprincipled political prostitutes have chosen to spend their electoral mandate from the American people.

Have these Republican whores accommodated the wishes of their strongest allies, the Christian Right, by drawing on the support of more than 70 percent of the populace to ban the disgusting and murderous abomination that is partial-birth abortion? No, they don't wish to appear extreme. Are they willing to fire the bureaucratic losers who totally failed in their responsibilities to defend the country on Sept. 11? No, it's more important to avoid offending Saudi Arabia and other financial supporters of violent Islamic expansion.

Do they speak out against clerics calling for the mass extermination of Jews? No, instead they condemn Jerry Falwell and Franklin Graham.

Republicans seldom do as they promise, nor do they ever live up to their professed ideals. The Department of Education still stands. National Public Radio and the National Endowment for the Arts still freely spread their toxic filth at taxpayer expense. Leviathan has grown so fast he has stretch marks. Bob Dole used to brag about carrying the Tenth Amendment around in his breast pocket, but as Jamie Lee Curtis once said, "The gorilla can read Nietzsche, he just doesn't understand it!"

Indeed, the act of selling one's Republican derriere is so common in Washington that it has become a verb, "to grow." So, which is worse, the whore who sells it or the skank who gives it away for free? I have more respect for the skanks—at least they are honest.

The most compelling piece of evidence that the Republican Party has sold its principles for power is the disgusting flexing of statist muscle that is the Homeland Security Act. It contains a whole host of evils, foremost of which is the Information Awareness Office, a diabolical creation intended to reduce individual Americans to naked, defenseless, easily manipulated bits in a federal Matrix. The IAO is even acronymically diabolical. Consider the following text from "The Gnostic Mass," conceived by the occultist Aleister Crowley in a perverse mockery of the Catholic Eucharist:

> Do what thou wilt shall be the whole of the Law. I proclaim the Law of Light, Life, Love and Liberty in the name of IAO.

But Admiral Poindexter's IAO surely has more in common with the Geheime Staatspolizei than with the life, liberty and the pursuit of happiness declared by Thomas Jefferson in the Declaration of Independence. Demonstrably the foremost Republican priority since the election, the Homeland Security Act is the most egregious act of war by the U.S. government against the Constitution since the War Between the States and the establishment of the Federal Reserve.

While I fully support America's war on Iraq, al-Qaida and the rest of our self-declared enemies, I believe that George Bush and his administration have made it quite clear that they are intending to use this war to advance their insidious goal of increasing the power of the central state at the expense of the individual.

Certainly, our elected whores and skanks alike appear to be more interested in waging war on the individual rights and freedoms of the American people than in defending them and their Constitution.

Deus le volt?

November 25, 2002

A LTHOUGH I DO NOT RESPOND to most of the e-mail which this column inspires, I do read them all. And while I prefer to avoid getting caught up in a continuing dialogue—instead of moving on to new subjects—occasionally a reader will ask an astute question which I believe requires a public address.

A recent question was:

Since I openly recognize and condemn the danger posed to American freedom and liberties by the federal government in wartime, how can I possibly lend support to the ongoing wars against Iraq and against violent expansionist Islam? A good question about an apparent dichotomy.

To answer this, it is first important to understand the distinction between the U.S. federal government and the American people. The two are not the same—while their interests may at times run in parallel, they are frequently divergent and sometimes even opposed.

In the case of violent expansionist Islam, the interests of the federal government and the American people are the same. The jihadists have declared war on both parties—indeed, they are at war with the entire Dar al-Harb. This is not a war the American people have sought, nor, interestingly enough, has the federal government accepted the reality of this war, choosing instead to deny its very existence. Thus, the official U.S. stance is that Islam remains a religion of peace even as civilians, women and children are slaughtered around the world on the basis of their non-Islamism.

But it is this war which I fully support, and I only favor the war on Iraq as being an important foundation upon which ultimate victory in the more central conflict will be built, despite the administration's insistence on making a distinction between these two wars. As with the Israeli debacle at Oslo, it was the failure of the previous Bush administration to finish the first war in the Gulf, combined with the Soviet defeat in Afghanistan and a lack of response to a variety of deadly provocations, which convinced terror groups such as al-Qaida and the Islamic Jihad that America was decadent and would easily collapse before the jihadist onslaught.

While the U.S. government turns a blind eye to the religious element, it is very aware of other threats to its interests. Indeed, the proposed adoption of the gold dinar as a means of settling accounts throughout the Islamic world poses a far more significant threat to the dollar imperialism of the global financial system than all the Islamic terror groups combined. The fact that China has recently opened its first gold market and is following the development of the gold dinar with interest is especially worrisome to the federal government and other fans of the imperial dollar.

But the desire to preserve economic hegemony is no excuse for war. Then again, I do not know that the administration's real reason for invading Iraq is in defense of the dollar—it is even possible that the Bush administration does not believe its "religion of peace" nonsense any more than I do.

Unfortunately, the administration's actions last week in ramming the abominable Homeland Security Act through Congress indicates that the federal government is more interested in warring against the rights and liberties of the American people than against Iraq, the Axis of Evil or those who kill in the name of the religion of peace.

Thus, the American people find themselves at war on two fronts, neither of which they have chosen. But the fact that the federal government hopes to rob you of your inalienable rights does not change the fact that violent expansionist Islam seeks to rob you of either your faith or your life.

Evil must be confronted and defeated, one evil at a time. But no people born in defiance of their own parliament, with the scalps of the English monarchy, the Nazi hierarchy and the Soviet oligarchy hanging from their belt, should ever fear it. Furthermore, take heart in remembering that the One who graced us with those inalienable rights is still with us, and is not only greater than those who would steal our rights, but is greater than he that is in the world.

The Myth of Woman

December 2, 2002

I ENJOY SCIENCE FICTION. I especially like the sort of book that allows one to get into the head of an alien being, that allows one to experience something so exotic and fundamentally foreign to the reality of one's own existence that even the simplest, most everyday thing becomes exciting and new.

This must be why I quite enjoyed "The Divine Secrets of the Ya-Ya Sisterhood". Not the movie, you understand, but the novel by Rebecca Wells. While male reviewers have broadly panned both the movie and the book—mostly for legitimate reasons which are well-articulated—I feel that they have generally missed the more significant point. "The Divine Secrets" are not about relationships or gender ghettos—nor, as it might superficially appear, the contentious nature of the mother-daughter bond. No, above all, it is about the central Myth of Woman.

There is a reason that what others have described as the Oprahfication of American culture has found such fruitful soil in the hearts and minds of millions of women. "The Divine Secrets" is a most appropriate title, for it not only presents what is an exemplary example of this mysterious phenomenon, but it also provides a key to understanding it for even the most testosterone-befuddled observer.

At this point, I imagine you might think that I am mocking the book, which is not at all the case. I loved it. In fact, I have now read it three times. The writing is colorful, the characters are absorbing and one even feels a genuine tension as the darkness lurking at the heart of Siddalee's childhood is slowly, exquisitely revealed. And is there any question so pertinent to the male mind as the truly fundamental one—will she or won't she? Just as one enjoys a flower all the more for being a flawless specimen of its genus, one cannot but admire what must surely be the archetype of its genre, never to be surpassed.

It is the genre itself with which I take issue, and, even more to the point, the reason the genre holds such marvelous appeal for so many women. It is related, I think, to the strange cult of Diana (the late princess, not the Huntress), to the peculiarly feminine nature of modern neo-paganism and to the doctrine of feminist infallibility. It also answers the lingering question of why women, despite surpassing men in almost every measure of scholastic achievement, still appear to have retained a distinctive distaste for science and mathematics, and why the Academy Awards continue to be considered a genuine form of entertainment.

What "The Divine Secrets" ultimately reveals is that the true Woman, namely, a female possessed of the requisite equipment who favors chick flicks over action movies, Oprah over Aristotle, "Friends" over the "X-Files," and the local TV news over the Internet, craves nothing more than to be Taken Seriously. Which, for the average guy, is best translated as Unquestioning Reverence For All Actions and Utterances.

It was only after finishing the book for the second time that the truth struck me. This story was not one that was new to me, indeed, I had seen it many, many times before. Like many a college girl of my acquaintance, the characters in the book are uniformly paralyzed by the notion of decision-making, because they believe that every choice Matters. Not matters in the sense that every choice has consequences, which is true to the point of tautology, but Matters, in the sense that it is an epic event of cosmic proportions.

I suppose this is where the neo-pagan aspect enters the picture. Because every decision is clearly of cosmic import, a Woman cannot be less than a goddess, despite all evidence to the contrary. And because to be a goddess is to be divine, she cannot be accountable to those of us who are mere mortals. Thus, as is clearly explicated in "The Divine Secrets" it is not only acceptable, but a measure of greatness that an alcoholic mother abandons, assails and otherwise screws up her child, because she does it with style, which, as we know from the Academy Awards, is all that truly Matters.

'Out, damned Lott!'

December 16, 2002

COUNT ME NOT AMONG THOSE who believe that wearing a "racism sucks" t-shirt is an act of praiseworthy morality. I have no trouble with discrimination per se, indeed, the ability to discriminate between the good and the bad, the wise and the foolish, and the worthwhile and the useless is a talent indeed. And as far as superficial things go, I have little doubt that were everyone to have exactly the same shade of skin, we would use eye color, hair texture or the ability to curl one's tongue to separate ourselves into clannish, warring sub-groups.

Nor do I believe that many of the Senate Majority Leader's loudest critics are anything but hypocrites. It is tempting, is it not, to defend the man simply on the grounds that irreverent Jesse "The Preacher, The Playa" Jackson is attacking him. Yes, it is the famous lover of "Hymietown" himself who cast the first stone. Beautiful! All we need is Al Sharpton—check!

But the fact that a pack of racist African-American buffoons are baying for Sen. Lott's hairspray-hardened head does not mean that we should not serve it happily to them on a platter. Consider the man's long and massively undistinguished record. He has spent his entire career collaborating with the left in feeding Leviathan and urinating upon the principles of freedom, liberty and smaller government for which the party he leads is supposed to stand.

There are those who defend the man on the principle that a single misstep should not sink a career. But there are two problems with this defense. First, this is not the first time that the Senate Majority Leader has inserted his foot into his mouth while speaking on racially charged issues. Second, as I have written before with regards to abortion, life is rife with extremely severe penalties for a single, momentary mistake.

American politics is blood sport, and a senator who is stupid enough to say, in the year 2002, that the country would have been a better place without the civil-rights movement is as dead in the arena as a Roman gladiator sans sword and shield. His fitness for leadership aside, he should be disqualified on the grounds of sheer political idiocy.

I sincerely hope the senior senator from Mississippi will see fit to do the right thing and resign. A poster boy for sham Republicanism, he is a statist in sheep's clothing, and the American people would be much better off without this unprincipled political prostitute holding any position of leadership in their government.

One suspects that Sen. Lott will find, like Lady Macbeth, that the taint of that which is unseemly will cling inexorably to him, a deadly spot which cannot be washed away.

Out, damned Lott! Out, I say!—One apology: two: why, then, 'tis time to do't.—Hell is murky!—Fie, my lord, fie! a senator, and afeard?

The King of Christmas

December 23, 2002

I LOVE EVERYTHING about Christmas. The white snow, the rainbow of lights and the dawn vision of presents piled under the tree. It is a happy time for my family, a time of joy. Some of our most cherished memories stem from this time of year. But we also remember the inspiration for the celebration, a truth both wonderful and grim.

We remember that Jesus Christ had to come into this fallen world because it was, and is, under the rule of a cruel and malevolent prince, who tempted Him, who slew Him when He would not submit, and who watched in helpless horror as He rose again in power.

The world is still under the rule of that cruel prince, the results of which can be seen every day in the news. Murder, war and tyranny continue to oppress many millions throughout the world, but we who refuse to submit to the ruler of this world are no longer bound by him, for we claim that truth that sets us free, the resurrection of the Lord Jesus Christ.

Jesus Christ of Nazareth is the true king of Man, yet I remain convinced His Father is a libertarian. Not only did He send His Son to set us free, but He allows us, no, He forces us to decide between acknowledging His Son or seating ourselves upon the throne of our own lives. And that freedom of choice, in the end, is the central liberty; it is the only liberty that matters.

A friend once asked how I could be so cheerful while America rots from within and endures attack from without. The answer is that despite my love for America and my passionate allegiance to the ideas upon which it was constructed, I know that its fate is immaterial. Our country, our homes and even our lives are all things of shadow which will one day disappear in the light of the glory of Jesus Christ.

Despair is the natural state of the thinking man. This is why intellectuals grasp so readily at even the feeblest straw promising hope for Heaven on Earth.

But there will be neither peace nor harmony until the revolution begun in a Bethlehem manger is complete, until the murderous ruler of this world is finally deposed. Then, at last, there will be peace and goodwill to men.

Merry Christmas.

The failure of democracy

December 30, 2002

DEMOCRACY must have a good PR agent. While war in the national interest is considered questionable at best, war in defense of democracy is held to be admirable and, indeed, the only way to get the anti-American left behind a military action is for the United Nations to invade a sovereign, albeit insufficiently democratic country in the name of establishing democracy.

I'm against it—democracy. I'm especially against the mutated variant enshrined as its highest form here in America and I'm pleased to withhold my consent from the fraud which purports to be a fairly elected representative government by exercising my right to not vote in federal elections.

Now, I realize that this flies in the face of some of our most cherished national myths, but hear me out. The system envisioned by the Founding Fathers restricted the right to vote, not primarily out of sexism and racism, but out of a historical awareness that providing a voice to society's less productive always ends in tears. It was not only blacks and women who were denied the original vote, but also the majority of white males, for this very reason.

Was this elitism? Certainly. But there is elitism in every political system, primarily because it is the elite who are most capable of gaming whatever system in which they find themselves, and openly acknowledged elitism is far preferable to the hidden sort. Since the dawn of time, it is only the elite, (admittedly, a small percentage of them), who have shown themselves capable of thinking beyond their own narrow interests. The wealthy patrician George Washington turned down the crown that was offered him as did the aristocrat Cincinnatus before him—one has a hard time imagining a Boston fishwife or Roman slave doing the same.

Do you really think that an elite does not guide our so-called democracy? Then consider how the federal judiciary routinely steps in to find "unconstitutional" any legislative measure of which it does not approve, regardless of whether the measure a) has anything to do with that which is written in the Constitution, or b) reflects practices which were demonstrably acceptable to those who wrote the Constitution. Interesting to note that democratically enshrined laws which favor the statist and deconstructionist cultural agendas are immediately cast in stone, while those which oppose them are undermined repeatedly until they are destroyed.

This critique of democracy does not even begin to delve into the gerrymandering of House seats which has resulted in less turnover in the Congress than in the British House of Lords, or the nepotism which recently set two second-generation politicos against each other in the presidential election. An analysis of the near-identical governing practices of the two parties in our two-party system would require a book—not a column—but it would show that the two are, for all practical purposes, effectively one.

Do I recommend a return to the past? Not exactly. But I would limit the right to vote to the productive, defined by those whose living does not depend on government of any level or on another individual. If you were a subsidized farmer, a welfare recipient or a stay-at-home mom, you would not vote. Even soldiers would not vote—history shows that those paid to fight have a strong, (and quite understandable), tendency to avoid it whenever they are given a choice in the matter. I understand Al Gore already favors this.

Outrageous? Perhaps, but for those of you who would defend democracy, I have a simple question: If mob rule is such a desirable thing, should we not work toward expanding it in order to realize its full benefits? Modern technology obviates the need for representative democracy, which is clearly an outmoded relic of the 18th century, and tradition aside, there is no good reason every bill that goes before Congress should not be voted on by the entire American people.

Thanks to the Internet, there is no logistical problem. The information load? Please, representatives and senators don't even pretend to read the massive tomes on which they are voting. It's time to look democracy in the eye, people. Is it to be one man, one vote—or not? And if not, why not?

I will take the notion of democracy's inherent virtue seriously when its self-styled defenders do. Until then, I stand by my assertion that modern American representative democracy is nothing more than a fig leaf on the inexorable advancement of the global state.

Bring it on!

January 6, 2003

B EFORE I BEGAN WRITING for WorldNetDaily, I was, like many of you, a voracious reader of socio-political commentary. Thus, I understand the frustration of writing to a columnist who does not write you in return and I know the outrage you feel when a writer who is generally sound in your eyes happens to go off the deep end on occasion.

But now that I'm writing a column myself, I understand why columnists so seldom write back to their readers—it simply isn't possible! I estimate it would take approximately 10 times longer to respond to everyone who writes than it does to write the column in the first place, even though more than three-quarters of the e-mail I receive doesn't really ask a question or otherwise require a response.

This is not to say that I don't appreciate your e-mails, because I do! Your questions and corrections have caused me to sharpen my thinking and devote more effort to precisely articulating my words. I especially enjoy e-mail from outraged parties who are deeply offended that I've skewered one of their sacred cows. Some have called me Young Nasty Man, but that's not me, that's my boy Timmy. I'm Wonderboy, and this is not that song, this is just a tribute.

Note to editor: Insert guitar solo here.

However, the fact that I don't wish to engage in lengthy e-mail debates or provide remedial historical education does not mean that I am altogether opposed to the notion of writer-reader interaction. In fact, I have an idea which I think promises to bring an entertaining new edge to this column on a monthly basis.

Here's what I'm thinking. Once a month, 350 words, (46 percent of the column), will be devoted to one fortunate correspondent (translation: sacrificial lamb) interested in challenging me on any subject, significant or trivial. Anything, from the moral superiority of supporting the Minnesota Vikings to the ontological argument for the existence of Cthulhu, is fair game. I will exert columnist's privilege in choosing from among the entries received, of course, and the latter half of the column will consist of my response to the reader's contribution.

For my part, I will commit to not selecting easy prey, unless, of course, I receive something so egregiously stupid that it would make for good humor in the inevitable dissection. I will play fair and will do my best to answer all of the issues raised, although I will assuredly not play nice. There's no flag for taunting in this league! I will also refrain from editing your submissions except in the case of unprintable language or overly confusing punctuation, so keep that in mind if you don't wish to look like a maleducated buffoon.

What I will require of those of you who wish to enter the arena is as follows: 1) No preaching to the choir. My general views are fairly well known by now, so don't write a half-column on the evils of taxation or gun control and expect to trigger a debate. 2) Make your case. This is not a TV talk show, so a hysterical screed of name-calling will not pass for a reasonable argument. 3) 350 words is the limit. Your word processor has something called Word Count under the Tools menu. Use it. 4) Don't expect mollycoddling. If you expose a weakness in your argument, I will rip it apart, not necessarily in a kindly manner. Deal with it. 5) Send the text in the body of the e-mail, as I never open attachments. Put "350 words" somewhere in the title. 6) Tell me if you wish to be identified by name and city, or only by initials. Your e-mail address will not be divulged in any case.

Keep in mind that I'm only going to do this once a month, so it will not be possible to respond to all half-columns submitted. We'll see how it goes, perhaps this will prove interesting to everyone, perhaps not. If it turns out to be lame, let me know and we'll certainly bag it. But it should be an interesting experiment, so if you ever wished to take a shot at a radical pro-life Austrian-school neo-capitalist Jacksonian techno-libertarian Southern Baptist Christian, here's your chance.

As they say in the Octagon, let's get it on!

The diversity disaster

January 13, 2003

I DON'T CARE much about whether the president decides to weigh in on the upcoming Supreme Court case on the constitutionality of racial preferences in college admissions or not. The notion that a Bush administration might decide to sacrifice principle for politics is not exactly a concept unthinkable in this universe.

One of the reasons for my indifference is that regardless of how the issue is decided, it is certain that the giant rock which covers the pernicious insects of affirmative action will be removed one day. Then it will be interesting to see some of the most shameless cockroaches of American culture scurrying for cover when the harsh light of truth exposes the devastating impact of their self-serving arguments.

I do not subscribe to the belief that personal experience is a substitute for logic. But for those of you that do, I will say that I happen to know far more about the problems faced by American blacks seeking higher education than the average white boy. This is because as a NCAA Division 1 athlete competing in an area dominated by blacks of West African descent, I was in the distinct minority. There's not a lot of melanin-challenged individuals in the sprinter-jumper-hurdler group at that level, so to paraphrase Jack Kemp, I've showered with more black men than many of you have ever known.

But the fact that I was down with P.E. before they went political or that I can still drop the lyrics of NWA's "F— Tha Police" upon request is irrelevant. What is relevant to the debate is what I saw happen to my teammates, who, thanks to the drive for diversity at our elite institution, were thrown into an impossible situation and left to flounder by the very people who claimed to have their best interests at heart.

Thomas Sowell, Walter Williams and Ward Connerly have written volumes about the theoretical flaw with affirmative action in education—namely, that it systematically sets up young men and women for inevitable failure. I, like many others, can testify that this flaw is not theoretical, but real, and furthermore, it affects the majority of black students seeking college degrees. There is a very solid reason that black dropout and failure rates are so much higher than those of other races, and it has nothing to do with discrimination, past or present.

I particularly remember a required statistics course in which I had little interest. The material was basic and I was rather occupied with an interesting independent study so I didn't even bother going to class most of the time. Two of my black teammates happened to be in the same course, but despite excellent attendance, doing all the homework and studying very hard, they ended up with Ds. I don't recall ever getting less than B+ on a test, on the other hand.

These girls weren't stupid, nor were they poorly prepared or suffering from bad study habits. But as I learned when I tried to help them, it was quite clear that they simply weren't operating at the intellectual level required to keep up with the rest of the class. It was sad to see how they fell further and further behind as the class blew through a new chapter every week. The situation was no better for most of the black students on campus, as despite the daily study sessions which the two black fraternities made mandatory at the library, many of their members spent their entire college career on some form of academic probation. But we had diversity!

There was one success story, however. A good friend of mine from the soccer team had attended a top prep school and done very well on his entrance exams, but he chose our university over a more prestigious choice because of our school's notorious dedication to Greek symbols and fermented beverages. He had no problem with his classes, graduated from medical school and established a successful practice in a difficult specialty.

But he should have been failing out of Harvard, I suppose. Does it serve anyone's interest to have kids who could succeed at the state schools bombing out of the private colleges, while those who would have been fine at the second-tier schools struggle at the elite institutions?

Only the insects of affirmative action who wish to wield the whip as overseers for their race, and those who seek to keep black Americans on a political plantation.

The raping of America

January 27, 2003

I HAD THOUGHT TO BEGIN THIS COLUMN with a mea culpa, as on Dec. 2, 2002, the NASDAQ index briefly crossed the 1,500 barrier to peak at 1,521.44 before being again washed away by the Great Bear tide. After checking the archives, however, it turned out that my August prediction was that the S&P 500 would see 500 before 1,500. So forget the apology, I'm still on target like Luke Skywalker in the Death Star trench.

Why should you care about any of this? Because even if you belong to one of the 50 percent of households which don't own equities, you are still profoundly affected by the financial machinations of the Political-Financial Cabal if you happen to have a job, a bank account or a house. And unfortunately, due to the idiotic and economically ignorant arrogance of this PFC, America is in for a very hard time in the coming decade and beyond.

In the immortal words of BTO, you ain't seen nothing yet.

Here's what happened. In 1996, facing the prospect of a bust cycle which was naturally following the expansion of credit that fueled the '90s boom, Greenspan and the PFC chickened out. They chose to try avoiding the consequences of their past actions and delay the oncoming recession by massively expanding the amount of Federal Reserve credit available to banks, which is best understood as selling money for a penny a dollar. The banks loaned the money to telecoms, Internet startups and people refinancing their houses, thus creating a boom on top of a boom which resulted in the biggest financial bull market of all time.

This is why your house is worth twice as much as it was 10 years ago. It's called asset inflation. Don't get used to it.

Since the bust began in March of 2000, the three major markets have declined from an average price-to-earnings ratio of 67.43 to 28.87. This has led all the media cheerleaders to hope that the worst is over. But it isn't. Prior to the Great Crash of 1929, the Dow's P/E ratio was only 32.6, while the historical market norm is a ratio of 14 and the average bear-market bottom is reached at 7.6. In other words, even if one somehow concludes that the biggest boom of all time will not be followed by the biggest bust of all time, the markets still have to fall more than they have already fallen simply to remain in line with the expected averages.

Here's another interesting indicator. In January 1980, one ounce of gold could buy the Dow—then at 820. In January 2000, it took 41 ounces of gold to buy the Dow at 11,723. Only three years later, it takes just 22 ounces of gold to buy the Dow at Friday's close of 8,131. Dividend-yield analysis also supports these negative trends—the increase from 1.2 to 1.96 percent is still nowhere near the bottom average of 8.3 percent.

It is important to understand that this ongoing financial catastrophe is not only predictable, but inevitable. It is a natural result of paper money, which, since its introduction to the world in 1690 by the colony of Massachusetts, has always gone through a natural life cycle of credit-fueled expansion followed by inflation leading to either default or hyperinflation. In fact, the dollar can even be considered a successful anomaly, as its adoption as a global standard of trade allowed it to exceed the average lifespan for a paper currency.

It's hard to know exactly how the imperial dollar will die. It is possible that the gold-backed Islamic dinar may replace the dollar as the global trading standard or that China or the European Union may seize the moment to offer the world a stable replacement currency. What I do know is that no amount of economic stimulus, be it tax cuts, spending increases or interest-rate cuts, will allow America to avoid paying the piper for four years of spectacularly ill-timed malinvestment.

The party is over. Prepare yourself.

If you are interested in reading in more detail than this column space can provide, I cannot overstate the importance of "A History of Money and Banking in the United States" by Murray Rothbard. Another excellent resource is 321 Gold which features the incredibly insightful essays of the invaluable Adam Hamilton.

Spiting their pretty faces

February 3, 2003

A RECENT STORY floating around the variety section of a newspaper I still read occasionally reminded me of a conversation I had with a college girlfriend about six months ago. She's a pretty woman—slender, petite, well-educated and intelligent. She has an excellent, high-paying job and even owns her own house.

She is, in short, the epitome of feminist success. And yet, she is profoundly disappointed with her life. She has, in her own words, continued to stumble upwards while somehow missing out on the only thing she truly wanted—a husband and a family.

Nor is she alone, in anecdotal or statistical terms. Not only do the majority of women who were in our college social circle remain unmarried, but according to Barbara Dafoe Whitehead, author of "Why There Are No Good Men Left: The Romantic Plight of the New Single Woman", a 30-something woman is three times more likely to be unmarried than her 1970's counterpart. While some might argue that this is a good thing, most demographics experts would disagree, as would, it appears, an awful lot of those 30-something single women.

While Whitehead correctly identifies the general problem, she is as clueless as the next feminist as to how to go about solving it. Instead of recommending that individuals change the one thing within their power—namely, their behavior—she advocates altering the entire system of courtship. Given this typically fascistic feminist approach, I am, of course, shocked that her six 30-something daughters and nieces all remain available.

But, as I told my friend, the root of the problem is that the kind of man she wants is precisely the man who is smart enough to stay away from her. Smart, educated women aren't willing to date down on the social scale, so the higher they rise, the more they cut down on their available pool of men. Furthermore, the smarter a man is, the more he is likely to realize that being romantically involved with an intelligent, educated, upper-middle-class American woman steeped in 20 years of feminist indoctrination is about as desirable as being flayed alive and rolled in salt.

Consider the premarital professions of the women in my social circle, all of whom are now stay-at-home moms happily married to intelligent, successful men: Farmgirl. Nanny. Teacher. Office manager. Nanny. Pipeline worker. Professional student. Church volunteer. That's eight quality men who won't be marrying a high-powered career girl right there.

The advice I gave my friend was succinct: In any given dating situation, think about what your instincts are telling you—then do the opposite. It's like football… if the run is getting stuffed, then throw the darn ball.

So, in the unlikely event there happens to be a 30-something single woman reading this, here are a few pointers which might be helpful while you wait for Ms. Dafoe Whitehead and company to change the dating culture:

Your rights are delineated in the Constitution. Everything else is a privilege.

Your family has to put up with you. For everyone else, it's optional.

Southern belles always get what they want. Watch and learn, grasshopper.

Sex as an incentive is fair enough. Using its deprivation as a punishment will backfire hideously.

Mocking your man in public creates a no-win situation. He can either slice and dice you verbally, which is no fun for you, or keep his mouth shut and look like an idiot. In the case of the latter, it doesn't mean that you've won, or that he's forgotten.

Men love happy women. Act happy and you may discover how to be happy.

If there's any doubt, choose the most optimistic interpretation. That's what he meant.

Honey, honey, honey—a thousand times honey. Never vinegar.

Conflict is not passion. It isn't any fun, either.

Limit yourself to five complaints and demands a day. If you're not counting, you're over the limit.

If no one ever taught you the traditional arts, find an older woman to be your mentor.

Your feelings and objectively verifiable facts may be different. Learn to distinguish between them.

Now, I'm not saying that applying these principles to your dating scene will turn frogs into princes or anything, but they will get you in the game. And if all else fails, just tell your next first date that you're thinking of quitting your job and returning to your former career as an aerobics instructor. He'll be intrigued, trust me.

Who let the dogs out?

February 10, 2003

L AST WEEK'S COLUMN drew a lot of fire, but you'd probably be surprised at how many women supported what I wrote. The hundreds of e-mails, in fact, ran 4–1 in favor, and that was the women. The male e-mail was, unsurprisingly, unanimously favorable.

A few points deserve addressing. The statistics are from Barbara Dafoe Whitehead, not my imagination. I was not writing about all 30-something women, just the upper-middle-class, college-educated, single women who don't want to be single. I am not single. I do not hate women. I do not suffer fools gladly, especially not critics who can neither read accurately nor write grammatically.

Now, it is important to keep in mind that while 30-something women certainly exacerbate and perpetuate their problem, they did not create it. Their feminist forebears did. But there is another group that adds fuel to the fire, and that is predatory young men. I know this very well, because, were it not for the grace of God, I would still be one of them.

It does not take long for the smart young male to learn that nice guys finish last where women are concerned. Young women in their teens and 20s, for the most part, simply don't respect men who treat them well. But, the observant young male soon learns, if you keep a girl guessing, keep her off-balance and insecure, you can summon her for a late night booty call whenever you want. Thus the once-lovestruck puppy becomes a dog.

Desirable women keep fan clubs of "friends" who wish to date them, holding them in reserve for those times when they need an armpiece or for long-term backup should Prince Charming fail to eventually appear. Desirable men, on the other hand, keep stables of willing women to provide them with sex on demand. Two or three is normal, but a Big Dog will have four or more at his disposal.

He does so without conscience, because it is impossible to provide him with any rational reason he should not. Having been taught since grade school that there is no connection between sex and morality, he is unmoved by appeals to traditional right and wrong. Sex education has wrongly taught him that women enjoy sex as much and as often as he does, and the vulgar, provocative front put up by college girls leads him to believe that they are as casual about it as he is.

He does not respect them, of course—why should he? They are simply there for his use. If a woman turns him down, he will simply shrug and move on. In fact, he may well move on should he not receive adequate satisfaction on the very first date. Those he is using are terrified of admitting their true longings for love and romance to him, as they know he will lose no sleep over informing them that he will no longer be requiring their bodies for his physical pleasure.

Marriage? It doesn't even occur to him. He knows women seek most divorces and is in no hurry to risk losing his future house, savings account and children. After college, he will often live with a woman for a year or two, only to move on to the next if she brings up the M-word too often. By the time he reaches 30, he usually has received and passed on at least one sexually-transmitted disease, hence the popularity of colposcopies in these latter days.

The Big Dog has no problem plucking another girl off the Girl Tree whenever one is needed. He is generally quite content with himself and his life, and he lacks for nothing, except honor. But without it, he is incomplete, because he has not learned that a man is more than the sum of his desires. He is a predator, without morals or mercy, stalking the bars and nightclubs as inerrantly and as voraciously as a great white shark.

He can change, however—he will need a good woman to help him do so. Her education, brains and success do not matter, but her character does. She does not represent a challenge, to him, but inspiration for what he can become. She is, almost surely, not an insecure, bitter, highly educated and career-oriented woman.

Answering the question of who let the dogs out is not difficult. The blame lies with those who decided that the patriarchy would best be undermined by debasing man's oldest currency: sex.

It is good to hate the French

February 17, 2003

IN THE YEAR 800, Charlemagne, or Karl der Grosse if you prefer, was crowned Holy Roman Emperor by Pope Leo III. This was not Charlemagne's preferred title, however, as the crowning was little more than a naked attempt at a Church-imposed stricture on his power. But the power of Carolo Augusto did not hail from the pope, but instead from his lordship over the Franks, and, to a lesser extent, the Lombards.

But the power of the Carolingian Franks did not stay united for long. When Charlemagne's heir, Louis the Pious, died 40 years later, the kingdom was riven in two. Louis II, the German, ruled over the eastern Franks, while Lothar claimed the west. The Franks, now divided into French and German variants and fought their first of many civil wars—two of the most notorious being World War I and World War II.

Still, the dream of Pax Carolingus lives on, even today, 1,203 years later. What centuries of failed Italian adventures, what the ignominious ends of Frederick Barbarossa and Napoleon did not teach, clearly cannot be learned. That Chirac and Schroeder are no more than infected pimples on the buttocks of Frankish history in comparison with these historical giants does not, however, change the fact that once again, the Franks are attempting to impose their will on their recalcitrant neighbors.

As I have written before, the European Union is nothing more than an attempt by French and German fascists to achieve by stealth what Napoleon and Hitler tried to do by force. Profoundly undemocratic despite its pretensions, the EU regularly violates its own rules and procedures any time the Old European duo finds them troublesome. Witness the way that Chirac and Schroeder made free to throw around the notion of European opposition to the ongoing Anglo-Turkic-American action against Iraq despite the fact that the matter had not even been discussed in the EU's facade of a parliament.

And, of course, the fact that the leaders of the United Kingdom, Italy, Spain, Denmark, Poland, the Czech Republic, Hungary and Portugal were reduced to writing an open letter to express their support for U.S. policy on Iraq only goes to show that the French and German leaders have exactly the same respect for freedom and representative government formerly demonstrated by their socialist and imperialist forebears.

The current rift with France and Germany is only the first of many conflicts toward which the United States is headed. In the distant future, I expect that far more than words will be exchanged. The heirs of Charlemagne will not go quietly into history's dark night, and the ease with which the ominous walls of union have been quietly erected around Europe indicates that despite their seeming weakness, the new Eurofascists will make for a more dangerous opponent in the long term than the dysfunctional Arab monarchies.

There are, of course, many other reasons to loathe the Axis of Weasels, particularly the French. No nation which has inflicted Jean-Jacques Rousseau and Jean-Paul Sartre on the world should hold its head high, but to lionize both pathetic cretins as intellectual giants is simply scandalous. No nation which took the American revolutionary cry for freedom and twisted it into the sadistic mayhem of Jacobin murder should ever lecture anyone on national morality.

But most of all, no nation which owes its very freedom to an unallied savior should dare to even think of refusing to come to the aid of its treaty-bound allies. The Axis of Weasels have shown conclusively that nations have no permanent friends, only permanent interests. The Iraqi conflict notwithstanding, it is time for Americans to recognize this and end the disgusting and expensive charade of our ties to both NATO and the United Nations.

United, we stand for freedom, liberty and justice for all. America needs no other ally than the truth. He who will not stand with us can stand against us and be doomed.

Bomb the U.N.

February 24, 2003

AMIDST ALL THE TALK about French perfidy, German weaselry and Turkish demands for bribery, one vital point has largely escaped the attention of the chattering class. For what may be the first time in U.S. history, the leadership of a major American political party has openly advocated the subversion of U.S. national interests to a foreign body.

This is nothing less than treason.

Last week, Sen. Carl Levin, a Michigan Democrat and ranking Democratic member of the U.S. Senate Committee on Armed Services let the treacherous cat out of the bag. He went so far as to declare on *Fox News* that President Bush could not act unilaterally against Iraq. When Brit Hume asked the senator how he could say that the president was acting unilaterally when 18 European countries were expressly supporting U.S. action, (not to mention the small, but significant fact that British, Turkish, Iranian and Jordanian troops are already fighting alongside our troops inside Iraq), the senator said that no American military action could be considered multilateral without the consent of the United Nations.

This despicable statement is not only a wildly incorrect use of the word "multilateral", but also goes conceptually far beyond the "entangling alliances" against which Thomas Jefferson warned the new republic he helped create. It is bad enough that Congress has delegated its war-making power to the executive branch—it is not only utterly unconstitutional, but criminally stupid to give a supranational organization any influence whatsoever over the exercise of American military power.

For decades, voices on the fringe have loudly opposed the deadly threat the United Nations poses to America, and for decades they have been dismissed by the mainstream. The skeptical conservative view has been that the U.N. is an international debating society, useless, perhaps, but generally harmless, whereas the optimistic Left sees the U.N. as a progressive development which will eventually lead to world peace.

Both views are wrong. Mark my words. The only peace the U.N. will ever confer is the peace of the grave.

The U.N. is not a debating society, it is an embryonic world government. It is antidemocratic, as the vast majority of governments it accepts as valid national representatives are not elected by the will of their peoples. It is anti-American, as its constitution explicitly denies the rights articulated by the American Constitution—whereas an American's rights are inalienable, the rights granted in the U.N.'s Universal Declaration of Human Rights are held only at the whim of the U.N., and "may in no case be exercised contrary to the purposes and principles of the United Nations" according to Article 29, section 3 of the Universal Declaration. It is anti-human, proven by its strident enthusiasm for worldwide abortion and global population reduction.

It is worth noting that global population reduction is the one goal toward which the U.N. has successfully worked. There are certainly fewer people infesting the planet following U.N. interventions in Rwanda, Somalia and Bosnia.

The United States should not pull out of the U.N. because it is an expensive boondoggle, though it is. The United States should not pull out of the U.N. because it appeases dictators, though it does. The United States should not pull out of the U.N. because it elevates totalitarian governments to positions of leadership, though it has. The United States should not pull out of the U.N. because it has failed to provide world peace, though it has not.

The United States should pull out of the U.N. because it is the greatest threat to life, liberty and justice that humanity has ever known, and it has now begun to attempt to exert its will over the American people and their government.

Think about it. Even if you regard the U.N. as a force for good in the world and hope that it one day achieves its stated goal of global governance, consider the possibility—which, if history teaches us anything, is a very high probability—that it will someday be corrupted. Global governance in the hands of Hitler, a Lenin, a Pol Pot, a Mao, a Mengistu, a Mugabe, an Amin, a Genghis Khan, a Duvalier or a Committee of Public Safety would be a disaster unparalleled in human history. Only this time, there would be no army of the free West to rescue the oppressed.

As America's pilots prepare to launch their smart missiles at targets in Iraq, here's hoping they'll save a few for One United Nations Plaza and excise the globalist cancer that threatens to one day kill the United States of America.

Janeane Garofalo is a short fat idiot

March 3, 2003

I HAD TO LAUGH when I caught Ms. Garofalo's little debate with Brian Kilmeade on *Fox News* the other day. It reminded me of some of the more clueless hate mail I receive from time to time. She refused to answer direct questions but instead responded with questions of her own, denied easily verifiable fact and became quite emotional when presented with an obvious historical parallel. I will say that she did a little better than Ms. Streisand would have, though, as she didn't confuse Iran with Iraq.

And then, there was the ludicrous lie, which scored a solid 7.5 on the Goebbels scale by claiming 32 million members for the anti-war group Win Without War. Just to put this in perspective, the largest Protestant denomination in the country, the Southern Baptist Convention, has 16 million members. Given that the current U.S. population is only about 290 million people, this figure is clearly absurd, even more so than the 600,000 claimed for the recent peace protest which was only inflated by a factor of 10.

I'm not saying that one cannot be in principled opposition to the ongoing war, but you certainly can't do it Ms. Garofalo's way—not if you want to retain any shards of intellectual integrity. Stick a fork in her, she's done.

The most amusing thing about the whole situation is that celebrities like Ms. Garofalo are becoming rather defensive about their right to hold an opinion. Of course you have a right to speak out, poor darling, but those of us who have actually read more than six books in our lives have the right to tell you that your opinion is baseless nonsense as we laugh at you.

It's nice to see that the administration is finally starting to admit to the war's real purpose, which involves replacing the Arab monarchies and dictatorships with governments capable of ending their support for international terrorism. For 30 years, America's leaders looked the other way and hoped for the best as Arab terrorists wreaked general havoc across Arabia, Asia, Africa and Europe and murdered hundreds of Americans in the process. Now, President Bush is planning to put a cocked and loaded gun at the head of every Arab country in the form of a conquered and occupied Iraq. Do you think Saudi Arabia will still find it so hard to crack down hard on murderous Islamists once there's 200,000 U.S. soldiers sitting across the border ready to go al-Qaida hunting? I don't.

The one thing it isn't about is the oil. Follow me on this, it's not rocket science. What do we pay for oil? Dollars. They send us oil and we give them dollars. And where do dollars come from? The Fed creates them— $10.348 billion worth in reserve credit just last week, which, thanks to the reserve requirement, means that banks were able to lend out $103.48 billion of money that did not previously exist. That $100 billion goes to pay for a lot of things, including all the oil that the oil companies wish to import. The oil companies then sell the oil, and book the difference between the selling price and the cost of the oil plus the low-interest cost of the loan as profit.

As long as the world operates on the dollar standard of exchange and foreign investors continue to buy federal debt, America won't fight for oil simply because it is essentially free to us as a nation. Furthermore, wouldn't it be a lot easier to simply drill in the ANWR than go to all the trouble of sending troops halfway around the world? It's not about the oil... it never was.

Note: the title of this piece is a Hollywood homage to Al Franken's book on Rush Limbaugh. As some of you have noted, I can usually do much better than "short fat idiot" when dropping vitriol.

Jesus Christ and war

March 10, 2003

SINCE THE DRUMS of war began to beat, I have been asked on numerous occasions how it can be that I, an outspoken Christian, can support significant aspects of the ongoing war on Iraq. That my position is a carefully nuanced one, previously explicated here, here, here and here, does not change the fact that there is an apparent dichotomy between it and my faith.

First, do note that I am not making a Christian case for this particular war—I am simply attempting to articulate how it is possible to be a Christian and also favor military action.

The notion that being a follower of Jesus Christ is synonymous with always favoring world peace is a common one, bolstered by the pacifist positions of many denominational leaders around the world. It stems from biblical roots, primarily the oft-mistranslated commandment "Thou shalt not kill", Jesus' command to love one's enemies and his admonishment of Peter in Gethsemane.

The first problem is that these divine directives apply to individuals, not nations—the Bible distinguishes clearly between the two in both the Old and New Testaments. Indeed, while salvation may be claimed by the individual, the soulless nations remain under the sway of the prince of this world who once offered them, without success, to Jesus. Thus, these commands cannot apply to a nation-state. It would also be highly illogical to assert that a nation which prides itself on the separation of church and state should be somehow subject to the same Christian morality which it may not impose on its citizens.

It is important to understand that the peace of which the Bible speaks is not the peace for which the world is protesting. Christian peace is a fruit of the

Spirit, it is the harmony of individuals, not nations. The blessed peacemakers who will be called sons of God are not riotous leftists protesting war in San Francisco, but those loving souls who make peace between individuals. Even such peace is not always possible due to man's inherent evil, otherwise Paul would not write:

If it is possible, as far as it depends on you, live at peace with everyone.

Jesus' own words on war are scanty, yet surprisingly practical.

Or suppose a king is about to go to war against another king. Will he not sit down first and consider whether he is able with 10,000 men to oppose the one coming against him with 20,000? If he is not able, he will send a delegation while the other is still a long way off and will ask for terms of peace.

On another occasion, He tells his disciples "if you don't have a sword, sell your cloak and buy one."

Hardly Clausewitz, true, but neither are they the words of one intrinsically opposed to self-defense, on an individual or national basis. Indeed, Revelation 19:15 prophesies that Jesus will make war on the nations Himself one day.

The truth is that the world will never know peace without the Prince of Peace, and to work for peace in the absence of Jesus Christ is to directly contradict the fundamental foundations of the Christian faith. Of wars and rumors of war, "do not be alarmed, such things must happen," Jesus said—so peace between nations is simply not a significant concern for the Christian. One might even do well to say that the Christian should leave to Caesar such responsibilities that fall to Caesar. As Paul writes of the one in authority, "he does not bear the sword for nothing."

But if world peace should not be a concern for the Christian at this time, then what should? The same things as always: to feed the poor, heal the sick, cast out demons, raise the dead and, above all, to spread the good news of salvation through Jesus Christ of Nazareth. War is only one of the many evils of this world, and if we have learned anything from the 20th century, it is that war is not the worst of them.

If what I have written here seems outlandish, keep in mind that Jesus Christ has confounded the wisdom of this world since the beginning of His ministry. I have no doubt that the King of Kings will continue to do so until he once more graces us with His royal presence.

Breaking little hearts

March 17, 2003

MTV VIDEOS are about as close as one can get to the cultural nadir, with the possible exception of Internet pornography. But even as wisdom may come out of the mouths of children from time to time, a meaningful and poignant message can occasionally find its way up from the gutter.

While I don't follow music much anymore, my exercise club always features MTV in the weight room and, last summer, I happened to notice a recurring theme I hadn't previously noticed. In Puddle of Mudd's "Blurry" and Nickelback's "Too Bad" singles from two very successful rock bands, the thematic focus is on how the separation of father and son wreaks emotional devastation on both.

The "Blurry" video is almost hard to watch, as the images of a lower-class father having fun and playing video games with his son contrast starkly with the pain of again being forced to return the boy at the end of the weekend to his mother, from whom the father is clearly estranged. While one should never mistake MTV reality for the real thing, the song's rage and heartache are palpable, the more so as the child in the video is lead singer Wes Scantlin's 5-year-old son, Jordan.

As Scantlin says of "Blurry", it is "a really personal and emotional song for me that I wrote about my son and how much I miss him … the whole concept was about kind of being kept from my kid."

"Too Bad", on the other hand, traces the bitter results of a man abandoning his family, and particularly his young son. The video climaxes with an attempted suicide-by-car, although there is an uplifting note of hope for reconciliation at the end, as the act of desperation forces the father to return and face his injured, now-adult son.

One finds it hard to imagine similar songs being written 20 or 30 years ago, before divorce became so easy and so socially acceptable, much less finding such resonance in the culture as to propel them to the top of the charts. But the terrible costs of divorce linger on, not only in the lives of the divorcing parties but also the lives of the children and the lives of those with whom the children become emotionally involved. For the child of divorce, every fight is potentially the fatal one, every conflict is potentially calamitous and there is no confidence that, at the end of the day, all will be well.

Although the Baby Boomer generation has much for which to answer, their self-centered embrace of casual divorce may well have the most lingering impact. It is not only a few angry pop-rock songs which indicate the problem, as a closer look at the 1993 study published in the *Journal of Family Psychology*—which is sometimes cited to show divorce isn't so bad for kids—actually demonstrates that boys and girls from divorced families are 260 and 340 percent more likely to be in the "problematic range" (in other words, requiring psychological help) than children from stable marriages.

Proponents of divorce like to argue that sometimes the children are better off following a parental split, and this is certainly true in extreme circumstances. But most of the time, divorce is nothing more than a selfish decision on the part of one parent, as 80 percent are classified as unilateral. No-fault is a poisonous notion—even worse is the awarding of sole custody, which, in combination with child support, is proven to dramatically increase the rate at which women seek divorces, primarily due to "personal unhappiness".

Since no one ever seems to trouble to listen to the children, who in the overwhelming majority of cases are bitterly opposed to the separation of their parents, allow me to do so on their behalf. If you believe that divorce—even in the case of verbal abuse, marital infidelity or great personal unhappiness—is better for your children than staying together and suffering through the misery, you are either ignorant or deluded.

The man who is determined to sacrifice his children on the altar of his happiness is totally unfit to be a father, and the woman who will not put her children's lives ahead of her own emotions does not deserve to be a mother. Life is not only about happiness, it is about many things, sacrifice being one of them. And being a parent requires the greatest sacrifice of all, to live one's life for the love of another.

Letter to an Apache pilot

March 24, 2003

D EAR CHIEF _____,
As the long eve of war gives way to a fiery dawn, I wanted to express my personal gratitude for the noble service you are providing to me, to the American people and to the world. It is difficult, I know, for you to be away from your wife and children, and harder still are the doubts you face about the terrible things you must do.

But as you do your martial duty, I hope you will keep the following thoughts in mind.

First, I thank you for volunteering to serve your country—not because serving one's country is always a desirable thing, but because this particular country is founded on a shining ideal of freedom that is still a rebuke to the darkness that engulfs the world. That America has oft fallen far short of this ideal does not change the fact that of your own free will, you volunteered to uphold our Constitution and to defend those liberties we hold most dear.

I thank you for being willing to put your life on the line for mine. Our enemies have warned that every American is a target, and so I thank you for being willing to intercede for me and my family, for being willing to stand in the gap and defend us, even in the face of death.

I also thank you for the courage you have shown in confronting your fears. Bravery is not the absence of fear, it is the willingness to persevere in the face of it. And yet, you need not be afraid that practicing excellence in your craft will damn you—for just as there is nothing you can do to win salvation without Jesus Christ, there is next to nothing you can do to lose it with Him. Neither David nor Paul were innocent of bloodshed—even murder—and yet the Lord loved them both and chose to use them in awesome ways.

Jesus does not love only prostitutes and tax collectors, He loves soldiers too. He knows who you are and what you do, for He, Himself, is a warrior who came, not to bring peace, but a sword. Remember that the Lamb of God is also the Lion of Judah. And did He not once tell an officer of an army occupying a country in the Middle East that He had not seen such faith in all the country before healing the man's son? Lean on His words and not on your own understanding, because death is nothing more than a gateway—not only for you, but also for those you must perforce send through it.

God works in mysterious ways, and one thing I have learned is that sometimes we are the unknowing instruments He uses to answer the prayers of others. Surely there is at least one Iraqi who has prayed for the liberation of his people, one Kurd who has prayed for vengeance upon the oppressors of his nation. Often, the rightness of your actions cannot be known until their fruits have ripened. Keep your eyes open and be on the alert for the hand of God guiding you to do His will.

Come back safely. Come back whole. Come back to the heartfelt gratitude of a nation, with the praise and thanksgiving of a newly liberated people ringing in your ears.

Know that I—and many others—will be praying for your victory, for your safe return and that you shall one day know the peace of Jesus Christ in your heart.

In gratitude,

Vox Day

The rightness of America's war

March 31, 2003

THE ITALICIZED SECTION is a half-column from a reader from Arizona, who submitted this under the guidelines of my challenge in January. It's quite good, actually, and my response follows.

Reader's perspective:

Invading Iraq doesn't protect our liberties—it weakens them—permanently. The Apache pilot swore to defend the Constitution, yet serves in an undeclared, unconstitutional war after Congress again shirked its duty.

Randolph Bourne's World War I-era observation: "war is the health of the state," is still true. Our latest undeclared war, the euphemistic Patriot Act, massively increased federal deficit spending, and random searches of free people and vehicles at airports and roadways, are all signs of a growing state. It's ironic how we must limit our liberty to make it easier to "protect" our freedom. "Operation Iraqi Freedom" bombs people so they can "freely" select leaders meeting our approval.

How does the pilot defend your family by invading a country we've bombed and embargoed for a decade? Wouldn't safety be better served with the pilot defending our American borders? Perhaps removal of our troops from the over 100 countries in which they're stationed might lessen hatred of us as invaders, and again make us a shining example of freedom.

You use David and Paul as examples of men still loved by God despite killing others to prove to the pilot he will not be damned for doing the same. But Paul stopped persecuting and murdering Christians after accepting Jesus, and David was punished when he killed for his own purposes. So unless the pilot knows he kills for God, your proof doesn't apply.

Nations, and terrorists, believe they do God's work. The Romans even made a god of their emperor, making their brutality divinely inspired. Does rationalizing our war as God's handiwork make use of God's Word to suit God's purposes—or man's? Surely more Iraqis are praying not to be bombed right now than for "liberation". The results of the war seem more the handiwork of the "god of this age" than of God—why help him?

Did the Prince of Peace need men to fight for him? Paul, too, says that Christians fight a different kind of war. I say to the pilot: "Come back safely; come back now."

While I very much agree with the writer's core beliefs, I take issue with his conclusions, which, in my opinion, stem from some flawed assumptions. The worst of these is the implied notion that America was attacked because of our troops stationed overseas. While I definitely support bringing home our soldiers from Germany and Korea, and ending all support for U.N. peace-keeping as well, it is grossly ignorant to think that violent expansionist Islam is attacking us because of troops stationed in Saudi Arabia or the Philippines.

Islam, from the very beginning, has been a religion of conquest. Modern Islamic terror began in Kashmir after the partition of India, migrated to the West during the French Algerian War in 1954, and has since slaughtered people from the African Sudan to the Zurich airport. America is hated because she is the most powerful part of the Dar-al-Harb, and will be attacked until she either submits to the Dar-ar-Islam or defeats it.

This war is not truly about oil, Israel, Pax Americana or even Iraqi liberation. This war, as I have written before, is about ending Arab-Islamic terror by destabilizing the Arab governments which support it and allow it to thrive. Of all the Arab states, only two—Egypt and Jordan—do not finance Islamic terror, and that is only because they have survived violent attempts at revolution by the Muslim Brotherhood and the Palestine Liberation Organization, respectively. This is why Iraq, being low-hanging fruit from a political perspective, followed Afghanistan, why the House of Saud and the Iranian theocracy will likely fall, and why Syria worries openly that it will be next to face the wrath of the West.

I, too, am appalled by Congress's dereliction of duty and the twin abominations of the Patriot Act and the Homeland Security Act, but I reject the idea that this long-delayed clash of civilizations should be put off longer because of governmental failure. Since the federal government has been acting in an unconstitutional manner for more than 100 years, one could hardly expect it to do otherwise now. Still, America is not its government.

This is not a Christian war, but of course, we are not a Christian nation. The rightness of a nation's war-making can only be judged on geopolitical realities—not on that which is only concerned with the individual's soul. This war is simply one of those things that must happen in a fallen world.

With regards to the Apache pilot, do you really think he wants to be there, or is murdering for his own purposes? Of course not—he is simply doing his job, as did that Roman centurion on his mission of occupation 2,000 years ago. I also pray that our pilot comes back safely, but when his job is done and this latest manifestation of violent expansionist Islam is as broken as was its historical antecedent by Charles Martel and Don John of Austria.

The stink of America rotting

April 7, 2003

T HE BULL MARKET IS DEAD. It was shot in the head and gutted—and its decaying carcass has been smelling up the neighborhood for the last three years. Even last summer, I can recall so-called investment experts who claimed that the bull was just taking a nap—it is now in fashion to insist that because of the success of the war in Iraq, a reinvigorated economy and revitalized bull market are just around the corner.

This, ladies and gentlemen, is nothing more than the ripest, rankest bovine excrement.

The first lesson is: Believe nothing from the financial media. They make the *ABCNNBCBS* news cabal look honest—Friday morning, the consensus prediction on a decline in March Nonfarm Payrolls was 29,000. But hours after the release of the data, which was 372 percent worse than predicted, the same news source was citing "a whopping loss of 108,000 jobs vs. the expected loss of 60,000 jobs in the U.S. economy in March."

Even worse, the headline was an attempted spin to the positive, "Blue chips move higher despite jobs data." Let's see, should we write about the massive and unexpected loss of jobs, or the Dow going up one-third of one percent? That's easy! Buy! Buy! Buy!

Here's the facts. The average market-weighted price-to-earnings ratio at a bear-market bottom historically averages 7.4. The current P/E ratio for the Dow is 22.9, down from 44.7 at peak—and that's if you buy into the official earnings with their fictional pension returns and unexpensed options—the real P/E is probably close to 70 right now. Furthermore, the average dividend yield at a bear market bottom is 8.3 percent, whereas the Dow blue chips are yielding all of 2.3 percent. Yeah, them's some real cheap stocks right there!

Now, I have no doubt that the Federal Reserve, believing as it does that a failure to print enough money caused the Great Depression, will eventually cut interest rates to zero and print scads of money too. But it won't work. Growth through inflation has not worked since the first king got the bright idea to debase his gold coins, and it won't work now. The bull market of 1999? It's called asset inflation, and it's going on right now in a house near you. The truth is that the Federal Reserve, also known as the Magic Inflation Machine, is an unmitigated disaster. Yes, it's unconstitutional, and yes, it's nefarious, but even worse, it's hopelessly, stupidly incompetent!

Which is frightening to consider, when you realize that the Fed's main task at hand is shock-starting the bull market. Ignoring the stink of rotting flesh, the director of the Fed's Division of Monetary Affairs recently came right out and said:

> *If asset prices don't adjust sufficiently to stimulate spending, then open-market purchases of long-term Treasurys in sizable quantities can move premiums lower.*

Translation: If the markets don't go up soon, we're going to inflate the smack out of this dead pony!

I tell you truly: Any rally given momentary life by a 250-amp monetary infusion will not so much be a bull as a shambling, undead zombie beast with horns. So here's a prediction you can hang on your refrigerator: By the time this Great Bear has finished shredding the viscerals of the American equity, bond and real estate markets, the Dow will be at 1,500 and you will be able to purchase the entire index with a single ounce of gold. This process will take years and will be extremely painful for the vast majority of those concerned.

So what to do? Save, don't spend, but hold your savings in gold, not cash. If you refinance your house, use the savings to pay down your mortgage to provide cushion for when the real estate crash hits. Subscribe to Zeal Intelligence. Read the the Mogambu Guru. Ditch your tech losers and mutual funds and invest something like the Prudent Bear Fund. Above all, don't believe the hype!

Personal note: Readers of this column know that I stand second to no one in my contempt for the mouth-breathing mainstream media. But Michael Kelly stood out from the pack—a lion among jackals, with his common sense and genuine interest in the truth. He was a talented writer and a warm-hearted man whose love for his family and his country never ceased to shine through his writing. May he rest in peace.

Beating down a woman

April 14, 2003

I'VE BEATEN DOWN A FEW WOMEN in my time. I'm not writing metaphorically here. I'm talking about punching a girl in the face, doubling her over by kicking her in the stomach, then putting her down on the ground with a right cross to the side of the head. I can't say I didn't enjoy it—an adrenaline rush doesn't know gender.

Now, before my inbox overflows with outraged accusations of criminal Neanderthalian misogyny, I should probably point out that this all took place in the brutal full-contact martial-arts dojo that was my home away from home for almost six years. I still remember my first day there, seeing all the fighters in their black robes and the savage gleam in their eyes as they warily circled each other before exploding in a paroxysm of violence. It was truly a place apart—a broken ankle was a cause for mockery and uproarious laughter, and if one was so unfortunate as to get knocked out during a sparring session... well, to that ignominy was added the expense of buying the victor's drinks that evening.

Of every 10 newcomers, one remained a month later. Few—very few—ever reached the highest level, as the punishing belt tests were not so much sought as fearfully avoided at all costs. They were tests of skill and discipline, but more than anything, they tested one's willingness to get back on one's feet after being knocked down, again and again.

There weren't many women in our midst, understandably enough. But I was close to one in particular, we called her "Penthouse" because of her long, flowing mane of hair and her not-quite-ready-for-Playboy prettiness. She was a single mother who'd been pushed around by her ex-husband one too many times and she was determined to learn how to defend herself. After three years, she was called on the carpet to test for her green, and I was one of those selected for her sparring test, which consisted of six consecutive two-minute rounds against three high-level fighters, none of whom had just been through a grueling three-hour demonstration of every strike, kick and kata in our repertoir.

By the fifth round, she was exhausted and bruised, barely able to keep her hands up to her chin, much less defend herself. She was nearly helpless, but she must have sensed my desire to take it easy on her, because she snarled at me not to dis her like that, that she'd earned the right to be treated as a fighter and a Dragon. And she had, so it was with genuine affection and admiration that I dropped her twice in the next two exchanges, leaving her with a black eye and a bloody nose. It was a wonderful performance on her part, as she never hesitated to pick herself up, unaided, from the concrete floor. A few months later, the entire dojo cheered her on as she mercilessly destroyed the competition and won her first tournament—never having fought a woman before, she said afterward that she couldn't believe how weak and slow her opponents were, how easy it had been when compared with her training.

But if my time in the martial arts taught me to respect the inherent toughness and mental resolve of women, it has also taught me that combat of any sort is no place for them. It may be easy for a woman who hasn't taken a straight-line headshot from a 200-pound man to spin airy myths of martial equality, but no woman like "Penthouse" would ever believe them, and only a man who hasn't felt for himself how easy it is to smash a woman to the ground would take them seriously for a second.

Modern combat may be less strenuous than it was in the age of the heavily-armored Greek hoplite, but it is still physically punishing. The fluid nature of America's new uberblitz tactics means that the attacking forces must carry more of their own supplies on their backs, and indicates that the supply lines will often be operating behind enemy lines.

The capture of Jessica Lynch and Shoshana Johnson and the fact that a significant percentage of our casualties came from a maintenance company does not support the foolish myth of the American Amazon. Instead, it proves that women should be excluded from far more elements of the U.S. military than they are today.

The wrinkled whores of Wall Street

April 21, 2003

AT TIMES, ONE IS FORCED TO WONDER if the financial media operates on some sort of Orwellian contrarian basis, wherein every word's meaning is wholly inverted. After all, the "inevitable" postwar rally left the Dow 183 points lower than it was when the pre-war rally ended, and the "lackluster trading" that was sure to characterize the lead-in to the three-day Easter Weekend somehow managed to pump the NASDAQ up 5 percent on "light" volume that was 18 percent higher than the monthly average.

There's a reason for all of this, of course. The truth is that America's capital markets are in no way free—they are massaged more carefully than a Dow component's books the week before earnings season. There's been quite a debate on the existence of the Plunge Protection Team—it's interesting to read arguments for and against the existence of this notorious beast, but the fact that the financial media avoids discussing the issue like the plague is surely decisive proof that someone, somewhere, is trying to prop up the markets.

I tend to be skeptical of human nature, so I don't find the notion of a PPT incredible simply because there are so many people who profit from the notion of the eternal bull market. Also, being a serious night owl, I've watched the NASDAQ futures jump noticeably on small volume in the Asian markets while said Asian markets are dropping like stones. Coincidence? Sure, once or twice, perhaps, but not when the same thing keeps happening repeatedly.

It's hilarious to watch the European markets get faked out of their cleats like a hapless cornerback trying to tackle Barry Sanders in the open field—this repetitive chicanery is why the German DAX is now up 29 percent compared to the NASDAQ's 12 percent since March 12. It's profitable, too, as a short picked up on the opening highs can clear 100 percent by the afternoon. And speaking of shorts, did I mention that the DAX was up 17 percent over the NASDAQ?

So, why complain if I'm riding the system? First, the corruption offends my sense of justice. A free market should be free, not secretly managed for the benefit of inside players or even for the economy as a whole.

Second, this charade gives me the same nausea as walking into one of those palatial Vegas casinos and seeing the blue-hairs losing their meager pensions in the slots. The people who suffer most are those who can least afford to lose.

Third, and by far the worst, this market managing leads to inefficient capital flows, exacerbating the lingering malinvestment problem that is already pounding the tottering U.S. economy. Inflating the money supply and temporarily propping up equity prices will only extend the bust and ensures that the inevitable payback will be that much more painful for all concerned.

I'm no technician, but a wily old trader once told me to ignore the news and trust the charts. What's interesting is that every technical chart and buy-sell indicator—and every whisper of a hint of desperate Plunge Protection Team activity—is now screaming that the markets are heading for a brutal fall. It may not begin too hard or too fast, but before November, equity prices will blow past last year's sub-800 lows like the Marines going through the Republican Guard. The PPT has failed in its valiant, but hopeless 4-month effort to extend the October rally, and the time to abandon ship is now.

But what about last week's impressive performance? Wasn't it a powerful demonstration of market resilience in the face of downbeat economic data? Weren't earnings surprisingly super-duper? In a word, no. I won't bore you with my exotic analytics, but here's an anomaly to ponder: The NASDAQ-100 is down 77.5 percent since the bear first roared in March 2000, but has closed up 61 percent of the time during short weeks—45.2 percent more often than the statistical average would indicate. How lackluster indeed! You see, the streetwalkers of Wall Street like to make their hay when the sun is shining and anyone who might be paying attention is on vacation.

Wall Street has many sins for which to answer. But what the market makers truly don't seem to understand is that neither people nor markets can be controlled for long, and with every well intentioned stabilization exercise, they risk killing the goose that lays the golden eggs.

R.I.P. Connor Peterson

April 28, 2003

THE PETERSON MURDER CASE is an magnificent example of America's continuing cowardice and moral occlusion. But for once, a bright line has been drawn which prevents the supporters of "a woman's right to choose" from hiding behind tortured definitions, incomplete phrases and naked appeals to selfishness, and forces the neutral majority to realize their complicity in America's greatest shame.

Indeed, I am grateful to those few abortionettes, like Mavra Stark of the Morris County, N.J., chapter of NOW, who are bold enough to publicly articulate what is the ultimate position of their pro-death camp—that a woman has a right to kill her child at any time.

There is no possible half-measure. Either an unborn child is human, or it is not. If abortion is not murder, then neither can it be murder for a stranger to end a woman's pregnancy with a savage kick to the stomach. If abortion is not murder, then it is only Laci Peterson's fate with which the law must be concerned, for we need not trouble ourselves anymore about the swelling growth in her abdomen than we would about a wart on her foot.

But abortion is murder. More than that, it is the most vile and despicable of murders.

I have written before that calling a feminist a feminazi is an insult to National Socialism—I say this because the National Socialists were targeting for dehumanization those they considered to be a deadly enemy, the members of a race with whom the Aryan nation was competing for the throne of the world. American feminists, on the other hand, have dehumanized the most innocent portion of the human race in the prosaic pursuit of sexual pleasure and career advancement.

Dehumanization is always the first step in any planned massacre, which is why feminists stubbornly cling to the word "fetus" and are panicked when an event like the Peterson killings puts the lie to their contention that the unborn child is somehow something less than human. Their defense of atrocities such as the abomination that is partial-birth abortion places them on the moral level of a concentration-camp employee.

Now, it has become commonplace today to engage in transtemporal judgementalism, which is why the Founding Fathers are denigrated for their recognition of slavery and why modern Germans are still tainted by their grandparent's acceptance of National Socialism. Consider, then, how future generations will damn America for the 40 million unborn children legally murdered since 1972.

Legality is not morality. It was legal to murder a black in 1840, a Jew in 1944 and it has been legal to murder an unborn baby in America for the last 30 years—in 50 more, perhaps it will be legal to murder a Christian, a Frenchman or a feminist. But morality is eternal, and regardless of the current state of the law, such actions will always be immoral.

Spare me any defenses of this madly sadistic blood-orgy. I have heard them all, and I could not care less that we do not yet know the precise moment at which life begins. I am unmoved by the thought that the country might be deprived of another International Relations major if an upper-middle-class girl is not able to finish her degree due to the easily foreseeable consequences of her actions, and I have no more pity for the hypothetical woman seeking a back-alley abortion than had the U.S. 157th Regiment for the Waffen-SS guards they captured at Dachau.

As for the red-handed doctors, nurses and organizations that profit by stealing life from the unborn, better I say nothing. My thoughts regarding them are unprintable, and, I will confess, less than perfectly Christian.

Just this morning, I held a little girl in my arms, a beautiful little girl younger than Connor Peterson would be now, and when she smiled at me I was able to see the pure joy that was in her soul, even at such a young age. Wanted or unwanted, every child is precious and if a claim on privacy can be manufactured from constitutional penumbras and emanations, then surely an imperative to be born can be discovered in the inalienable right to life, liberty and happiness.

I hope that the sad and tragic fate of Laci Peterson and her little son, Connor, will help America wake up from its long, shameful national nightmare. Abortion is murder. Abortion must end.

Mailbox Vox: Abortion, the Dow, Mensa, more

May 3, 2003

As I've written before, I truly appreciate hearing from you—well, from most of you, anyhow. This Mailbox will be a regular weekend feature where I'll answer some of the many questions which I receive from you all. A special thanks for all the great blessings from the plethora of fervent pro-lifers who e-mailed this week.

> *I am assuming that you understand that the moment of life begins the moment our sinful nature does what the Holy Spirit through David defines as being at the moment of conception?*

> —Ed

I don't know when life begins, precisely, nor does anyone else. This is one reason why abortion must end, since no one is even capable of knowing that exact moment at the present time. I am sure, however, that it starts sometime before birth.

> *The truth is, it is hard to face the fact of murder or complicity in murder without a hard and cold heart. What is left is for America to decide is whether we will countenance murder and call it sympathy for the mother, or set a new paradigm making the issue of "abortion on demand" a question once again, and perhaps we can get the answer right this time.*

> —John the Marine

You can always trust a Marine to cut to the heart of the matter! We'd better get it right or, more to the point, President Bush's next Supreme Court nominees better get it right and trash those emanations and penumbras that sprang from the hallucinating hive-mind of the Supremes 30 years ago.

> *I came to a point in my life once where I thought abortion was the answer, as probably many others have done. Unfortunately, that is the decision that I made, and I am faced with that every single day of my life. A "Christian" would not remind others of their mistakes. It is so very easy to point your finger, isn't it? If we were all as "perfect and morally correct" as you seem to think you are, then the world would be a much better place!*

> —H.

It is not my intention to make those already conscious of what they have done to feel guilty, but to drive the truth of the abortion home to those who are either unrepentant, considering it, or are supporting it politically. I do not think I am perfect, especially since I am informed on a weekly basis by my readers, among others, that I am not. However, as Christians we not only have the right, but the responsibility to speak out when others go astray. See James for details.

> *If I'm to e-mail you in the future and remind you that the prediction (of Dow 1,500) was a failure, which might prompt you to re-examine some of the beliefs which led you to that conclusion, I need some kind of time frame for the prediction… Do you have any faith at all in what you said?*

> —Steve the Taurophile

S&P 445 by Oct. 31, 2005. That precise enough for you? Here's a freebie—the Vikings won't win the Super Bowl that year.

> *So what did the U.S. 157th Regiment do with the captured Waffen SS guards?*

> —Richard

After the camp was surrendered, the outraged U.S. troops shot most of the SS and allowed the inmates to finish off the rest. Five hundred, twenty of the 560 Waffen-SS were killed; the regular Wehrmacht soldiers were mostly unharmed. Patton had no problem with it; I can't really say that I do either.

Regarding Mensa: Do not advertise it. I surely would not join that arrogant group, where the average reported IQ is depressingly low to claim such superiority. You are surely better than that.

—Bob

Don't worry, Bob, I've never even been to a meeting. Now, Mensa is not the only group for which I qualify, but it's the only IQ outfit with which everyone is familiar, and it serves to preempt leftist hate mailers from making one of their two arguments, which is that they are smarter than me. This leaves them only the moral superiority argument, which is always amusing to hear from a defender of moral relativism.

Great article… Informative stuff. How exactly do you think the "PPT" are propping up the equity markets? Is it mainly through money inflation? Where should one "abandon ship", as you put it? Go long in bonds? More gold?

—Jeffrey

A lot of you were curious about the markets in general, and what I recommended once the latest money pump hits diminishing returns and the down wave begins. I'd suggest unhedged gold stocks as the easiest way to ride the wave out, with pretty much any HUI index component such as GG, GFI, NEM or GLG being a good bet.

As for "Down with Madden", all I'm going to say is that it's not a disease, and I'm just fine!

Nightmare on PC Street

May 5, 2003

We can gamble to the break of dawn, nigga
Money long, nigga
Pass up the skirt to talk to the thong, nigga
Some say I'm wrong, but f— it I'm grown, nigga
If you ain't bout money then best be gone, nigga.

—Nelly, "E.I."

THERE IS an interesting dichotomy in the public discourse. Even as the PC police clamp down ever more tightly on every expression of traditional values and religious beliefs, as they more strictly censor the textbooks of the schools through which most children are passing, the youth culture becomes ever more deliberately and contemptuously venomous in response to this totalitarian cultural whitewashing.

Thus, while the media attempts to ban references to God and the race of Man—excuse me, species of hupersonity—and feminists go red in the face should one refer to a woman as a "girl", much less a "chick", their children have become accustomed to using the terms "bitch" and "ho". While the endless debate of Colored/Negro/Black/African-American/Person of Color is now into its fifth decade, young black men have chosen the simple expedient of going back to a variant of the trusty old word "nigger". And the Queer/Gay/GLBT rigmarole is bypassed in favor of the disdainful standby "fag".

It seems that Rick Santorum, the Republican senator recently assaulted by the PC police, has a lot to learn from the likes of Nelly, Dr. Dre and Eminem. One couldn't help but notice that although Sen. Santorum was not only speaking sober legalisms in the remarks that spawned the most recent tempest in a teakettle, but doing so in a delicate, decorous manner, he came in for the full-court PC press.

The PC cops can never be avoided, you see, because their objections are not to the words that offend, as they would have it appear, but the ideas of which they do not approve. Thus the solution for successfully defeating them is not to retreat and apologize, but to confront them and turn up the heat instead. They are like Freddy Krueger of "Nightmare on Elm Street" fame—they have only as much power as one allows them to take.

It is amazing to see how quickly a PC cop will retreat in disarray when one does not immediately wither before their petty and controlling objections. If they object to "girl", drop "bitch" on them. If they protest "black", rap out a verse or two of NWA. If they complain about a reference to God, then tell them of the resurrected Lord Jesus Christ of Nazareth, who died for them, that they might have eternal life.

Believe me, they'll shut up faster than Jeff Gordon. They can't win, you see, because our thesaurus more accurately reflects the world in all its colorful reality than their pallid dictatorialism.

Moby, you can get stomped by Obie,
You 36-year-old bald-headed fag, blow me…
Now, let's go, just give me the signal
I'll be there with a whole list full of new insults.

—Eminem, "Without Me"

The media may try to excuse such errant sentiments as "reflecting the reality of the grim streets" or whatever, but that is utter nonsense. The PC-violating quotes above are from platinum-selling CDs, recorded by massively popular artists on major labels who sell to suburban white America and whose lives are about as grim as Queen Elizabeth's.

While to some readers this column may a priori appear to be some sort of post-adolescent rebellion, the ongoing attempt to control the language is a very serious matter, and overt resistance, as demonstrated by the vulgar youth culture, is the sole viable defense. Only a complete refusal to submit to the PC cops will defeat them, for as the Santorum affair proves, it is not the words which are the PC movement's ultimate target, but control over the minds which articulate them. At this point, I would even go so far as to suggest that the movement's sensitivity has been raised to such a level that if one is not offending, one is at least subconsciously submitting.

The Bible says that a soft answer turns away wrath, but we are not dealing with anger here—we are confronting a totalitarian movement that aims at nothing less than the wholesale destruction of history, intellectual freedom and traditional values. In this instance, I think Nelly, echoing the sentiments of Public Enemy, has the right of it.

Should we apologize?
Nah f— 'em, just leave 'em pissed.

—Nelly, "E.I."

Mailbox Vox: Adoption, cheese and articulate lefties

May 10, 2003

I WAS A LITTLE TAKEN ABACK by some of the mail I received after last week's column; for a group of readers who appear to have absolutely no idea what "Down with Madden" could mean, a lot of you are surprisingly knowledgeable when it comes to hip hop. Even stranger, the mail was unanimously positive, save for Craig, who is a man of few, albeit pungent words.

> *you're a f—— a——*

> —Craig

This critique, so typical of the Left, is presented in its entirety. Notice the lack of any charge of inaccuracy, logical failure or intellectual dishonesty, the total absence of any attempt at debate, honest or otherwise. Indeed, there is nothing but the pure ad hominum attack of the self-styled moral superior. Sadly, Craig left out the required aspersions of bigotry, stupidity and undereducation, so the best we can give him is a gentleman's C.

> *I was wondering about one thing you said. You said no one knows when life begins. Because, obviously, the sperm and egg are both alive, so life has already begun, so to speak. But as to the beginning of an individual human being's existence, it's not true that no one knows; any biologist, physician or embryologist knows, whether they'll admit it or not, individual human life begins at conception, when the individual human genome is formed and a unique individual human comes into being.*

> —Jeremy the M.D.

This may come as a massive shock to those of you who cherish the notion that I think I know everything, but I am incredibly ignorant when it comes to biology, among other things. I mean, I pretty much grasp that babies are not, in fact, delivered by the stork, but that's pretty close to the limit as far as it goes—I'm still trying to get over the fact that cloning is no longer just another science fiction staple.

Anyhow, the fact that the baby has discernibly different DNA from the mother at conception is close enough to proof that I'm quite willing to accept this as the point at which life begins, with the caveat that I am, as mentioned in the previous paragraph, no student of biology.

So you're against abortion, fair enough I suppose. Now that leaves a question, where do the unwanted kids go? Are you one of the many against abortion who would force a socialized adoption system on the taxpayers?

—Mike

Adoption is certainly preferable to infanticide, in my opinion, and considering the two-year waiting lists and the number of child-seeking couples who travel to China and Eastern Europe to adopt, I believe that a reasonable percentage of the increased supply would find demand. I would never support a taxpayer-supported socialized adoption system, though; I would instead suggest the novel concept that mothers and fathers be held responsible for the welfare of the pre-natal child just as they are held responsible for the welfare of their post-natal children.

If you don't want to become a father or a mother, then don't do the one thing that will cause you to become one. This is not exactly rocket science. As for not wanting a child, well, it's not like you can avoid paying your credit card bills simply because you don't want to deal with them either. And speaking of rocket science…

I figure you have already got a lot of irons in the fire, and are already pretty good at verbally shooting your enemies full of holes, but if you ever want to know how to insult the flavor of French cheese, based on the chemistry of it, give me a shout. I have done some rocket-science research in flavor chemistry, which will no doubt help to define what makes American cheddar the king of cheeses… By the way, do you like cheddar? I just can't get enough of that extra sharp Vermont stuff.

—Joe the Ph.D.

Joe, I do like cheddar, and should I ever need a cheese expert, for any reason, I can think of no one better to consult. Personally, I am rather partial to the Cotswold variant.

Sounds like you are getting into technical analysis. Any favorite books or websites? Technical analysis seems more like an art than a science.

—Ron

It is an art, certainly, and its beauty is in the eye of the beholder. A lot of people are still e-mailing with questions about the markets. It turns out that I'd inadvertently developed a crude variant of basic Elliott Wave principles, which is arcane, but intriguing stuff. I have more confidence in wave theory than in the generic technical analysis, which I feel is far too simplistic and easily manipulated by would-be market makers. As for sites, 321Gold, PrudentBear and SentimenTrader are good places to start.

The condottieri of capitalism

May 12, 2003

THE FIVE MAJOR POWERS OF ITALY—the duchy of Milan, the Serene Republic of Venice, the kingdom of Naples, the Florentine republic and the Papal States—were not known for their military prowess. While Florence had a militia of sorts and Venice was known for its navy, for the most part they relied upon condottieri for their defenses—mercenaries who not only had no significant attachment to the city-state that employed them, but often were not even Italian.

Indeed, the most famous condottiero, Sir John Hawkwood of the White Company, was an Englishman. Like most mercenaries throughout history, the condottieri were reluctant to risk their lives, without which their pay was useless, and so combat on the Italian peninsula evolved over time into a bloodless pageantry of parade drill and political intrigue.

This system appeared to work well, for a time, but the foolishness of placing Italy's fate in the hands of indifferent mercenaries became clear in 1495 when King Charles VIII of France marched south and easily claimed the throne of Naples, and his successors made Milan into a virtual French protectorate.

Much has been written about the failure of capitalism with regard to the chicanery practiced by the executive officers of companies like Enron, Worldcom and Tyco. But it is not the capitalists who were guilty of misdeeds in any of these situations—for in a free market system, it is not the executives who are the capitalists, it is the shareholders.

Management is not ownership. While there is occasionally some overlap between the two, the average CEO holds only a very small percentage of a company's total shares and those only because they have been given to him by the ownership. But America's capitalists have been imprudent to place their trust in a group of mercenaries with no more loyalty to their shareholding employers than had Francesco Sforza to the Visconti of Milan.

The furious debate about stock options is only the most recent demonstration of the conflict of interest between owners and executives. While CEOs such as Craig Barrett of Intel and John Chambers of Cisco simultaneously argue that a) it is impossible to value stock options granted to employees, but b) valuing stock options would have cost a third of their companies' profits this year, billions of dollars are traded every day on the Chicago Board of Options Exchange, which seems to have no problem putting a price on the time value of options using the Nobel prize-winning Black-Scholes model.

One of the biggest myths in America is that big business is an enemy of big government. The opposite is true, because big business, which is primarily led by the management class, is tireless in demanding that government protect it from the consequences of its own actions and from the natural fluctuations of the business cycle. It is the capitalist class of small business entrepreneurs that is usually opposed to government, which frequently acts as a defender of big business in seeking to maintain the competitive status quo.

But this is a violation of what Schumpeter accurately described as the capitalist process of creative destruction. This is dangerous, because it is the protection of giant corporations and their rapacious, self-seeking stewards that not only threatens to lead to a Japanization of the economy—wherein profitless zombie organizations continue to drain the lifeblood of the economy, precious capital from the savings pool, like monstrous business vampires—but creates a strong inclination toward unproductive growth through acquisition and a focus on short-term quarterly financials instead of the long-term health of the business.

Still, excessive CEO pay, be it through options, cash or shady "loans" is only a symptom, not the problem. The condottieri of capitalism are a cancer, certainly, but as with most things, the cause of this cancer can be traced back to government interference—in this case, with the free market. This interference, through the tax laws and S.E.C. rules and abetted by investment-bank preferences, creates a constant bias toward the elevation of the management echelon at the expense of the shareholding owners.

As the bear winds grow increasingly colder, it is important to remember that the difficult times ahead are not a crisis of capitalism, they are instead the inevitable result of anti-capitalist machinations on the part of corporate management, the banking community and the federal government.

Mailbox Vox: The bane of man

May 17, 2003

Who do you think you are to criticize France as you are doing? How an American dare to say that France "inflicted" Rousseau and Sartre to the world? French people respect American great authors, who are few you must admit, so why do you despise France's like that? What do you think of Molière, Voltaire, Flaubert, Maupassant, Balzac, Ronsard, Zola, Camus, Valéry, Hugo, and the others?

—Marianne

TO PARAPHRASE THE IMMORTAL WORDS of the undead metal poet, I am the ripper man, an American-style locomotion mind, and I am not even close to being done. The fact that the mad syphilitic and student of Flaubert, Guy de Maupassant, was quite possibly the finest writer of short fiction the world has ever known does not change the fact that Rousseau's words shall survive as the preposterous droolings of a childish mind, as free of logic as they are of wisdom. Camus is the interesting and semi-literate aspect of existentialism while Sartre is the flip side of the coin that may or may not exist, the pretentious, sophomoric aspect which holds such appeal for Philosophy 101 students. Voltaire is amusing. Hugo is compelling, although his work contains more tangents than an algebra textbook. As I promised, Marianne, I will eventually get around to Zola. But, in the meantime, you're quite right—there are few great American authors.

Like you, I am very much Christian in my philosophy and, by logical extension, libertarian in my political beliefs. We are in extremely dangerous times and most have lost sight of the truth. People don't understand that mega-conglomerate global corporations don't represent the best or the ideal of what capitalism is, or does, or means to those of us with a real conscience. We've gotten a raw deal, and it's going to get a lot rawer.

—Chuck, California

Unfortunately, Chuck is correct. Global corporations and free-market capitalism have about as much to do with one another as chipmunks and integrated circuit design. The irony of mutations like phone book-sized tomes such as NAFTA is that a real free-trade agreement only has to be about a sentence long: Congress shall pass no laws with regards to trade with (fill in the blank here). Of course, we all know how much respect the three branches of the federal government have for simple, easily understood sentences written in this format.

Knowing the history of violence, radicalism, coercion and tyranny in social-ism, the violent rhetoric and mischaracterizations by socialists deeply disturb me. Maybe it is paranoia. Maybe I am being ridiculous, but I just can't see any good coming from this.

—Sarah, Canada

Very little good, if any, has ever come out of socialist philosophy. Socialism is the bane of man; it is the cancer of his dreams. Socialism has given us the gas chamber, the gulag and the Great Leap Forward, and has racked up a body count that would be the envy of any barbarian ruler. Show no more respect for a socialist than you would for a sociopath; indeed, all the sociopaths throughout history have probably done less damage than have socialists in any country in which they've come to unrestrained power. Which leads me to wonder if perhaps socialism is not a form of intellectualized sociopathy.

Hello, great king. You are great master of strong nation. I will be happy if we can create alliance between us. Are you interest? We can easy together rule the world! Please agree.

—Saxony

The sad thing is, this is an actual e-mail. Even sadder, I know exactly what he's talking about. Once a gamer, always a gamer. Get behind me, Saxony, the mighty Sultan of Ayyub needs no friends! Crows and vultures shall feed until they burst upon the livers of his foes!

I've been meaning to e-mail you regarding Elliott Wave Theory for a while now, and when you mentioned it in your article, I got pretty excited (yeah, I know, I have to get a life)! I wanted to know your opinion of Elliott Wave.

—Rob

Elliott Wave Theory is intriguing. The short summary is that human action viewed collectively tends to result in progressions of five distinct waves—three trend, two countertrend—which tend to conform to certain specific patterns. The theory was developed for the investment markets, but has been applied to a number of different social concepts, including disease, among other things. Last week's call of a Dow top at 8770 was particularly impressive, as it survived five serious challenges, including two that failed less than six points short.

From my perspective, the jury is still out, but I am very interested in the causal relationship the EWave theorists are attempting to make between fear and disease, which is the inverse of how one would normally think of it. What is particularly fascinating about this is that it is a purely secular description of a Christian principle of spiritual warfare, namely, that it is our sin and our fear which allows evil to exercise power over us, power that we inadvertently and unwittingly grant it.

The slide into oblivion

May 19, 2003

I HAD A PLEASANT EXCHANGE of e-mail this week with a nice lady who happens to be a columnist at the newspaper I grew up reading. Like most major papers, it has long been a stronghold of the American left—it's never seen a Democrat it didn't like, or a Republican that it did—and as the opinion leader for the People's Republic of Minnesota, I've often heard friends refer to it as the Red Star, or the Star and Sickle.

But over the years, I also noticed that unlike most of the left, a few of this paper's writers harbored a genuine regard for the truth, buried though this might be beneath the stinking mass of mindless mediathink that otherwise permeates the paper. Thus, I saw no disingenuousness in the shock and dismay expressed by the aforementioned columnist, not so much at the discovery of Jayson Blair's misdeeds as at the public's blase response to the news of his wholesale forgeries.

Now, the idea that the mainstream media's product is often nothing more than a bizarre collection of misrepresentations, poorly digested half-truths and outright fiction is yesterday's news to those who inhabit the Blogosphere or read WND. But for those who have never heard of the Krugman Truth Squad, who have never seen how quickly Internet readers will gleefully pounce upon even the smallest mistake and who obtain their news from a combination of the local paper, the local TV news, *USA Today*, *CNN*, Tom Brokaw and the water cooler, this is a stunning revelation.

Thanks to the *Times*'s scandal and the fact that the ratings war between *Fox News* and *CNN* bears more resemblance to a prison rape than a horse race, the establishment media is finally beginning to wake up to the thought that perhaps the wider public's disdain for it does not stem solely from the great unwashed being too stupid, uneducated and mean-spirited to follow its shining path to the enlightened society.

The Gray Lady is certainly an appropriate moniker for the *New York Times* now, although the Sclerotic Dinosaur would be a better one. The truth is that the Jayson Blair scandal and the institutional failures of the so-called newspaper of record are only symptoms of what will prove to be a terminal disease for many conventional news organizations. The establishment media has grown lazy and complacent due to a lack of competition and the result of this hegemony is that it is now spectacularly unfit to survive the changes wrought by the ongoing technological revolution that is the Internet.

Just as, according to current scientific understanding, the dinosaurs were unable to cope with the great changes that came toward the end of the Cretaceous period, the establishment media is structurally and conceptually handicapped in a myriad of ways that the New Media are not. We of the right—libertarian, paleocon, neocon or otherwise—have had to be sharper, harder, faster and more accurate from the very beginning. Operating on the outskirts, without margin for survival, we are forced to be responsive and to learn quickly from our mistakes.

Think of it as evolution in action. It is interesting to note that even the traditional media's remaining strengths contain inherent weakness. For example, access to those about whom one writes has its benefits, to be sure, but it has its shortcomings too. I have no fear of politicians snubbing me, because no one was ever going to talk to me in the first place. Therefore, I can articulate my thinking in complete freedom, without any concern for reprisals.

It is certainly possible that elements of the establishment media will learn from the continuing train wreck of its popularity and salvage something from the destruction. It can do so by abandoning the arrogant and false pretense of its pure objectivity, by beginning to study the intellectual foundations of its opposition's thinking and by resolving to pursue the truth instead of consistently massaging the facts to fit a predetermined script.

But who are we kidding? The ink-stained successors to Plato's Guardians are unlikely to learn from their mistakes until it is far too late, when their wide audiences have been irretrievably lost. *MSNBC* is already dying, how long will it take the network that spawned it to follow suit? The tide is turning—remember, it was not so long ago when one could safely dismiss unpalatable ideas as being "off the Internet" and therefore dubious, if not a downright joke.

So, who is laughing now?

Mailbox Vox: Articulation on confiscation

May 24, 2003

I have a very simple question. What happens to all the personal property that is confiscated at airports? I ask because my husband travels on business with his tools a lot. He and his colleagues constantly report that their tools are being confiscated. My husband had some valuable ones confiscated out of his carry-on, but he has also had tools confiscated from his checked luggage as well.

I know that we are not allowed to come back and claim the confiscated property, nor pay to have it shipped back to us. We are not even given receipts for it. So what happens to it? And what law (constitutionality aside) permits the government to take it from us without compensation?

—Sarah

I HATE TO DISAPPOINT you Sarah, but I simply don't know. I rather suspect the tools are claimed for personal use by those who are doing the confiscating. This behavior is very much in keeping with the various seizures being practiced on all levels of government around the country, in violation of numerous state constitutions and laws protecting private property. As American property rights decline, it is becoming more and more clear that government is usually little more than a massive criminal gang feeding off the populace.

I wrote a letter to Joseph Farah. It generated no reply, and as far as I know, it was not posted. Somehow, I get the feeling that the length of my letter was not the real problem. Since I, too, am a Christian, with libertarian leanings,

I thought you might have some insider view of WND which might explain WND's non-response.

—John

OK, everybody, relax! Joseph is not selling out his principles, he is not blowing people off because he's getting above himself and there is no dark secret behind every failure to respond to someone. It's just that Mr. Farah gets a massive amount of e-mail and he's incredibly busy keeping WND's ball rolling. It takes him a month just to send me a one-word answer to one of my e-mails.

What happens to the money contributed to the Social Security system when a person dies before retirement age? I figure the honest thing to do would be to roll that money over to the surviving family members but it appears instead that the government just walks with it, nobody thinks anything of it and it's never mentioned. It appears that there were approximately 2,400,000 deaths in the U.S. in 2000. Let's say that 400,000 of them were between the ages of 40 and 60 with an average contribution amount of $30,000. That would mean the government is walking with $12,000,000,000 of technically unaccounted for tax (retirement) dollars per year.

—Phil

Great question! That's an excellent point, Phil, and one I wish I'd come up with myself. Since Social Security is actually a tax set up like a Ponzi scheme, the money that was paid in was long ago spent on benefits for retirees or other government programs, but I don't know what is the official government rationale for allowing itself to keep the benefits of the deceased.

For those of you who were interested in the Elliott Wave theory, Elliott Wave International has a comprehensive website. According to them, the markets ended the March rally last Thursday. You have to subscribe to receive the detailed reports, but there's a lot of free information in their Club EWI.

She came, she saw, she got crushed

May 26, 2003

ANNIKA SORENSTAM appears to be a decent individual. Her remarks before and after the tournament were appropriately humble and void of the usual girly trash-talk which the women of my generation can't seem to resist despite never being able to walk the walk. She's an excellent lady golfer, if occasionally prone to the chokies when playing the majors, though hardly on the scale of lefty or the Great White Shaak.

She is not, however, even close to being able to play with the big boys.

That's no shame, neither am I. Nor do I take any issue with her playing in a PGA tournament on a sponsor's exemption. It's legit by the rules, but let's face it, the crowds attracted to the novelty of watching Annika play are no bigger than they would be if Pamela Anderson Kid-Rock were out there swinging in a bikini, and they're no better for the sport of golf.

Then again, is golf actually a sport? I submit that it is only a game masquerading as an athletic event. Have you ever seen Davis Love's arms? They're like rubber toothpicks!

So, she played and she was spanked. The actual event was fine, but what was offensive was the constant barrage of condescending politically correct jabber leading up to it, and the instant condemnation of anyone who dared to voice opposition to a woman playing on the men's tour. Vijay Singh, who backed up his talk rather nicely with a win the week before, was labeled a Neanderthal by sportswriters who collectively got the vapors at the notion that any man, anywhere, would object to this "inspirational story"; this "gallant", even "heroic", sporting endeavor.

They couldn't imagine why any man would object to Sorenstam's inclusion, and to be fair, Annika was totally unobjectionable as she refused to portray herself as the Amazon warrior for which Martha Burk, the National Organization for Women and the Title IX Nazis were wishing. Even so, and despite the fact that it would be a mathematical impossibility for me to care less about golf, I hated seeing her in the Colonial field and so did a lot of other guys.

Why? Because as long as I can remember, my generation has had the myth of female superiority shoved down our throats. Turn on the television, and if there is an athletic competition of any type involving a man and a woman, the woman will win. Every single time, with a smile and a shrug as she confesses that she used to play in college or whatnot. This is sheer gynomythology, of course, as anyone who is even half an athlete knows that there's a reason that runs /throws /hits like a girl is considered to be an insult.

Furthermore, it sticks in my craw that two men cannot sit in a room, smoke cigars and shoot the breeze without a woman brandishing a lawsuit and wanting in. And yet, we have women's colleges, women's fitness centers, women's business conferences, women's symposiums and women's golf tours, all of which blithely practice exactly the same gender-based discrimination which women have supposedly been protesting for years.

Now, this may come as a shock to some of you, but I not only like women, I enjoy them on their terms. I know the difference between Valentino and Versace. I know which dresses passed muster on the red carpet, and which ones didn't. And I've not only read "Divine Secrets of the Ya-Ya Sisterhood" but thoroughly enjoyed it! OK, I still don't get the whole Oprah thing.

But like a lot of guys, I am seriously annoyed with being labled a prehistoric brute who doesn't get it every time a woman has a minor disagreement with me. Equity feminism was one thing, but this gender feminism, this quasi-pagan anti-intellectual misandric vaginacentrism, is straight from the bottom of Hell's bell curve. I mean, after reading Catherine MacKinnon, I was absolutely convinced that the Founding Fathers were right to deny women the vote.

Then I came down thanks to Camille Paglia and a little Ann Coulter, and I eventually reached the conclusion that if women don't blame us for Marx and Rousseau, we shouldn't hold them collectively responsible for MacKinnon, Susan Faludi and Marilyn Friedman.

Nevertheless, men and women really are different. Can anyone imagine Tiger Woods bursting into tears after missing a cut? But fair enough, Annika's had her shot, so now let's see how Brian Kontak fares against the big girls of the LPGA.

Bears and belles

May 31, 2003

I imagine that you would be concerned with the potential effects your writings may have on others. I am speaking in particular about your comments regarding investments, i.e.: spiraling asset deflation, DOW at 1500 etc. While I don't completely dismiss the possibilities presented by you on any of these subjects, I do believe that a bit of restraint is in order. I agree… the buy guys are playing their own game too, and CNBC's Squawk Box is the Three Stooges of economic reporting. I guess I don't bother challenging any of them because I know that would be a waste of time.

—Bob

I THINK IT'S WORTH NOTING that while I'm willing to defend my assertions and reject them when they are demonstrably wrong, you'll never hear the financial media do anything but declare that now is the time to buy stocks. If equity prices are high, it's time to buy since momentum is with the markets. If they're low, then it's time to buy since the markets are cheap. I'll freely admit that stocks are proving more resilient than I expected, but, a) the Fed pumping money during a short week almost always provides a five percent lift, and b) the previous bear market rally rose 24 percent in 37 days to peak. On day 56 of the current rally, we're at 20.36 percent. Time is running very short and some important indicators have already turned south.

As a woman myself, age 61, I have been fed up for years of hearing the feminist garbage and the male bashing. Today's women are aggressive and whiney. The true feminine qualities and attributes are mostly lost on this new generation. They don't have that inner womanly beauty that used to come from the softness and dignity that used to make woman so attractive.

—Barbara

Though I shouldn't be, I'm always surprised by how many women write to tell me of their support for my supposedly misogynistic stance. Women of my generation are often whiney and aggressive, simultaneously convinced of their own superiority attendant with a right to a complete lack of self-responsibility. This dichotomy is a lethal combination which is a massive turn-off for the vast majority of men. It is certainly one factor in the preference of many black and white men for Asian women, whose upbringings still tend to reflect more of the traditional values held by their immigrant parents and grandparents.

Feminism is a sorry excuse for addressing real issues that many women had to face in the old days. Now, since the '60s, it's run amuck and makes me ashamed. I wonder what the world would be like if women were still denied the vote? I can't help think it might be a more normal world still.

—Dianne

Since the infamous Gender Gap is, statistically, less a Republican problem with women than a Democratic problem with men, I don't believe that any Democratic presidential candidate since FDR would have won without the women's vote. While the blame for the ills of modern welfare state Big-Brotherism lies solely with the men who conceived it, the system could not have been implemented were it not for the collectively gullible nature of women, who still buy into the charade to a much greater degree than men.

Switzerland is an interesting example of this, as its greater emphasis on individual liberty and responsibility compared to its European neighbors is a direct result of women only receiving the right to vote in 1972.

Women are killing men in the education field. They have a much better GPA, SAT and intelligence scores than the men. More bachelors, masters, and Ph.D.s than men. And more females attending law and medical schools than men. What is your reaction to this?

—Bernie

First, this illustrates the silliness of the glass-ceiling notion. The reason that women don't tend to reach the top of the corporate ladder, just as they don't tend to inhabit the extremes of the IQ bell curve, is that most don't value that particular form of success as much as men. No one reaches the top without making incredible sacrifices of opportunity cost with regards to personal relationships with both friends and family—foolish sacrifices, for the most part, in my opinion. Money is an absolute necessity of life in today's society, but it is certainly not the most important thing.

However, this does make me wonder about the women who are determined to have their own success, but also demand an even more successful mate. There's a fundamental contradiction there, as the higher one climbs, the stiffer one's competition and the worse one's odds. This shouldn't be news, it's just simple logic.

What does "down with Madden" mean? I'm new to WND and your column, so if you have explained it before I missed out.

—Josh

As one reader who did manage to wheedle an answer out of me on the subject concurred with my original notion that the not-knowing was preferable to the knowing, I shall refrain from adding to your store of knowledge.

Gynomythology

June 2, 2003

I N WHICH WE EXAMINE a few of feminism's favorite fairy tales.

Feminism is about choice.

Feminism is actually about having your choices made for you. Feminism is nothing more than a gender-based form of fascism, which attempts to control the behavior of individuals through government fiat. Fortunately, feminists have not been able to amass the power required to send unrepentant males and recalcitrant gender-traitors to the pink gulag. In the words of feminist icon Simone de Beauvoir:

> *No woman should be authorized to stay at home to raise her children. Society should be totally different. Women should not have that choice, precisely because if there is such choice, too many women will make that one.*

The reason that women have accomplished very little of note throughout history is primarily due to male oppression.

There is an element of truth to this, as the vast majority of women were denied access to the higher levels of education; then again, so were most men. However, it is also true that those women who did obtain excellent educations often chose to engage in light intellectual amusements instead of contributing anything of significance to the arts or sciences. There was nothing to stop the educated hetaerae of Greece from writing a "Metaphysics" or a "Republic", nor anything preventing the mistresses of the famed Parisian salons from compiling, like Diderot, their own "Encyclopedia"; the fact remains they did not.

But the most damning argument against this myth is the appalling behavior of the leading female pseudo-intellectuals over the past 30 years. Instead of taking advantage of their intellectual freedom and unprecedented access to education, the feminist vanguard has embraced an anti-intellectual dogmatism that imprisons the current generation of young women in the academic convent of Women's Studies, robbing them of both foundational knowledge and the capacity for rational linear thought, thus ensuring that this generation, like its foremothers, will also fail to accomplish anything worthy of historical regard.

Women entering the work force has been good for America.

The entry of women into the work force accomplished only one thing. It significantly lowered wages by doubling the size of the work force. According to the iron law of supply and demand, increasing the supply of X while demand remains constant means that the price of X will fall. The primary impact of women entering the work force in quantity has been to lower the price of labor so that two people must now work in order to maintain a household instead of one, as before.

While America does realize the benefit of the contributions of women whose talents might have otherwise been wasted, it pays a heavy price in terms of children who are abandoned to be raised by day-care centers, the state schools and television. And those many women who would like to make the choice to remain home with their children cannot, since their husband can't earn enough money to support a family alone due to his wages having been lowered because of the increased supply of labor.

Anything men can do, women can do better.

This myth raises the question of how the nefarious Patriarchy could possibly have come to be established in the first place. Were the women of yore less intelligent, less aware, or otherwise less able than their modern counterparts? A lovely example of nonlinear fifth-stage thinking.

The Sexual Revolution liberated women.

It actually freed men from the responsibilities that traditionally accompanied access to sex. Whereas a man once needed to all but promise marriage before taking a lover, he now can freely expect a woman to satisfy his desires on the third date, if not the first. The real revolution was the wholesale transference of power in the male-female dynamic from women to men, and now any reasonably handsome young man can effortlessly rack up more sexual conquests in four years of college than did the legendary Casanova in a lifetime.

A woman has a right to control her own body.

This baseless assumption flies in the face of hundreds of long-standing American laws. A woman can be jailed for putting certain unapproved chemicals into her body, for failing to put certain required chemicals in her body (military vaccinations), for selling portions of her body or renting out her body on an hourly basis, or for displaying her body in public in an unapproved manner. The fact that some of these laws are, in my opinion, ill-founded, does not matter; they still serve to demonstrate the fallacy of this particular pro-abortion gynomyth.

Feminists lose their breakfast

June 7, 2003

The reason women entered the work force was World War II. The fact of the matter is, the shortage of men needed to arm our troops required women to take their places in the factories. It is not women that caused wages to go down. The fact is wages have not gone down... Sorry, guys, but on this point, Vox Day has been slam-dunked. And by a woman. Oh the shame of it!

—Jill

GET THAT BOVINE BYPRODUCT outta here (sound of KG smacking a ball into the fifth row)! Jill has her facts wrong. As she mentioned, there was a labor shortage during World War II, so clearly the women who entered the work force then couldn't have affected the wage rate, since they were replacing the men who were away fighting. From 1950 to 1998, women's participation in the work force rose from 33 percent to 59.8 percent, and is projected to peak at 61.9 percent in 2015. Real wages did not drop immediately, but they peaked in 1973 and have declined since then.

Why did wages not peak sooner? I was puzzled by this until I dug a little deeper into the labor statistics. It turns out that at the same time women began entering the labor force in significant numbers, men started leaving; in fact, the percentage of men working has fallen 11 percent since 1950 and is expected to fall a further 6 percent in the future. Is this because men can't compete with women? That's possible, but it's more likely that older men are simply taking the opportunity to retire and collect Social Security, as most of the men who've dropped out are the 65-and-older crowd, whose labor participation has fallen from 45.8 percent to 16.5 percent. So, it seems that women are working primarily in order to fund the retirement of old men—maybe there is a Patriarchy after all!

Now, I will readily admit that this is a gross simplification. There are many other factors involved, including immigration, taxation, inflation, the shift from a manufacturing economy to a service economy, globalization and the abandonment of the gold exchange standard. But it would be almost impossible for a virtual doubling of the labor supply to have zero impact on its price—I can't imagine that anyone with a knowledge of even the most basic economics would seriously attempt to argue that.

> *Vox Day ... sums up with what may be the most immortal paragraph of the generation. "It's hard to know exactly how the imperial dollar will die. It is possible that the gold-backed Islamic dinar may replace the dollar as the global trading standard or that China or the European Union may seize the moment to offer the world a stable replacement currency. What I do know is that no amount of economic stimulus, be it tax cuts, spending increases or interest-rate cuts, will allow America to avoid paying the piper for four years of spectacularly ill-timed malinvestment. The party is over. Prepare yourself."*

> *The only dispute I have with Mr. Day is his calculation that we have had only four years of "spectacularly ill-timed malinvestment." Looking at my watch, I figure that it is close to almost 50 years, as it took that long to run up a deficit of the newly-discovered $44 trillion dollars of un-funded, un-thinking, un-economic, un-common sense, and ultimately un-payable commie-think idiocies.*

> —The Mogambo Guru

I won't argue with the Mogambo Guru. First, he knows far more about markets and the economy than I do, and second, it's downright dangerous! If you don't read him, you really must. I'm flattered beyond words to learn that he reads this column.

Women's accomplishments may not be in the same areas as men, but they still should be considered noteworthy and of value… (list of female artists from the Bronte sisters to Alice Walker, including Amy Grant and Madonna).

—Carol

Women absolutely must be valued, as they are the civilizing force of society, indeed, without women society would barely exist. But under no circumstances should anyone attempt to equate the works of Alice Walker with those of Fyodor Dostoyevsky, or favorably compare the musical accomplishments of Madonna with Mozart, or even, for that matter, William Orbit. A desire to be valued is quite understandable, and women have surely earned the right to be respected for their very real contributions to humanity, still, this does not justify ludicrous comparisons of artistic worth; to do so only causes one to question a woman's judgment, if not her sanity. I love Ministry, but I would never suggest that "Jesus Built My Hot Rod" is an aesthetic masterpiece worthy of the same regard as the Brandenburg Concertos.

I must say you caught my attention, looking beyond the hair-cut, a very handsome man… I do not think I need a man, but you sure would be one I'd love to learn from.

—Nancy

Hark, what's that I hear? Ah, yeah, it's feminists across the country losing their breakfasts. Thanks very much, Nancy, but I have three words for you. Dorothea and Casaubon. Learning and love don't mix well, and furthermore, I'm off the market.

Friday, the fat lady sang

June 9, 2003

I DIDN'T SEE THIS RALLY COMING. Neither, it seems, did a lot of the institutional investors who missed out on the all-important initial stage of the rally, which is typically where 50 percent of the gains are made. And, like a lot of bears, I got hammered when the expected snap-back didn't happen in late March, then again last week, when despite the indicators turning south, the final blow-off top drove inexorably upward for an almost unprecedented 11 days out of 12.

But I've been wrong before and if there was no risk, there would be no reward. What's important is to realize that there are two possibilities from this point. Scenario A is that the *CNBC* cheerleaders are right to be jumping up and down, excitedly waving their pom-poms, and the October lows mark the start of a new bull market. Their arguments are that inflation and interest rates are low, the economic indicators, while negative, are not worsening at the same pace as before and are therefore positive, and that corporate earnings will increase dramatically in the fall thanks to the economic growth that is just around the corner. This will justify the optimistic pro-forma earnings-based valuations, which in Generally Accepted Accounting Principle terms again exceed those of pre-crash 1929.

This scenario is not only rosy, but is about as likely as monkeys flying out of Alan Greenspan's beknighted butt. I'm down with Scenario B, which is that this is just another bear-market rally—the sixth since the bear first growled in early 2000.

While the impressive scope of this rally, 27.71 percent on the S&P 500 in 61 days, exceeds the average bear rally, (24.10 percent in 28 days), this only indicates that the present rally is a rather labored one due to collapse of old age and exhaustion. And despite taking more than twice as long to reach these heights, the Dow's peak is still .29 percent short of average, and the Nasdaq-100 is 11.61 percent short.

But averages only indicate probabilities. What is perhaps more important is to understand the actions of the market makers. You see, when the Fed talks about its fears of deflation, it is not talking about deflation in the general economy, it is talking about deflation in the asset markets, since by any reasonable measure, the U.S. economy is in the deadly grips of massive inflation. Inflation is when the money supply increases faster than the economy grows—it is not, as most people think, an increase in consumer prices as measured by the CPI—and the Fed's three measures of money supply have all been growing around 13 percent, far faster than the feeble 2 percent increase projected in the GDP.

So, until recently, have the Fed's market operations, which is the money it loans out to banks that use it to buy stocks or currencies, then sell them and repay the Fed, usually the very next day. It's worth noting that in the last two weeks, the Fed has reduced this liquidity pool by 40 percent. This isn't a definitive sign, but in conjunction with the rally's age and performance, it suggests that the Fed feels that it has done its job of stabilizing the situation and can safely allow the market to decline for the next two or three months without fear of a terminal crash.

This isn't conspiracy theory—the Fed openly manages the bond and mortgage markets, so why would one believe the equity markets are magically off limits? Especially since there's nothing the least bit unusual or illegal about the central bank lending money to its member banks in the first place. Remember, since the Fed is considered responsible for managing the economy, it would be downright derelict in its duty if it simply ignored one of the more important markets.

Finally, for those who only pay attention to price action, last Friday was truly intriguing. Just as on Dec. 2, 2002, the Nasdaq-100 raced up more than 2 percent at the start, only to reverse abruptly and finish well below its peak. The significance is that Dec. 2 marked the end of the last rally, so if we see a similar 9 percent decline in the Nasdaq this week, that will be all the confirmation we'll need to know that, on Friday, the fat lady sang.

Mailbox Vox on Catholics, cannibals, porn, and Porsches

June 14, 2003

I find it most odd that you think a Christian has an obligation to take any side on a matter of war. You're simply saying that a Christian should make an individual choice and that it best be on the side of the nation that one happens to live in. Then the German Christians—who went along with Hitler—were doing the Christian thing by doing so?

—Michael

THAT'S A VERY reasonable summation of my position, Michael, assuming you've first been hitting the crack pipe. I did not say a Christian has an obligation to take sides in war, in fact, I said precisely the opposite.

Contrary to common understanding, Jesus Christ was neutral on war. He said war was inevitable in a fallen world and He told His followers not to be troubled by it. He did not tell them to devote themselves to working against it. Regarding the present situation, violent expansionist Islam has already declared war on both America and Christians around the world. War, unlike the tango, does not take two.

Someday, the sky will fall, hopefully long after each of us is gone, and then our progeny can dust off your predictions and say, "Yep, that Vox, he was right all along… but I'm sure glad we didn't miss all those millennia of living, waiting for him to be right." I envy your talent, but not your outlook. Choosing to live positively is not stupidity—it is just one of the choices… free will, if you will.

—Steve

Look, I'm not saying that we're about to descend into cannibalism or anything. Japan has seen its markets drop by more than 75 percent and it survives—there's just far fewer Ferraris parked in front of the night clubs than there were in the days when I was prowling Roppongi. But no society has ever become wealthier by destroying its currency, decimating its savings and encouraging its people to go heavily into debt.

But if things do fall apart completely, we appear to be fortuitously well prepared for a descent into cannibalism judging by the plethora of plump posteriors wandering the malls. See, I am an optimist!

As a fellow Mensan, I read your WorldNetDaily column with some interest, and tend to agree with your political opinions. When it comes to economics and equities, however, I find your knowledge to be sorely lacking. With all due respect, you have nothing on the pundits whom you seem to berate. And your analysis of the current situation regarding equities will, I think, prove to be simply wrong.

—Stan

I imagine we'll find out soon enough. I do, however, note that as of last week's close, the markets have not made it back to the Jun. 6 highs. While I freely admit that I have been wrong about the markets in the past, and will likely be wrong about them on occasion in the future, I do take exception to being compared with the *CNBC* cheerleaders.

Just today, I heard one gentleman, who had been denigrating bonds, respond to a question about any potential downside risk to equities. His answer? There is none. My column may have many flaws, but I have never written anything that mind-bogglingly stupid or gut-wrenchingly dishonest.

Time is running out. The Pentagon plans to convert the concentration camp in Guantanamo Bay into a DEATH CAMP—this is just a glimpse of what is to come. The Vatican will destroy millions of lives, in order to make way for a TOTAL REIGN OF CATHOLICISM in the Western hemisphere.

—Mike

There are a lot of things about which I am concerned, but the total reign of Catholicism, in any hemisphere, is fairly close to the bottom of the list. Then again, it's entirely possible that Catholic imperialists have been cunningly lying low for, lo, these many centuries. Because at this point, nobody expects the Spanish Inquisition.

Now, I want to know what the hell is wrong with men and the porno crap at work. Since you have such insight into women's screwups these days, maybe you can enlighten me about the porno-viewing men.

—Jerri

It's not exactly a secret, but men really do quite like to look at pretty women with hot bodies which aren't particularly well covered. Since real women don't tend to appreciate this sort of attention unless they're being paid for it, and because the law takes a dim view of men wandering into women's changing rooms, inanimate pictures are usually the safest bet.

This may sound pathetic, but it is, so there you go. Furthermore, a lot of men don't really appreciate or enjoy their jobs. Throw an Internet connection into the mix, and you have one very unedifying picture of the depths to which men can sink without the inspiration and support of a good woman with strong Judeo-Christian morals. Or, at the very least, a boss with a clue.

It's all about the visuals, ladies. Visuals are like scented candles, expensive restaurants and the smell of leather in a new Porsche all rolled into one as far as men are concerned.

Saint Hillary of Hell

June 16, 2003

HILLARY SAYS she has written another book. She's on a book tour. But as usual for this ghastly revenant of American politics, that isn't true. She no more wrote "Living History" than did you or I, although I have no doubt that she edited it very, very closely. After all, without careful precautions, it was always possible that one or two elements of the truth might inadvertently slip out.

But this column is not a fiction review, so I'll ignore the book. What interests me more is the response of other women to the latest charade of this fraud. Consider, for example, the words of Erica Jong in the New York Observer:

> *The woman is stronger than Queen Elizabeth I of England, a greater strategist than Catherine the Great of Russia, braver than Boadicea or the Amazons of old.*

Apparently, Ms. Jong is not only afraid of flying, she is also woefully ignorant of history. File this one under Exhibit 3,567(b) in my catalog of contempt for feminists. So, let's have a look at the comparisons, shall we?

Before she was ever crowned, Elizabeth faced the very real threat that she would be murdered by Catholic fanatics concerned about her sister's inability to provide for a Catholic heir. She survived several assassination attempts by her cousin's partisans, faced down the French over their massacre of the Huguenots, and with the help of a timely storm, defeated the Spanish Armada. Under her reign, English power and English literature flowered as never before. While putting up with Bill Clinton for years no doubt required superhuman strength, I think the nod here goes to Good Queen Bess.

Can you even imagine the concept of Good Queen Hillary? The mind reels.

Boadicea was an earlier British queen, who led the Celtic Iceni in a two-year uprising against the imperial Roman army after her daughters were raped and she herself was flogged by soldiers. Her husband, the king, was already dead, so Boadicea took matters into her own hands and vengefully orchestrated the slaughter of tens of thousands while razing Colchester, St. Albans and London. While this does sound like something very much in Hillary's line, I don't think braving the Vast Right-Wing Conspiracy quite rates with battling Roman legions in terms of sheer valor.

While Boadicea was a warrior woman, the Amazons were not, primarily because their existence is wholly fictitious. Not unlike the idea that Hillary is an author, or, for that matter, human.

It is true that one might well question how Catherine the Great rates as a strategist. After all, how cunning can a woman be, whose former lover selects all of his subsequent replacements? Nor did she lead her armies personally, as did her imperial antecedent, Peter. However, her very survival on the throne was a strategic masterpiece, since she started as little more than a German princess with a very tenuous claim to the Russian empire. But she held her throne, and went on to establish schools across the country, triple the number of factories, turn the empire's budget deficit into a surplus and found Russia's first school of medicine.

Whereas Hillary Clinton managed to fail, in spectacular fashion, at the only executive responsibility she has ever held in her life. Unlike Catherine, Hillary's only interest in medicine was her failed attempt to destroy it in America. Fortunately, she proved to be as painfully inadequate in exercising power as she is ruthless in pursuing it.

Hillary the Great? Hardly. And yet, I'm only surprised that Ms. Jong did not compare her, favorably, of course, to St. Francis of Assisi.

Because it is not enough for Ms. Jong to raise Hillary above these three women of historical fame. She is angered—bitter—that we do not follow her example and fall to our unworthy knees before the lizard queen.

The fault, dear readers, is not in Hillary, but in our ghastly mass media, which only applauds brainy women when we are reduced to tears.

But it is more truly we the people Ms. Jong would fain see reduced to tears. She, and other minions like her, will not be content until we have the

Hillary Channel, Hillary-span, and CNBHillary—all Hillary all the time—until at last we look upon that eerie lidless gaze, and, with tears of fear and joy streaming down our faces, proclaim our love for her.

The lizard queen and bad boys

June 21, 2003

"[U]ntil at last we look upon that eerie lidless gaze, and, with tears of fear and joy streaming down our faces, proclaim our love for her." So, is this a reference to the ending of '1984'? I am reminded of the pigs in 'Animal Farm' when I see Hillary.

—Tom

YOU GOT IT—it's just a paraphrase, really. I have to say, I am tremendously disappointed that no one mentioned the Monty Python quote. It was even topical!

On Hillary of Hell: I got quite a chuckle from your missive and must say that I concur. I do think you exercised restraint in your assessment which I will have to attribute to your obvious enlightened upbringing in a Christian home.

—Dennis

Yes, I'm quite notorious for my restraint. Dennis, with all due respect, have you ever read my column before?

You are trying to completely dehumanize Hillary Clinton. In fact, you challenge the fact that she is human. Well, she is married to a man and gave birth to a seemingly human daughter. I guess biologically she is no less of a human being than you, sir… I mean, you are entitled to have your enemies and choose them as you please, but it is not a good style to treat them with such utter disrespect.

—Boris

I can only note that even Boris feels the need to qualify the lizard queen's ability to spawn convincingly human progeny with the word "seemingly".

The admittedly courageous and brilliant Iceni queen, Boadicea, was put in her place at the Battle of Mona Island in 61 AD. There, 10,000 Roman soldiers led by the even more brilliant Suetonius Paullinus defeated the 80,000 troops of Boadicea and routed them, probably the last time Italians were ever good soldiers. The Iceni queen, humiliated by the defeat of her army and the deaths of her daughters, took poison.

—Patrick

Must… not… respond…

I have begun reading your columns recently and they are as entertaining as they are informative. My only comment is that hair growing on either side of your head will not affect your ability to write. I've shared some of your articles with some office idiots. Their comments are never directed towards your words, only that you look like a Nazi. That's OK, I suppose, I have a full head of hair and they think I'm a Nazi, too. Do you ever appear on TV? I would like to see you debate with the morons on the left.

—Steve

The National Socialists had mohawks? Who knew? I've yet to do a television appearance, and I suspect it would likely be a disaster anyhow, as there's no time for any depth or support for one's assertions. I'd probably clock the first doorknob who said they didn't agree with my facts based on their opinion, as I once heard a woman tell John Lott. Some are called to be writers and others read teleprompters, I suppose. TV may help with fame and fortune, but fundamentally, it blows.

Do you think CAIR is a terrorist organ as Daniel Pipes says? Pipes is Bush's choice to add to his Near/Middle East advisory board and CAIR has opened an office here. Wouldn't mean as much but the head Islamics here are both unknowns and one claims to be from a place that is nowhere to be found.

—Gary

The Council on American-Islamic Relations is an apologist voice for many Islamic organizations, including Hamas and other known terrorist groups. I've been the beneficiary of their e-mail barrages myself in the past. I've yet to see anyone successfully refute Mr. Pipes's statements about CAIR, as he documents the refutations and his convincing responses to them on his website.

What in the H-E-double-hockey-sticks was Mike talking about? Catholic imperialism? How do you put up with these kinds of insane letters?

—Kim

You're kidding, right? They make my day! That was a classic, and I even got to work in the Spanish Inquisition.

Sensitive, good-looking men are like scented candles, long hot bubble baths, mink coats and chocolate all rolled into one as far as women are concerned. Vox, I agree with everything you said, except for the notion that without a good woman, men are more able to fall into these things. Unfortunately, women are held accountable for their actions while men use excuses.

—Mandy

I think you're forgetting that what women enjoy, what gets them going, tend to be things in which they can indulge freely without notice. A woman can get together regularly with a man, even engage in serious flirtation with him, and no one is aware that she is thinking X-rated thoughts about what she'd like him to do to her. A man, on the other hand, can't even walk innocently into a strip club without a presumption of lascivious intent.

Oh, relax, I'm kidding! But speaking as a retired and reformed member of the bad boys' wolf patrol, I can state with some authority that women don't like nice, sensitive guys half as much as they think they do.

Harry Potter and the Harbingers of Doom

June 23, 2003

I'M QUITE A BIT behind the times on this one. I just read the first two Harry Potter novels last week, and, let me tell you, it was a bit of a shock to sail through J.K. Rowling's simple, straightforward prose directly after navigating past the treacherous shoals of Perez-Reverte's latest work.

But please understand: This is not to denigrate the phenomenon that is Potter, as I very much enjoyed the books and their massive appeal is easy to comprehend. They are magical escapism, ideal for the young boy or girl who would like nothing better than to disappear for a time from what can be a very difficult period of life. If they lack the mythical depth of Susan Cooper's *The Dark is Rising* or even the poignant whimsy of Lloyd Alexander's *Chronicles of Prydain*, what of it? They are easy, enchanting and amusing reads.

Well-meaning Christians have attacked Harry Potter because of the idea that the books make the occult appear fun. But this is like attacking pornography because it makes sex appear fun. The problem with this approach is that sex is fun, as is getting drunk, gossiping and a whole host of other things that are accounted sin.

Sin, in general, is fun. And so is the occult. Aleister Crowley, at least, knew how to party. "OK, guys, and for the altar, we'll use a hot naked redhead!"

While pornography can be dismissed as an evil temptation on its own, reading for simple pleasure cannot. Thus, the question becomes: Does reading Harry Potter and other books of similar ilk cause one to become involved in the occultic arts? I am willing to believe that magical fantasy might foster an interest in the supernatural, to be sure, but an interest, even a belief, in the supernatural is exactly what a Christian should hope to foster in one's children!

The basic challenge facing Christians in the West is not that too many people believe in the supernatural, it is that too many people do not! As Christians, we believe in spiritual forces, in demons, and, yes, in magic too. Sorcery may be forbidden to us, as is astrology and fortune-telling, but it is an element of our worldview. If Harry Potter does indeed inspire one to think of the world beyond the pure material, then he is at least operating within the boundaries of the Christian worldview, if not in the precise manner that the Christian parent might prefer.

Of course, it is absurd to argue, as do Harry's defenders, that the mere fact that children are reading the books makes them inherently worthwhile. Simply substitute The 120 Days of Sodom for Harry and the argument drowns in a viscous puddle of bodily fluids. Nor can one attempt to argue Harry's morality on some feeble notion of good triumphing over evil. Harry is not a virtuous protagonist as he is a practitioner of explicitly forbidden arts, and if he is a lesser evil than Lord Voldemort, that still does not make him righteous.

In this, Harry Potter reflects the real world, wherein evil battles evil far more often than it is confronted by good. Indeed, it is ironic to think that some of the very same concerned parents who would ban Harry Potter from their children's libraries blithely send these same children to schools where they are daily force-fed secular dogma and sexual technique as they learn to worship at the shrine of the material world. There are many malignant influences on children, but if the Harry Potter series is not the least of these, it is surely close. One would do far better to ban television, movies, pop music and the Internet than these fat little fantasy novels.

Indeed, I am myself a published novelist, and I can testify that if Christians—especially the Christian media—spent half the time discussing authentic Christian children's literature and overtly Christian fantasy that they do in jousting this Potter windmill, the publishing industry would be turned upside down.

Harry Potter, like most things in this world, is neither good nor bad in himself. The books are simply books, entertaining fantasies, not a gateway into the Dionysian worship of the chthonic Great Mother and not a paragon of moral virtue either. If Harry Potter seriously troubles you, best stay far, far away from the works of Homer, Virgil, Dante, Spenser, Shakespeare, Coleridge and the vast majority of the classical canon.

Did Harry Potter take the Mark of the Beast?

June 28, 2003

Many sincere Christian organizations, like Focus on the Family, have been quick to condemn Potter, then proudly point readers to The Chronicles of Narnia. *And that's great, except that is all they can point to. Which leads me to the heart of the Christian media malaise in general: Where are the great Christian authors, filmmakers, screenwriters, producers, artists, and what is being done to train and nurture their craft? Until we put more effort here, Christians will remain on the sidelines, confined in their cozy churches, throwing an occasional grenade or two at the next Potter or Matrix, then return to their potlucks.*

—Hilber

I TOTALLY AGREE, except that I would point out that a closer viewing of "The Matrix", the first movie, is basically a violent technorwellian retelling of the Christian story with an emphasis on spiritual warfare. Since I'm an author, I am no doubt biased, but I find the fact that the Christian media would rather complain about secular novels than devote coverage to those books written by and for Christians is tremendously annoying. I can't speak for other authors, but I can state for a fact that my publisher, a major New York house, sent out books to over 50 Christian media outlets and not a single one bothered to review it, despite the fact that Publisher's Weekly did. But they've got plenty of time to complain about what non-Christians are writing for non-Christians. Go figure.

I think you are sickening, and it is sad they give you a voice… Sin is fun? A redhead on the altar is something to joke about… wonder what the Lord will think of your comments and endorsement of Harry Potter books when you stand before Him?

—Kathy

Believe me, that column is pretty close to the bottom of the list of things for which I'm not looking forward to being held accountable. However, I stand by my assertion that sin is fun. If it wasn't, we wouldn't ask God to help us deal with the temptation.

Yes, there are far worse things to worry about than Harry Potter… However, I subscribe to the broken window theory… Warning people about Harry Potter may be considered a small thing, but it's not unimportant. Informing people that this is not a positive influence on our kids is appropriate and not wolf-crying.

—Brian

We'll just have to disagree. I have witnessed several of these Christian panics, from Dungeons and Dragons to Magic: The Gathering and now Harry Potter, and I do not see that the pagan revival, which is real, has much, if anything, to do with these products. I believe that the spiritual poverty of secular humanism, which is being taught in a much more specific and comprehensive manner to the children of America, is primarily to blame for this. I'll listen to anti-Potter arguments from homeschooling parents, but anyone who thinks a single fiction series can have a more deleterious impact on children than 40 hours of secular humanist indoctrination a week for 12 years is truly living in their own fantasy world.

You are soooooooooo brilliant and fine looking, please marry me. I'll convert.

—Beth

Thanks, Beth, but as I mentioned a few weeks ago, I'm off the market. But it's great to feel as if you have a fan club, especially on a week with heavy hate mail.

No matter how innocent the Harry Potter stories seem, they only serve to inoculate younger children to believe that receiving a mark on your forehead makes you special like the good wizard, Harry, and that anyone who refuses to take such a mark is just like a muggle-a non-magical person. If you cannot understand why this is evil, then you are either an idiot or a liar.

—Matthew

This is ridiculous. The Mark will have far more to do with your credit card, your driver's license and your health insurance than any special feeling of elitism, and furthermore, it will be required by law. There will be no need to convince people that it is worthwhile, as the vast majority will accept it as readily as they give their children Social Security numbers.

I heard recently on the "Rich Dad's Cashflow Quadrant" that money has lost 90 percent of its value since 1950. I read a similar statistic in Thomas Sowell's "Basic Economics" that 20 bucks could get you more in 1960 than a hundred bucks can today. But what I have yet to hear is a clear-cut explanation why?

—Matt

The answer is pretty simple. I've read that the average lifespan of a paper currency is only about 70 years, because the temptation to create more spending power by printing money is simply too tempting for politicians and central bankers. It all comes down to the basic law of supply and demand, when the supply for dollars increases faster than demand requires, then the price must fall.

Since the creation of the Federal Reserve in 1913, so much money has been printed that 95 percent of the value of the dollar has been destroyed. In other words, a nickel then is worth a dollar now—and that's according to the Consumer Price Index, which massively understates actual inflation, which is more accurately defined as the expansion of the money supply over the growth in gross domestic product.

Supreme post-morality

June 30, 2003

HOMOSEXUALITY has always been, to some extent, an Apollonian death cult. As safe-sex advocates learned to their despair, flirting with destruction is a fundamental aspect of the homosexual ethos, because the very real possibility of receiving a beating or worse is the heart of the masochistic titillation inherent to the cruising vocation.

Unfortunately, by insisting on the fabrication of a constitutional right to engage in same-sex relations, homosexuals have now opened the door to a Pandora's box that will wreak havoc on sexual and familial relationships across America, and contribute to the acceleration of America's decline into decadence and ultimate bondage.

Homosexuals have long argued that their private behavior has no effect on the vast majority of the population that is normally oriented, and though arguable, this is a reasonably defensible position. But by using the Supreme Court to achieve their aims instead of the state legislatures, the homosexual movement has sown a wind that will reap a devastating whirlwind that will, in the long term, destroy it.

Since the Supreme Court, in its inimitable lack of foresight, has decided to expand the fictitious right to "privacy" that it invented in Roe v. Wade, it will now be impossible to legislate against any behavior that can be reasonably described as consensual. How can a state possibly defend statutes against prostitution, when the transaction is made between two consenting adults in private? How can a state defend its laws against incest, bigamy, polygamy or bestiality, as long as such acts are committed outside the public view?

They can't—not anymore. Because of the self-serving manner in which the judicial system gives precedence to its own decisions over statutory law, anyone challenging a law against prostitution or any of these behaviors long held to be socially deviant will simply need to cite Lawrence v. Texas in order to trump whatever case has been built by the prosecuting state.

If the justices of the Supreme Court were not so manifestly thoughtless with regard to the logical consequences of their actions, you would suspect they were intentionally trying to destroy the social fabric of the nation.

While the wisdom of attempting to support morality through legislation can be rightly questioned, preventing such attempts on specious grounds when they are the expressed will of the majority in support of centuries-old tradition is deranged foolishness of the kind seldom encountered throughout history. One does not have to believe that prostitution, or any of these other activities, should be illegal to recognize that making them government-protected rights are likely to lead to serious negative repercussions for the entire society as it spirals into full-blown decadence.

The war on tradition, morality and civilization will not end here. Without a change of at least one justice on this renegade Supreme Court, the worst since the Warren era, we will soon see the concept of marriage redefined, completing the destruction of the family that began with the so-called sexual revolution, Roe v. Wade and the easing of divorce laws. Lawrence v. Texas is not a cause, it is merely a symptom, but it is a warning sign of a fatal disease.

Post-moral tradition-hating libertines might do well to pause in the midst of their celebrations to consider this. Cultural embrace of homosexuality is a late-stage pre-imperial phenomenon. Once the republic collapses, which will surely happen within the next 200 years if the Roman example is any guide, and a lot sooner if Alan Greenspan doesn't kick off before he completely destroys the global financial system, a harsh anti-libertine reaction will take place, one without the traditional moral constraints that were dismantled over the last 100 years.

The American Augustus will be no friend to freedom, but he will also view libertine decadence as cultural weakness, thus an impediment to the national greatness that will be his monument to himself. And he will stamp it out, as ruthlessly as did Hitler and Stalin before him. The infamous closet of old will look like a paradise in comparison.

The basic family structure has survived for thousands of years, across cultural and religious boundaries. It has always destroyed its competitors, probably because it is rooted in the most basic human instincts. It will also survive this latest assault, but I suspect the inevitable backlash that will restore it again to unquestioned supremacy will be ugly. There is seldom an action without an eventual reaction.

I enjoyed reading Gibbon's Decline and Fall of the Roman Empire. I'm not, however, taking much pleasure in watching the sequel unfold before my eyes.

Mailbox Vox: Homosexuals, the Byzantines and a dead-cat bounce

July 5, 2003

The Supreme Court's finding of sexual privacy is entirely in step with the American public's values and opinions. I grew up in Texas and Oklahoma, and I can't recall hearing even the saltiest old cowboy say anything other than "What I do in my bedroom is no business of the government." Your (and Bill Frist's) appeal to hostility towards gays as a class will find ever-diminishing appeal.

—TJ

I T MAY WELL BE IN STEP with the American public's values and opinions—of course, that's exactly what THE LEGISLATIVE BRANCH is for. If the American public truly feels as you assert, then why haven't sodomy laws been overturned by all the various state legislatures, as they were in Minnesota a few years ago? With regard to Bill Frist's appeal, if the Defense of Marriage Amendment passes as quickly as the Defense of Marriage act did, I expect his political star will be shining rather bright.

As for my appeal, I could not care less.

Actually, the fictitious "right of privacy" was invented in Griswold v. Connecticut; that decision was then cited as precedent by Roe v. Wade et al.

—Jim

That's right. I should have mentioned Griswold as well.

So let me get this straight, even though you claim to be a libertarian, if the court ruled in a way that agreed with your libertarian attitudes and values, you would still oppose the ruling if it failed to comply with a particular ideological interpretation of the Constitution, despite the fact that the ruling increases personal liberty? You don't seem to support liberty so much as you oppose the federal government.

—Michael

That sums it up pretty well, yes. I am a stronger anti-statist than social libertarian, as I am far more concerned for those liberties that defend people's lives and property against the central state than I am for those relating to interpersonal behavior. The Supreme Court decisions on currency and taxation are far more inimical than the recent Lawrence monstrosity, however, they were made long ago and are not part of the current news cycle. Still, all three decisions tie closely into my theme of American decline.

Not that it's not painfully obvious where your frustration and animosity is coming from. But that's our little secret, isn't it?

—JP

I think it's amusing that homosexuals still believe hurling charges of homophobia, bigotry and secret homosexuality have any impact on anyone. Even the feminist hate mailers are more creative—this lot sounded like catty 13-year-old girls, only sillier.

When you argue against homosexuality, you are aiding and abetting a future totalitarian government. You are laying the philosophical groundwork, convincing the people that we are falling into decadence because we are allowing people the freedom to define their own values. You are spreading a fear of freedom, convincing people that liberty is frightening, harping on the point that when people are free, they do things we don't want them to.

—Marjorie

No, people always do things the government doesn't want them to. That's why the more a government attempts to control the populace, the more likely it is to start killing people, since there are always those who resist control without concern for the cost. However, you are mistaking behavioral freedoms for basic freedoms. Imperial Rome and many other societies demonstrate that even the most hedonistic behavior is quite compatible with a repressive totalitarian government, however, sacrosanct private-property rights, a stable currency and an armed populace are not. Regardless, Marjorie, would you seriously argue that we are not falling into decadence?

I've just read your piece "Supreme post-morality". Surely you jest—you can't possibly believe it might take as long as 200 years for the Republic to collapse!

—Colin

Two hundred on the outside. The speed of societal change has increased in the last two millennia, and unanticipated change usually has a way of taking conventional wisdom off guard.

What about the Byzantines as an extension of the Roman world?

—Howard

The Republic of Rome lasted 421 years, until Gaius Marius seized control of Rome during the first civil wars. After a period of unrest and various dictatorships, the Roman Empire began with Octavian in 27 B.C. and survived another 1,480 years, in one form or another, until Mehmed II sacked Constantinople in 1453. I don't care how long a totalitarian successor state might call itself the United States of America, it would still not be the America in which I believe.

Do you think this bear market is over?

—Bernie

Not even close—this is just another bear-market rally and it's over. It even appears that I nailed the call on the Nasdaq top in my June 9 column, though I was a week early on the S&P 500. But whether one uses Elliott Waves, put-call ratios, volatility indicators, price-earnings ratios or Fibonacci timeframes, this rally is toast. Don't be fooled by the little pre-Fourth jump—the Fed always pumps in money during the short weeks, and a meager 2 percent gain on a four-day week is perhaps the most powerful sign that this rally is not only dead, but approaching rigor mortis.

Remember that the financial media always lie. For example, the "expected light volumes" for this holiday-shortened week were 12 percent higher than the previous week. Wall Street always likes to do its shady work when the masses aren't looking.

I'll leave you with an intriguing quote from Yahoo! Finance:

There's talk that the precipitous drop in the indices at around 10:40 ET was caused by an erroneous execution order, in which a major house sold 2000 SPX contracts instead of 200 and took the market down with it.

This is a very interesting explanation for Thursday's 100-point drop, since the financial media, who always claim the markets cannot be manipulated, rest their case on the notion that buying index futures cannot possibly drive the markets up.

Land of the fearful, home of the craven

July 7, 2003

ACCORDING TO THE NEW YORK POST, all New York City is abuzz with the failure of the latest Kennedy marital experiment. And when a married woman blows off her commitments to her husband and her children in favor of an affair with a married man, who is to blame? According to many people, not her, but the aggrieved husband, who refuses to hold a dignified silence that would allow everyone to quietly pretend nothing has happened until the whole mess fades away.

This attitude has somehow become the norm in America today in matters both public and private. Subjects once debated openly on the floors of Congress are now whispered only behind closed doors.

America is afraid. Most of her citizens may not realize it yet, but somehow, they have taken to heart the old Japanese dictum, the nail that sticks up gets hammered down. This is not the motto of a free people, it is a slogan of slaves.

In today's America, the media will not discuss the fraudulent federal income tax nor the peculiar jurisdiction of the IRS, because journalists are afraid to be audited. Lawyers do not protest how judges regularly ignore the law as it is written in favor of so-called precedent, nor do they speak up in court when a judge blatantly flouts the centuries-old right of the jury to decide on both the justice of the law and its application, because they are afraid of being disciplined before the bar.

Even the few members of the judiciary who are not corrupt are afraid—some have even articulated their fear of judging as directed by the law—because they fear the tumult and unrest that might well explode amidst a people who suddenly realize they have been cheated and defrauded for four generations.

Ask any tax accountant, any tax lawyer or even your neighbor where in the legal code it is written that a natural-born citizen of any state in the United States must pay federal income tax. They won't be able to tell you, because no such law exists. And yet, they play along with the charade on mere hearsay, because at heart, they are terrified that the evil eye of government will be turned in their direction.

This spirit of fear is not limited to taxation. Investors and economists write of the free market, but what American market is free? Certainly not the money market, where short-term rates are directly controlled by the quasi-governmental Federal Reserve, which openly threatens to manipulate the long-term rates as well. In the stock market, there are whispers too, most recently of a timely 5,000 contract order placed by Goldman Sachs last week at the behest of the Working Group to stop the market fall last Tuesday. But no one at the *Wall Street Journal*, *CNBC* or *Fox News* will ever mention this, not unless they wish to conclude their career in the financial media.

Conservatives are afraid to mention their deep concerns regarding the president and his incessant caving to Democratic pressure lest they be seen as lending support to their enemies. But what is the use of having a Republican in office if he has nothing to offer but tepid Democratism? Seven of the nine Supreme Court justices who authored the recent decisions so unpopular with conservatives were nominated by Republicans, after all.

Christians are afraid to speak of their faith for fear they will be accused of intolerance or bigotry. Never mind, of course, that Jesus said that the world would hate his followers just as it hated Him. And so they sit in their dwindling pews and watch, mute and helpless, as the moral foundation upon which the nation was constructed is slowly, carefully dismantled.

Even left-liberal America is afraid. They are afraid to speak the truths they know, lest their particular interest group lose influence. Feminists are afraid to denounce a serial harasser and rapist, homosexuals are afraid to admit the dangerous reality of their sexual practices, teachers are afraid to admit that the public schools are a massive failure and politicians of both parties are afraid to admit their desire to raise taxes and spend like a stripper with a stolen credit card.

America—all of America—is living a lie. We are no longer the land of the free, we are the land of the fat, feckless and fearful. We are no longer the home of the brave, we are the home of the comfortable, the cowardly and the craven.

Just say no—to government

July 12, 2003

It is incredible with the devastation around us that we are only now getting our diagnostic forums heated up. When do we move into prescriptive dialog? When does this movement get legs? When does someone who is a public figure finally call for action that is within the reach of those who listen and inspire them to move?

—Art

I AM NOT A PUBLIC FIGURE, but I have called for action before, and I will do so again. Evil always slavers for submission, so those who oppose the ongoing dismantling of our nation must refuse to submit. This has always been the positive model of those who have made a real difference in the world, from Martin Luther to Martin Luther King, from Jesus Christ to Thomas Jefferson. Refuse to submit to laws that contradict God's Law, refuse to submit to government agents exercising illicit power, and refuse to participate in the popular charade of democracy.

Does this require sacrifice? Absolutely, which is why this path is described as the hard one. There is a much easier path for those who prefer to be fat, lazy and complicit, of course, it is also known as the road to Hell.

Regarding the role of the jury. Your statement of their role is simply not correct. The jury's role has always been to make findings of fact, not conclusions of law.

—Stephen

The Jury has the Right to determine both the law and facts.

—Samuel Chase, U.S. Supreme Court Justice

The Jury has the power to bring a verdict in the teeth of both law and fact.

—Oliver Wendell Holmes, U.S. Supreme Court Justice

The law itself is on trial quite as much as the case which is to be decided.

—Harlan Stone, U.S. Supreme Court Chief Justice

Twenty-two states include jury nullification provisions in their state constitutions.

I know where it says Americans must pay an income tax. It is called the 16th Amendment.

—Vince, Ry, Dick and others

I have to say, I find this sort of shallow e-mail to be more offensive than the most hate-filled feminist diatribe. Do any of you truly believe I am unaware of the text of the 16th Amendment, the fact that it was never ratified, or the cases in which the Supreme Court has declared that a) it was ratified, and b) even if it wasn't ratified, it is nevertheless in effect? But the fact that Congress can write a law requiring Americans to pay a direct, unapportioned federal income tax does not mean that Congress has done so. There is a very good reason the tax code is so Byzantine; it is to disguise the fact that at heart, there is no there there.

Note that in numerous cases, including Brafman and Radinsky, the Supreme Court has also declared that without a signed assessment certificate, there is no tax liability.

My brother stood up and spoke out against corruption and racism within the United States Marshal Service, for doing so he got the treatment told of by the old Japanese dictum, the nail that sticks up gets hammered down. His fight for justice has ended up with his partner paralyzed for life and with my brother fearing for his life and for his family. He has gone without pay since October 2002, the USMS is denying him pay and benefits as they seek to destroy him, yet no one cares.

So tell me Mr. Vox, why should any American stand up bravely and speak out as my brother did? What has it gained him?

—Anthony

One might as easily ask what it gained the apostles to preach the Gospel, considering the lethal reward almost all of them received from the world. Your brother will never know how his brave stance has affected those who witnessed it and heard about it, or what effect it will have on their future actions. Furthermore, as was said in the movie, "Rob Roy", honor is a man's gift to himself.

Things might be different if I was free to speak or act without bringing down unpleasant consequences on others. But I have to consider that my actions can and will have repercussions which will touch my family and people that I love. For that reason, for now, I guess I'll remain a coward.

—Lee

There will always be a good reason to keep one's mouth shut, to avert one's eyes, to look the other way. But did the Germans of the Nazi era save their families by not speaking out? Neither will we. I cannot speak for anyone else, but my grandfather braved the swamps of Guadalcanal and the fire-swept beaches of Tarawa while fighting for what he believed was right, and I will not forget the lessons he taught or dishonor his memory by submitting to evil, injustice or my own fears.

3 cheers for jury nullification

July 14, 2003

AMERICANS ARE ACCUSTOMED to think of the courts of law as being a good thing. With our invariably simplistic tendency to summarize any given issue into Good vs. Bad, the courts are held up as the primary counterpoint to the criminal element of society. But just as there can be no Geheimestaatspolizei without a police force, one cannot hold show trials without a judiciary.

So, the courts are neither inherently good nor bad. But our positive view of the courts is relatively new, as a significant portion of the Magna Carta, which is a foundational element of our common law, is devoted to limiting the corrupt power of the king's courts. Indeed, the very existence of the jury can be traced directly to this need to harness a judiciary run amok.

Contrary to most people's understanding, and directly contrary to the courtroom instructions of most judges, the jury in any trial, civil or criminal, has the power to judge both the facts and the law in that particular case. This means that if any juror believes that the law is unjust, he has power and the duty to ignore it and make his decision according to his conscience alone.

Now, intellectuals of all stripes, even one of my heroes, Thomas Sowell, have written that this concept of jury nullification is a threat to the rule of law. But this a tragic misunderstanding of wherein the threat to the rule of law lies. The rule of law does not collapse when people do not obey the law; that is an end result, not a causal factor. The rule of law collapses because the law itself is unjust, and when those charged with ensuring its just application refuse to do so.

The proof, as always, can be found in the deceit. In the 1995 Gaudin decision, the Supreme Court wrote:

The question there [Sparf, 1895] was whether the jury could be deprived of the power to determine, not only historical facts, not only mixed questions of fact and law, but pure questions of law in a criminal case ... We decided that it did not. In criminal cases, as in civil, we held, the judge must be permitted to instruct the jury on the law and to insist that the jury follow his instructions. But our decision in no way undermined the historical and constitutionally guaranteed right of criminal defendants to demand that the jury decide guilt or innocence on every issue, which includes application of the law to the facts.

Thus, the official word from on high is that while the judge can tell the jury whatever he wants about the law and can even try to intimidate the jury into following his courtroom instructions, the jury still retains the power to decide whether it wants to apply the law in its particular case or not.

The dishonest historical revisionism of the anti-jury crowd can be seen most clearly in a 2002 article written to oppose the unsuccessful attempt of South Dakotans to join Maryland, Indiana, Georgia and Oregon in enshrining jury rights in their state constitution.

[U]nelected, unaccountable jurors will decide case-by-case, jury-by-jury, whether to apply our laws at all. Such a system is irreconcilably at odds with our '[nation] of laws, and not of men,' as stated by John Adams.

This is a particularly shady piece of propaganda, as there can be no question that John Adams, our second president, would have supported the right of the jury to decide matters of law, for in speaking of the juror, he wrote:

It is not only his right, but his duty ... to find the verdict according to his own best understanding, judgment and conscience, though in direct opposition to the direction of the court.

Freedom of the press would not exist without the jury nullification that took place in the celebrated Zenger trial of 1735. Jury nullification was also practiced with great regularity in the trials of abolitionists prosecuted for helping slaves escape and in the trials of Prohibition era drinkers as well.

Many have asked me what they can do to help stop the devolution of this country into tyranny. Here is one relatively easy action—don't avoid jury duty the next time you're summoned, but instead take advantage of the opportunity to exercise your power to rein in the corrupt judiciary and to educate your fellow members of the jury pool about their right to decide the application of the law as well as the facts.

Your future freedom may depend on it.

Mailbox Vox: Secret police and the sinking of the Itanic

July 19, 2003

> *There is no doubt in my mind that judges will try to influence the outcome of the jury even to the point of intimidation. Therefore, if a jury nullifies the law can they be punished for doing so by the judge?*

> —H. Lynn

NO, THEY CANNOT. The judge will occasionally declare a mistrial, or issue empty threats about the jury failing to live up to their so-called oath, but there's nothing the judge can do about a jury's refusal to follow his instructions. Laura Kriho was the first juror to be charged with failing to bring in a guilty verdict since the William Penn trial in 1670, and her conviction for obstruction of justice was overturned on appeal. Judges are paper tigers.

> *Two words that argue against jury nullification: O.J. Simpson!*

> —William

Ah, yes, another deeply reasoned retort. This flimsy pretense of an argument does not so much shoot itself in the foot as directly in the head. The fact that O.J. is walking free despite the seemingly overwhelming evidence against him is proof that the jury had the power to judge both the facts as well as the application of the law. If they did not have that power, then the judge could have overridden them and declared O.J. guilty—since he did not, it is quite obvious that, as the Supreme Court wrote in 1995:

...the jury decide guilt or innocence on every issue, which includes application of the law to the facts.

Furthermore, the civil jury found O.J. liable. Do you trust judges to bat better than .500? Based on the number of laws attempting to limit judicial sentencing leeway, most legislatures don't.

What a great article you wrote. I just graduated from law school, and never heard a word about jury nullification. After the bar exam, this is going to be one of the first things I research, as I want to go into criminal defense. Thanks for the heads up. Forgive me, but what does Geheimestaatspolizei mean?

—Andrew

I'm flabbergasted! What will we learn next, that education schools don't teach educators how to teach kids to read? In any case, good luck with the bar, Andrew. GEheimeSTAatsPOlizei = gestapo. It means secret state police.

Just a quick note to let you know that our prayers have been answered. My husband will be coming home Tuesday. I am one of the lucky ones. We lost 12 friends in this war, one of whom was in our wedding. I am so thankful that God kept him safe.

—K.

Some of you may recall my letter to an Apache pilot. I'm happy to report that the pilot to whom it was written is safely home now.

Are you saying then that judges such as the Supreme Court should rule on cases with what their hearts tell them and not adhere strictly to the Constitution?

—George

No, because I was writing about the rights of the jury. Juries are not judges. Judges are not juries. Anyone who finds this to be a difficult distinction would do well to remain silent on the matter even if threatened with hot irons.

Any government, verdict or regime which is based upon, or overtly allows for nullification by illegal means—whether jury nullification, terrorism [or] secession—has lost its legitimate rule of law, if that law and government was based upon reason, choice and votes. That jury nullification happens does not legitimize its use any more than the fact that not all murderers are captured makes the law against murder void.

—LAB

It always puzzles me when people attempt to argue the law while ignoring what it says. According to this logic, the government of the United States has had an illegitimate rule of law from the very start, since jury nullification is not only legal, but is a right enshrined in the common law, defended by numerous Supreme Court decisions, championed by a variety of Founding Fathers and remains an integral part of the American rule of law.

With regard to secession, it was generally considered to be a right of the states until Abraham Lincoln ended the discussion by resorting to military force, which is not exactly the most persuasive demonstration of the rule of law at work.

As a lawyer who has been involved in both civil and criminal cases, I know that judges—especially federal judges—don't give two hoots in hell about the law. But just because they do not care to follow their oaths does

not excuse a juror from his duty. Surely, the answer to corruption and perjury is not more corruption and perjury.

—Corbett

Sigh... again, the juror's duty is to "decide guilt or innocence on every issue, which includes application of the law to the facts." Jury nullification is neither corruption nor perjury, indeed it is a defense against both. If the judge imposes an oath on jurors that contradicts this duty, then it is the judge and his oath that are in error.

First, I want to say thank you for your column. You are one of a very small number of journalists with whom I consistently agree. Second, I am curious as to your thoughts on the future tech industry. I work for a major computer

*manufacturer, and I have been growing more and more optimistic about the
2–5 year outlook for the industry*

—Brad

I'm a little less optimistic. First, the tech industry is not the growth
industry it was 20 years ago, simply because it's impossible to grow a multi-
billion dollar company at exponential rates. With regard to the specifics you
mentioned, there are serious doubts with regard to Intel's new Itanium, (a
nickname like The Itanic is never a good sign), and the fact that screens
are bigger and fast processors are cheaper doesn't change the fact that you
don't need more speed for the vast majority of applications used by the
overwhelming majority of users.

While I am intrigued by the promise of Linux and open source solutions—
I run a dual-boot system on one of my machines—Linux may hurt the already
slowing computer replacement cycle, since the main reason computers need
to be replaced is to keep up with the inefficient resource pig that is Microsoft
Windows. Once people don't feel pressured into changing their operating
system every two years, they'll begin to realize that their applications run just
fine on their current machines.

Sex in secret

July 21, 2003

Girls don't like boys
Girls like cars and money

—Good Charlotte, "Boys and Girls"

I N THE MOVIE *Weird Science*, Anthony Michael Hall utters one of the all-time classic dating lies when speaking of his imaginary girlfriend*. "She's from Canada, you wouldn't know her." And the conventional wisdom that men regularly lie about their sexual experience is so commonly held that it has a noun of its own, locker-room talk.

But except in the case of big-talking junior-high kids desperate to score approval points by impressing their peers, I never bought that line. For one thing, men don't talk about sex in anywhere near the gory detail that women do. And for another, I have never known a single sexually active woman to tell the truth about her past. I don't know if women think men's relative lack of verbal skills equates to an equivalent deficiency of memory, but I always found it amusing to hear how a girlfriend's stories would inevitably evolve over time.

The strangest thing is that it's not as if I was an insecure control freak who demanded to know everything about a girl's history. Quite the opposite, actually—10 years ago I founded a band signed to the label that has gotten a lot of recent press thanks to the *New York Times* customarily inept reporting, Steve Gottlieb's TVT Records, and like most young guys who find themselves in the music industry, I was far more interested in the immediate present than the dusty past.

But when a girl asks you a loaded question of this kind, it's only natural to respond in like manner. And by the way, guys, the correct answer is: "I don't know, I've just never viewed a woman as some kind of trophy…"

The way women tend to hide their little flings from their friends has always made me suspicious about the veracity of the fair sex. Women, it seems, must walk a tight rope, balanced precariously between what they want to do to attract men, and what will provoke other women to speak badly about them. It's not an easy thing to do, whereas if a man can drink beer, talk about football and hold his own in a fight, he's all right with most guys, even if he's a transvestite homosexual poet.

So, I was interested to see that the *Journal of Sex Research*—which despite its name appears not to be an invention of Penthouse Forum or media hoaxer Joey Skaggs—has recently released a study which supports my suspicions: It's the girls who are lying, not the guys. The study found that women's stories change in keeping with the chances they'll get caught out, as the number of reported notches in a girl's lipstick case increase 69 percent when she thinks she's hooked up to a lie detector.

Speaking of lies, the answers reported by both men and women between the ages of 18 and 25 also exploded the notion that everyone is having wildly promiscuous sex. The polygraph-compelled answers indicated an average of only 4.2 partners per individual, which is significantly lower than one would imagine from watching television or reading the covers of women's magazines.

And perhaps young women are taking their deceitful cue from their favorite magazines. Liza Featherstone of the *Columbia Journalism Review* wrote:

> *It is the lifestyle magazines like* Mademoiselle, Cosmopolitan, Glamour, Marie Claire *and others that most often run the most features dedicated to sex and relationship conundrums … Just about everyone interviewed for this story said that these stories were embellished.*

There are some interesting implications to this story. First, conservatives should take heart from it, not only because young adults are far less promiscuous than advertised, but particularly because women still feel this pressure to lie. The culture will not be entirely lost until women, the traditional defenders of civilization, see no need to hide their abandonment of morality from other women.

Second, if it is indeed true that it is not men, but women, who disproportionately lie about sex, this would demolish the already creaking feminist gynomyth that a woman accusing a man of sexual assault is inherently credible.

If supporting studies show similar conclusions about a female predilection for sexual duplicity, justice will require the courts to assume a bias toward the accused in the all-too-common he said-she said case sans evidence.

Which would no doubt hearten Kobe Bryant and his defenders, if not the rest of the NBA.

Hall's geek character in The Breakfast Club *also makes a comment about a Canadian girlfriend.*

Tarts and penguins

July 26, 2003

> *Rape of women is under-reported, not over-reported. Another attempt to justify Bryant, sans any real facts.*

> —Patty

THE FACT THAT a new study shows that women are far more likely to lie about sex than men, in contrast with conventional wisdom, happens to lend some support to Kobe Bryant's story does not indicate that my column last week was an attempt to justify Kobe Bryant's behavior. This reader also sent in a manufactured statistic which claimed that only two percent of rape accusations are false, which is not only false itself, but as is usually the case with feminist-championed statistics, wildly inaccurate.

According to the FBI's Behavioral Science Unit's 1983 study on false allegations, 39.57 percent of the alleged rapes investigated were false. This is in accordance with the very low arrest rates reported in the 2001 FBI Uniform Crime Report, which shows that only 30.14 percent of reported rapes end in arrests, compared to the 85.44 percent of reported murders that do. This dichotomy is huge, considering the fact that investigators usually have the benefit of a witness and DNA evidence in the case of a reported rape, whereas in the latter case, they may well have neither.

In any case, Kobe will have to look for his defenders elsewhere, considering his 32.1 points per game against KG and the boys in last year's playoffs. Lock him up and throw away the key—please!

> *Women, as the upholders of society's sexual standards, seem equipped with an amazing ability to rationalize their sexual behavior. A promiscuous man usually does not bother much with rationalizations… Not so with women.*

Except in the most atypical and extreme cases, women are never truly proud of promiscuity. Oh, she may dress like a tart and sleaze around a bit, but a woman deeply wishes to be thought of as essentially moral.

—Stacy

Not being a woman, I can't say what any woman truly wishes, but this certainly sounds plausible. Of course, the fact that very few people today understand that morals are not and have never been personal only adds to the confusion. Wendy Shalitt's demolition of the myth of the happy slut perpetrated by *Cosmopolitan* and its ilk is very telling in this regard.

How can a Christian conservative take heart in the fact that women are lying about sex? Whatever happened to honesty?

—Sinjin

The fact that someone hides their behavior indicates that they have a conscience, which is telling them that their behavior is wrong. A person acting against the dictates of his conscience is far more likely to experience remorse and change his future behavior than one who is remorseless. Conservatives should fear the day when women do not feel the need to lie about sex.

Computers are tools for business. If a business can extend the life of its tools, the company is then able to allocate resources to other more profitable ventures. The computer replacement cycle should reach equilibrium just as the vehicle replacement cycle or furniture replacement cycle has. There is no intrinsic reason to upgrade today's business computer every couple of years, and there is no reason to upgrade end-user productivity software with much frequency. Right now about the only IT company making

major profit is MS. But their profit is tied to an engineered-in product obsolescence.

—Michael

Which is why we call them The Evil Empire. I'm not saying that I support the government's ridiculous pursuit of Microsoft under antitrust law, but there is something inherently despicable about building a profit model around planned inefficiency. Linux is only two or three generations away from being a real home-user option, and I'm looking forward to that day.

You seem like the kind of intelligent guy that would use a Mac. I'm disappointed.

—SJ

I started out on an Apple IIe and moved up to the original Mac in college. But I'm a gamer, so I've been on the PC since Wing Commander and my first 386/25. I know Umberto Eco disagrees, but I nevertheless stand by my position that an operating system is not a religion—with the possible exception of those of you who worship at the temple of Steve Jobs.

The first time I was on a jury, after the judge had us swear to uphold and abide the law as it was written, I asked if jury nullification has been outlawed. He answered, "Yes." After the trial I sent him a letter asking for information of the elimination of jury nullification. The paperwork he sent me only stated that he had the right to not inform jurors of their right to use jury nullification … We need to start charging judges with perjury.

—Rich

I think it would be preferable to simply send them all to prison and start over with a new lot chosen at random. People tend to forget that the only reason juries even exist is because the judiciary was hopelessly corrupt—like any government entity, the judiciary has an inherent tendency to devolve into corruption over time.

We live in a world that is predominantly run by the sort of annoying losers who thought it would be cool to be junior high school president when they were kids. Think on that, and shudder.

The science of future prediction

July 28, 2003

F OLLOWING THE STOCK MARKET can be a real bear. There isn't a single person, signal or system I know that has not been spectacularly wrong at one time or another. Robert Prechter Jr. knows this, having first made his name with a wildly optimistic call in 1982 that turned out to be on the conservative side, he missed out on the 1996–1999 bull bubble but redeemed himself with a harshly negative prediction in 2000.

He is the leading champion of Elliott Waves, which are an esoteric, but respected theory of interpreting market movements, and recently published two books which he believes will found the basis for the new science of socionomics, which is based on the application of Elliott Waves to broader social trends.

In my opinion, the jury is still out on the usefulness of Elliott Waves for short-term trading—since May, the experts at Elliott Wave International have been predicting an end to the March rally followed by a steep decline that has not, as yet, appeared—but I think the fundamental notion that market movements are primarily reflective of social mood is a good one.

For example, the fact that Uday and Qusay Hussein no longer tread this mortal coil is assuredly A Good Thing, but to imagine that their deaths will have any impact on the economy whatsoever is absurd. If we are to accept the widely reported notion that the markets rose in response to the news of their demise, then social mood is the only realistic explanation for such movements.

Prechter has taken things one step further, though, in developing what could become an intriguing tool for social analysis. His thinking is logical— if social mood governs market movements, and if Elliott Wave theory allows for predicting market movements, then changes in the social mood and all of its attendant effects can be predicted using Elliott Waves.

Prechter coined the term socionomics to describe his new idea, and it is a big one. It reverses the conventional wisdom of social causality, which states that events govern mood. Socionomics, in contrast, insists that moods govern events. This makes a degree of sense in a historical context, as a historian can often see how shifting moods preceded the supposedly causal events, even if those living through them usually could not.

The impressive thing about socionomics is that it has a much stronger scientific basis than most accepted social sciences. By this, I mean that its conclusions are consistent with its premises, and its assertions are independently testable. In his two books, Prechter has assembled a list of things he considers to be important components of mood, as well as some cultural expressions of social mood trends that allow for easy examination of his theory on an ongoing basis.

Some of these cultural expressions of mood which fit a bull-market peak are save-the-world social concern, bright fashions, short skirts and individual style, fitness, revered politicians, religious tolerance, peace agreements and pop superstars. Bear-market peaks feature riots, drab fashions, conservative dress, indifference to physical fitness, hated politicians, religious fundamentalism and cults, war and a divergence in popular tastes. It is important to note that these are considered trend peaks, which means that the trend is about to reverse in the opposite direction.

Prechter is certainly not shy of making bold predictions. He calculates that we are presently at the beginning of Intermediate wave (3) of Primary wave 3 of Cycle wave a, which in English is a Very Bad Thing. Some of the implications he has drawn are: George Bush will not be reelected, American birth rates will fall, sexual ambiguity will increase, open homosexuality will be increasingly accepted and the Dow will fall below 6000.

Is he visionary, or is he a lunatic? Time will tell. But I must say, I did find myself raising an eyebrow when I looked up from reading Pioneering Studies in Socionomics to see the latest volume in the world's best-selling fiction series being unveiled on television a few months ago. The ominous blue shades of the cover, combined with a description of the text as being the "darkest" yet, did appear as if it might have the potential to mark a real shift in the social mood.

I can certainly recommend socionomics to the intellectually curious. It's an interesting concept, if nowhere nearly as precise as Hari Seldon's psychohistory. But if President Bush, whose approval ratings are currently running at 55 percent, is not re-elected, I'll have no qualms about using it myself.

Market predictions or just surfing trends?

August 2, 2003

Is Prechter claiming that in the middle of a bull market peak, social unrest begins and drives the market down? Everybody is living high, and they begin to riot and use their treadmills as coat-racks? If these events are most prevalent at peaks (indicating an ensuing reversal) then a) Prechter is merely noting trends, not predicting the market, and b) if he is predicting the market, then the height of social unrest and apathy would mean we are headed for a economic upturn!

—Alex

YOU'RE STILL CAUGHT UP in event causality. Turn it around. According to the socionomic theory, it is the social mood reversing from its positive peak, as indicated by the market, which will ultimately cause social unrest. Your point b) is correct. When social unrest hits its peak, that is the sign that economic upturn is on its way, just as the current euphoria that pervaded the stock market and the world in 2000 was actually a very negative sign going forward. The challenge is that peaks of both sorts are notoriously difficult to identify.

Vox, why don't you just admit your issues and stop hiding behind one study. You notice women don't need studies to tell you all about men? That's because with some of men's outrageous behavior, experience will always serve women better.

—Jill

I always enjoy how quickly some women will dive into pop psychology and anti-intellectual positions the minute a fact contradicts their feelings. This is a nice example of the nonlinear Fifth Stage in action. Talk about reverse causality! Yes, it's one study. That's because it's the first one. It's also why I qualified my statements and suggested more studies were needed. Forget the fake lie detector, just shoot the subjects up with Pentathol next time and use the real machines.

> *You don't know much about women. Well, I will tell you something… Men lie about love. Women lie on sex surveys. This is the "it's none of your business" syndrome. Rape accusation makes it everyone's business—the media, the state, your friends, your family. It is scrutiny women shy from. Any mention of sex in conjunction with a woman, even of non-sex, gains unwanted hostile attention. Women are taught that their sex life is supposed to be private.*

> —RT

I don't see how saying that women lie on sex surveys disproves my point that women lie about sex. And I agree, men do lie about love, the important difference is that women seldom get thrown in jail because men are lying about love. Given the choice between a broken heart and four years sharing precious moments with Bubba, I'll take the broken heart, thanks.

> *As high-tech bails out of the U.S. for a capitalist utopia of cheap labor in India, is it wise and safe to invest? Will India's masses be politically and culturally stable enough to support American capitalism in the long term or are the lefties in tech corporate circles lying to themselves about the superiority of third world governments, culture and people over "racist America"? I am not putting my money into left-wingers who are fleeing the reality of their dirty nest in the U.S. in the hope of finding a Third Way utopia in India.*

> —Jo

Since 71 percent of the surprise 2.4 percent jump in preliminary Q2 GDP last week was increased defense spending, I remain skeptical of the recovery line—especially since that 2.4 will likely be revised down, to 1.9 percent if it follows the example of the last quarter's corrections. I don't see any tech recovery, and the point about business fleeing to countries not handicapped by huge regulatory and tax burdens, which are certainly leftist in origin, is an apt one. The permabulls are trying to convince everyone that the rise in interest rates is a good sign, but of course, this directly contradicts everything they've been saying for the last four months. If mortgage rates are going up, this bear market rally is, as they say, an ex-rally.

> *Is it possible that the Elliott Wave has been skewed because of the manipulation of the Fed, profit taking, and the daffy duck reactions by the news media?*
>
> —Delese

Mr. Prechter considers that Fed actions are fully accounted for by the mood-driven waves, and while this makes theoretical sense in the grand scheme of things, intelligent and timely manipulation would certainly help account for some of the difficulties shown in the short-term Elliott Wave analyses. I've seen five of my non-wave trading signals broken in this rally, and there also appear to be a mysterious rash of timely trading mishaps as well. I have no doubt that the Market Stabilization force has been working overtime in July, and I have no doubt that they will ultimately fail. The only question is when.

> *I hope you go far, but don't sell out!*
>
> —Charles

I know if we do, we get the hell out.

> *If I were called to serve on a jury and had to swear to uphold and abide the law as written ... what could I do in such a situation if I firmly believe in jury nullification?*
>
> —Michael

You can uphold and abide the law and still decide not to apply it in your particular case. That's not only logically consistent, it is your right and duty as a juror, according to the Supreme Court.

Bambidiots

August 4, 2003

Bambidiocy—

1. *[n] To accept the assertion of an individual, corporation or government agency as evidence of fact, when the said individual, corporation or government agency stands accused of lying or fraudulent activity.*

2. *[n] To believe that men will pay more for paintball than prostitutes.*

I F THERE'S ONE THING you can count on, it's that across the political spectrum, the media will fall all over itself to cover anything involving naked women. Television producers loved the so-called "Hunting For Bambi" story because of the promise of eye candy. Liberals loved it because it made men with guns look like Neanderthals, and conservatives leaped at the chance to tut-tut predictably about the social decay of America.

Now, I like pretty naked women just as much as the next guy, I've met my share of scary hicks with guns and I am certainly of the opinion that America is not so much slouching towards Gomorrah as it is sprinting. However, the reason I never so much as mentioned the Bambi story that drew so much press interest of late is that I figured the only way it could have been more obviously a hoax is if the sponsor of the hunt had said "Baba Booey" or mentioned a certain radio star's genitalia while being interviewed.

I've marveled at the media's collective gullibility for years. I can still recall with pleasure the night when O.J. Simpson was trapped in his white Bronco, and Peter Jennings excitedly announced that *ABC* had an eyewitness to the breaking news on the phone. No sooner had the eyewitness announced "Oh my Lord, this is quite tenses" than my friends and I burst out laughing. The caller rambled on in an exaggerated black accent for a few minutes until Al Michaels finally informed Jennings that the call was a hoax. A decade later, all one of the gang has to do to crack everybody up is to say: "Ah see… OJ!"

The Bambi story was a sham from the get-go, and an obvious one at that. I have a friend who went straight out of high school and directly to the pros, as Nelly would say, and worked the high end of the scale in Hollywood about eight years ago. According to her, top girls earned around $1,500 per night, which is pretty good compared to the $25—$50 per session charged by an Amsterdam window hooker.

And yet, we were supposed to believe that men were paying up to $10,000 for the privilege of shooting a girl in the butt with a paint gun? Right, when for that kind of cash, a guy could fly in a top-flight European escort and keep her for a week. There's also the fact that the quasi-sapients to whom this sport would presumably appeal aren't generally known for having that kind of cash to blow on extracurricular activities.

I'm not saying that the media can't, or won't, get things wrong from time to time. Mistakes are inevitable, but stupid ones that only require less than five seconds of thought to avoid are not. But the Bambi debacle proves, once more, that a significant portion of the media is far more interested in covering stories that confirm their ignorant view of the world than in discovering the truth.

Many esteemed members of the media embarrassed themselves by thoughtlessly leaping in to opine on the matter, but bambidiocy in its purest form was demonstrated by the original KLAS-TV reporter, whose notion of fact-checking amounted to going back and asking the hoaxer if he was pulling her leg or not.

That's pretty funny. What is not so funny, though, is that this is standard operating procedure for how the mainstream media covers government. For example, when the federal income tax charade is covered, the usual procedure is for the reporter to mention a few of the many fraudulent actions that the IRS is perpetrating on the American people, then ask an IRS representative if the accusations are true. Shockingly, the IRS representative invariably says they are not, which, in the reporter's mind, is enough to settle the matter. Can you imagine if we depended on the news media for justice?

And yet, these same bambidiots are your Fourth Estate watchdog, protecting your rights and liberties against government encroachment. Better buy a shotgun—I wouldn't count on the toothless old mutt.

Time to go

August 11, 2003

I AM NOT AN EPISCOPALIAN, although I did attend an Anglican church in Europe for nearly two years. While my denomination, the Southern Baptist Conference, does not have much stylistically in common with the Anglican liturgy, I have always respected and enjoyed its solemn and beautiful traditions.

But, as the Apostle Paul warned, an enemy lurks within every church, always alert for an opportunity to destroy it. This destruction can take many forms, and it never ceases to amaze me that church leaders of all denominations devote so little time to performing one of their central duties—indeed, perhaps their primary duty—in guarding their flock from the wolves who would slip in amongst them.

It's not as if this day should have been a surprise to anyone. It has been a long time in the making, as evil always labors long and hard to drive out good. The slippery slope is not a paranoid straw man, it is the primary way in which a weak, but determined minority exerts its will on a more powerful, but less disciplined majority. The English Anglican and the American Episcopal churches have long been flirting with disaster, and with the approval of Mr. V. Gene Robinson as a bishop, the Episcopal church has finally signed its death warrant.

The issue is not the homosexuality of Mr. Robinson. The issue is the willful decision of the bishops' convention to raise a man openly flaunting his sin to a position of senior church leadership. Such a man cannot speak out against sin, for he is publicly embracing it for all to see. Indeed, it is difficult for him to do so much as preach the Gospel, for what is the point of Jesus Christ's sacrifice for humanity if sin does not matter? One does not need to be redeemed from an irrelevancy, after all, and the world has no need of a church that cannot bring itself to condemn sin, even in its leadership.

The good news is that Christianity is not Episcopalian, it is not Catholicism and it is not Southern Baptist. Jesus Christ does not live in buildings, or denominations, but in the hearts and lives of His followers. There is no need of vestments, bishops or cathedrals to worship Him, only a repentant heart and a will to follow.

Nor is there any need to rescue the Episcopal Church. It has been dying for a long time, and though it may take a while for the corpse to cease its flopping around, it is now, as they say, an ex-church. But what of that? Let it rot and fade away upon the winds of time. Denominations are trivial things anyhow, they are spiritual nothings. What is important is that Jesus Christ lives, and everywhere that men and women gather in His name, there is a place for those who wish to worship Him and help each other learn to live according to His teachings.

But the ongoing suicide of the Episcopal Church should be an object lesson for other mainline denominations which attempt to curry favor with the world by watering down the message of the Gospel. A man cannot serve two masters—eventually, you will be forced to choose. And if the way is easy, and if the praises of the world ring in your ears, you have almost certainly chosen the wrong path.

Episcopal Christians, it's time to go.

Hitler and Hillary

August 18, 2003

U NTIL HERSCHEL'S DISCOVERY of Uranus in 1781, it was considered a matter of certainty that there were six planets. But the fact that everyone knew this to be true did not make it so. In like manner, college students and other insufferable connoisseurs of all human wisdom "know" that the historical Nazi Party epitomizes the extreme right-wing.

It is informative to first note an academic definition of communism:

A social, political and economic system characterized by the revolutionary struggle to create a society which has an absence of classes, and the common ownership of the means of production and subsistence and centralized governmental control over the economy.

And yet, the definition of its supposed opposite, by the same academic source, is rather different.

Nazism: The ideology and policies of Adolf Hitler and his National Socialist German Worker's Party from 1921 to 1945.

Isn't it a strange sort of opposite that claims to be a socialist worker's party, as opposed to, well, a socialist worker's party?

Consider 13 of the most relevant points from the Nazi Party's 25-point program of 1920, its Munich manifesto:

- *We demand that the State shall make it its first duty to promote the industry and livelihood of the citizens of the State.*

- *The activities of the individual must not clash with the interests of the whole, but must proceed within the framework of the community and must be for the general good.*

- *Abolition of incomes unearned by work. Breaking of the thraldom of interest.*

- *We demand the nationalization of all businesses which have been amalgamated.*

- *We demand that there shall be profit sharing in the great industries.*

- *We demand a generous development of provision for old age.*

- *We demand a land reform suitable to our national requirements, the passing of a law for the confiscation without compensation of land for communal purposes, the abolition of interest on land mortgages, and prohibition of all speculation in land.*

- *We demand ruthless war upon all those whose activities are injurious to the common interest.*

- *The schools must aim at teaching the pupil to understand the idea of the State. We demand the education of specially gifted children of poor parents, whatever their class or occupation, at the expense of the State.*

- *The State must apply itself to raising the standard of health in the nation…*

- *We demand legal warfare against conscious political lies and their dissemination in the press. In order to facilitate the creation of a German national press … It must be forbidden to publish newspapers which are damaging to the national welfare.*

- *We demand liberty for all religious denominations in the State, so far as they are not a danger to it. The Party… does not bind itself in the matter of creed to any particular confession.*

- *That all the foregoing requirements may be realized we demand the creation of a strong central national authority; unconditional authority of the central legislative body over the entire Reich and its organizations in general;*

These supposedly right-wing extremists were calling for national health care, social security, state-run schools, communal land development and centralized government control. They were determined advocates of gun control. And if they did not believe it took a village to raise a child, they were certainly enthusiastic about public youth programs. And then there were the complaints about vast conspiracies in the private press. Sounds familiar, doesn't it?

While some argue that the National Socialists became "conservative" as a result of their rapprochement with the great German industrialists following the final defeat of the Strasser wing of the party in late 1932, this conveniently skates over the fact that a) the 12 years concerned represents half of the Nazi Party's lifetime, and, b) Many elements of the avowedly socialist 1920 program were retained after 1933 when the National Socialists took power. Once in power, Vladimir Lenin, too, made capitalistic compromises with his New Economic Program, but this somehow never caused him to be defined as a man of the Right.

The National Socialists were not as radically left as the Soviet Communists, nor are most American Democrats as far left as were the National Socialists. But an examination of their ideological cores reveals the undeniable philosophical kinship between these three parties of the Left.

Perhaps the Democratic Party should consider a new battle cry should their most famous face decide to enter the presidential race in 2004. Sieg Hillary!

The United Socialist States of America

August 25, 2003

T HE ASSERTION THAT AMERICA is well along Friedrich von Hayek's ominous "Road to Serfdom" may sound as outlandish as the notion that the Nazis were left-wing extremists, but a great body of evidence suggests that America—despite its capitalist principles, ideals of liberty and constitutional protections for the individual—is already a quasi-socialist state.

There can be no doubt that America lacks some of the traditional trappings of a socialist state. With the possible exception of Massachusetts, we have no people's republics. Our national flag is not red and yellow, and it does not sport the dread hammer-and-sickle. We have two major parties, and neither one of them calls itself social or socialist, much less refers to itself as a front. Karl Marx is not deified here, and none of our leaders have ever attended Patrice Lumumba University in Moscow, although I have my suspicions about Howard Dean.

But consider the following evidence. Socialism is, more than anything, concerned with central state control of the economy. In the perfect worker's paradise, there would be 70 beautiful virgins—sorry, wrong paradise—that is to say, the government would control 100 percent of expenditures, or in modern economic terms, account for 100 percent of GDP (gross domestic product).

Marxists, like Christians, must lament the fact we live in a fallen world, as the closest any society has yet come to realizing this communist nirvana is that of Cuba, which last year could boast of its government accounting for 60.2 percent of its GDP. Even the standard bearer of international socialism, the Soviet Union, fell far short of this achievement, with its government outlays totaling a mere 29.37 percent of GDP in 1990 despite the benefit of 73 years of totalitarian rule by the workers' vanguard.

And where does the United States fall? The answer might surprise you. Of the $10.4 trillion U.S. economy, 19.5 percent is federal spending, more than four times higher than in that bastion of capitalism and individual freedom, the People's Republic of China, where the government only controls 4.7 percent of the economy. Add in the 12 percent controlled by state and local governments, and we have an American economy which is almost one-third given over to government of one form or another.

This was not true historically. As the chart below shows, in 1930, government spending accounted for only 5.3 percent of the economy. This changed rapidly with the ascension of Franklin Roosevelt, who—in addition to seizing the nation's gold—tripled the level of government spending even before the start of World War II.

Fortunately for America, her economic growth was such that even the incredible expansion of her government could not keep pace with it, thus mitigating somewhat the sclerotic effects of socialism on an economy. A more accurate picture of the metastasizing federal cancer can be seen in the comparison of government spending with population growth. The chart below shows how federal spending per capita has increased 250 times over the last 73 years. This figure does not correct for inflation—nor should it—since inflation is caused by the Treasury and the Federal Reserve printing money and is a form of government confiscation in its own right.

Nor is government spending the only statistical evidence that America has devolved into a quasi-socialist state. Over 703 million acres of American land are not private property of any kind, but are owned collectively by the federal government. This vast acreage amounts to 31.1 percent of the United States. With the addition of land to which title is held by state governments, the total amount of American land owned communally is 39.8 percent. This shows that significant progress has been made toward the communist goal of abolishing private ownership of land, at least in America.

But I do not believe that such progress is predestined. I do not believe in the inexorable hand of History. I do not believe in the inevitability of the United Socialist States of America anymore than I believe in the inevitability of the Napoleonic empire, the Third Reich or world revolution.

The argument that "we can't go back" is nothing more than a propagandistic lie. What goes up not only can come down, it will come down. Even if the socialist structure is constructed in its entirety, it will one day collapse of its own self-defeating contradictions. It would be much, much better, though, if it is never allowed to be completed in the first place.

Note: Data sources used were CIA World Factbook 1990, 2002; U.S. Bureau of Economic Analysis, "Summary Of Receipts, Outlays, And Surpluses Or Deficits (-) As Percentages Of GDP: 1930–2005" table 1.1, also table 1.3; U.S. Bureau of the Census; the Heritage Foundation; the National Wilderness Institute.

Christian and Libertarian

September 1, 2003

E VERY WEEK, someone asks me what it means to be a Christian Libertarian. Almost as often, I hear from Republicans disgusted with their party's abandonment of its purported principles of small government, social conservatism and adherence to the Constitution, who are nevertheless afraid of switching their allegiance to the godless Libertarians.

It has been said that a conservative is a liberal who's been mugged. In like manner, a libertarian is a conservative who's been mugged by the government. There is no criminal gang or collection of scam artists who perpetrate even a small fraction of the crimes that the federal government commits and abets—from the forgeries and inflationary confiscations of the U.S. Treasury to the cowardly corruption of the judiciary, from the extra-Constitutional executive orders of the president to the treasonous signings-away of national sovereignty by Congress.

One need not be an atheist or a devotee of Shub-Niggurath to oppose these things. Indeed, I suspect the problem many Christians and conservative Republicans have with making the leap to Libertarianism is that they still see a connection between the concepts of legality and morality. But there is no inherent relationship between the two; indeed, it is becoming increasingly obvious that it is not possible to honor both in many aspects of American life.

"It's the law!" is not a moral argument. It is an argument based on the threat of force. Yesterday the law required one to return an escaped slave to his owner; tomorrow it will require one to have an implanted Social Security number when one simply wants to buy Cheerios at the supermarket. The law is not only "an ass", but in a secular society, its moral neutrality is the best for which one can hope. And the law is impossible to obey, even for the most servile citizen—no one truly knows the laws because no one reads them, not even the politicians who pass them!

Then there are those conservatives who simply do not have a real commitment to individual freedom. They believe that government power is like a light switch, to be switched on to enforce policies they favor—such as banning private development on scenic lands—but switched off in the case of policies they do not. This is optimistic lunacy, since the argument for limited government does not rest upon the notion that the government always does undesirable things, but on the idea that if it can, it eventually will.

The same government that has the power to ban a private house on the beach also has the power to sell the beach to Wal-Mart or build a nuclear power plant on it. Since the Founding Fathers understood that a Marcus Aurelius was always followed by a Commodus, they tried to construct a system that would prevent either. Good central government, even when it exists, is a short-lived beast.

And Libertarianism is not inherently godless. In fact, it is the only political philosophy that is truly in accordance with Christianity. The Christian religion posits an all-powerful God who nevertheless permits humanity to turn its back on Him. This shows an extreme respect for free will and for the very sort of individual choice that is banned by Democrats and Republicans alike as they attempt to enforce their will upon the people through the power of government.

The basic principle of Libertarianism is not anarchic. There are real limits. My free will ends where yours begins. Neither the community nor I have any claim whatsoever on your property or your life, and a libertarian legal system would be structured around that principle. Do not be misled by the false "pro-choice" rhetoric of the infanticidal abortionettes; when one individual decides the fate of another, it is nothing more than the ancient law of tooth and claw. Still, their very terminology is the homage vice pays to virtue.

And what of the Christian element? Christianity is integral to the philosophy, as without the spiritual core of its demand for free will responsibility, libertarianism has a tendency to devolve into simple utilitarianism, which eventually leads to the very collectivism it was conceived to oppose. The occasional perversions of princes of the various churches notwithstanding,

Christianity is timeless and so provides the inexhaustible spring of moral refreshment that is necessary to any political ideology that hopes to resist corruption over time.

To love Jesus Christ and individual freedom; that is what it means to be a Christian Libertarian.

Defining the left-right spectrum

September 8, 2003

ALTHOUGH THE MEDIA regularly apply some form of the adjectives "left" and "right" to nearly everyone from the Chinese politburo to Baptist ministers, as is often the case with mainstream journalists, they do so in almost complete ignorance of what the words represent in terms of political ideology.

The most common error is to postulate a Communist left-wing extreme opposed by an extreme Nazi right wing. Not only does this leave out a substantial body of political and philosophical thought, but the construction falls apart the moment the two socialist ideologies are compared. Any reasonable comparison inevitably forces the confused advocates of such a definition to assert that the spectrum is actually a circle, in which case the terms left and right, much less left-wing and right-wing, are wholly nonsensical.

Nor is the original usage of much utility today, since it represented the fundamental division of the pre-revolutionary French national assembly. Since very few nations feature a monarchy these days, and even fewer political parties espouse positions with regards to the Bourbon kings, this definition is now defunct. And the notion of basing the spectrum on progress, of course, begs the Marxian question. In other words, progress toward what? The worker's paradise?

To find a stronger foundation for a proper political spectrum, it is necessary to delve into intellectual history. Looking back to ancient Greece, one finds striking similarities between the collectivism of Plato's Republic and modern leftist thought. And likewise, the close relationship between the Aristotelian regard for the individual, the American Bill of Rights and today's Libertarian Party is equally hard to escape.

Taking this fundamental dichotomy between the supremacy of the community and the primacy of the individual as a starting point, it becomes relatively easy to determine where an individual or party happens to fall on the political spectrum if communism is accepted as the anchoring point for the extreme left wing. The figure below illustrates where some of the most familiar political philosophies fall upon the spectrum based on an analysis of what I consider to be the ten most significant elements affecting individuals and their relationship to their government, followed by a point-by-point breakdown of how these positions were determined.

	COM	NAZ	DEM	REP	LIB
Religious Freedom	0	3	4	8	5
Right to Life	0	0	3	8	5
Gun Control	0	2	4	6	10
State Money Standard	0	0	0	0	10
Private Property	0	4	3	6	8
Freedom of the Press	0	1	3	7	10
National Sovereignty	0	4	3	4	7
Standing Army	0	0	6	2	10
State Schools	0	3	3	5	10
Central State Authority	0	0	3	6	10
TOTALS	0	15	36	52	85

Despite left-liberal chest-beating with regard to the Freedom of the Press, I noted it is primarily Democrats who support government-run media and the limitations on the individual inflicted by federal regulation of the airwaves and campaign-finance reform. National Sovereignty reflects both a willingness to sacrifice it in favor of international treaties and governing bodies as well as a lack of respect for the sovereignty of other nations or national borders. The last item, Central State Authority, represents the general tendency of the philosophy to support or oppose increased central state power through its policies.

This political spectrum of freedom is by no means complete, and I would certainly welcome any suggested modifications or additions from thoughtful readers. What it does provide, however, is a reasonable starting point for a discussion of the left-right political spectrum based on identifiable facts and philosophy instead of ignorance, deception and half-baked history.

Satanic Schwarzeneggerians

September 15, 2003

> *I have gone back and forth on Schwarzenegger, so much that I almost have whiplash. But my new—my current—position on him is: To hell with him.*

> —Jay Nordlinger, *National Review*

I LIKE ARNOLD, the bodybuilding evangelist and the movie star. But I have no regard for Mr. Schwarzenegger-Kennedy, the evasive politician. He's a man of the people now—give him a little more time and he'll be feeling our pain and doing everything "for the children". Fortunately, it didn't take long for Arnold to destroy himself as a viable candidate in the eyes of thinking conservatives everywhere. He was already suspect, indeed, anathema to those of us who believe in principles over party.

But he damned himself even with the pragmatists, those who care more for power, party and position than principle, with his dismissal as "right-wing crazies" those who support Proposition 54, which bans the state's collection of racial statistics on the population. How eminently fitting that a son of a National Socialist would fail to see the dangers in compiling such data! After all, without it, how can the state be expected to find those pesky Jews and Japanese in case it serves the interests of the children to round them up again?

The Republican enthusiasm for Arnold was initially based on his star power. It was nice, for a change, to see a Hollywood entity throw in with the GOP for once instead of barking mindlessly at it with the usual combination of vacuous accusations and cretinous insults. But his real support stemmed from his presumed electability, which sufficed to prevent numerous Democratic grandees from throwing their hats into the ring.

The problem is that the concept of electability is a massive crock of fumet. The Bush administration is demonstrating this truth in real-time, as its compassionate big-government neo-conservatism expands the federal leviathan at a pace faster than anyone since FDR. Would President Gore have been worse? Perhaps—but then there would be an opportunity to elect a man who actually opposed the rising tide of government in 2004 instead of surfing it like a cattle rancher gone beach-boy stoner.

Schwarzenegger, far from representing the salvation of California's Republican Party, stands for its complete immolation. He does not offer a philosophical alternative to California's self-destructive Democratic socialism; instead, he is a form of life-support for it. Instead of swearing to cut spending, he vows to beg more money from the federal government—demonstrating very clearly that this Republican is no republican!

Republicans in the state legislature have held their ground against the rapacious taxes proposed by Gov. Davis, and their obdurate political Manichaenism will allow them to do the same against Bustamante. But they will not be able to resist the same tax increases which would be proposed by a future Gov. Schwarzenegger. Furthermore, California Republicans will then be tarred by the same fiscal irresponsibility that now sticks only to their Democratic rivals, which, combined with their contemplated Schwarzeneggerian abandonment of cultural conservatives, will leave them wholly without a raison d'etre.

Pragmatism in politics is self-defeating in the long run. It is a euphemism for the slow sacrifice of one's principles. The constant substitution of "electable" moderates for principled conservatives is what repeatedly kills the Republican Party and prevents it from ever realizing even a small part of its platform when it is in power. It is particularly ironic when the electable moderates show themselves to be nothing of the sort, which in this particular case has already happened when the managing editor of the seminal *National Review* abjures the Great Teutonic Hope in no uncertain terms.

And those so-called Republicans who would drive a principled conservative like Tom McClintock from the race should hang their heads in shame. If they cannot fight for this candidate, they may as well abandon the battle altogether, for they are useless soldiers. It is better to spend 40 years in the political wilderness than to forsake one's soul for all the kingdoms of the world, much less four years in Sacramento.

Still worse, however, are the right-side commentators who urge conservatives to abandon their principles and line up behind this false Republican god.

To sacrifice your own soul to the naked pursuit of power is bad enough, to tempt others to do likewise is not just the ultimate in negative campaigning, it is pure political Satanism.

How to battle the Left at universities

September 22, 2003

ONE OF THE MOST outrageous claims made by the Left is that its inability to consistently command the allegiance of the masses it claims to champion stems from its innate decency, which precludes it from utilizing the hateful methods of its evil foes.

Thus, the prodigious failures of left-liberals at talk radio and cable news cannot be laid at the feet of the Left or its unpopular causes, but because conservatives, libertarians and the rest of the right are wily, mendacious manipulators of the gullible public. How we can manage this while at the same time being stupid to the point of drooling dysfunctionality—another favorite leftist libel—is beyond me, but then, intellectual consistency is the hobgoblin of small right-wing minds such as mine.

As with most unfounded accusations, the truth of it is to be found in the accuser, not the accused. The American Left, in politics, academia and entertainment, is invariably guilty of the very methods that it imagines and decries being used by its foes. That the average leftist has the emotional maturity of an undisciplined 2-year-old only exacerbates this tendency to wantonly project upon others that which they know to be true of themselves.

One of the reasons the Left engages so freely in wild accusations is that on a subconscious level, they know their intellectual foundation is built on factual sand. If one examines their paranoid accusations in any depth, it soon becomes clear that one of the Left's great fears is that conservatives will resort to using the same sort of proactive measures against them that they regularly use against their opponents. So, give them what they fear, I say, and David Horowitz, in company with Colorado Gov. Bill Owens, has shown the way toward breeching of one of the Left's most powerful strongholds— academia—with his Academic Bill of Rights.

The irony of diversity, that silly idol of universities and newsrooms across America, is that it is only tolerated in the most superficial manner. As long as one has the requisite numbers of women, blacks and homosexuals, one is safely diverse; never mind that there isn't a ruble's worth of ideological distinction between them. The university is easily the worst offender in this regard; the purported champions of intellectual freedom are those who hate it most.

But the Academic Bill of Rights does not go nearly far enough in assaulting what is today little more than a government-funded left-wing arsenal. What is needed is a federal Academic Fairness Doctrine, which would require every institution of higher learning in the country to establish ideological quotas for their faculties. Or perhaps I should say, ideological affirmative action. Each professor would check off one of eight boxes, Socialist, Green, Democrat, Republican, Constitutional, Libertarian, Other (Left) or Other (Right), and a college with a faculty that was not equitably balanced between the parties of left and right would suffer the loss of its federal funding.

Of course, there would be a need for an investigatory body to examine those professors who were attempting to hide their ideological roots in a vain attempt to cling to their tenure. This body, the Academic Fairness Agency, would respond to student complaints and the suspicions of fellow faculty members aroused when a purportedly Libertarian professor of literature gives a lecture on why Che Guevara had to die so that we might have universal health care. Unconstitutional? By no means! What is good for the taxpayer, the businessman and the broadcaster is surely good for the professoriat. Are they not Americans, too?

You might think I'm joking about this, but I'm not. Since the right does not require the aid of government to force-feed our views down the throats of an unwilling public, enacting this legislation is the ultimate win-win situation for Republicans and the rest of the right. But isn't this the very sort of pragmatic sell-out I regularly decry?

Not in the long run. It could be characterized as such, to be sure, except that this is an obvious case of one step back, a giant leap forward. Five years after the passage of the federal Academic Fairness Act, I guarantee the Left will be squealing for an end to all federal funding for higher education. Sometimes, one must lose the battle to win the war.

Al Franken is an irrelevant sissy

September 29, 2003

AL FRANKEN IS STANDING UP for the manhood of the Democratic Party. The task falls to him, it seems, since he is one of the last white men remaining in that collection of hypersensitive racists, outdated labor unions, infanticidal feminists and globalist socialists not named Kennedy.

Al Franken is more than a former comedian, he has now devolved into a media parasite worthy of note. His latest best-seller, *Lies and the Lying Liars Who Tell Them*, is in much the same vein as his previous book on Rush Limbaugh, showing him to be a literary mosquito dependent upon sucking blood from the efforts of others.

This is not to say that the book is entirely useless. Mr. Franken does an admirable job of exposing some of the more risible gaffes, exaggerations and, yes, lies of several current media stars. Nevertheless, like an increasing number of Americans, I'll take the quasi-conservative blowhard O'Reilly over the moribund leftist cadavers at *CNN*, despite his purple pen. So, too, with regard to Sean Hannity, although his failure to grasp the proper calculation of percentage differences is almost as cringe-inducing as O'Reilly's fiction.

But Franken's critiques are, for the most part, irrelevant. It is particularly so with regard to the case of leftist media bias put forth by my favorite columnist, Ann Coulter. Indeed, if Franken were an exterminator, one can easily imagine the scenario proceeding thusly:

House Owner: There's an animal in the house!

Al Franken: (steps gingerly over massive pile of steaming elephant dung) This, in the corner? That's not a rat, it's a dust bunny.

House Owner: Hmmm, I guess you're right.

Al Franken: (ignoring loud trumpeting from the next room) No rat, no problem. Quod erat demonstrandum!

In this case, the rather significant point that seems to have escaped Mr. Franken is that in order to dismiss Ann Coulter's claim that the mainstream media is run by lefties, it does not suffice to point out that Miss Coulter was incorrect with regard to the paternal lineage of *Newsweek*'s Evan Thomas. To prove the media is not run by lefties, it is necessary to demonstrate that the mainstream media does not repeatedly and reliably support the socialist principles expounded by Karl Marx in the "Communist Manifesto".

Not only is this an impossible task, but it is one Mr. Franken is rather unlikely to undertake since he supports those Marxian principles himself. "National park system—really good Social Security—hottest." Some of the other avowedly Marxian causes for which he has sympathy include: "A heavy progressive or graduated income tax" (*Lies*, p. 291) and "Abolition of all right of inheritance" (*Lies*, pp. 298–302). Mr. Franken did not explicitly elucidate his enthusiasm for "free education for all children in public schools" (*Lies*, pp. 93–94), but it is implied.

Al Franken is an intelligent man, but his education is obviously neither deep nor wide. This, in addition to his heavy reliance on the 14-man Team Franken and various friendly experts, causes him to consistently fail to see the forest for the trees. He lambastes John Ashcroft for spending $8,000 that could have gone to fighting terrorism without realizing that government fiat money is not a zero-sum game. He points to the era of Clintonian prosperity, demanding to know what, if not Bill Clinton's budget discipline, could have brought it about, without considering the effects of the Federal Reserve's concomitant 56.86 percent increase in M3.

It is said there is pain festering below the surface of many a funny man. In Al Franken's case, there appears to be only seething rage. The Rich Lowry episode in chapter 38 exposes the ugly bully in him, as the genteel *National Review* editor's bewildered response when challenged to a fistfight only proves him to be "a tad on the wimpy side" according to Franken, and "a wuss" according to the like-minded spawn of Franken, Joe.

Therefore, Mr. Franken, let me state that I not only believe the Democrats have feminized politics, I believe they have feminized the American male and are responsible for the evolution of the so-called metrosexual as well as the homosexualization of American culture. And I'm calling you out—fight-club rules. Any time, anywhere, although I'm amenable to waiting until you finish your book tour. After all, it's hard to do a reading with your jaw wired shut.

I'm just kidding about the jaw, of course. Kidding on the square.

Step back, black quarterback

October 6, 2003

WHILE I WAS SURPRISED that Rush Limbaugh elected to take advantage of his elephantine media status to become an NFL commentator, I wasn't surprised that he brought the same willingness to confront sacred cows that has made him such a massive success in the world of politics to the world of sports.

It is shocking, however, that he chose to resign so quickly, rather than force *ESPN* to show its timorous hand by firing him for daring to speak out on an issue around which the cowardly sports media has danced so delicately for decades. And as a fan of pretty much all of the parties concerned, I thought it was worth examining the facts about the controversy.

First, there is no question that the NFL aggressively promotes at least one racist agenda. Can you imagine the howls of indignation that would surround the New York Stock Exchange if brokerage houses were fined for a failure to interview a white candidate for an open stockbroker's job? And yet, the sportswriting community not only does not criticize the racist policy requiring interviews for black would-be coaches, it celebrates it.

Peter King of Sports Illustrated, among others, is disingenuous when he claims that the sporting media has no particular interest in black success at quarterback. Anyone who has followed the NFL for a long period of time will remember Joe Gilliam and James Harris, black quarterbacks who played long before the massive hoopla that surrounded the Washington Redskins' Super Bowl win over the Denver Broncos. Doug Williams's monstrous game not only fired up the media's cheerleading for black quarterbacks, but also led to the great Public Enemy line: "We got a black quarterback, so step back!" It also led to what may have been the dumbest question in the history of the sports media: "How long have you been a black quarterback?"

After Williams's success, it was as common to read about the so-called lack of black quarterbacks as it is to read about the supposed shortage of black coaches now. So certainly, there was, and is, a certain amount of media desire for black success at quarterback.

But does that suffice to explain McNabb's superstar status and prove that Rush was right? I don't think so. Donovan McNabb is not the NFL's only starting black quarterback. In fact, there are seven with a reasonable amount of experience. And looking at the career quarterback ratings for these seven starters, it's surprising to note that McNabb is not even in the top five.

Rating	Name	Team	Division
86.3	D. Culpepper	Vikings	NFC North
82.8	S. McNair	Titans	AFC South
79.6	A. Brooks	Saints	NFC South
79.2	J. Blake	Cardinals	NFC West
77.6	M. Vick	Falcons	NFC South
77.5	D. McNabb	Eagles	NFC East
71.3	K. Stewart	Bears	NFC North

McNabb has led his team to the NFC championship game, but so has Culpepper, and McNair has not only been to two AFC championship games, he's actually won one. Is McNabb handicapped by a lack of quality receivers? I don't see that Burress and Ward helped the magic INT machine also known as Kordell Stewart all that much in Pittsburgh.

The answer to McNabb's media fan club is to be found in the league schedule. McNabb plays in the NFC East, home to the New York Giants and the Washington Redskins, and he is televised at least twice a year in each of the two American media centers. He also plays regularly against the Dallas Cowboys, who, despite their currently humble state, are still the beneficiary of more media coverage than most NFL teams, or U.N. member states, for that matter. Meanwhile, Steve McNair—a black quarterback with a comparable QB rating in 2002, who also led his team to the conference championship game—plays in a division featuring teams in Nashville, Indianapolis, Jacksonville and Houston, and did not even make the Pro Bowl.

Bias is to blame for McNabb's undeserved stardom, but not racial bias. In truth, it is nothing more than that old sporting standby, the East Coast media bias. This not only explains McNabb's prominence, but also that of the greatest tight end in the history of football, New York's Jeremy Shockey, who has all of three touchdown catches in his career.

Rush got it wrong, but then, so did his critics. And once again, we see that in the home of the brave and the land of free speech, some things remain unmentionable.

The end of art

October 13, 2003

THERE CAN BE LITTLE DOUBT that Western Art is in decline. Any comparison of the great masterworks of the past 500 years with the pathetic soup cans of Andy Warhol, not to mention the flayed cows and elephant dung creations that now pollute our museums, indicates that the artistic culture has progressed well beyond decadence and is now sliding down an increasingly steep slope toward total creative rigor mortis.

Architecture devolved into primitive geometrics some time ago, but actually appears sober in comparison with the delusional self-parody of modern sculpture. The art of painting has not only been stripped of beauty by its artless practitioners, but the basic techniques have been lost as well, producing works that are cruder to the eye than the pre-perspective images of medieval times.

Music, too, has fared poorly. A top producer such as Dr. Dre could no more write an orchestral score than could Britney Spears tackle Verdi's "La Traviata". I say this with confidence, having penned two Billboard-charting dance hits myself, despite barely being able to read music. About poetry, the less said the better, as even the treacly, but delightful wordsmithery of A.A. Milne looks downright epic in comparison with the state-subsidized, overpoliticized tripe published today.

Of all the arts, it is only the novel that has held up well. This may be in part because it is a younger art, and one more amenable to modern sensibilities. If there are no sculptors to compare with Michelangelo, no musicians to compare with Mozart and no poets to compare with Byron, there are still novelists, who, while perhaps falling short of true literary greatness, may at least be mentioned in the same sentence as their historical antecedents without provoking mirth and scorn.

It is true that the works of Umberto Eco, Salman Rushdie and Neal Stephenson may not quite rate with Tolstoy, de Balzac, Austin, Bronte, Flaubert and Dostoevsky, but the comparisons are not wholly absurd. Even so, I was troubled after reading "The Rice Mother", an excellent first novel by Malaysian writer Rani Manicka.

This was not due to any dearth of writing skill—which is considerable—or an absence of character development, plot or story arch. Her portrait of Malaysia is realistic enough that one can virtually smell the jungle surrounding the pathetic wooden huts constructed on stilts, which provide joint habitation for a family as well as the chickens that sustain them. Her description of the intrafamilial poison that is passed from one generation to the next is disturbingly lifelike, and the characters who populate the novel are masterfully drawn.

"The Rice Mother" is a beautiful and brutal book. At times, it could almost pass for an Oprah Book Club novel, chronicling the self-absorption and petty martyrdoms of the modern American woman. But the genuine cruelties of reality intrude too harshly and too often to force the book down that mysteriously popular literary dead end.

What is sad is that for all Manicka's Eastern heritage and well-honed artistic talent, the power of her art has been drained by that great vampire of Western literature, amorality. Ted Chiang, the award-winning science-fiction writer, has written that "Hell is the Absence of God," and this certainly is true for the author who aspires to literary greatness. There is no drama without conflict, and "The Rice Mother" offers very little of either, as both the author and her characters are wholly bereft of any moral vision against which the reader may contemplate their actions.

Thus, even the book's most ghastly events are stripped of their horror, and so of their dramatic power as well. Where would be the drama in "Oedipus Rex" if the incestuous usurper simply murmured an embarrassed apology about the terrible misunderstanding and quietly replaced his queen with a more appropriate lover? Would the reader follow the twisted meanderings of Raskolnikov's mind with such interest, if, after taking an axe to Alena Ivanovna, he ate a sandwich, watched television and forgot about the matter? And without the Puritanical strictures on adultery, would there even be enough color to Hawthorne's famous letter to render a short story worth while?

The horror of "The Rice Mother" is the way in which it reveals that our most talented artists have been stripped of the most vital tool of their trade. An amoral society may have its advantages, but a fertile field for literary greatness is not one of them. This is the end of Art.

Breaking up with Bill

October 20, 2003

WHILE I WOULD NOT go so far as to say that I regard computers as an absolute necessity in life, I have to admit that if given a choice between giving up my computers and giving up food, my first instinct would be to ask how long you had in mind.

The Apple II was my true love, although the first computer in our house was the original IBM PC. Thus, I was intimate with Microsoft from the beginning, though I always had a cheater's heart. I was enamored with Apple games such as Akallabeth, Castle Wolfenstein and Wizardry—yes, that's right, I know my Mahalito from my Tiltowait—and my parents sent me off to college with the original Macintosh.

I was working at a computer graphics company when Windows 3.0 was released. We'd seen all of the previous versions, which were ugly, hard-to-use jokes, but I can still remember after we fired up 3.0 for the first time, a few of us looked at each other and nodded as we realized that Microsoft had finally done just enough to give DOS-heads a reason to migrate to a graphical user interface.

I'd already abandoned the MacOS by then, since great games like Wing Commander and the Ultima series required DOS VGA. And I've obediently upgraded Windows in step with the masses, from 3.11 to 95, 98 and finally, 2000. But no more.

Now, understand that Microsoft is not a monopoly. The fact that it does a very good job of hooking the technologically clueless makes it an astute competitor, not an antitrust violator. It is, nevertheless, an evil empire, and moreover, one that is antithetical to human freedom.

Whereas Microsoft once represented freedom of choice, it now does everything in its power to reduce one's freedom to choose. It does not give one the ability to choose to update one's software or not—you can update now or you can update later, but you VILL UPDATE, HEIN! Security holes and bugs abound, but Microsoft whispers soothing lies and insists that there's nothing to worry about, drop $50 on Norton Anti-Virus and everything will be fine.

Even more disturbing are the routine violations of privacy that Microsoft abets and sometimes demands. Microsoft is paving the easy path, promising more ease-of-use, a calmer, happier computing experience, and all that you need to do in return is turn off your brain, hand over every detail of who you are, what you do and with whom you do it, then slide down the user-friendly interface to Hell.

One week ago, after wrestling with a nasty virus that took down my entire ISP, I'd had enough. It was the first virus I'd ever encountered despite never using anti-virus software, and it was the last straw as well.

It wasn't just the virus, or the thrice-weekly crashes, or the forced upgrades or even the massive, bloated resource hog that Microsoft Office has become. It was the realization that Microsoft is building the Great Eye That Never Sleeps, which, in combination with your government identification number, will be used to track you, verify you and determine if you are a properly obedient little wage-serf. As Chuck D says, I rebel with a raised fist. And, I might add, a solitary finger.

Now determined to break out of the system or fry my machine trying, I sat down and fired up my dual-boot system on which I'd installed Red Hat Linux a few months ago in a previous spasm of irritation with a serial-crashing laptop running Windows 2000. This time, though, I chose Linux and I followed through. I mounted my hard drive. I got my wireless network up and running. I downloaded my favorite browser—Opera—as well as a few other needed sundries.

It wasn't a piece of cake, but it honestly wasn't hard and I was fully operational by the second day. In fact, I'm writing this column on OpenOffice.org 1.1.0 Writer, which reads and writes to all of my Word documents without a murmur of complaint. Goodbye, sweet Bill.

Four days into Linux, my conclusion is that the casual computer user will not be able to make the switch yet, but the power user can. And should.

I've chronicled my migration experience on my new daily blog Vox Popoli, and I encourage you to take a glance at it if you have any interest in breaking the chains of Microsoft and riding the Linux penguin to techno liberty.

Follow me! Follow me to freedom!

Shadows, sex and sorrow

October 27, 2003

I LOST A FRIEND during the New York City blackout. We were not especially close—the last I'd seen of her was a year ago, as she walked off into the night after an evening's reunion on the rue Roger Verlomme. But her death by her own hand hit me harder than I would have imagined, perhaps because she was one of the most vivacious women of my acquaintance.

A pretty redhead with laughing, mischievous eyes, she was always strikingly alive. I met her at a Thanksgiving dinner when I was in college—she was several years younger, but traveled up to pay a visit a few months later, in the spring. We went out every now and then, and stayed in contact over the years thanks to some mutual friends.

Strange, to think that of the six people at dinner that night, three of them are now dead.

My friend graduated from photography school in New York, and, like many artists, plunged into a libertine lifestyle with more than a little enthusiasm. She was the only woman I ever knew who considered bodypaint to be a suitable Halloween outfit, and one of her favorite self-portraits was a picture of her holding an old rifle, wearing a 10-gallon hat and cowboy boots… and nothing else. No one who met her was likely to forget her.

If I had to choose one adjective that best described her, it would be adventurous—she was, in every sense of the word. She lived for pleasure, with such exuberance and charm it was almost impossible not to be swept up in her wake. But pleasure is like a drug. The more you indulge, the more you require, until ultimately even the most dedicated hedonist begins to learn that pleasure and happiness are not one and the same.

I abandoned my single-minded pursuit of pleasure when I became a Christian. I can't say I never had any regrets or harbored any doubts about my decision, but on the whole, I've been surprised to find that trying to walk the harder path in pursuit of a higher purpose has proven to be more personally rewarding and more satisfying than I would have imagined.

I told my friend of my new faith a few years ago. She was accepting of this, of course, as she was of everything, but made it clear that she was uninterested in such ethereal things as offered little in the way of immediate excitement or amusement. She had other things on her mind, such as a wedding and starting a glamorous new chapter of her life in Paris.

I don't know if her vivacity was a desperate attempt to escape a shadow that had long oppressed her, or if the shadow crept slowly upon her over time. She wasn't the kind of person with whom you had that sort of conversation, and even in retrospect, even when I look for it, I can see little hint of darkness in her eyes or in her smile.

She died, as she lived, on her own terms. I admire her for that, even as I mourn her decision, because there is a certain cold logic in its remorseless nihilism. If not only our faith, but our hope, is in Jesus Christ, then we cannot be surprised or dismayed to know that those who deny Him and focus their eyes solely on the evil of the fallen world that surrounds us will sometimes feel overwhelmed.

If you will indulge me, I should like to say to you what I wish I had known to say to her. The shadow is an illusion. It is like the pleasure—it passes, it waxes and wanes with time. Only that which you consider to be fairytales is the reality, it is that hope that is the truth, and only through that blinding light can the shadow be entirely banished. And if you feel that you must give in, that you are no longer strong enough to stand on your own, then surrender to the light, not to the darkness.

I will miss my friend. The world is a less vivid place for her loss. She was a brightly burning candle, extinguished far too soon by the weight of her own shadow.

Bypassing government

November 3, 2003

F EW WOULD QUESTION that the free market has been one of mankind's greatest blessings. Having produced life expectancies that more than double those of our historical antecedents and widely enjoyed riches that even the wealthiest king of yore would have envied—what price a hot shower and flea powder in the stinking court of the Sun King—capitalism has enriched the world.

Even its most notorious critic, Karl Marx, spoke surprisingly well of capitalism, saying that it "has accomplished wonders far surpassing Egyptian pyramids, Roman aqueducts and Gothic cathedrals." And few would deny that America is a capitalist society… but is it?

After all, NAFTA-sanctioned trade can hardly be characterized as free. A real free-trade agreement requires but a single page, saying something to the effect of "Congress shall make no law…" And for all that the denizens of Wall Street are considered the vanguard of global capitalism, the extreme level of government interference, barriers to entry and bureaucratic cronyism is hardly indicative of a free and open market. No one who has ever witnessed the exegeses that follow every sibylline Greenspan pronouncement can fail to miss the significance of the interest-rate whip that keeps the Wall Street beast well-tamed.

It is quite possible that the reality of the modern corporation has become incompatible with free-market capitalism. Global corporations now embrace government regulation as an aid to stifling embryonic competition, and government spending is an important source of their revenue. The concept of big government versus big business is outmoded, a 19th century fossil as hopelessly beside the point as Howard Dean, Madonna or the labor theory of value.

Indeed, we seem to have fallen into the rabbit hole of the corporatist Third Way, halfway between socialism and capitalism, a concept first dreamed up by Benito Mussolini before being revived by Tony Blair and Bill Clinton.

But the Third Way is no more inevitable than the death of its two progenitors, which in both cases have been announced prematurely. Like its capitalist father, the Third Way is inextricably tied to the technological development required for economic growth, and therein may lie the contradiction of corporatism. For the advancement of human freedom, this contradiction presents both an opportunity and a threat.

Already, the technological imperative is looming ominously over one of the great champions of the Third Way, Microsoft. It is ironic, to be sure, but due to corporatist restraints on competition, the open-source movement was forced to develop outside the corporate environment until products such as the Linux operating system reached a point where corporations could no longer afford to ignore it.

And where open source leads, open markets can follow. Neal Stephenson's "Cryptonomicon" paints a brilliant and entertaining portrait of the development of an independent data haven operating outside the bounds of government, and therefore corporatist, intervention. An intriguing notion, especially when one considers that international money is nothing but data.

It sounds impossible today, of course. But who would have thought a free operating system cobbled together by techno-enthusiasts could pose a threat that is taken very seriously by the world's reigning technology company? On a similar note, who would have imagined 20 years ago that a large percentage of private investors would begin to ignore their stockbrokers and invest their assets directly? The stockbroker has already been cut out of the process. How long will it be before the inherent inefficiencies of the investment banks and government-regulated exchanges are likewise cast aside?

The implications go far beyond who makes a buck on the middleman's cut. A world where the entrepreneurs behind Google do not have to hand over large slices of equity to investment banks and wait years before cashing in on their success, and where other talented young minds can make their case directly to investors via the Internet, will represent a real shift of financial muscle that cannot help but make a significant impact on the American economy and political system.

After 70 years of failure, Soviet and Chinese communists finally came to recognize that the free market is more powerful than socialist dictatorship. In like manner, the corporatist debate will revolve around whether it is possible to harness the power of the market without permitting the concomitant freedom that it engenders and demands.

One hopes that America elects to align itself with the forces of freedom and the markets, not against them.

Are you a Nazi?

November 10, 2003

1) Do you agree with the 59 percent of the European Union that believes Israel is the country that presents the greatest threat to world peace?

A) No; B) Yes; C) Only 59 percent? Damn Jewish pollsters!

2) Do you believe it is important for the government to fund newspapers, radio stations and television channels in order to counteract the influence of the independent media?

A) No; B) Yes; C) Yes, because everyone knows that Jews run the media. Didn't you see that poll?

3) Is the federal government's primary responsibility to promote the industry and livelihood of its citizens?

A) No; B) Yes; C) Yes, as long as they are pure-blooded Aryans.

4) Should the federal government be permitted to confiscate private property in order to convert the land to communal purposes?

A) No; B) Yes; C) Yes, especially if it belongs to Jews.

5) Does the federal government have the responsibility to execute individuals whose activities are injurious to the common interest?

A) No; B) Yes; C) Yes, especially if they're Jewish.

6) Should the education of poor children be provided by the government?

A) No; B) Yes; C) All education should be provided by the government.

7) Should the federal government apply itself to raising the standard of health in the nation?

A) No; B) Yes; C) Yes, except for the health of Jews, Catholic priests, homosexuals and enemies of the state.

8) Is it the responsibility of the federal government to provide generously for the elderly?

A) No; B) Yes; C) Yes, unless they're Jewish.

9) Should the federal government require the registration of all privately owned firearms?

A) No; B) Yes; C) No Jew should be permitted to own firearms.

10) National sovereignty is:

A) A right to be defended; B) An outmoded relic hindering progress; C) An affront to the right of the Aryan race to lebensraum.

11) Euthanasia is:

A) State-sanctioned murder; B) Sometimes in the best interest of the individual being euthanized; C) An excellent way to punish enemies of the state.

12) Christianity is:

A) The truth; B) A dangerous myth that threatens progress and the social order; C) A Judeo-Bolshevist pathology of decadence.

Give yourself zero points for every (A), two points for every (B) and five points for every (C). A score of 24 means that you are in perfect, 100 percent accordance with the policies and positions of the National Socialist German Worker's Party, or NSDAP, known colloquially as the Nazi Party.

A score of 40 or more suggests that you made it to Argentina before that traitor Doenitz betrayed the Führer's memory and the honor of the Volk by surrendering the Reich.

The irrational atheist

November 17, 2003

T HE IDEA THAT HE is a devotee of reason seeing through the outdated superstitions of other, lesser beings is the foremost conceit of the proud atheist. This heady notion was first made popular by French intellectuals such as Voltaire and Diderot, who ushered in the so-called Age of Enlightenment.

That they also paved the way for the murderous excesses of the French Revolution and many other massacres in the name of human progress is usually considered an unfortunate coincidence by their philosophical descendants.

The atheist is without God but not without faith, for today he puts his trust in the investigative method known as science, whether he understands it or not. Since there are very few minds capable of grasping higher-level physics, let alone following their implications, and since specialization means that it is nearly impossible to keep up with the latest developments in the more esoteric fields, the atheist stands with utter confidence on an intellectual foundation comprised of things of which he knows nothing.

In fairness, he cannot be faulted for this, except when he fails to admit that he is not actually operating on reason in this regard, but is instead exercising a faith that is every bit as blind and childlike as that of the most unthinking Bible-thumping fundamentalist. Still, this is not irrational, it is only ignorance and a failure of perception.

The irrationality of the atheist can primarily be seen in his actions—and it is here that the cowardice of his intellectual convictions is also exposed. Whereas Christians and the faithful of other religions have good reason for attempting to live by the Golden Rule—they are commanded to do so—the atheist does not.

In fact, such ethics, as well as the morality that underlies them, are nothing more than man-made myth to the atheist. Nevertheless, he usually seeks to live by them when they are convenient, and there are even those, who, despite their faithlessness, do a better job of living by the tenets of religion than those who actually subscribe to them.

Still, even the most admirable of atheists is nothing more than a moral parasite, living his life based on borrowed ethics. This is why, when pressed, the atheist will often attempt to hide his lack of conviction in his own beliefs behind some poorly formulated utilitarianism, or argue that he acts out of altruistic self-interest. But this is only post-facto rationalization, not reason or rational behavior.

I am saying nothing new here. It is an ancient concept. More than 2,000 years ago, the first atheist martyr, Socrates, declared "The only good is knowledge and the only evil is ignorance." Being fully aware of the repercussions of this teaching, he also argued that it was necessary to keep such virtuous knowledge to the elite.

> *"I mean", I replied, "that our rulers will find a considerable dose of falsehood and deceit necessary for the good of their subjects … these goings on must be a secret which the rulers only know, or there will be a further danger of our herd … breaking out into rebellion."*

The Romans, ever practical, understood this as well. Seneca the Younger wrote: "Religion is regarded by the common people as true, by the wise as false, and by rulers as useful." It is more than useful for a civilized society, though, it is a downright necessity.

Even the great champions of reason accepted this bitter truth. Alvin Bernstein writes of Voltaire:

> *He regarded belief in God and in an afterlife of rewards and punishments as requisites of ethical behavior.… Voltaire was convinced that the lower classes must fear God in order to be ethical. His religious outlook … is a stepping-stone toward a full secular outlook in which moral judgments have nothing to do with religious and spiritual abstractions.*

This is not to say there are no atheists who are rational, that there are none who are true to their godless convictions. Friedrich Nietzsche is the foremost example, but there are certainly others who do not fear to determine their own moral compass. Today, we call them sociopaths and suicides.

Without God, there is only the left-hand path of the philosopher. It leads invariably to Hell, by way of the guillotine, the gulag and the gas chamber. The atheist is irrational because he has no other choice—because the rational consequences of his non-belief are simply too terrible to bear.

Why Hillary won't run

November 24, 2003

MORE THAN ONE SAGE has expressed an opinion that Hillary is only lying in wait, not unlike a crocodile lurking at a waterhole, before announcing an unexpected bid for the presidency. I disagree. In my humble opinion, there are a number of reasons why the Lizard Queen will choose to sit on the sidelines in 2004.

First, none of the four major theories of history support her candidacy at this time. The Great Man theory dictates that in this time of crisis and war, George Bush will rise to the occasion, like many an underrated man before him, and tower over the electorate like an unassailable Colossus until the danger is past. The Accident theory is chancy and in any case would seem to favor Howard Dean, or, more amusingly, Al Sharpton.

Given the Marxian reduction of everything to class interests, it is obvious that a petit bourgeois arriviste such as Ms. Rodham-Clinton can neither command the allegiance of the proletariat nor enjoy the trust of the capitalists. Furthermore, the economic climate—or at least the perceived economic climate; I've read novels containing less fiction than the recent claim of 7.2 percent growth in GDP—is not one that lends itself to electoral upheaval, much less class struggle.

Even the Conspiracy theory, which usually fits all things Clintonian like a condom, does not point to Hillary. The Old Guard is nothing if not sexist, and while it's not exactly unheard of for a Rhodes Scholar to replace a Jolly Roger, one finds it hard to imagine them permitting a former Girl Scout to do the same. Not even one who is in the direct matrilineal line of Lilith, daughter of Asmodael, Hell Baron of the Seventh Circle.

While I have much respect for the raw animal cunning and devious creativity of America's most famous foot-fetishist, I honestly think that Dick Morris is forgetting something about his former client. The Lizard Queen is cold-blooded. She is not a risk-taker, at heart, and she is far more prone to finishing off the sick and wounded than taking on an alpha male in a full-frontal attack.

Her carpet-bagging defeat of an unready, ill-prepared Rick Lazio may have proved her electability, but it was a risk-free run in one of the most left-liberal states in the country. To maintain her momentum, she had little choice but to throw her hat in the ring somewhere while her husband and his allies still controlled the Democratic National Committee. And was it boldness that helped her propel her husband's campaign in 1992, or simply a Wellesley snob's desperation to escape Little Rock?

In 2004, however, she has much to lose. Not only would a late entry anger significant powers within the Democratic Party, but a loss would dramatically reduce the wattage of her star. A bad loss—or worse, a failure to win the nomination—would finish her as a serious contender altogether.

President Bush 2.0 should not be confused with his predecessor. He has not yet won his war, but he shows no signs of prematurely letting up on the gas. His domestic timidity may be the result of more pressing issues or simply a lack of conservative conviction, but in any case, his willingness to pull the trigger on Afghanistan and Iraq shows that, when pressed, he will go for the jugular. And for all that she has the nimble feet of a survivor, Hillary has no armor.

Last week's Goodridge decision should cement Hillary's decision to stay on the sidelines. No candidate will now be able to finesse their position on this ludicrous redefinition of marriage, and upcoming debate over the inevitable Defense of Marriage Amendment will significantly weaken the Democratic Party, as a large portion of its remaining Christians and conservatives—of all colors—abandon it. The decision of the Massachusetts court will likely prove to be every bit as significant in the re-election of George Bush as was the decision of the United States Supreme Court in his election.

So, the Lizard Queen will continue to lurk quietly in the gaseous morass of the Senate, biding her time, waiting for the right moment to strike an unsuspecting America and drag it beneath the dark waters of her totalitarian vision.

Shoot 'em in the face!

December 1, 2003

L IKE MOST WHO HAVE GRADUATED from college, I have endured many pious and pedantic secular sermons from various members of the self-appointed moral elite. From the day I set foot on campus, I was lectured on my proclivity to rape women who might or might not be saying no, the need to be tolerant of the idiosyncratic behavior of others, and, above all, to know that I, as a campus conservative, was a crypto-Nazi slavering for the chance to commit violence on others.

The incidents of politically correct left-wing campus totalitarianism are too numerous to be chronicled here. But I too have encountered the unholy trinity of left-liberal students, leftist faculty and PC administration.

As a result of some histrionic accusations of being "sexist pornographers" and sexual harassers, my friend and I were rousted from our beds by the campus Gestapo at a ridiculously early hour. My friend was dragged off in his underwear to face the university inquisitors. Only after openly accusing the dean of students of lacking some vital male organs that were all too conspicuous in the case of my friend did the dean agree to look into the facts of the matter before punishing us. And after the woman admitted to lying, our names were finally cleared.

But the campus left is seldom content with merely lying. Sukhmani Singh Khalsa found this out the hard way at the University of Tennessee. He wrote an opinion piece published in the Daily Beacon, complaining about the left-wing bias of the university's Issues Committee and its activities, which include inviting campus speakers. He claimed that Tucker Carlson was the first conservative invited "in about five semesters" whereas the other four speakers invited that same semester were Scott Ritter, Howard Zinn, Ralph Nader and Sy Hersh.

For this, he was viciously mauled in an intra-committee exchange of e-mails, which became public thanks to the techno-idiocy of the committee members. This was protested to the dean of students, Maxine Thompson, who somehow saw no harm in the desire of various committee members to torture and murder the "raghead" who had dared to criticize them in a public forum. And when the College Republicans held a petition to protest the behavior of this university-funded committee, the associate dean of students, J.J. Brown, called the cops on them.

Fortunately, the Knoxville police appear to understand the basic concept of human liberty rather better than the upholders of academic freedom at the University of Tennessee, quickly determined that the College Republicans were doing nothing wrong, and left them alone.

After reading the aforementioned e-mails, I had several questions. Unfortunately, the student head of the committee was only willing to say that some statements had been misconstrued before informing me that she could not speak to the press. And so, I wonder:

Was Mr. Khalsa insufficiently open-minded with regard to the idea of torture that would "put the Spanish Inquisition to shame" for the Issues Committee to accept him as a member?

What was the good that the committee ultimately concluded torture would not suffice to provide with regards to Mr. Khalsa?

Since Mr. Denning asserts that the committee understands "what goes on in the committee" and "why it is liberal leaning", would someone be so kind as to share this with the Tennessee taxpayers?

Mr. Comstock's statement about the Issue Committee's performance is sadly devoid of details. What are his reasons for asserting that the committee is "doing a f—— incredible job"?

How was Mr. Rubinstein's comment "if you see one of those ragheads, shoot him in the f—ing face" misconstrued? What is the correct way to construe such a comment when made with regard to a turban-wearing Sikh?

The entire affair is nothing but another tempest in a teakettle, of course, but it is valuable as it demonstrates the totalitarian mindset lurking beneath the tolerant facade of the left. It also demonstrates the rampant hypocrisy in academia, which leaps at any chance to punish conservative students while blithely ignoring far worse offenses from their leftist counterparts.

Most of all, these e-mails reveal the shocking state of higher education. The UT administration should not only fire the two irresponsible deans and replace the entire Issues Committee, it should get rid of the professors who failed to teach these arrogant children how to write.

Don't trust your computer

December 8, 2003

I T IS UNDERSTANDABLY DIFFICULT for Americans to worry much about the future. We are the wealthiest, most powerful society in human history, and as many astoundingly silly expert predictions have proven, it is notoriously difficult to imagine the future as being anything but a linear projection of the status quo.

But an ominous new technology is appearing like a small cloud on the horizon. It is being embraced by a consortium of the world's largest technology companies and it threatens to completely overturn the computing world as we know it.

Twenty years ago, Microsoft was an integral part of the personal computer revolution, and fulfilled Bill Gates's daring dream of a personal computer on every desktop. But now, Microsoft has gone to the dark side and embraced an evil vision. Instead of liberating individual creativity through the personal computer, Microsoft hopes to use a Trusted Computer to chain the individual into the digital bondage of consumer serfdom.

The Totalitarian Control Group is a consortium, led by Microsoft, intended to force all computer users into a new computing paradigm. This new paradigm, based on the Non-Governmental Social Control Box or NGSCB, will be the new PC standard, according to Bill Gates, and "will allow computers to be used in ways they currently aren't secure enough to be used for."

How are computers insecure? In many ways. But the only ways that actually concern the TCG are those relating to the use of software and other digital products in ways that the TCG does not approve. A Trusted Computer containing the NGSCB will place a digital stamp on all files created on that machine, which can be encrypted so that only another Trusted Computer can open them. So far so good, and no different than GnuPG or any other private encryption scheme.

However, a Trusted Computer can also—and will—be set so that a document or file produced on an unTrusted Computer will not open or run. This is designed to not only eliminate the ability to run pirated software, but also to put pressure on those who do not have Trusted Computers to migrate to Trusted technology.

Today, for example, I can write a letter in OpenOffice on my Linux machine, save it in Microsoft Word format, attach the document to an e-mail and send to someone using Microsoft Office on a Microsoft XP machine. That person will have no trouble receiving the e-mail or opening the document. If the TCG gets its way, my recipient will neither be allowed to receive the e-mail in the first place—it comes from an unTrusted computer—nor will they be able to open the document.

The scheme is diabolically brilliant. Since Microsoft has learned that it cannot compete effectively with the Open Source movement, it has decided to change the game entirely. In one fell swoop, the Evil Empire can hope to achieve the following goals:

Lock users into a permanent upgrade cycle.

Turn the movie-music cabal from an enemy into an ally by converting software from a de facto product into a per-use license.

Slow, and perhaps reverse, the move to Open Source application software.

Eliminate future challenges to its desktop supremacy.

Sell software licenses in Asia.

Win the favor of governments everywhere.

While the first two goals are the most immediately irksome, it is this last goal which is the most troubling. Trusted Computing spells the end to all privacy in individual computing. Your ISP—which is already required to divulge all information about you when hit with a subpoena—will know exactly what you downloaded, to which machine you downloaded it, and on which machine whatever you downloaded was first produced.

Or to put it in words that hit closer to home, gentlemen, Trusted Computing spells an end to anonymous porn. Among other things.

That's why I'm not really too terribly worried about the likelihood of the TCG's nefarious plan succeeding. In one corner, we have the most powerful entertainment and technology companies in the world, in the other we have little but the male desire to look at pretty naked women. Obviously, the totalitarians don't stand a chance.

But how do we fight it? There is only one answer. Refuse to use all things Microsoft, in your work or in your home. Cleanse yourself. Purge your system. Microsoft delenda est.

How to teach your child to read

December 15, 2003

AN ESTIMATED 22 PERCENT OF AMERICANS are considered functionally illiterate. SAT scores have dropped so low that the test was rejiggered. Huge percentages of children are failing the oft-mandated reading comprehension tests despite the low scores required to pass them.

But it is no mystery to me why so many children have a difficult time learning how to read. Unlike the vast majority of Americans, I have adult experience in learning how to read using competing whole-word and phonetic systems.

Japanese features three reading systems: hiragana, katakana and kanji. Hiragana and katakana are both phonetic syllabaries, wherein each of the 46 symbols equates to one phonic. Kanji, on the other hand, is a whole-word system wherein one pictograph or combination of pictographs equals at least one word.

I mastered both kanas in about six weeks. After six months, however, I only had about 250 kanji down, less than 1 percent of the approximately 50,000 total, and not quite 8 percent of the 3,000 required to be newspaper-literate. It proved to be too arduous a task, and I finally gave up.

From this experience, I conclude there is simply no comparison—if you want to teach a child to read, you must use phonics, not whole language or sight reading or whatever they're calling it now.

Nor is it difficult to teach a child to read if you use phonics. A computer with Impress or Powerpoint is ideal, but paper flashcards will also suffice. Here's how to do it:

Create two slideshows, one consisting of the small letters of the alphabet, one in capitals. Use Times New Roman fontsize 200 to help them get used to serif characters. Run through each twice every day. Once they have mastered an alphabet, randomize the slides. Don't move onto the next step until they are reliably perfect with a random slideshow. You can begin doing this pretty much anytime after the second birthday.

Create a slideshow of base phonics, one for each letter. Add a clipart picture of an animal for each letter. Run through it twice every day, saying b—buh— bear and e—eh—elephant and having them repeat it. Once they know them all, drop the letter—just say the phonic—and also randomize it to confirm their mastery before moving on.

Create a slideshow of around 50 combination phonics. CA as in cat, DO as in dog and so on. It may take a while before the light bulb goes off on this concept, so don't be impatient. They will determine the speed of progress, not you.

Create a slideshow of simple three-letter words. C-A-T. D-O-G. At the same time, create a slideshow of all 200 English phonics and begin running through them. Be prepared for some skepticism regarding the "silent gh".

Buy Bob Books A1 and begin having the child read them to you. They start out very simple and get progressively more difficult.

This process works very well. In one year, I have seen a 3-year-old go from reading a page consisting of "Mat sat" to:

> "Thank you, Mouse," Toad gratefully said. "No problem," said Mouse, as the two went into the house. "I am always happy to help a toad across the road!"

> —Bob Books C1 "The Visit"

The entire process never takes more than 15 minutes a day, and can be used for any language. Some languages, like Italian, are even easier for the children, as there are fewer phonetic irregularities than in English. If you're interested in classics, it's very easy to teach them to read Greek at this time, since to them all the symbols are equally meaningless. They don't know that they're supposed to believe that zeta or pi is strange—although for some reason, the children I've been teaching find tremendous humor in upsilon, and the whole notion of two sigmas is downright hilarious.

Of course, you can always wait two or three years and hope your child will pick up reading through osmosis and mass whole-language drill.

There is a potential downside to teaching your child to read this way, of course. Seeing the profound intellectual development of your child in comparison with his peers may cause you to wonder if it makes any sense to place him in a classroom where everyone is several years behind him.

"The King Returns"

December 22, 2003

B OROMIR'S DESPERATE STRUGGLE to redeem himself by saving Merry and Pippin was my first exposure to *The Lord of the Rings*. I was at a Boy Scout overnight event, and it was with extreme reluctance that I returned the book to its owner when he discovered me reading his copy of *The Two Towers*, some 20 pages in.

The following morning, I pestered my mother into running out to the library and picking up the three books, which I devoured without regard for school, friends or food. That Christmas, a set of the three paperbacks plus *The Hobbit* became one of my most prized possessions. The books sparked a love of literature, particularly fantasy, which has never died and, over time, I have become a teller of such tales myself, albeit one who is not fit to sharpen J.R.R. Tolkien's pencil.

I do not like movies. They are shallow and incompetently written, for the most part, stocked with characters who feature the emotional depth and range of tinned sardines. The plots are absurd—contrived beyond all possible suspension of disbelief, and there is less fantasy in Robert Howard's entire "Conan" oeuvre than in the average action extravaganza or chick flick.

The sad state of Hollywood only highlights the mind-boggling achievement of Peter Jackson in giving visual life to the epic vision of J.R.R. Tolkien. He shames the arrogant directorial elite by his humble devotion to the written word, and in doing so has raised tenfold the standard expected when translating a book into film. Never again, one hopes, will a Paul Verhoeven or his haughty ilk be permitted to blithely urinate upon a genre classic under the aegis of directorial hubris.

The great accomplishment of Peter Jackson is to have produced a cinematic saga that features more exciting action than *Raiders of the Lost Ark*, more emotional power than *The Godfather*, and deeper insight into the nature of

Man than *One Flew Over the Cuckoo's Nest*. All of the book's great themes are present, including, most importantly, the central Christian message that lies not far beneath the surface of Tolkien's epic masterpiece.

This is true of the trinity that is the film in its entirety. As to *Return of the King*, Jackson's particular gifts serve him very well here. His taste for horror underlines the terrible nature of war, which makes the willingness of his heroes to sacrifice themselves for those whom they love all the more powerful. His humility in approaching the text is echoed by Aragorn, the true king who does not fear to kneel before the least of his subjects, in imitation of one who was not too proud to wash the feet of those who followed him.

The film is not without its flaws. For all that Theoden's restoration and victorious death were perfect, I was disappointed with the reduction of Faramir and the petty lunacy of Denethor—in the books, a truly tragic figure. And the willingness to sacrifice military verisimilitude for the sake of a single aerial shot was surprising.

Still, these are minor points. Peter Jackson has made a film for all time, but also one that is uniquely apropos today. As John Rhys-Davis, the actor who played Gimli, has said:

> *I think that Tolkien says that some generations will be challenged. And if they do not rise to meet that challenge, they will lose their civilization.*

Today, our civilization faces just such a challenge, with enemies within and without. America, the champion of the West, is challenged by the orcs of violent Islam, the would-be Sauron that is the United Nations, and its Nazgul—France, Germany, Russia and China. Nor should we forget our globalists in government, who, like Saruman, would betray everything to which they are sworn in an attempt to win the favor of the growing shadow.

We cannot all be Aragorn. But, perhaps we can each strive to be a Frodo, shouldering our lonely burden for the sake of those and that which we love. And we can hope for loyal companions such as the trusty Sam Gamgee, who will walk by our side, always ready to lift us up and carry us when we falter.

In this manner, we will persevere... until the return of the King.

Hellfire and Howard Dean

December 29, 2003

A S ALIEN AS THE CONCEPT MIGHT SEEM to the sneering editorialists of the *New York Times*, the words Christian and Democrat are not inherently antithetical. Not even in Europe, that secular socialist dystopia, so slavishly aped by the American left.

In fact, one is far more likely to see the two words joined together in the Old World than in the New. Christian Democrats are one of the major political parties in Germany, Switzerland and Sweden, although the religious reference has, unsurprisingly, been excised from the collective E.U. variant, which is now known as the European People's Party.

Based on recent comments by Howard Dean, it's pretty clear that one of the more astute members of the Dean campaign has read Rod Dreher's brilliant article in *Touchstone* magazine, titled "The Godless Party". The article is profound, explaining why Christians in general, and evangelicals in particular, have been leaving the Democratic Party in droves.

And why should they not, given how openly hostile the party of the left has become to every social issue embraced by Christians as well as the most trivial public expressions of Christianity? Were significant elements within the Democratic Party to have their way, every mention of Christmas would be banned, every Christian would be barred from public service and every homeschooler would be forcibly thrown to the lions of the public schools.

Indeed, there is no ember of faith too insignificant for a Democrat-appointed judge to stamp out, while the mere hint of sincere religion is enough for the Democratic leadership to justify barring even the most qualified judicial appointee. This is the new secular inquisition.

Howard Dean is many things—he is not a fool. He sees how the secular inquisition threatens to devour itself. It has moved too far, too fast, in a country still predominantly comprised of individuals who have a regard for the trappings of Christianity, even if they do not hold to the faith itself.

And having wrapped up the loyalties of the small, but vicious anti-Christian left, Dean knows he now must tack hard to the religious right to have any hope of winning in November. He cannot hope to win the evangelical vote, but since many are unhappy with George Bush, he may be able to persuade a few million of them to stay home. Like Jean-Francois Kerry, Dean imitates the French; la maison blanche vaut bien une messe.

Therefore, a man who raised his children to be Jewish, who does not attend church and who left his congregation over a petty triviality, now begins to speak of the power and extraordinary example of Jesus Christ. Of course, some of his first words on the subject involve giving to Caesar, which leads one to conclude that the left-liberal media, who never met a tax they didn't like, will not harp on their belief in the unsuitability of candidates who openly discuss their religious faith, as they did with George Bush four years ago.

I suspect many Christians will understandably view Dean as a shocking hypocrite, even as a wolf in sheep's clothes. They will see his talk of Jesus and Christianity to be superficial and insulting, and they will be tempted to condemn him. But they should refrain from doing so, for as the apostle Paul wrote:

> It is true that some preach Christ out of envy and rivalry, but others out of goodwill. The latter do so in love…. The former preach Christ out of selfish ambition, not sincerely⊠ots But what does it matter? The important thing is that in every way, whether from false motives or true, Christ is preached. And because of this, I rejoice.

So, I take great joy in the fact that in the Year of Our Lord 2004, even a man who bears the red standard of the American left is willing to publicly preach the gospel of Jesus Christ. But do not be confused, I do not say that evangelicals should support Howard Dean for president—the true metric of a man and his beliefs are his actions, not his words. And by these fruits, Howard Dean has rendered himself utterly unfit for office.

A mass may have won Paris for Henry of Navarre, but a hundred baptisms across the South will not be enough to save Howard Dean from the lonely hell of the defeated presidential candidate.

Haters, haters everywhere

January 5, 2004

THERE CAN BE no doubt that the Jewish people have been the most persecuted people in history. They have been used and abused by everyone from Pharaonic Egypt to modern Paris, have been slain in Slavic pogroms and in socialist programs, and been targeted by everyone from debt-ridden Christian kings ruling by divine right to atheist architects of a secular world order. It is a wonder they survive at all.

Today, as they face an implacable enemy—one that has fought four wars against Israel and slays Jews everywhere around the world—it is also a wonder to see how there are those who don't believe the Jewish people have enough enemies and seek to invent more.

For example, Joel Mowbray, a muck-raking conservative writer and Bush administration supporter who has done excellent work dissecting the State Department for its appalling bias toward Saudi Arabia after 9-11, published an article on Dec. 31 tearing into retired Gen. Anthony Zinni, USMC, for "tarnishing" his three-decade service history with "idiotic remarks" that Mowbray claims are anti-Semitic.

Discussing the Iraq war with the Washington Post *last week, former Gen. Anthony Zinni took the path chosen by so many anti-Semites: He blamed it on the Jews.*

Really? I read the article and I didn't happen to notice any such blame being assigned. That's probably because, according to Mowbray, when Zinni said neoconservative, he actually meant Jews. Mowbray says this is eerily similar to remarks made by Malaysian Prime Minister Mahathir Mohamad, who said: "—today the Jews rule the world by proxy. They get others to fight and die for them."

What did Gen. Zinni actually say? Down toward the bottom of the article, he says:

> *The more I saw, the more I thought that this was the product of the neocons who didn't understand the region and were going to create havoc there. These were dilettantes from Washington think tanks who never had an idea that worked on the ground.*
>
> *I don't know where the neocons came from—that wasn't the platform they ran on. Somehow, the neocons captured the president. They captured the vice president.... What I don't understand is that the bill of goods the neocons sold him has been proven false, yet heads haven't rolled.*

Now, the general is absolutely correct. President Bush did not run a campaign promising war on Iraq. The neoconservatives in the administration do come from Washington think-tanks. They inarguably have an influence that is disturbing to the hysterical Democratic left as well as to the conservative and libertarian right, not historically known for supporting Wilsonian-style military adventurism.

However, since Zinni himself identifies precisely zero individuals from the neocon camp, Mowbray is forced to turn to Business Week, which distinguishes between Jewish "neocons" such as Pentagon official Paul Wolfowitz and non-Jewish "key allies" such as Secretary of Defense Donald Rumsfeld, to explain Zinni's anti-Semitism. This is absurd, as there is no connection whatsoever between Zinni and Business Week. But Mowbray assures us that it's all typical, so drawing imaginary lines to slur someone's reputation is OK since everyone knows that "neocon" is a code word for Jew.

But Joel Mowbray is not the only one who can find a Jew-hater in a haystack. When Pat Robertson wrote critically of international bankers after the Mexican and Russian bailouts—which involved American taxpayers protecting giant banks from the consequences of their bad loans to the two governments—the unsuspecting public was likewise informed that "international banker" is also a codeword for Jew.

It seems that to some deluded minds, straightforward capitalism, classical conservativism and libertarianism are all anti-Semitic. Movies about the Gospel, of course, are also anti-Semitic according to the Anti-Defamation League; so is the New Testament itself. We are still somewhat in the dark as to the status of the National Football League, the Linux operating system and Winnie the Pooh, although I understand that "halfback", "grep", and "Roo" are all code words for Jew as well.

Which no doubt sheds a harsh new light on the hidden purpose behind Roo's being stranded in that tree with Tigger. Not to mention the run blitz. In any event, the Jewish people are facing enough difficulties without manufacturing imaginary ones. Anti-Semitism, or Jew-hating as it should more rightly be known, is reprehensible. But a false and unsupported accusation of it is equally unconscionable.

Maybe Bush is Hitler

January 12, 2004

I N 1934, four years before Germany annexed his native Austria in the Anschluss, the economist Ludwig von Mises left Vienna for the safety of Geneva. The great enemy of socialism—his damning critique, "Socialism", was published in 1922—had seen clearly how the winds were blowing with the rise of the National Socialists. In 1940, he emigrated to the United States, where he warned of the rise of quasi-socialist statism in his 1944 book, "Bureaucracy".

Unlike Mises, most people are taken by complete surprise when their government turns on them. This is the only explanation for how a person living in the 20th century was 4 times more likely to be killed by his own government than in war or civil war, and 17.3 times more likely to be legally killed by an employee acting on behalf of his legitimate government than to be murdered by a criminal acting on his own. But, as the example of Mises shows, such a fate is not unavoidable. The future is no mystery to those who see with the eyes of history.

In my unfinished book, "The Red Hand of Government", I have developed a theory of socialist crisis. Not all governments turn on their people in a lethal manner, but 35 percent of the 191 United Nations member states have murdered at least 10,000 of their own citizens in the last century, with an average of 122,565 victims apiece. Socialist countries are particularly prone to slaughter, as 58 percent of self-identified socialist regimes have committed democide, and these socialist mortacracies are responsible for four-fifths of the 169 million victims of government murder in the 20th century.

Although the United States does not view itself as socialist, as I have previously demonstrated, it is a semi-socialist state by most measures. Furthermore, as the paper dollar approaches its 33rd year, the risk of a breakdown into the hyperinflation that has ended all previous paper money mechanisms increases. This would not be overly worrisome, were it not for the fact that constitutional protections for Americans have been egregiously weakened under the current administration.

While taking a break from destroying the social fabric of America, the United States Supreme Court has decided that there is no First Amendment protecting political speech. It has also tacitly upheld the Ninth Circuit's decision that there is no Second Amendment guaranteeing the right to bear arms. Meanwhile, in Texas, a federal judge conducts show trials, announcing that the word of John McBryde supersedes the written law as he openly directs the verdict in what is supposedly a trial by jury.

In other words, Americans no longer have the ability to protest against their government, they can no longer expect justice in their courtrooms and they will soon lose the ability to defend themselves against their government as well.

The handwriting is on the wall. Watch Brazil as a harbinger of things to come. Only months after electing the socialist da Silva to power, Brazil has passed a law requiring the registration of all private firearms, with a complete ban to be considered next year. If the socialists manage to consolidate their hold on power, there is a probability that some level of democide will begin there within 10 years.

I am not entirely pessimistic. It is quite possible that the danger can be averted. Perhaps the paper dollar will survive another 33 years without support. Perhaps the Federal Reserve can pull another economic boom out of its hat, after all, some of the nation's finest minds are hard at work trying to keep the machinery of the global financial system working smoothly. If there is no socialist crisis, there will be no bloody democide, merely more of the quiet drift toward total state control that we have enjoyed for the last century.

President Bush is not responsible for all of this. Indeed, it is ironic that he is attacked as a Hitler by those who advocate policies almost identical to those of the historical National Socialists. Unfortunately, George Bush has not only done nothing to reduce the danger from future Hitlers, on his watch he has allowed the danger from the enemy within to grow unchecked.

George Bush is no Hitler. But if he does not respond as vigorously to the threats posed from within the United States as he has to those without, he may prove to be Paul von Hindenburg.

Wesley Clark and the curse of intelligence

January 19, 2004

MIKE MARTZ, the head coach of the St. Louis Rams, is widely considered to be one of the smartest men in the National Football League. He is the architect of The Greatest Show on Turf—an explosive offense that set numerous records for offensive production—and the word "genius" frequently appears in the same sentence with his name.

His team, however, has again fallen short of its Super Bowl expectations, mostly because the brilliant coach made a boneheaded decision that shocked even beer-befuddled couch potatoes across the country, only the latest in a series of inexplicably bad decisions that have cost the Rams dearly over the last three years.

John Madden, on the other hand, is hardly known for his acumen. His butcheries of the English language are legendary—"few yards are better than none yards"—but he has the diamond-encrusted ring that has so far eluded Mike Martz. And few would argue that Madden's Raiders had more talent than Martz's Rams. So, how is this possible?

The truth is intelligence is not synonymous with success. A certain amount can be very helpful, to be sure, but beyond a certain point, the ability to see diverse possibilities starts to become a hindrance. It is much easier to weigh the odds of three or four options than it is to balance 10 or 12, and it takes less time, too. As data gathering and processing capability increases, the ability to focus and ignore unwanted information becomes increasingly important. Otherwise, there is a tendency to become either paralyzed with doubt or divorced from reality as one gets lost in elaborate probability models.

George Bush is cut from the John Madden mold. He is not a stupid man—his estimated 125 IQ puts him well above the norm—but he is by no means brilliant. Like JFK, who is known to have had an IQ of 119, he has an ability to focus on the actual situation at hand, even if he does not have a gift for beautifully articulating it.

Smart politicians such as Bill Clinton, Al Gore and Richard Nixon, whose IQs come in at 137, 140 and 143, respectively, have for the most part been failures at the highest level. Their ability to incorporate information also gives them a strong tendency to micromanage, which is a disastrous characteristic for any executive. Note that Jimmy Carter, an unsuccessful president by any standard, was the most intelligent president of the modern era.

There is another danger, too, for the intelligent presidential candidate. To the average man, one of the great mysteries of life is how brilliant academics can be so reliably stupid. This is because there appears to be a strong correlation between one's level of intelligence and the importance one places on the abstract as opposed to quotidian reality. Thus, a brilliant Marxian economist can dismiss a century of total socialist failure with a wave of the hand, because none of the historical real-world applications precisely matches the theoretical vision in his head.

Both leading Democratic candidates appear to be highly intelligent men. Howard Dean is a doctor; Wesley Clark is a Rhodes Scholar. But it is becoming increasingly apparent that both men are more wedded to their abstract internal visions of the world than how it actually operates according to objective reality. This is how Gen. Clark can make bizarre statements about a European right of first refusal on American national security and Howard Dean can believe that raising taxes is good for the economy despite two millennia of evidence to the contrary.

Neither man makes any sense to the logical observer, but that is unimportant. It makes sense in some ideal place in their heads, and for such men, that is all that matters.

Based on the two men's comments over the last few months, I am quite sure that Wesley Clark is the most intelligent of the candidates for the Democratic Party nomination. He has said almost nothing capable of withstanding even the most cursory analysis, and his globalist view of the world appears to have more in common with Star Trek than with what history suggests is a Hobbesian free-for-all of ambitious, power-hungry men wrestling for wealth and influence. More than most, Gen. Clark appears to suffer from the curse of intelligence. America would do well to avoid him.

George Delano Bush

January 26, 2004

G EORGE BUSH met with some skeptical listeners in his recent State of the Union address, but he truly convinced me of something. He convinced me that the Republican Party, as the party of small government, is dead. Oh, I understand very well that in terms of electoral votes, the Republicans have seldom had a future that looked more immediately promising, but the party is nevertheless a soulless zombie of an institution.

Or rather, make that a vampire. For the Bush administration is sucking the lifeblood out of the United States with every raising of the federal debt roof, with every new federal entitlement, with every new Clintonian promise to end someone's pain somewhere, somehow. Consider the following federal spending increases:

- Education, 60.8%

- Labor, 56%

- Interior, 23.4%

- Defense, 27.6%

This is not even Clinton-lite, this is simply armed left-liberalism. Note that the increase in domestic departments dwarfs the increase in defense spending during a time of war. This is astounding!

Now, the president's defenders argue that President Bush has no choice, that the exigencies of the War on Terror require that he accommodate his Democratic opposition in order to free his hand for his duties as commander-in-chief. But this is precisely backward! Wars do not prevent chief executives from driving the domestic agenda—in fact, history supports the opposite premise.

Did FDR refrain from his radical program of nationalization once the Japanese bombed Pearl Harbor in order to accommodate his conservative opposition? On the contrary, he put the pedal to the metal and increased government spending to the greatest share of the economy it has yet known. From this, I conclude that President Bush is doing exactly what he intended from the start, but he is using the war as an excuse to placate his hoodwinked conservative allies instead of using it as a political weapon to bludgeon his enemies on the radical left.

But if the Republican Party is dead, where can those who believe in republicanism, small government, individual freedom and the Constitution go? Right now, there are two places: the Libertarian Party and the Constitution Party. Either, in my opinion, are vastly preferable to the empty charade of the GOP.

Ultimately, both parties must eventually merge into one Freedom Party, which will certainly require some level of initially uneasy assimilation. Some libertarians will need to accept that abortion is a violation of the unborn child's unalienable right to life, while conservatives will need to recognize that drugs are not an appropriate target of federal warfare. Christians will have to understand that using the state to enforce traditional morality will always backfire in the end, and everyone will have to wake up to the fact that government largesse is nothing more than poisoned bait.

George Bush has not destroyed the Republican Party by himself, he is merely the culmination of 24 years of false promises. Actions speak much louder than words, though, and his resemble none of his predecessors so much as Franklin Delano Roosevelt, expanding central government and eradicating individual liberties during a time of war. He could have been George Jefferson Bush, or even George Reagan Bush, instead, he chose to become George Delano.

As the November elections approach, there are those who will say that one must simply accept the inevitable and vote for the lesser of two evils. To them, I will only say that regardless of whether it is big or small, supporting evil is anathema to any man who seeks the good, the right and the true. Three political generations of Republican promises of future virtue to follow the whoring of Republican principles should be enough for any honest conservative to abjure the party once and for all. I did so 12 years ago—I have never regretted it for a moment.

It is painful to admit that one has been betrayed. It is even more painful to see the rock roll down the hill, and know that one must begin pushing it back up again. But every journey begins with a first step, and sometimes wisdom requires embracing what the world believes to be folly.

A legacy of betrayal

February 2, 2004

I DON'T KNOW if it was finally being off the drugs that did the trick, but it's nice to see Rush Limbaugh has woken up to the fact that it doesn't really matter if you call yourself a conservative—compassionate, neo or paleo—if you embrace a progressive vision that revolves around the notion of giving ever more power to the federal government, you are a de facto left-liberal.

A new and metastasizing federal drug entitlement wasn't enough to convince Rush of this—neither was allowing a Republican Congress to go hog-wild with the national credit card. Blatantly ignoring the Constitution he was sworn to uphold as commander in chief didn't do it, nor did the de facto amnesty proposal, the proposed Mars boondoggle or having sex with an intern in the Oval Office. No, wait, that last one was Clinton, wasn't it. I'm having a tough time telling the difference.

But amped-up spending on the National Endowment for the Arts appears to have at last caused the scales to fall from Rush's eyes. Apparently, the notion of another chocolate-smeared lesbian, urine-soaked crucifix or embedded bullwhip being fraudulently passed off as art on the taxpayer's dime was finally too much Jonah for the Republican Party's great white whale to swallow.

Mr. Limbaugh wrote:

Well, they're getting it done, all right. They're sticking a fork right into America's back.

I am no political strategist, and my daily audience is less than one-one hundredth the size of Mr. Limbaugh's. But I could have told Rush that the Republican Party had absolutely no intention of effecting any change in the long-term direction of the nation back when I left the party—disenchanted—in 1992.

Unlike most people my age, I had the chance to see the sausage-making up close and personal. Through family connections, I knew a few party players, though no one terribly major—they were mostly at the level of the third circle. But at one national convention, I got to know the Houston coterie much better than I would ever have expected through a girl I was dating at the time. It is very surreal experience to find yourself at a party with 30 people when two of them are Donald Trump and Henry Kissinger.

Even at the time, it was very obvious to me that these were not people who were interested in ideas or ethereal, abstract notions of human liberty. The language of small government and freedom was not an article of faith for them, but rather, a rhetorical device with which the power they craved could be wrested from the powers-that-were in the Democratic Party.

Like the vast majority of Republican politicians who have scrabbled their way to the top of the heap, George Delano Bush has a far greater commitment to his immediate power base—those who raised him to significance—than to the conservative voters who subsequently elected him. Unlike Ronald Reagan, who for all his amiable public persona was a private intellectual, George Delano has no strong ideological principles to counterbalance the massive political pressures on him.

Last week on Vox Popoli, I lampooned a cynical George Delano, who amuses himself by yanking the chain of conservative columnists and making bets with Karl Rove on their reactions. Although the poodle-like, tail-wagging reactions of some conservatives to even the president's most outrageous actions have surpassed my most skeptical expectations, it's a relief to see that Mr. Limbaugh has seen fit to declare that far too much is, at last, enough.

Power is useless—totally useless—if it is not wielded justly in the cause of the right and the true. Pragmatism in politics is nothing more than a means of cutting your own throat in the slowest and most excruciating manner. Do not listen to these assassins of principle when they tell you that a vote for a third party is a vote for a Democrat.

If the last three decades are any guide, it is a vote for a Republican that is a vote for a Democrat, and a vote against the Constitution of the United States of America at that.

Why men don't respect women

February 9, 2004

THERE IS A RATHER INFAMOUS blog on Salon with the arresting name, "Why Your Wife Won't Have Sex With You". The author, an intelligent woman and self-described formerly frigid wife, provides a long laundry list of explanations for this unhappy state of affairs. She has entire sections devoted to: Disgust, Discomfort, Distraction, Insecurity, Anger, Fat, Misunderstanding, Boredom, Infidelity, Technique, Motherhood, Aging and Depression, Bad Company (as in toxic friends), Religion and Childhood Abuse.

Indeed, one wonders that women have sex at all after plodding one's way through this morass of marital misery.

Now, Ms. Deckham Grey, the author, is no man-hater—the Tiger Beat pictures of Wesley Clark alone would disprove that—and perusing her material makes it clear that she's fairly reasonable. But something about her blog reminded me of an e-mail I once received from a single male reader in response to one of my own more infamous columns, entitled "Spiting Their Pretty Faces". This reader belonged to a church singles group, and after hearing an encyclopedic list of the ways in which modern men fail to live up to women's expectations of their responsibilities, he said: "OK, that's what men should do. Thanks. Now, what is a woman's responsibility in a marriage?"

Total silence.

In the movie, "As Good As It Gets", Jack Nicholson's character, a romance novelist, is asked how he is able to write such effective and believable women. He responds: "I think of a man, and then I take away reason and account-ability."

Why is it that three disparate sources should all echo this same theme? Is it nothing more than a coincidental combination of overly demanding spouses, toxic spinsters-to-be and overactive Hollywood imaginations? Or is it possible that there is a fundamental difference between men and women when it comes to the notion of personal responsibility? And if so, could it be this, and not some outdated notion of physical prowess that accounts for what both men and women perceive as a lack of respect for women?

I suggest that this may well be the case. A weightlifter will certainly scorn a spindly-armed accountant's inability to lift more than a pencil, but he is unlikely to carry that same lack of respect over to matters outside the weight room. And yet, even the most ardently sensitive New Age male, awash in feminist propaganda from kindergarten through university, usually finds it difficult to show even the most accomplished women the respect that they deserve.

Let me state that I don't know why this is, I only suggest that it appears to be the case. Perhaps men are irredeemably sexist—although I fail to see how the husband-as-child motif so popular in soccer-mom circles is any less so. Perhaps women have been spoiled by a lifetime of freely saying things to others that would have earned a man doing the same a black eye. Perhaps it is the coddling of parents and teachers, which has led to things like female recruits in boot camp being permitted to turn in blue cards to their sergeants on days that they can't deal with being yelled at.

It is strange, too, because women are by no means the second sex. As Camille Paglia conclusively demonstrates, women are without question the dominant sex in our society. No one who has ever seen the desperate attention-seeking of teenage boys or intricately-shaped lavender soap in the private bathroom of a rich and powerful CEO can doubt it. It is usually not much more than a decade, somewhere in the years from 15 to 30, that a man is not under the strong influence of a woman.

There is a saying, that a woman is, and a man must become. Perhaps it is this need on the part of males to become, this sense of a battle fought and won, that separates the sexes more than any other.

Or perhaps it is that women simply do not understand that male respect is never given freely, it must always be earned. And the only way it is earned is by taking complete responsibility for one's words, one's actions and one's decisions. Avoiding responsibility for these things may be a successful strategy in the short term, but it will inevitably cause most men to regard you as a lightweight, little more than a child, whose opinions can be safely ignored at will.

God and Man in the NFL

February 16, 2004

W E'VE ALL HEARD IT and winced at it before. The quarterback has just thrown for 300 yards and three touchdowns against the most ferocious defense in the league in leading his team to victory. No sooner does the ubiquitous sideline reporter stick the microphone into his face and begin asking a stunningly trite question when the quarterback segues into a mini-testimony of his religious faith.

First, Ahmad, I've got to thank my Lord and Savior Jesus Christ...

There's also a myriad of lesser forms of this behavior. The receivers who kneel in momentary prayer after catching a ball in the end zone, the defensive backs who pound their hearts and point to the sky after bringing one back the other way. This more subtle form of acknowledgement of the Divine doesn't seem to offend people as greatly, but many still find it distasteful.

Why is that?

A number of *ESPN* writers recently had a discussion of both the phenomenon and their feelings about it, and it was interesting to see that most of them, on both sides of the issue, missed the point entirely. While there may be some players who seriously believe God has chosen the victors in advance—indeed, how can the Almighty not have chosen a side if he is the omniscient control freak that many Christians believe him to be—I've heard this example brought up and denigrated by more critics than I've ever heard in more than two decades of copious football watching.

I've certainly never heard a reporter ask a player to clarify whether he is thanking God specifically for the victory, or for creating life, the universe and everything.

*Through him all things were made; without him nothing was made that has
been made.*

—John 1:3

Indeed, the only time one sees an interview ended more abruptly is when
John Francois Kerry is asked how far he has gone in imitating the philander-
ing behavior of the man whose initials he happens to share.

Some of the *ESPN* writers defended the overtly religious on the grounds
of advertising. After all, sports is used to advertise everything from Sharpie
pens to beer, so why should the players not use it as a platform to advertise
their faith? This point was grudgingly accepted, although not without some
grumbling about how reducing the glorious ineffable to the level of the Coors
Twins is not really appropriate. Of course, there were plenty of those who
looked askance upon Jesus Christ's willingness to associate with the harlots
of his day too.

The essential point, in my estimation, is to recall we live in a society that
glorifies and worships the famous. Not for nothing do we call them idols.
While there are those who slaver to bathe in the esteem of others, there are
many who do not—especially those who have been taught that all praise and
glory and blessing and honor belong to the Lamb of God alone.

I do not see that these various gestures are designed to draw attention—
how could they be when the eyes of the crowd are already focused upon the
player? They are, instead, sincere efforts—however clumsy—to deflect glory
to where it is more rightly due. Of what importance is a touchdown, even one
upon which an entire season hangs, in comparison with the fate of mankind?
Nor is it necessary to share these beliefs in order to respect the honest and
humble intentions of those who demonstrate them so publicly.

It is hardly reasonable to expect those who worship God to accept pagan-
style idolatry directed at them with equanimity. The apostle Paul, facing the
same situation, tore his robes with horror.

Are these athletes hypocrites? Of course they are, for we are all hypocrites.
There is only one kind of man who is entirely successful in living up to his
standards and that is the man who entirely lacks them.

But if Janet Jackson can bare her breast to sell her music, I do not see why anyone should have a problem with those who merely bare their hearts to share what they believe to be the truth.

Bring them home

February 23, 2004

I AM, AND ALWAYS HAVE BEEN, a supporter of the U.S. military. I have had friends and family in every branch of the military, at all ranks and rates from seaman recruit to five-star general. Two of my proudest possessions are two Purple Hearts, one belonging to my grandfather, the other belonging to my uncle, both Marines. I am, and always will be, a cheerleader for the United States Marine Corps.

I state this only so that you will understand that I do not say this lightly: The policy of Pax Americana enforced by our troops stationed around the world is not only a failure, it is leading to the corruption of the American military.

There is no question there are various countries and non-governmental organizations at war with America. Official voices of Iran, al-Qaida, the Palestinian Authority, Hezbollah and Saudi Arabia have all declared themselves to be at war with the United States. Much to the shame of the Bush administration, these declarations have been brushed aside as mere diplomatic noise even as American soldiers, officials and civilians are killed.

I was willing to support an open and declared war on Iraq and other self-declared enemies of America as a means of ending this clash of civilizations that began in the 1970s—or 1950s if you view the post-independence violence that took place in India as the rebirth of jihad. War is the health of the state, true, but unlike the tango, it does not require two. However, it has become clear that the neoconservative utopians in the administration do not see this undeclared and unconstitutional war as a reactive strike in self-defense, but more as a means of reshaping the global order. I expect this attempt to work about as well as Woodrow Wilson's did in 1918.

It is not only the inevitable failure of this vision that concerns me. A military machine is a delicate creature, designed to do one thing very well—

destroy the opposition. It is a well-known fact of military history that fighting troops and garrison troops are two very different things, and attempting to turn the former into the latter significantly impedes their ability to perform their primary mission.

Consider that the U.S. military accomplished its mission in Iraq—taking Baghdad and destroying the Hussein regime—with the loss of 106 soldiers in battle and accidents. Since then, the occupation has cost another 437 American lives lost to combat, accidents and suicide. Consider also that the wars for Kuwait and Afghanistan cost 247 and 76 combat deaths, respectively.

The beheading of the Hussein regime sent a powerful message to America's enemies. The subsequent elimination of the Saudi and Iranian regimes would have cost fewer American lives and been an even more powerful demonstration of American might, perhaps strong enough to bring a generation of peace. But instead, America has chosen to play Israel's futile game of one step forward, one step back, allowing its enemies to regroup in safe havens, then come back and attack troops who are pinned down like sitting ducks on orders from above. This is an old game, dating back to the Korean police action, and it has never played out well, demonstrated most clearly by the continuing threat posed by North Korea.

And the notion of bringing democratic republicanism to an Islamic tribal culture is ludicrous, particularly as our constitutional rights and liberties are being simultaneously eroded at home. Congress and the Supreme Court are far more dangerous to America than al-Qaida could ever be.

Stationing troops in 144 of the 191 U.N. member states around the world has not brought peace. History proves that no utopian vision, however sweeping, will ever bring a permanent peace. Let us then abandon visions of a global Pax Americana, bring our soldiers home, and only send them forth when war is necessary and declared. And when the war is won and the enemy is destroyed, bring the troops home again immediately. They deserve no less.

Bring them home from Germany, from South Korea and Italy. Bring them home from Kosovo, from Afghanistan and Kuwait, from Turkey, Spain, Iceland and Belgium. Bring them home from Panama, Portugal and Japan. Most of all, bring them home from Iraq. Now.

Our matchless soldiers have won the war—they cannot win the peace.

Divorcing the State

March 1, 2004

I T WAS NOT UNTIL relatively recently, in historical terms, that marriage was considered the legitimate business of state government, still less the federal government. Prior to 1987, in Turner v. Safley, when the Supreme Court described marriage as "a relationship that can receive tangible benefits including government benefits and property rights," there was still some lingering question of the federal government's power to intervene with the formerly sovereign states of the Union in defining the concept.

The involvement of government in the form of the state in concerning itself with marriage is also relatively new. Virginia's first legal code consisted of the Lawes Divine, Morall and Martiall, enacted in 1610 by Sir Thomas Dale. In this code, Virginia's Christian ministers were required to record all christenings, marriages and burials they performed. Not until 1631 did the House of Burgesses create marriage licenses.

But these licenses were not required for marriage, and not until 1853 was the Virginia licensing procedure taken away from the churches and given to the county and independent city clerks. Other states made marriage licenses mandatory sooner—in Indiana, for example, county marriage licenses were became necessary in 1800 although the state government did not become directly involved until 1958.

As is almost always the case with everything upon which government lays its venomous hands, it did not take long for the lethal effects of the transformation from a religious sacrament to a government contract to appear. Divorces per 10,000 population rose from .38 in 1900 to 2.4 in 1960, then peaked at 5.3 by 1981.

Divorce rates have fallen slightly since then, to around 4.9 per 10,000, but this is mostly due to the decision of young men and women to delay marriage if not avoid it altogether.

There is a significant difference between marriage—the religious commitment between a man and one or more women—as it has been known in every historical society for at least 6,000 years, and the modern concept of state-granted civil marriage. Self-styled conservative "defenders of marriage" justify their support for state involvement, mostly in the form of tax breaks and social security benefits, in much the same way that left-liberal justify everything—it's all for the children.

As usual, however, this mistaken notion has worked out about as well as every other government intrusion into the economy and culture. The number of children being produced in the United States has dropped to its lowest level since 1909, when birthrate figures were first calculated. The number of children living with two parents is also at an all-time low, while 33.8 percent of all children are now born to unmarried mothers. So, by every metric, the idea that government can support or defend marriage is a complete failure.

And now, of course, governments from coast to coast have begun to define the concept so widely as to eliminate it altogether. However, cultural conservatives should not dread this—nor do I think they should attempt to circle the wagons in one last attempt to thwart the lavender tide by passing yet another amendment that the corrupt courts will confound with a disingenuous circumvention of logic, reason and reading comprehension.

Instead, if they are truly interested in restoring marriage and the family to their proper places as the twin bulwarks of civilized society, they must leap at the opportunity to remove the state, at all levels, from the process entirely. Marriage is a sacred trinity of a man and a woman before God, there is neither room nor reason for a fourth party to enter into the relationship, still less one that corrupts and destroys the tripartite relationship.

Marriage survived for 6,000 years without government, in less than 1 percent of that time, the government has nearly managed to destroy it in this country. There is nothing to fear from removing government from the equation—indeed, doing so will only strengthen true Christian marriage.

As for the other, non-sacramental commitments that may be announced, what of them? With or without a government document, they cannot and will not be married, exactly as they weren't before government became involved in the process. And it is only through the illegitimate power of government to counterfeit a redefinition of the concept that these anti-traditionalists have a hope of creating these charades in the first place!

The State and Marriage is a joining made in Hell, conducted by the Devil. This is one divorce that conservatives should embrace with all alacrity and enthusiasm.

The Axis of Liberal

March 8, 2004

D EMOCRATS ARE MASTERS OF AVOIDANCE. Ever since Walter Mondale was massacred by Ronald Reagan, thanks to his foolish truthfulness in telling the nation exactly what he planned to do to it, Democrats have attempted to obscure who they are, what they stand for and what they hope to do to the country.

Even the dictionary is evasive. Compare these two definitions of liberalism, the former referring to the word in its proper, classical sense, the latter being the Mondale-Dukakis-Kennedy-Kerry axis-of-liberal meaning of the word:

1. *an economic theory advocating free competition and a self-regulating market and the gold standard.*

2. *a political orientation favoring progress and reform.*

The question inherent in liberalism is thus: Progress toward what? A little research into Democratic speeches, legislative initiatives and party platforms provides the answer. Progress toward total government control, where private-property rights have been abolished and every possible threat to the State's complete hegemony has been crushed into dust.

Not that the Democrat's new standard bearer will admit this, although it is the logical and etymological foundation of his progressive philosophy—as well as the predictable conclusion of his specific policy positions and voting record—taken in the collective.

American liberalism has transformed itself into the L-word, a curse to be avoided even by some of its foremost champions, such as John Kerry and Nancy Pelosi. But the poison is not in the word, the poison is in the meaning that lurks behind the word. In modern America, liberal is progressive is globalist is socialist.

They all represent precisely the same freedom-hating concept, constructed on the notion that all rights spring from government, that the government's primary roles include: a) providing for the needs of its people, b) serving as a referee between competing group interests, c) acting as God, High Priest and Supreme Judge in bringing cosmic justice to society, and that all property belongs collectively to society through the agency of the government.

In a recent discussion on my blog, Vox Popoli, a self-described liberal declared that the notion of taxation being theft was only a metaphor, because under the social contract, taxation is nothing more than the price of belonging to society. Even if we ignore the most obvious flaw—it is actually the social contract which is the metaphor, as neither you nor I have ever signed any such document—the argument rests upon the proposition that it is not only the property being taken, but also the individual member of society being taxed, that is the property of the State.

Now consider the words of the French intellectual who popularized the concept of the social contract, Jean Jacques Rousseau:

> [E]very malefactor, by attacking social rights, becomes on forfeit a rebel and a traitor to his country; by violating its laws he ceases to be a member of it; he even makes war upon it. In such a case the preservation of the State is inconsistent with his own, and one or the other must perish; in putting the guilty to death, we slay not so much the citizen as an enemy.

Seen in this red light, we are all criminals, who insist that individual rights are unalienable. Death of freedom or death of the State is the progressive metric—this is why those who advocate social progress ineluctably find themselves slaughtering large numbers of individuals when they obtain the reins of absolute power. John Kerry doesn't want you to know that he's a liberal because he'd just as soon not have you realize his political philosophy is a red-handed death cult such as to put Jim Jones and David Koresh to shame.

Is there any wonder he wants to take your guns away? The butcher seldom sees much interest in allowing the herd to be armed.

So, call it progress or call it liberalism. By any name, the Axis of Liberal stinks of the gulag, the guillotine, the gas chamber and the grave. It is nothing more than latter-day socialism, dumbed-down to the point that it is too stupid to recognize itself in the mirror.

Deadly echoes of antiquity

March 15, 2004

T HE SPANISH AUTHORITIES are not the only ones hoping the 10 bombs that killed an estimated 192 people in Madrid on Thursday were set by ETA, the Basque terrorist group. They were quick to point the finger at ETA—not only because hardline elements within the Spanish government wish to step up their long-running war against the separatists, but because the alternative is too terrible to consider.

But a statement released by the Brigade of Abu Hafs al-Masri claimed that its death squads had penetrated "one of the pillars of the crusade alliance, Spain." It went on to state:

> *This is part of settling old accounts with Spain, the crusader, and America's ally in its war against Islam.*

The bombings sound a truly ominous note for Europe, which had hoped that with its Muslim-friendly immigration policies, it would escape the wrath of the reawakening jihad movement that had slumbered for almost 1,300 years following the conquest of the Iberian peninsula in 718. While Americans, whose tenuous grasp of history begins more than a thousand years later, have a tendency to assume that the Crusades were fought entirely in the Middle East, both Europeans and Arabs know very well that the Reconquista, too, was a crusade of sorts.

The Reconquista ended in 1492 when Isabel of Castile and Fernando II of Aragon, the married Catholic monarchs of united Spain, expelled Boabdil of Granada, the last of the Moorish rulers, from the newly formed country. This is the most egregious of the old accounts to which the Brigade refers, and the cause of many a furrowed brow across Europe today.

For like the Reconquista, most of the Crusades were a reactive martial effort against the dynamic and fast-growing empire of "the Turk". There are few medieval documents which do not refer, in one way or another, to the ever-present danger posed to Christendom from Poland to Sicily by the expansionist imperial armies. As for the Holy Land itself, it was first taken from the Byzantine Empire in 637—the crusaders reclaimed it from the Seljuk Turks in 1099, only 24 years after the Seljuks themselves had seized it from their fellow Muslims in 1075.

Moving forward in time, the last 30 years have seen a peaceful movement of peoples from Arab nations to European lands, one that has worked out remarkably well for both parties… until recently. But the realization of shifting demographics combined with the stark division between the half-hearted support of European governments and the vehement opposition of European Muslims for the U.S. wars against Afghanistan and Iraq has divided Europe in two.

If these Madrid bombs do, indeed, represent the first strike of violent Islamic forces against their European hosts, then the world has reached a new and ugly stage in what some have predicted as an inevitable clash of civilizations.

The European mood, for all of France and Germany's well-known recalcitrance on Iraq, had already begun to shift. The List Pim Fortuyn, a Dutch party founded by a left-wing homosexual, swept into power not long after the assassination of its eponymous founder largely on the strength of advocating immigration restraints far harsher than the most anti-immigration Republican could imagine. And even before the bombings, the electoral success of the List was likely to be soon replicated by parties in other European countries, especially Germany, France and Denmark.

A country surely has the right to decide who is permitted to immigrate and become a citizen of that country—that is not the issue. The question of the day is what is likely to happen as the peaceful detente between aging European nations and their Gastarbeiten begins to break down on the treacherous fault line of religion. Europe has never been kind to those its rulers view as troublemakers.

So, while there is still hope that this is nothing more than a peculiarly Spanish affair, I am not so optimistic. We will have the answer soon enough. If the horror of Madrid is followed by similar scenes in Berlin, Paris, Oslo or Rome, it will be difficult to place the blame at the bloody feet of the Basque terrorists.

For almost three years, George Bush has been insisting he is not fighting a Crusade. The bombs of Madrid and the rulers of Europe may soon force him to rethink that insistence.

The yellow bus

March 22, 2004

IT WAS a fine September day,
   When my sweet poppet came to say,
   Oh Daddy, could we please discuss
The purpose of that yellow bus?
I see the children get on board
While our house is always ignored.
It looks like fun, it looks so cool,
To ride upon it off to school!

Her little face was serious,
And naturally curious
About this strange phenomenon
Her friends had all departed on.
With some misgiving then I knew
An explanation now was due.
I placed a hand under my chin
And wondered how I should begin.

Then I remembered my school days
Now dim in memory's fading haze
The good times, and the bad times too,
When everything was bright and new.
And yet my main recollection
Was a sense of disaffection.
Endless boredom, a parody
Of learning, farce and tragedy!

Do you know what they'll learn today?
She shook her head without delay.
They first will learn the alphabet…
But Daddy, don't they know it yet?
She interrupted in surprise,
Amazement in those big brown eyes.
Ten letters is the minimum,
I said, that's where they're starting from.

She blinked and looked somewhat perturbed.
So, what would I do, next I heard.
I know my letters, phonics too,
Today I read a book—no, two!
And yet, they're gone for the whole day
Do they do nothing there but play?
That sounds so fun, can I go there?
I think that would be only fair!

They do play, my lovely flower,
But for just one single hour.
Then all the rest they sit in class
And wait as the long hours pass.
For no child can hope to move on
'til all is learned by everyone.
But Daddy, that's ridiculous.
Surely, it could never be thus!

It's worse than that, (I thought it through),
As they teach things that are not true.
They will not let you learn of God
And instill logic badly flawed.
It's not so much education
As naked indoctrination.
For little is more blindly cruel
Than sentencing a child to school.

Of course, these thoughts I did not share
As she stood innocently there
Their parents love your friends, I'm sure
But Mommy and I love you more.
These next years will suffice to show
How freedom helps a mind to grow,
And you, my dear, will always be
A child of God and liberty.

Did she fathom?
I cannot say.
She'll tell me so
One day, I pray.

How to argue like a liberal

March 29, 2004

IT IS INARGUABLE that liberals—in the modern American sense of the word—are the most flawless human beings on the planet. They are smarter, better-educated, wealthier, kinder and morally superior to those benighted quasi-Neanderthals called conservatives, who would like nothing better than to drag society back to the Middle Ages, or, according to some high-minded liberal theorists, the Iron Age.

How do we know this? Why, liberals tell us so!

Perhaps it has escaped me, but I have not personally witnessed any call for a return to the monarchy, much less land grants held in fief, on the part of even the most conservative Republican. And the last time I looked, the Bush administration was very much in favor of steel—certainly the U.S. steel industry appears to be most appreciative of his efforts in enacting a 30 percent tariff on their behalf.

But being a liberal means never having to worry about the facts. Facts can be uncomfortable, and of course, anything that makes anyone uncomfortable is a violation of our constitutional rights. The only fact that matters is the foundational fact that you can only feel what is right, so if a fact happens to contradict your feelings, obviously that fact must be wrong. Sentio, ergo rectum.

Due to this inescapable and irrefutable logic, I have finally been convinced that I will be healthier, happier and wealthier if I join the large-brained ranks of the morally superior elite. I have therefore decided to become a liberal. Already I have benefited greatly from my decision—whereas many previous discussions ended in a frustrating impasse, now, being inestimably more clever and better-looking than before, I am able to win any argument with the greatest of ease. Let me share with you the secret of my success.

1. Make an untrue statement, preferably on the subject of something about which you know nothing.

2. Express astonishment that your source could possibly be inaccurate.

3. Demand what motivation your source would have to lie.

4. Assert that the other party's inability to articulate this motivation is tantamount to proof that your source is not lying.

5. Question the motivation of the contrary source.

6. Argue that all sources are equal and that therefore the contrary source is irrelevant.

7. Change the subject.

Alternatively…

1. Make an untrue statement.

2. Deny that you said what you said.

3. Deny that the other party understood what you said.

4. Deny that the words you used mean what the other party claims they mean.

5. Redefine your definition and hope the other person forgets the previous one. Repeat as needed.

6. Assert that since definitions are irrelevant and subjective, the other person is mean-spirited, racist, sexist, intolerant and obsessive.

7. Change the subject.

Remember: As long as you haven't admitted you're wrong, you are right. Any attempt to demonstrate otherwise is evidence of criminal hate and probably mental imbalance, too. Never forget that an answer to a question you have asked should always be regarded as a personal attack if the answer is something you don't like, and that the answer to all evils personal, spiritual, moral and societal is more government money.

Now, if you don't mind, I should probably go exercise my newfound moral superiority. The world won't save itself, after all—not without the fount of all that is good and wise and smart and cute, which is to say, me.

Ominous lies

April 5, 2004

ARK TWAIN'S FAMOUS STATEMENT about lies and damned lies was a condemnation of how a dishonest man can take a statistic and interpret it in a manner that serves his purpose. But what does one call a statistic that, by its own lights, is openly and verifiably inaccurate? This is particularly troublesome because it is these very statistics on which the managers of the American economy base their Olympian decisions.

The Keynesian theory of economics is the prime justification for federal control of the economy. (Yes, I said control.) It dictates the use of monetary and fiscal policy to artificially expand the economy in bad times and, in theory, keep it from getting out of control in good times. Even Keynes admitted that, in the long run, this wasn't going to work, but the excuse his theory provided the politicians to do what they love best—spend taxpayer money—was simply too useful to ignore.

Of course, since Keynesian theory has dominated the American economy for almost 60 years now, one begins to wonder just when this long run, in which we are all dead, can be expected to kick in.

The Austrian theory of economics, championed here in the United States by the Mises Institute, teaches to the contrary that macroeconomics statistics are largely fiction and that the chairman of the Federal Reserve can no more control the economy than he can command the weather. This is not to say he cannot stand on top of Wall Street with a garden hose and convince derivative-sotted traders that it is raining, (and fractional-reserve banking is one Godzilla of a hose), but he has no more control than a tick riding the back of a dog.

Which theory is correct? The Keynesians are back in boom mode as, by their metrics, the economy is growing at a solid 4.1 percent rate with mild

1.2 percent inflation. According to them, these are, if not the best of times, pretty doggone good times about which you'd have to be a fool to complain.

Call me a fool, then. Let's look at one example, courtesy of the raving genius that is Mogambo. The U.S. Treasury announced it purchased $64 billion in debt last month. Annualized, that is $768 billion, which amounts to 7.3 percent of the $10.5 trillion American economy. And yet the projected deficit for 2004 is only $478 billion, or 4.6 percent of the economy. Which number would you guess is cited by the economists and used to make political decisions?

So, if a dollar is borrowed to buy something off-budget, is any money actually spent?

It gets much worse than that, of course. Adam Hamilton has calculated that according to the historical link between commodity prices and the 10-year Treasury bond, which has a long-term correlation of more than 90 percent, interest rates should be over 10 percent already. Yet the Fed, in its desperate attempt to keep a monetary finger in the dyke, has kept rates so low that the 10-year is trading below four. And anyone who has pumped gas recently does not need to understand the arcane mechanics of hedonic adjustment, substitution and rental equivalence to be suspicious of the CPI as a measure of inflation.

What do the Austrians have to say about all this chicanery? First, that it is inevitable. Those with an interest to concealing the precariousness of the situation and the power to do so will always take every opportunity to hide their failures. As surely as bust follows boom, every artificial stimulus designed to put off judgment day will only worsen the reckoning when it finally arrives.

When will that day come? I can no more predict it than I can foresee the date of the Second Coming. But in both cases, the wise can see the signs. Nine months ago, I was totally wrong about the immediate need to exit the stock market, although my advice to go into metals at the time was impeccably sound. (Gold is up 18 percent and silver an incredible 72 percent since then). And a suspicious mind, seeing that 10 percent of the Dow stocks have just been swapped out for new blood, might contemplate what happened the last time this took place.

Does November 1999 happen to ring a bell?

Bush misses the mark

April 12, 2004

THERE CAN BE LITTLE DOUBT there was sufficient cause for the American military to invade Iraq, unfound WMDs and United Nations' resolutions notwithstanding. Saddam Hussein had violated numerous elements of the 1991 ceasefire, any of which sufficed to allow the president to ask Congress to declare war against Iraq. Nor can there be any doubt that the removal of Saddam Hussein from power was a positive step for the various Iraqi peoples, who suffered under decades of his savage tyranny.

Still, the defeat of two minor military powers by the greatest military machine history has ever known does not make George Bush a great wartime president. Indeed, the jury is far from in on the question of whether he can even be considered successful at this juncture. It is even possible that he will come to be judged a complete failure in the execution, just as Bill Clinton failed at the preparation.

The primary reason for my concern about the conduct of this so-called war—still undeclared—stems from this quote from Clausewitz, the military theorist:

> *Our position, then, is that a theater of war, be it large or small, and the forces stationed there, no matter what their size, represent the sort of unity in which a single center of gravity can be identified. That is the place where the decision should be reached; a victory at that point is in its fullest sense identical with the defense of the theater of operations.*

The administration is either being disingenuous or deceptive about the theater of what it calls a war on method. The very concept is wrongheaded on its face, as there can be no unity or identifiable center of gravity to amorphous terror. This would seem to indicate deception and conjures images of "1984", with its endless war that justified Big Brother's "boot in the face forever." But even if the administration is innocent of all malevolent intention and the Patriot Act is as innocent as its freedom-loving Republican supporters claim, this lack of focus is troubling.

For if the war is not against terror, but against violent expansionist Islam as the jihad claims is the case, then Iraq is a strange place to try and win it. It is clear that the theater of the war is the breeding ground of the jihad's global soldiers, the seething cauldron of the Middle East. And there are only two serious candidates for a place of where it can be said: "In this one enemy we strike at the center of gravity of the entire conflict." Neither is Iraq.

Iran is the operations center of global terrorism. The mullahs of the Islamic Republic fund and control Hezbollah and Hamas as well as the Mahdi militia of al-Sadr. Even more important, though, is the spiritual center of the jihad in Saudi Arabia, where government clerics preach war against America as the government funds the establishment of mosques worldwide in the deliberate attempt to lay the groundwork for global Sharia.

The conquest of Iraq no more brought about an end to the global jihad than did the conquest of the Rhineland-Palatinate mean the end of World War II. Nor could it have. Berlin had to fall before the defeat of Nazi Germany could even be contemplated, and it's bizarre to suggest that the occupation of a peripheral Arabic province could end the war while the Clausewitzian center of gravity remains unmolested.

The commander in chief must either make the case to the Congress and the citizens of America about the true nature of the struggle in which they find themselves engaged, or continue to obscure the truth. He would do well to remember that for all his power, he is not capable of forcing the nation to engage in war. The president can no more dictate the hearts and minds of American citizens than he can control the hearts and minds of the Shiites at the center of the current battle.

If George Bush chooses to continue to leave the American people in the dark and ignore the Constitution as he fights his own war, against an enemy he refuses to identify, he will surely lose. Moreover, he will deserve to lose.

Iraq is not the end, it is only the end of the beginning. What that end will be, only time will tell.

What men want

April 19, 2004

THERE IS PROBABLY no question so universally feared by men the world over than one heard throughout the living rooms of the world on a nightly basis. "What are you thinking about?" True, "Do I look fat?" is arguably more laden with inherent danger, but there the answer is obvious: "No."

Now, this is not the typically self-flagellating column about men written by a man in a degrading attempt to appeal to female readers—the literary equivalent of the repugnant canine habit of rolling on one's back and urinating. Rather, it is a brief attempt to decrypt the male psyche for the benefit of women who might be interested.

First, men require respect the way that women need love and affection. For some reason, many women operate under the misconception that treating the men in their lives disrespectfully is cute or somehow scores them social points. But not only does this behavior lower the woman in the eyes of those witnessing it, rest assured that it causes bitter resentment in the man so treated, even if he refuses to speak out in his own defense.

Remember that stoicism is a male virtue. Whereas a woman is unlikely to remain silent when she is angry, male silence in the face of provocation is often a serious statement that is dangerous to ignore. Men don't like to talk things out, they prefer to think things through. A man who is silent while being abused is a man who is considering his options and, often, preparing to act.

Men are not as complex as women. Whereas a woman speaks for reaction, to test and gauge what her next words should be, men, being generally less verbally skilled, have a greater tendency to articulate their meaning as precisely as they can. The more a woman pushes and probes for clarification, the further she is like to diverge from the message intended. This does not mean there is never a subtext, but in most cases, text and subtext are the same.

A man defines himself by his responsibility, and one of them, strange as it may seem, is the mood of his woman. A man whose woman is unhappy considers himself a failure, and the short-sighted woman will use this knowledge to her temporary advantage. But even the sharpest tool grows dull with use— the wise woman will eschew such manipulation and instead choose to regard her man as a potential refuge from her troubles rather than the inherent cause of them.

A man may feel he is responsible for a woman's feelings, but the truth is that he can do very little about them even if he wants to. Most of the time, happiness is a choice. Making the choice to be happy whenever possible, even in spite of difficult circumstances, can be the difference between a lifetime of shared bliss or mutual misery.

Male confidence is always attractive to a woman, which is why tearing it down almost always leaves a woman dissatisfied with the result. It is said that whereas a woman is, a man must become. Without the confidence to become what he is meant to be, a man remains incomplete. The woman who can learn to read her man, to see when his confidence is shaken, and assure him that even if he cannot believe in himself at the moment, she still does, that woman will inspire loyalty that would shame a dog.

Finally, it is not a bad thing to encourage the boy within the man from time to time. The man who cannot put aside the cares of supporting a family from time to time is a widow waiting to happen. The woman who not only accepts, but supports the male friendships of her husband will always be the most popular woman among the married men in her social circle. And learning even a little about football and holding a staunch opinion on which Sports Illustrated Swimsuit model is the prettiest will go a surprisingly long way in ensuring acceptance by the boys.

If a woman treats a man with civility and respect, maintains a cheerful attitude toward him and encourages him believe in himself, he will not only respond with love and affection, but will consider it an honor to lay down his life for her, both metaphorically and, if the occasion demands it, literally.

Low IQ, low-tech

April 26, 2004

ALTHOUGH thanks to Universal Press Syndicate I am now—somewhat to my astonishment—a nationally syndicated columnist, my media perspective remains with the New Media, the Internet and the blogosphere—not the mainstream media. What does this signify?

It means I do not believe my opinion is inherently objective, thanks to a course or two in Olympian Perspectives. It means I view editors as being more thought-police than fact-checkers. It means I know I am responsible for my own errors and no one is going to hide them for me behind a bland statement by a geriatric ombudsman made weeks after the fact. It means I am free.

Fred Reed, the longtime military and police reporter for the *Army Times* and the *Washington Times*, wrote a wonderfully contemptuous column explaining why the newspaper media is almost universally awful. He gave six reasons for its increasing tendency toward mediocrity and irrelevance.

1. Print reporters aren't very smart.

2. Everyone at a newspaper is frightened of offending someone.

3. The media is inherently self-controlled. Outsiders are not allowed to speak freely.

4. Ruffling feathers leads to diminishing the all-important access.

5. Superficial diversity in the newsroom brings about less diversity of opinion.

6. Corporate ownership influences coverage.

It's true reporters are not very smart. Even worse, they're usually not very well educated, even in the areas of their supposed specialty. Ask the average business reporter what hedonic adjustment is and he won't be able to tell you, even if he often writes about the Consumer Price Index. In my experience, reporters operate under the assumption that having heard of something is equivalent to actually understanding it, which is one reason why newspapers regularly make one bizarre prediction after another, none of which ever comes to pass.

Television news is even worse. Brenda Buttner, the host of Fox's "Bulls and Bears", said last week: "If you actually adjust for inflation, the inflation numbers aren't so bad." I would hesitate to bring up what one would hope was a simple verbal slip, except that her guests—media experts all—immediately agreed with her.

Indeed, on the few occasions I watch the television or read the mainstream newspapers at all these days, I am struck by a weird sense of going back in time. By the time a bit of information cracks the mainstream news cycle, it has often been circulating the blogosphere for days, sometimes weeks. This is not to assert that Internet news is always accurate, but in a time when mainstream reporters and editors are dropping like flies thanks to their predilection for fiction—three *USA Today* editors being the latest casualties—it's clear one cannot judge the message by the medium.

If you're not yet familiar with the brave new world of the Web log, I highly recommend an excursion into the wild, chaotic newsflow of the blogosphere. Stop by Vox Popoli, my blog, where libertarians and conservatives spar enthusiastically over anything and everything from atheism to the Legend of Zelda. Or get a closer view of the war in Iraq through the military blogs, such as Blackfive: the Paratrooper of Love, Citizen Smash and From The Halls to the Shores. Those looking to understand the coming economic storm would do well to check out the Mises Economics blog, which occasionally features WorldNetDaily's own Ilana Mercer.

It's not hard to see that Fred Reed's six points of media mediocrity simply don't apply to the Internet media. WorldNetDaily, TownHall and other Internet sites feature the best national writers, not the local hacks. And even a cursory glance at the blogosphere quickly demonstrates;

1. The intelligence of bloggers and their regulars is often frightening.

2. As is the willingness of many bloggers to say precisely what they think. Even if you wish they wouldn't.

3. Every blog with comments provides outsiders with an open mike. See point No. 2.

4. You can't lose what you haven't got. In any event, access is usually a synonym for acting as a public-relations mouthpiece.

5. The blogosphere is nothing but genuine diversity—of almost everything.

6. No corporations, just free individuals speaking freely.

We may not be approaching singularity and posthumanity, but the day of the input-only news consumer is over. As one media scandal flows into the next, it's becoming increasingly clear this is no great loss.

The slow suicide

May 3, 2004

I N ROBERT HEINLEIN'S NOVEL, "The Moon Is A Harsh Mistress", the revolution-leading professor tells his fellow revolutionary a story of a government functionary:

> *"Manuel, once there was a man who held a political make-work job like so many here in this Directorate, shining brass cannon around a courthouse."*
>
> *"Why would courthouse have cannon?"*
>
> *"Never mind. He did this for years. It fed him and let him save a bit, but he was not getting ahead in the world. So one day he quit his job, drew out his savings, bought a brass cannon—and went into business for himself."*

It is no secret that working for the government has a corrosive effect on the employee. The great Ludwig von Mises wrote the seminal work on bureaucracy back in 1944, demonstrating how the absence of the laws of supply and demand and the abolition of the profit motive in the government's non-Smithian virtual world brings about perverse institutional goals severely at odds with those common to private corporations and individuals.

These perverse institutional goals instill a warped mindset in the employee, where financial and other resources appear out of nowhere by some inexplicable magic, a mystical largesse to be distributed from the central locus of power by the managerial elite. This is a fundamentally socialist model—it is no coincidence that Hannah Arendt damned the banality of the National Socialist evil even as C.S. Lewis portrayed the ultimate malevolence as a faceless bureaucracy in "That Hideous Strength".

The government employee's perverted frame of reference, therefore, becomes antithetical to the principles of freedom, liberty and limited government that are enshrined in the American Constitution and the Republican

Party platform. And yet, the Republican Party leadership—selling out its principles in the pragmatic pursuit of temporal power—has been steadily increasing the population of those most likely to be hostile to the party's stated goals.

When George Delano took office in 2001, government employees at federal, state and local levels consisted of 18.9 percent of the national labor force. Three years later, in 2004, that percentage has increased to 20.1 percent, an increase of 670,000 government workers in a time when total employment has dropped by almost 3 million.

While government's percentage of the labor force is still lower than it was in 1994—when men were men, women were women and Republicans took out a Contract on big government—at 20.8 percent, at the present rate, it will not take long to surpass that figure. Government employment is expected to grow 2.62 percent in the first quarter alone, adding 562,000 more employees, creating nearly as many government jobs in three months as were created in three previous years.

These numbers might seem insignificant in a nation of 300 million people. But when you consider both the close margin of the 2000 presidential election as well as the fact that only 106 million people voted, the potential for future disaster becomes clear. We are not talking about butterfly wings and hurricanes here, but rather, large turbines and a stiff breeze.

This is not to say that every government employee checks his brain and his principles at the door when he punches in for the first time. But long-term steeping in the morass of bureaucracy, at any level, will have an insensible effect on most individuals over time, and one that is highly unlikely to lead toward supporting republicanism.

In pursuing pragmatism over principle, Republicans are unwittingly sowing the seeds of their destruction as a party in both ideological and practical terms. The ideologists of liberty—columnists such as Joseph Farah, Ilana Mercer and myself—have already left for freer pastures in the Libertarian and Constitution parties. This may well be seen as insignificant by the Republican leadership—one seldom builds a popular party around intellectuals.

But the practical result of creating more bureaucrats will not be so easily ignored. As the voting population continues to become more dependent upon government paychecks, arguments for reducing government expenditures will become naturally less and less popular. This will pull the Republican

Party to the left, reducing the entire political debate to one simple question: Not "Is this right?" but instead, "How much?"

Abandoning one's principles for pragmatism is repugnant, but understandable in an imperfect world. But abandoning one's principles in order to commit a slow and unnecessary suicide is simply stupid.

Hard landings

May 10, 2004

THE SAME VIDEO kept appearing on the music channels. It looked like Slipknot, but as my regular viewing companion has about the same tolerance for Zeros metal as I do for Celine Dion, I couldn't be sure. Also, I don't recall anyone from Slipknot wearing a mask that looks like a cross between a dissected lizard and Frankenstein's monster.

Now, it's hard for a band to get on MTV, and you have to be pretty popular to make it into heavy rotation. Light rotation on Spanish MTV was as far as my band ever got—*ole*! What is the significance of this? Perhaps nothing, although it is interesting in light of the Dow's laborious struggle to get back to the 11,000 mark.

For Bob Prechter's theory of socionomics declares that music, like the Dow, is an important measure of social mood. Of course, there's no shortage of pop princesses to be found, but as we move into what Prechter's Elliott Wave theorists posit is the start of a downward intermediate wave (1) of primary wave 3, it's intriguing to see that the little darlings of the 1999 top are now getting Dirrty, Naughty and Toxic.

I've been wrong about the markets before, so I'm not going to offer any specific entrail-readings, but it's important to note the implications go far beyond your 401k. First, despite all the economic good news that is being reported, the fact that the Federal Reserve is still keeping rates at 1 percent is not a healthy sign. When you factor in that the fractional reserves of our banking system are now 1/109—that is to say, $1 is now loaned out 109 times—it begins to look as if The Powers That Be are deeply worried about something wicked this way coming.

Wars have long been known to accompany bear markets. For historical and military reasons, I have previously asserted that the present conflict in Iraq is a Phony War of sorts, a prelude to the real show that is basically invisible to the nation at quasi-war. Socionomics dictates that as the 2004–2006 primary wave 3 will be to the 2000–2002 primary wave 1, so the coming conflict will be to the present one. Not a particularly nice thought, so here's hoping a series of cheerful boy bands begins topping the charts soon.

Speaking of crashes, thoughts of *Air America* insensibly enter my mind. It looks as if the employment rate will be rising soon by the 100 or so employees of the ill-fated leftist talk-radio network, which was doomed from the start. Considering that Alice Franken—who still hasn't been so good as to answer my call to fisticuffs, hence the appellation—was not offering anything you couldn't hear on NPR, read in the *New York Times*, or watch on the *ABCNNBCBS* cabal, the network never had a chance.

Of course, one hardly expects a group composed entirely of fluff-head leftists to understand the complexities of the law of supply and demand.

I'd like to luxuriate in the joys of what Jonah Goldberg calls Frankenfreude as *Air America* loses executives and misses payrolls. But that's not possible now that Alice is bruiting about the idea of running for the Senate. In any other state, that might be laughable, but not in Minnesota. It's the one state where he could actually win. Do the words "Gov. Jesse Ventura" ring a bell?

First, Minnesota is one of the most reliably leftist states in the country. Second, the Star & Sickle, otherwise known as the Star Tribune, already loves Alice to distraction. Third, never underestimate the desperate Minneapolitan appetite for celebrity. You can't appreciate the meaning of trying too hard until you've read a local columnist hyperventilating over Minneapolis being compared to Des Moines instead of Paris. Fourth, Paul Wellstone. It could happen.

And frankly, socionomics appears to predict it. I can't think of anyone, short of the Lizard Queen herself, better suited to help that grand supercycle wave get rolling.

G.I. Jane does Baghdad

May 17, 2004

PFC LYNNDIE ENGLAND isn't exactly a Vivid-quality porn star. Even so, word is she put on quite a show there in the squalid surroundings of Abu Ghraib, although some of her audience may not have been in a position to fully appreciate it, considering that they were wearing pillow cases over their heads at the time.

"Almost everybody was naked all the time," said one member of Congress, presumably disapprovingly, although the *New York Post* was not clear on this. "It was pretty disgusting, not what you'd expect from Americans. There was lots of sexual stuff—not of the Iraqis, but of our troops," said Sen. Norm Coleman, causing observers to wonder if the Minnesota senator had ever encountered either the Internet or cable television at any point in the last decade.

Since the psychological pressures of warfare have already been used to excuse the abuse of prisoners—by reservists who never saw any actual warfare, I might add—I suppose we can expect to see this one chalked up to the Iraqi heat. Perhaps the air-conditioning wasn't working, leaving the poor prison guards no choice but to take their clothes off. Then a bad sound track kicked in with a whocka-whocka-whocka, somebody pulled out a camera and things got a little crazy. Somewhere in California, a producer is thinking: "Hmmm, G.I. Jenna—I can see it!"

Now, I don't think that "Girls Gone Wild" was exactly what George Bush was promising the Iraqi people as the sweet fruits of freedom. But what do you expect when you take a large group of half-trained young men and women and throw them together, in close quarters, in what has to be one of the most boring places in the world? Better yet, add the possibility of danger and sudden death—that'll keep their pants on.

One wonders what the Islamists are going to make of all this. One minute, they're shaking their fists about the danger of Britney Spears and pierced belly buttons, and then they learn that Britney might as well still be a Mousketeer compared to what else we have on offer. This isn't enlightened democracy taking on benighted medievalism, it's pornocracy vs. theocracy. But at least they should be clear on the fact that it's not a Christian crusade.

The truth is that these sort of shenanigans goes on all the time, wherever there are women in the military. Since the average reporter doesn't know anyone actually in the military, they're unaware that military wives absolutely hate their husbands going off on assignment with the co-eds. This is not without reason, as an astonishing percentage of women become pregnant while on assignment, when they're not getting pregnant in order to avoid going on assignment.

A friend of mine was the ombudsman, or civilian liason, for a 350 man-and-woman ship on a six-month tour a few years ago. There were nine pregnancies in all, and seven children were born during the tour. This was nothing compared to the infamous Love Boat, or USS Eisenhower, which had 60 of 492 women become pregnant or miss deployment due to pregnancy. If simply telling people not to have sex didn't work for the far more powerful Catholic Church during medieval times, it's not likely to work for the U.S. military either.

This is not to say that the porn patrol is all the fault of the tempting little minxes in uniform. It takes two to tango, though perhaps in light of Miss England's oeuvre one should say that the activity requires a two-soldier minimum. However, one sex or the other is going to have to stay back home in order to shut this down and I don't see us converting to an all-Amazon force anytime soon.

It's been clear for years that women cannot measure up to the physical requirements of military duty. Now, it's beyond obvious that they completely destroy military discipline and wreak havoc on day-to-day operations. If soldier-porn isn't enough, what is it going to take to end one of the most idiotic social experiments of all time?

I salute those well-meaning women in the military who only want to do their patriotic duty and serve their country to the best of their ability. I strongly suggest they do so by acquiring honorable discharges at the earliest possible opportunity.

Symbolic war

May 24, 2004

C ENSORSHIP AND RESTRICTIONS on the free flow of information have long been a part of war. For example, a powerful element of America's rush into the Spanish-American War of 1898 was due to the ability of William Randolph Hearst and Joseph Pulitzer to wield such significant influence over the coverage of the events that led up to the war.

Nowadays, such a drumbeat to war is more problematic. The promulgation of digital cameras and videocams combined with the instant global access of the Internet means that the mainstream media no longer exerts monopolistic control of martial imagery. It still wields great power, of course—note how the potentially inflammatory images of 9-11 were quickly eradicated from the nation's television screens—but the speed with which images of the Nick Berg murder spread across the Internet demonstrated how the media can no longer hope to definitively dictate the symbols of a given situation.

In his great work, "Tragedy And Hope", Georgetown professor Carroll Quigley explains how the spread of weapons technology affects freedom. As weapons become cheaper and more easily produced, they are acquired by more men. Freedom tends to increase when individuals have access to weapons of the same quality as governments—the great age of liberty began when private men were able to afford better long-barreled rifles than the muskets of the royal British troops.

This concept suggests some interesting notions, even as the public worries about nuclear briefcase weapons and various chemical and biological agents falling into the hands of private individuals like bin Laden.

Quigley, were he alive today, would likely point out that the same argument can be applied to cameras as well. Public access to the truth increases as the price and availability of information production and distribution puts them in the hands of people around the world—a nameless Iraqi blogger has the potential to have more influence on public opinion than the *New York Times* and the *Washington Post* combined.

One of the many mistakes the Bush administration has made in waging its war-on-method is to ignore the supreme importance of symbols in a war which is, more than anything, one of semiotics. When even the very name of the enemy is couched in code, it is the height of folly to imagine that the usual technique of crude jingoism and empty sloganeering will suffice to ensure the enthusiastic support of the American people.

Infowar is real, but it is a much more unpredictable thing than conventional war. For one thing, the number of variables is several orders of magnitude higher, as the mere fact of a porn princess pretending to get raped in Romania can have a significant impact on how the U.S. Marines are used in Iraq. Chaos theory clearly applies to global conflict.

In conventional war, reality is the only reality that matters. In symbolic war, perception is the only reality that matters. Given the clumsiness of the Bush administration in dealing with the relatively simple challenge of the mainstream political media, it is difficult to be optimistic with regards to its prospects of successfully addressing the far more complex issue of semiotic war.

What was advertised as freedom and democracy vs. terrorism has insensibly devolved into pornocratic do-gooders forcing benighted medievalists unwillingly into the modern era for their own good. Little wonder, then, if the American people should fail to be inspired by this.

It is too soon to be sure, but it certainly appears as if the symbolic war has been lost. This is not due to Abu Ghraib or the anti-administration media, but a vast combination of variables, some of which were beyond not only the control, but even the imagination of the parties involved. And yet, how foolish was it for the administration to embark on an enterprise of this kind knowing full well that it would be staring down the barrel of its most powerful weapon—the mainstream media—at the first sign of trouble.

George Bush is no conservative, but in this strange new world, he is perceived as one. And so the irony goes full circle, as the anticonservative American media applies the old Arab proverb about the enemy of one's enemy being one's friend to the global jihad,

The 3 I's of liberalism

May 31, 2004

S OME OF YOU MAY BE AWARE that I am a member of the SFWA, a poorly constructed acronym for the Science Fiction and Fantasy Writers of America. As such, I tend to find the occasional foray into the mentality of the American liberal to be a fascinating exercise in alien thought.

It is truly interesting to swim in the deep morass of a complete absence of logic, historical knowledge and consistency. Some might consider this to be an unfair overstatement, but it's pretty easy to prove that this is anything but the case.

Take, for example, the notion of the Iraqi war and occupation. At the onset of war, the left-liberal's protests revolved around the "No blood for oil" cry. This one idiotic phrase manages the trifecta—and please bear in mind, I have been calling for an end to the occupation for some time now.

We'll start with logic. The notion that the president ordered the invasion of Iraq to take control of its oil supplies does not make sense on two counts. First, we pay for oil in dollars, which except for the cost of inflation, are essentially free to the U.S. government. But since Alan Greenspan was preaching we were teetering on the brink of a deflationary precipice, even that minor cost was no constraint in 2002. It's not necessary to invade if you can simply run the printing press at will. Second, the price of oil, at $41 per barrel, is $16 higher than it was prior to the invasion, which completely defeats the postulated purpose of invading to ensure cheap oil supplies.

History, too, was ignored. America already held the oil fields of Kuwait and Iraq in its grasp in 1991. There was nothing to prevent the U.S. military from retaining its control over the oil fields—the fact that it readily relinquished what was already in its possession strongly indicated that Americans have no need to take what it can buy, especially if it can buy it in paper dollars created out of debt.

Finally, the lack of consistency demonstrated in the "no blood for oil" cry is illuminated by left-liberal opposition to drilling in Alaska. Oil pumped from there would cost no blood, and, according to the theory postulated by liberals, the increased supply would thereby relieve America of any need to go to war. Thus, deceit is revealed along with the illogic, ignorance and inconsistency, as "no oil, period" would be a more honest battle cry.

In the context of the three I's, John Kerry is the perfect standard bearer for American liberalism. He is supremely illogical, calling for the United Nations to manage a situation that is far more potentially explosive than the many tamer situations in which it has completely failed in the past. Indeed, the despicable depths to which the United Nations sank in its Iraqi oil-for-food scandal is exceeded only by its sex-for-food scandal in Guinea, Liberia and Sierra Leone.

John Kerry also has ignorance down pat. No one of any political stripe who condemns tax cuts during a time of potential recession can claim to have even a glimmering of an economic clue, as this is straight out of the Keynesian textbook—if you're easing the money supply, you should also be cutting taxes and increasing spending—and, of course, we Austrians always favor more money in private hands.

And as for inconsistency, anyone with a lifetime ADA rating of 93 who tries to claim that he is not a liberal well deserves the title of Monsieur Flip-Flop. This is in addition to his much-chronicled flip-flops on the Iraqi war, the marriage penalty, the Patriot Act, homogamy, the death penalty, affirmative action, gasoline taxes, abortion, election reform and NAFTA.

George Bush does not deserve re-election. I'd much rather see a man of confirmed principle such as Michael Peroutka of the Constitution Party or Aaron Russo of the Libertarian party in the White House. But as the great work of the public schools remains incomplete, the president is fortunate that only those handicapable individuals possessed of the Three I's of Liberalism will be supporting his main rival.

The cowardice of his convictions

June 7, 2004

G EORGE BUSH practiced a little self-censorship the other day. In what appears to have been an attempt to draw parallels between the public-approved invasion of Normandy 60 years ago and the unwise decision to occupy Iraq, he quoted Gen. Eisenhower:

> *Soldiers, sailors and airmen of the Allied Expeditionary Force. The eyes of the world are upon you. The hopes and prayers of liberty-loving people everywhere march with you.*

Stirring words, but the president happened to drop a phrase from the middle, that phrase being:

> *You are about to embark upon the Great Crusade, toward which we have striven these many months.*

Apparently the president didn't wish to offend those sensitive individuals who are currently attempting to murder Americans around the world. But there is some truth to the notion that the current conflict in Iraq is no crusade. After all, the Crusade was a nominally Christian endeavor to take back Christian lands with the blessing of the pope, whereas the current occupation of Iraq is a secular effort to pacify an Islamic land sans papal approval.

One of the biggest myths in American politics is that George W. Bush is a courageous leader. He isn't. Indeed, he is remarkably timid for a president who until recently enjoyed some of the highest approval ratings of all time. Even when compared to Bill Clinton, not exactly a paragon of political courage, George Bush falls short.

Consider how Clinton attempted radical restructurings of the American health system and the American military. These initiatives would have been calamitous, to be sure, but they were hardly timid. Furthermore, Clinton sparred openly with the Republican majority in Congress even prior to his impeachment.

George Bush, on the other hand, has somehow managed to kowtow before the minority party, while at the same time producing only a single initiative of note. Unlike Clinton, he succeeded, unfortunately—the creation of a new federal entitlement is not exactly the revolutionary rollback of federal power for which conservatives were hoping. George Bush has been a go-along-to-get-along president from the start. While it is disheartening to see he wages war in like manner, it is hardly surprising.

It is fascinating to see how previously staunch supporters of the administration are finally beginning to come around to this view of the president, rosy-glassed observers such as Peggy Noonan notwithstanding. If the president hopes to win re-election on his performance as commander in chief, he is doomed to disappointment, although I expect the anti-charisma of John Kerry will save him from himself.

Still, the president is either lying or hopelessly and utterly wrong in saying, as he did on May 24:

> *Our terrorist enemies have a vision that guides and explains all of their varied acts of murder. They seek to impose Taliban-like rule, country by country, across the greater Middle East. They seek the total control of every person, and mind, and soul; a harsh society in which women are voiceless and brutalized.... None of this is the expression of a religion.*

What idiocy! *All* of it is an expression of a religion. The president cannot possibly subscribe to the notion that the Taliban was nothing but a philosophical discussion group. Indeed, the jihad itself has become a religion, which is why most of its leaders are clerics, why its propaganda is couched in apocalyptic religious terminology and why all attempts at negotiation and reasonable accommodation are doomed to failure.

Ironically, it is those who most fervently cling to the myth of the bold George Bush who argue that the president has no choice but to dissemble, to declare that France and Saudi Arabia are our friends, that the Iraqi people want American troops to occupy their country and that we can co-exist peacefully with the religion of peace. In doing so, of course, they sabotage their own position, as it is speaking the truth without fear of consequence that is the mark of courage, it is the willingness to confront popular opinion that is the stamp of bold leadership.

To suggest that the successful occupations of Iraq and Afghanistan could ever bring peace is tantamount to believing that the reclamation of France and Holland would suffice to bring down the Third Reich. George Bush has neither the courage to fight the global jihad nor to admit that the nation is unready to fight it at this time. Either option is valid, but instead, he follows in the disastrous Clintonian tradition of doing as little as possible, hoping the problem will somehow resolve itself in time.

Is marriage worth it?

June 14, 2004

A READER, who happens to be a single man of marriageable age, wrote in to ask me a simple question: "Does anyone out there feel that marriage is worth it?"

After some reflection, I decided to answer him thusly: A marriage to the right person is worth it. A marriage to the wrong person is not. How does one decide who the right person is? Aye, there's the rub...

This is not to say that one cannot determine who the right person is, only that it requires a certain amount of analytical detachment about the relationship that is difficult for most people. Some of the more important factors for a man to consider, in my opinion, are as follows:

- Is she a woman of genuine faith? A woman who seriously believes that marriage is a sacrament—be she Christian, Jew or Muslim—will have a very different view of the institution and the commitment she is making than will a secular or casually religious woman. As for irreligious men, I see no purpose in marrying whatsoever—why put oneself at serious risk for a sacrament in which one does not believe? If you're marrying her simply because she demands it, don't be surprised when you're forced to accede to other, even less palatable demands, like a divorce.

- Does she accept the notion of personal responsibility? A woman who is constantly blaming others for her problems in life will soon begin to see her husband as the source of all her problems. These women always blame whoever they are around the most instead of themselves—if she's constantly complaining about her coworkers or her family, don't even continue to date her. If you do, soon enough you'll discover that she has a new target at which to aim her barbs.

- Are you comfortable with her? Passion is no substitute for genuine compatibility. Hot sex is delightful, but there is the other 99 percent of the time to consider, too. If you and your potential wife are not capable of several hours in the same room together without talking or otherwise interacting directly, you may not be comfortable enough with one another.

- Can she entertain herself? Men need their downtime. This becomes problematic if she sees your free time as a violation of her time with you.

- Does she genuinely put the interests of others first? I love a beautiful, self-centered drama queen as much or more than the next guy, but I would never want to marry one. They're fun to watch... from a distance. Keep your distance.

- Do your friends and family think she's good for you? Those around you are not likely to be blinded by the rose-tinted lenses of infatuation and will often have a better read on her true personality than you do. If you find yourself defending her by saying things like "Oh, but you just don't know her," then you are flirting with long-term trouble.

- Does she attempt to control you? This tendency will only get worse with marriage, so any sign of this in a dating relationship is a red flag. Women have a strong maternal instinct and have a hard time grasping that most men loathe being mothered—can she back off when you tell her to?

- Does she treat you with respect, in public and in private? If she does, this is an excellent sign. If she's always putting you down, just "giving you a hard time" and "keeping you in your place", better find someone else. Marriage is not a buddy-cop movie.

- Are you in agreement on the larger issues? If she wants kids and you don't, forget it. If she wants to keep up with the Joneses and you want to save for the future, there is a seed of much future conflict already embedded in the relationship.

- Finally, do you know her? Really, truly know her? Do you know what she hopes her future will hold, even if she can't articulate it?

Marriage and family are definitely good things. But they are important and life-altering, and are not to be entered into lightly. If you are so fortunate as to find the right woman, don't let shallow concerns get in the way, pursue her and see it through. If neither you nor those close to you harbor any serious doubts about her, then marriage is likely the right decision.

Unsettling signs

June 21, 2004

FOR THE LAST THREE MONTHS, contrarian economists have been looking at the Fed's wild and crazy increase of the M3 money supply, which has been jacked up by $1.4 trillion since January, and wondering what in the world is going on. It has led some to conclude that the Fed is aware of an imminent disaster approaching as the Fed usually only cranks the printing presses up to high after an event like 9-11 or the 1987 Long-Term Capital Management disaster.

But what sort of event can you expect and plan for months in advance? Consider the other evidence. Last November, during a visit to Washington, Israeli Defense Minister Shaul Mofaz warned that Iran would reach a "point of no return" in its nuclear program within a year. On May 6, the House of Representatives passed a resolution to authorize pre-emptive military strikes against Iran, 376–3. On March 10, France, Germany and the U.K. "sharply criticized" Iran in a resolution presented to the United Nation's atomic agency, which is rather more than the cheese-eating surrender monkeys and the schnitzel-snarfing stormtrooper spawn were willing to do to Iraq.

Such developments make the assertion of the anti-war Sydney Morning Herald appear less stratospheric, as it has claimed that a plan for an Iranian invasion was completed last May, involving attacks from Georgia and Azerbaijan as well as Iraq. Debka, an Internet news site which throughout the Iraqi war demonstrated itself to be rather more credible than the mainstream newspapers, noted on June 17 that Iran was building up its forces along a 350-km stretch of its border with Iraq.

Now, all of this could be much sound and fury signifying nothing. It's entirely possible that, as one old trader told me, George Bush simply grabbed Alan Greenspan by the collar and said: "Look, you old fraud, you're not going to sink me the way you sunk my father" and ordered him to keep the money spigots open. Easy money in an election year is not a new concept, and it's not as if we invaded North Korea—another card-carrying member of the Axis of Evil—for the crime of possessing nuclear weapons either.

It is hard, though, to shake the notion that all of these tiny tremors and discordant sounds do not harbor some degree of chaos ahead. Having finished an uncharacteristic period of reflection following the loss of our late, great president, we are back to the throes of the silly season and a return to the never-ending love triangle of Bill, Hillary and Monica. Ah, if only Hillary would leave Bill for Monica—then our joy would be complete.

There are those market technicians who worship at the altar of Fibonacci, that Golden series of numbers. For months, they have been projecting June 15 as either a significant top or bottom, and now that the date has finally arrived, the consensus appears to be that it would appear, given the state of the market, to be a top. If they are wrong, we'll know soon enough, if not, then perhaps we will discover why the Fed has been printing all that money.

In any case, June 30 is not all that far away from June 15, and it would certainly be interesting if President Bush were to announce that American troops were going leave Iraq... as they moved next door into Iran.

While I have no objections at all to the forcible prevention of nuclear proliferation, especially with regard to terror-sponsoring states that direct murderous groups like Hezbollah, I do seriously question the wisdom of presenting the expansion of the war to a third nation-state without the involvement of the American people. It seems to me that if there is any likelihood of an attack on Iran—and it is entirely possible that there will be no such action—that there will be no avoiding the reality of a global clash of civilizations that the administration has been attempting to sweep under the carpet since 9-11.

I make no predictions. I have no answers. All I can say is that I hope God will grant President Bush wisdom in these difficult times, and that he will follow the Constitution and ask the will of the American people before committing the nation to a course of action that may threaten not only what we stand for, but who we are.

Flunking Fascism 101

June 28, 2004

T HERE ARE FEW WORDS the American Left loves to fling around with such abandon as the word "fascist". According to them, social conservatives, libertarians and the Religious Right are all various brands of fascism, that political ideology which came into such disrepute following the demise of il Duce, Benito Mussolini.

And yet, is the accusation legitimate? Who better to judge than Mussolini himself, not only the founder of the Fascist movement, but also the author of its manifesto. The Manifesto of the Fascist Struggle is not so well-known as the Communist Manifesto—and deservedly so, being markedly lacking in memorable phrases such as "a spectre haunting Europe"—and is not even as well-known as the Munich Manifesto of Germany's National Socialists.

In fact, one can seldom find a direct translation of the Fascist manifesto, as it is usually summarized quickly before being swept aside in favor of contorted explanations of how its socialist theoreticians, including Panunzio, Gentile and Mussolini himself, are actually right-wing extremists influenced by the Catholic Church. It is fortuitous, then, that I happen to speak Italian, and so I present herein an original translation of The Manifesto of the Fascist Struggle, published in The People of Italy on June 6, 1919.

Italians! Here is the program of a genuinely Italian movement. It is revolutionary because it is anti-dogmatic, strongly innovative and against prejudice.

For the political problem: We demand:

> - *Universal suffrage polled on a regional basis, with proportional representation and voting and electoral office eligibility for women.*

- *A minimum age for the voting electorate of 18 years; that for the office holders at 25 years.*

- *The abolition of the Senate.*

- *The convocation of a National Assembly for a three-years duration, for which its primary responsibility will be to form a constitution of the State.*

- *The formation of a National Council of experts for labor, for industy, for transportation, for the public health, for communications, etc. Selections to be made from the collective professionals or of tradesmen with legislative powers, and elected directly to a General Commission with ministerial powers.*

For the social problems: We demand:

- *The quick enactment of a law of the State that sanctions an eight-hour workday for all workers.*

- *A minimum wage.*

- *The participation of workers' representatives in the functions of industry commissions.*

- *To show the same confidence in the labor unions (that prove to be technically and morally worthy) as is given to industry executives or public servants.*

- *The rapid and complete systemization of the railways and of all the transport industries.*

- *A necessary modification of the insurance laws to invalidate the minimum retirement age; we propose to lower it from 65 to 55 years of age.*

For the military problem: We demand:

- *The institution of a national militia with a short period of service for training and exclusively defensive responsibilities.*

- *The nationalization of all the arms and explosives factories.*

- *A national policy intended to peacefully further the Italian national culture in the world.*

For the financial problem: We demand:

- *A strong progressive tax on capital that will truly expropriate a portion of all wealth.*

- *The seizure of all the possessions of the religious congregations and the abolition of all the bishoprics, which constitute an enormous liability on the Nation and on the privileges of the poor.*

- *The revision of all military contracts and the seizure of 85 percent of the profits therein.*

As with National Socialism and Communism, it is easy to see that far from being a right-wing ideology, fascism is simply another variant of leftist worship of the State. I found the first plank in the above platform to be particularly amusing, as last week on my blog, Vox Popoli, a five-day debate sparked by a post on the historical consequences of women's suffrage caused some hysterical leftists to label me a fascist. And yet, the only serious question is if it is more ironic to tar a libertarian or a member of the Religious Right with the fascist brush, as one seldom hears James Dobson calling for the government seizure of all church-owned property.

In 1925, Mussolini encapsulated the heart of fascist philosophy in a memorable phrase:

Tutto nello Stato, niente al di fuori dello Stato, nulla contro lo Stato.

This means "Everything in the State, nothing outside the State, nothing against the State." Now, I ask you, in the Year of Our Lord 2004, does that sound more like a Libertarian, a Republican or a Democrat?

The end of America

July 5, 2004

D R. UMBERTO ECO is one of the great minds of our time. He is an eminent classicist, a best-selling novelist, the world expert on the science of symbols and writes a weekly column in the Italian magazine *L'espresso*. He is, like most European intellectuals, a man of the Left, but of the dwindling breed of the sober and freedom-loving Left.

Recently, Dr. Eco wrote a column entitled "To appear more than to be", which highlighted the campaign advice given to Cicero in a letter written by his brother, Quintus Tullius. (A rudimentary translation is here.) The Roman's advice is astonishingly appropriate to modern American politics; the instruction to "never expose oneself on any political issue" immediately brings to mind the Invisible Man, John Kerry, as one watches his attempt to quietly flip-flop his way to the White House.

Eco does not see these correlations as coincidence. He reminds the reader that Cicero was running for consul—president—in the very last days of the Roman republic. For while Cicero claimed his consulship in 63 B.C., only 14 years later Julius Caesar would cross the Rubicon with his legions. And as the vision of America's Founding Fathers was directly inspired by the republican model of Rome's limited government, these correlations are hardly insignificant either.

Societies, like the individuals that comprise them, have a lifespan. There is nothing guaranteeing the perpetual existence of the American republic. Indeed, the Supreme Court has been diligent of late in demonstrating that the U.S. Constitution is nothing but a piece of paper devoid of power. It might behoove us, then, to know how long its predecessor lasted before the rule of law devolved completely into dictatorship and the rule of force.

The Roman republic was born following the rebellion that overthrew the last Etruscan king, Lucius Tarquinius Superbus, in 509 B.C. Its republican system of limited democracy with limited suffrage began to die with the first consulship of Marius, in 107 B.C. Marius created legions loyal to him personally, violated Roman law by holding the consulship five consecutive times and ordered a series of bloody proscriptions that inspired his one-time lieutenant, Sulla, to wage Rome's first civil war against him. In 83 B.C., Sulla was victorious and became Rome's first extrasenatorial dictator. From republic to empire was a matter of 460 years, then, including the 58 years of violent transition.

The second great influence on the American republic, Athens, was rather shorter-lived, as it was only 185 years from the Cleisthenesian reforms of 507 B.C. to the Athenian Assembly's submission to Antipater in 322 B.C. Unlike the Roman model, Athenian democracy was brought down less by internal strife than by external empire building, which eventually resulted in its forced involvement in the Pan-Hellenic League of Corinth, which surrendered Athenian sovereignty to Philip of Macedon.

It has been 223 years since the Articles of Confederation founded the American republic. Already, our republic has surpassed Athens. Is it possible to hope that it will outlast the 460 years of Rome? The odds of success do not appear high. The social ills of illegitimacy, divorce and public homosexuality are already more reminiscent of the early empire than even the late republic. The politicians of both major parties run substance-free campaigns eerily reminiscent of those advised by Quintus Tullius, who prefigured Karl Rove and Dick Morris by two millennia.

And in Iraq, we are witnessing an attempt to build a Pax Americana in open imitation of the famous Pax Romana. What admirers of this effort tend to forget is that the Pax Romana, which is considered to have run from 27 B.C. to A.D. 180, was an imperial affair, beginning with Octavian's assumption of the title Imperator Caesar.

The laws of history are not as easily discerned as the laws of physics, but they are every bit as inexorable. Eco gives us one more reason to believe that we are living in the last days of the American republic as he closes his article with this ominous warning:

[O]ne cannot avoid the thought that Roman democracy had begun to die when its politicians understood that they no longer had to be serious about their principles but only needed to arrange to obtain the sympathies of those we might well call television viewers.

You can't fix a corpse

July 12, 2004

TIBETAN RELIGIOUS TRADITION has it that when the Dalai Lama dies, the Buddha of Compassion leaves his body and incarnates in the body of a young child. The monks immediately go out in search of this blessed child, and when they find him—as they inevitably do—he is tested by a group of high lamas and enthroned as the reincarnation of his successor.

Imagine, however, if the lamas refused to recognize that the Dalai Lama was, in fact, dead. Suppose that instead of going in search of the Buddha's new carnal home, they hooked the corpse up to a life support machine and waited patiently for the Holy One to awake and rise up. It's not hard to see that they would be doomed to disappointment, and furthermore, would fail to find the next Dalai Lama as well.

This is precisely our dilemma today, for America, as envisioned by the Founding Fathers, is dead. By every measure, large and small, the original vision of limited government by, for and of the people has been folded, spindled and mutilated beyond recognition. When one reads the Constitution, one simply marvels at the distinct difference between its words and our present reality.

Our paper Federal Reserve Notes are not Congress-issued gold and silver coins. Our direct taxes are not apportioned. We are entangled in a veritable web of foreign alliances, Congress shamelessly makes laws regarding speech, religion and guns, and the judicial branch has arrogantly assumed for itself unchecked supremacy over the other two branches.

Regardless of whether one see these changes as blasphemous treason against the Constitution, or as reasonable and necessary modifications to what was designed to be a living document that evolves with the times, it is impossible to deny that they have been made. It is likewise impossible to assert that a massive central government possessing eminent domain, owning over a third of the land and claiming more than a third of all income is either limited or small.

For many years, conservatives and other freedom lovers have placed their trust in the Republican Party, hoping that it would fulfill its promises to return America to its national birthright of freedom and individual liberty. Those promises, unsurprisingly, were broken by the party of Abraham Lincoln, who is most famous for converting what had been a voluntary Union of free association into a forced Union by military might.

Any last vestiges of hope in the Republican Party have been shattered by the current regime, wherein a Republican President, Republican House, Republican Senate and Republican-nominated Supreme Court have demonstrated that they have zero interest in the timeless vision of America's founders. Supporting them in the hopes that they will revive American liberties is akin to hoping that shock paddles will suffice to revive a month-old corpse. American freedom is not only dead, it has been rotting for some time.

There are those who say that a vote for a third-party candidate, such as the Libertarian's Michael Badnarik or the Constitution Party's Michael Peroutka, is wasted. Nothing could be further from the truth. Indeed, these are the only votes that are not wasted, for positive change will only come from those outside the corrupt bi-factional system. After all, it was neither the Tories nor the Whigs who fought for American independence.

Like the Tibetan lamas, we must go in search of those in whom the spirit of freedom and liberty burns. The revival of American liberty is still in its infancy, as only 482,451 people voted for the Libertarian and Constitution presidential candidates combined, 0.96 percent of those who voted for the victorious Republican, George W. Bush. But that is 482,395 more people than the 56 signers of the Declaration of Independence, and as for those who believe our present bipartisan system is eternal, well, tell it to the Whigs.

Or, for that matter, to the optimates and populares of Rome. The choice is simple, if not easy. A revival of liberty or the continued stink of an extinct republic as it decomposes into dictatorial empire.

America is dead. Let us go, then, and find her.

Waves of 'War and Peace'

July 19, 2004

I T IS EASY TO MISTAKE Leo Tolstoy's massive book, "War and Peace", for a novel. It is not. Instead, it would better be considered the world's longest satirical polemic, in the vein of Jonathan Swift's "A Modest Proposal". From beginning to end, Tolstoy's classic work is intended to illustrate the arrogant incompetence of human understanding and the inability of human reason to explain even the simplest of social phenomena.

With unrelenting precision and distinct overtones of mockery, Tolstoy dissects the notion that men dictate events. In one specific example, he examines, with minute detail, the four specific orders Napoleon gave to his army prior to the battle of Borodino:

> *These dispositions, which are very obscure and confused if one allows oneself to regard the arrangements without religious awe of his genius, related to Napoleon's orders to deal with four points—four different orders. Not one of these was, or could be, carried out...*

> *And it was not Napoleon who directed the course of the battle, for none of his orders were executed and during the battle he did not know what was going on before him. So the way in which these people killed one another was not decided by Napoleon's will but occurred independently of him, in accord with the will of hundreds of thousands of people who took part in the common action. It only seemed to Napoleon that it all took place by his will.*

In the second epilogue, Tolstoy goes on to brutally abuse both specific and universal historians, demonstrating how their explanations of various historical events is not only inevitably contradictory, but often constructed on base premises that do not withstand a moment's reflection. Tolstoy further underlines his case by the choice of the two heroes of the novel within the polemic, Pierre and Kutozov, both of whom achieve their respective dream of inner peace and Russian victory only by submitting their will to the great forces moving around them.

Writing 199 years after Tolstoy, the controversial technical analyst Robert Prechter echoes the count in scorning the common wisdom's basic explanations for why things happen. In the June Elliott Wave Theorist, he writes:

> *Almost every day brings another example of rationalization in defense of the idea that news moves markets. The stock market rallied for half an hour on the morning of April 20, peaked at 10:00 a.m., and sold off for the rest of the day. Almost every newspaper and wire service claims that the market sold off because "Greenspan told Congress that the nation's banking system is well prepared to deal with rising rates, which the market interpreted as a new signal the Fed will tighten its policy sooner rather than later." Is this explanation plausible?*
>
> *Point #1: Greenspan began speaking around 2:30, but the market had already peaked at 10:00.*
>
> *Point #2: Greenspan said something favorable about the banking system, not unfavorable about rates…*
>
> *Point #3: Greenspan's speech was not the only news available. Most of the other news that day was good as well…*
>
> *Point #9: There is no evidence that a rise in interest rates makes the stock market go down.*

Prechter takes things one step further than Tolstoy, as he posits that these massive forces that historians alternatively ascribe to individuals such as Napoleon—institutions such as the Federal Reserve and ideas such as the Brotherhood of Man—tend to operate in distinct patterns known as Elliott Waves. Developed for use in the financial markets as a model of mass human emotion, Prechter is attempting to make use of these patterns to not only explain, but predict the likely effect of massive waves of human emotion.

For example, in my column of July 28, 2003, I noted Prechter's assertion that we stood on the cusp of Intermediate Wave (3), which meant, among other things, that George Bush would not be re-elected despite a 55 percent approval rating. It's still too soon to know if the president will serve a second term or not, but it's surely worth noting that his approval rating has declined 11 points to 44 percent over the past year.

Neither Prechter nor Tolstoy claim to precisely understand the way in which the mysterious wheels of history are turning. What is certain, however, is that both men appear to provide a far better means of beginning to understand the process than the historians, journalists and columnists who unwisely attempt to explain the news with a wildly inappropriate use of the physical laws of cause and effect.

'The Fraud Factor'

July 26, 2004

NO ONE CAN DENY that Bill O'Reilly is a massive media success. However, contrary to the beliefs of some, he is neither conservative nor crazy. He is, instead, a complete fraud—a blowhard as devoid of principle as the iconic strawmen he sets up and knocks down with mind-numbing regularity. In other words, he is just another media whore, selling not ideas, but himself.

Mr. O'Reilly has mastered a confrontational style, which works as long as he is in control of his opponent's microphone. His usual tactic is to ask a question, cut off his opponent halfway through the answer, then feign an emotional overreaction to an exaggerated and often inaccurate extension of their position. The fact that he has taken on many leftist lightweights and exposed their essential silliness has led many to conclude that Mr. O'Reilly is a conservative and a genuine lover of American liberty, but this is not the case.

Television is an inherently deceptive medium. It is much harder to deceive in text, where the reader has the opportunity to easily review something that might have been passed over in a casual first read. After reading Mr. Reilly's first book, it was readily apparent this was not the product of a logical, intellectual or conservative mind, but rather a haphazard collection of muddled opinions which reflected a strong government moderate's typically hazy grasp of political reality.

For example, Mr. O'Reilly once attacked the president of the Gun Owners of America as a nutcase on the fringe due to the GOA's opposition to the assault weapons ban. This demonstrated three things:

"The Factor" does not understand the purpose of the Second Amendment, which is to ensure that the people are able to militarily resist their government. Of all people, a New England man should know that Lexington and Concord were fought by those resisting the attempt of the then-legitimate government to confiscate private weapon stores.

"The Factor" does not understand the Assault Weapons Ban, which does not concern itself with bazookas and machine guns, but pistol grips and magazine clips.

"The Factor" has no intention of allowing open debate on his program. It's his program, so that's his right, but it puts the lie to his "No-Spin" claim. Mr. O'Reilly is every bit the agitprop artist that Michael Moore is, the primary difference being that Moore lies and seeks the destruction of his targets in order to destroy them, while O'Reilly lies and seeks the destruction of his targets in order to sell himself.

Lately, Mr. O'Reilly has taken to apish chest-thumping in proclaiming that various individuals are "ducking" and "backing down" from him. This is rather ironic in the face of the following transcript from *Fox News*:

> *The ACLU held its annual convention, but The Factor was not invited. However, The Factor said, "Colorado Gov. Bill Owens, a Republican, was, and he debated our pal Howard Dean, who remains too frightened to appear on [this show]. The debate dealt with the Patriot Act. Dean claimed it robs us of individual rights." The Factor reminded, "If anybody has been abused by the Patriot Act, call us, please. We want to put them on the air."*

Upon hearing this, Michael Badnarik, the Libertarian Party's candidate for president, was quick to respond to Mr. O'Reilly's challenge, apprising "The Factor" personnel of his victimized status. But like bold Sir Robin, O'Reilly bravely ran away. When danger—in the form of a political candidate, who, unlike Bill's pal, is not primary toast, but will instead be on the ballot in all 50 states this November—reared its ugly head, he bravely turned his tail and fled. One of brave Sir William's minions sent the following e-mail:

> *According to producers, the "challenge" has apparently been misunderstood in terms of what Bill actually said on the air. There is no interest in having Mr. Badnarik on the show at this time.*

Oh, it was a misunderstanding! Did "The Factor" mean to say that he does not want to put someone abused by the Patriot Act on the air? Did he deny Badnarik's victim status? No to both counts. As you see, brave Sir Bill, he turned about and gallantly he chickened out. Bravely taking to his feet, he beat a very swift retreat. Bravest of the brave, O'Reilly!

The cowardly "Factor" should change the name of his show. As "Fear Factor" is taken, "The Fraud Factor" would appear to be apropos.

Closing the open door

August 2, 2004

I NDIVIDUAL FREEDOM is at the center of all libertarian thought. Ever a lover of human liberty, Ronald Reagan hailed libertarianism for that very reason. Unlike the neosocialist Democratic Party and the neoconservative Republicans, the Libertarian Party is driven by a devotion to an idea instead of an unprincipled pursuit of power.

But as is the case with academic theories whose connection to the real world is precariously tenuous, the sad state of freedom in America means that too many libertarian ideas go untested by reality. One idea, however, that has been tested to some extent, is the libertarian concept of open borders.

Unfortunately, in the United States, de facto open borders have had the net effect of increasing central state power, as immigrants legal and illegal eagerly sample the many services provided by the state and federal governments. One can recognize this most surely by the assiduous support for "undocumented persons" voiced by Democratic Party leaders, who recognize a potential constituency when they see one.

Advocates of open borders assert that this is only because of the attractions of the welfare state, as if it is not the mere fact of societal wealth that draws aliens to a new land. This assertion is not only unsupported by fact, but is historically dubious considering the amount of human migration that occurred throughout all of human history prior to the notion of an expected claim on government largesse.

Furthermore, if an ideological theory is accurate, it must be accurate in all cases, not merely the exceptional case of the United States. Consider Switzerland, for example, a nation of some 7.5 million people, surrounded by four countries containing almost 28 times as many people. Despite strict immigration laws—even marrying a Swiss citizen or being born in Switzerland is no guarantee of obtaining residency, much less citizenship—almost

20 percent of the population is alien. And, in contradiction to the welfare theory, this has occurred despite the fact that France's welfare system is more generous.

If a Libertarian Party were to open Switzerland's borders to free immigration, Switzerland would cease to exist within a year. It would be swamped instantly by the North African tide now threatening to engulf southern Italy. The United States, being almost 40 times larger and situated further from impoverished population centers, would require more time to meet the same fate, but it would be inevitable nevertheless.

If the borders are to be open, who can then tell 1 billion Chinese or Indian citizens that they are not permitted to immigrate? Either the government has the ability to close the borders or it does not. Libertarians must remind themselves that they are not anarchists, nor do they hold to a mutant Trotskyite vision of world libertarian revolution. Protecting the national border is one of the few necessary and proper duties of a national government.

Still, the open borders policy is half right. The chief hallmark of a free society is its voluntary nature. Even if entry is, necessarily, to be restricted, the exits must always remain open. The United States fails badly by this score, as its addiction to theft-by-government causes it to not only attempt taxing non-resident citizens, but even to claim a Soviet-style exit tax as well as additional taxes for 10 years following a former citizen's relinquishing of his citizenship.

This is precisely backward when viewed from the perspective of human liberty.

Conservatives often argue that we libertarians are seeking perfection in politics. That is manifestly untrue, as I support the Libertarian Party even though its appeal is hamstrung by its flawed logic and anti-libertarian conclusions on abortion and open borders.

The Libertarian Party is still young, by historical standards, and already its position on abortion is beginning to change, as science reinforces the baby's property claim to itself. I am optimistic that the same process will eventually unfold on the immigration issue, which, as with so many other issues, will give the American people a genuine alternative to the statist policies of the bi-factional ruling party.

Ideas which cannot stand the test of time and reason must fall. The 1971 platform was a beginning, not an end, and I am confident that through its principled dedication to reason, human liberty and individual freedom, the Libertarian Party will only grow stronger as opposition mounts to the metastasizing cancer of the central state.

Why Jennifer Lopez is a sex symbol

August 9, 2004

I HAVE TO CONFESS the J-Lo phenomenon was a difficult one for me to understand. Not that she's an unattractive woman or anything, but let's face it: She possesses a reverse of what most men would consider to be the ideal bust-to-butt ratio, if decades of Playboy, Maxim and the Sports Illustrated Swimsuit Issue are any guide.

It wasn't until reading an article by the expatriate sage, Fred Reed, that I finally began to understand why Ms. Lopez—or is that Lopez-Anthony now, I'm never quite sure about these things—should present such an appealing image to the young men of America. For, as Fred writes:

> *The embittered single American women in my town do not understand why, believing that men only want young Mexican bodies. Everything, they assume, must be sex. Yeah. Sure … In Mexico you don't marry one of the guys. You don't marry a child-support bomb waiting to explode without visitation. You don't marry a hundred pounds of irrational anger looking for an excuse. You marry a woman. The difference… my God, the difference.*

Jennifer Lopez is not Mexican, to be sure, but she is nevertheless the symbolic antithesis of the Single White Female. Nor does the fact that she is a career woman with what would appear to be a serious set of relationship issues—it's a tossup between her and Ms. Spears as to who will catch Liz Taylor first—change the fact that she symbolizes, a priori, something very different than what young American men have been taught to believe is the archetypical single white American female.

The modern American woman prides herself on being strong, intelligent and independent. She insists she is just the same as a man in those few areas where she is not superior. She demands the right to be accepted exactly as she is, while claiming the right to modify everything about any man who is so foolish as to become involved with her. She is a goddess—glorious and pagan—requiring nothing more than a mortal male satellite to reflect the light of her shining splendour.

She holds firmly to these beliefs, even as she drugs herself to the gills with Prozac and sees a therapist twice a week, all the while whining to everyone within earshot that the men around her are too intimidated to ask her out.

A gentle word of advice would perhaps be useful here. The fact that men smile nervously at you and sidle away quietly at the first opportunity does not mean that they are intimidated by you. It is also possible that they have simply concluded you are a lunatic.

I once dated a delightful Asian girl, the daughter of immigrants who barely spoke a word of English. It was instructive to discover how this brought out a disdainful racism in many of the upper-middle-class white girls of my acquaintance, of which I had hitherto been unaware. In this, they echoed the defensive contempt of their ancestors, the Imperial British, whose women forced their husbands to exclude from the ruling social circle those men who had "gone native".

The great achievement of feminism is twofold. First, it allowed young men to obtain easy sex without the price of marriage or a prostitute. Second, it allowed men over the age of 60 to exit the workforce and be maintained by the labors of their newly employed daughters. When one considers the evidence, one is forced to conclude that Ms. Steinhem and Ms. Friedan were either appallingly stupid or agent provocateurs of the dread Patriarchy.

Even so, I do not despise American women. Quite to the contrary, I very much admire those who possess the courage, the character and the feminine spirit to reject the poisoned propaganda of the self-destructive Sisterhood and be women. It requires far more genuine strength and independence for a young American woman to become a lady today than it does for her to devolve into a faux male—those who manage the feat are princesses for whom a man might well wish to slay a dragon or three.

Instead of regarding her ethnic rivals with ill-concealed fear and loathing, the wise SWF would do well to consider why they should hold such appeal to the modern American SWM. Otherwise… well… there's always those reruns of "Sex in the City".

The prophet of the waves

August 16, 2004

D
O YOU EVER WONDER what it might feel like to speak with Galen or Galileo? The thought crept into my mind as I interviewed Bob Prechter, the founding father of socionomics, while the bulls were being noisily slaughtered on Wall Street last Thursday. Prechter is the first to insist that his imprecise art of reading market entrails for clues about society is not yet a science, but he nevertheless speaks with the impatient assurance of one who sees clearly that which others do not even sense.

No historian would think to deny that there are patterns to markets and societies. But are the patterns at all predictable? Aye, there's the rub.

Question: The Nasdaq-100 fell 83 percent in the Wave 1 bear. It has dropped 19.5 percent since the end of the Wave 2 bull in January. How far do you expect the Wave 3 bear we're in now to extend downward?

Answer: Sometimes first waves can be extended. That may be the case here. Wave 3 will never be the shortest, so you're certainly talking somewhere in the 60 percent range minimum, assuming a mild third wave. Otherwise, 80 percent is possible.

The Dow has held up pretty well compared to the SPX and the NDX. Do you expect that to continue?

No, definitely not. The blue chips usually give way last in a bear market. A classic example is the first half of the 1970s. The overall decline started in 1966 but the blue chips held up and even made a new high in January 1973. Then, in two short years, they dropped 45 percent. The Dow Industrials will eventually catch up to the S&P 500, but not the Nasdaq. The Nasdaq is in a class by itself.

What are the implications for the housing market? It seems to have shaken off Wave 1 rather nicely.

Yes, and that's also typical. Pete Kendall studied the coincidence of real estate and stock market tops going back 200 years and found that there tended to be a lag, typically about two years between the two peaks. This lag has now been four years, which fits our thesis that the top is of larger degree than anything we've seen in the past 200 years. What we're seeing is how people give up on one [investment class] and say the other will save us.

Some people believe that diversifying into foreign markets will protect them. Do you think that's a viable strategy?

No. It's a very bad idea. One of the things I discussed in *Conquer the Crash* is what a burden foreign diversification can be when it's time to get out of your positions. All equity markets will suffer, but North America and Europe will get hit most severely.

What do you think of bear funds such as RYVNX and BEARX? They did pretty well from 2000 to 2002. Would you expect them to do well in 2005 and 2006?

Definitely. I think for the average investor, those are excellent ways to make money in the bear market. You avoid the time decay of options as well as the open-ended risk of being short an individual stock.

Mainstream commentators often mention the election cycle as a means of assuring that the markets will go up. That hasn't played out too well this year—do you expect a significant move upward into November?

Quite the opposite. I'm looking for a down into the election, probably a downward acceleration into the election.

What are some of the more unexpected socionomics trends that you expect to reveal themselves as Wave 3 plays out?

A lot of them have already begun. We told people several years ago that there would be religious conflicts and foreign attacks on U.S. soil in *At the Crest of the Tidal Wave*. That's old news now, but it wasn't then. As for things that haven't happened yet, two things I expect to see are secession movements and labor strikes.

How are you attempting to improve the art-science of assigning wavecounts and making socionomic predictions?

The biggest step toward increasing our accuracy is the work I did for *Beautiful Pictures*. Even in *The Elliott Wave Principle*, chapter 4, we steered people in the right direction, but here I think I've demonstrated it.

Krazy John Kerry

August 23, 2004

I BELIEVE GEORGE BUSH is a traitor to the American people and their Constitution. I believe he should be impeached for sacrificing American sovereignty to supra-national organizations and I suspect that he would be perfectly content to establish a neo-fascist corporatist state in which the government was allowed to trample individual liberties.

Now, have I sufficiently established my anti-Bush bona fides to write about John Kerry without being accused of being a Republican lapdog?

Bush is, without question, an execrable president. But that does not make John Kerry fit for the office. Nothing that Bush has done, or will do, has anything whatsoever to do with John Kerry's truthfulness, his character or his mental stability. Humans are not a zero-sum game.

And the truth is that John Kerry is a very, very strange individual. Bill Clinton was once described as an unusually good liar—Krazy John Kerry is proving to be an unusually weird one.

Although the mainstream media and the *ABCNNBCBS* cabal have done their very best to sweep the stunning revelations of Krazy John's former comrades-in-arms—the swiftboat veterans—under the carpet, enough word has leaked out from the blogosphere to wreak what would appear to be fatal damage to the Kerry campaign.

Even Kerry's most diehard defenders have already conceded he was not in Cambodia over Christmas 1968, regardless of what Krazy John has claimed was seared—seared—into his memory. We're still waiting to discover the owner of the hat which Krazy John says was given to him on one of his secret missions—missions so secret that his crew, his fellow commanders and his commanding officer all deny they ever happened.

Now Kerry's defenders are getting a little crazy themselves. The *Washington Post* ignored the exposure of Kerry's Cambodian lies in favor of reporting that the military records of Larry Thurlow, a swiftboat commander and one of the authors of "Unfit for Command", contradict Thurlow's own recollection of events. Apparently, we are supposed to see this as some sort of self-contradiction. However, the only thing it actually contradicts is Krazy John's version. For, as Thurlow explains:

> *I submitted no paperwork for a medal nor did I file an after action report describing the incident. To my knowledge, John Kerry was the only officer who filed a report describing his version of the incidents that occurred on the river that day.*

It's too bad the Hero of the Mekong Delta didn't bother turning on his ever-present camera on the river that day—surely that would settle the issue. Written, directed and starring… John Kerry!

Nor is the *Washington Post* the only media outlet determined to go down with the swiftboat. Two of Slate's biggest dogs criticized the vets' ad, saying:

> *Several Swiftvets then appear on the screen, saying they "served with" Kerry. This is a semantic trick. Edwards is talking about crewmates who, at one time or another, accompanied Kerry on his six-man boat. The Swiftvets served with Kerry only in the sense that they manned other boats in Vietnam.*

Well, except for Steve Gardner, who served in Vietnam six times longer than Krazy John, and had this to say about his former commanding officer:

> *How can Kerry possibly be commander in chief when he couldn't competently command a six-man crew? Kerry was erratic. He hardly ever did what he was supposed to do. His command decisions put us in more peril then he should have. But mostly he just ran. When John Kerry looked out the bow of the boat and he saw tracer fire coming after him, he'd turn and run.*

Kerry's propensity to turn and run is the one thing that Kerry and his critics agree upon. And Gardner's contention that Kerry "hardly ever did what he was supposed to do" is supported by Kerry's own description of his Silver Star-winning heroics, where he violated several swiftboat procedures and put his entire crew in danger in order to personally kill a wounded enemy, as if the boat's three .50 caliber machine guns would not have sufficed.

The strangest thing about Krazy John is not his overly vivid imagination, his propensity for self-serving fiction, or his creepy public persona. No, the most incomprehensible thing about John Kerry is the fact that anyone, Republican or Democrat, believes a single word that comes out of his mouth.

Traitor to the Constitution

August 30, 2004

L AST WEEK, I prefaced my elucidation of the fraud that is the John Kerry campaign with some statements about the president. A number of you, unsurprisingly, took exception to my labeling him "a traitor to the American people and their Constitution."

Unfortunately for these hear-no-evil, see-no-evil Republicans, events have a way of supporting those who view objective reality without flinching.

It is an article of faith that George Bush didn't really mean it when he signed the McCain-Feingold "campaign-finance reform" bill into law. He was expecting the Supreme Court to overturn it as unconstitutional, we are told, and was shocked—shocked—when they upheld this joint effort of the mainstream media and the political class to silence political speech from parties outside the pre-approved elite.

I didn't buy that story from the start. Nor should anyone else have done so, as on Thursday, George Bush made it very clear that not only does he support McCain-Feingold's restrictions on free speech, but he plans to make forceful use of them. Furthermore, it was announced that if his administration cannot make the Federal Elections Committee shut down the efforts of American citizens to express their political views, he will propose new legislation to do so.

Since the FEC failed to act, we would now be asking the courts to force the FEC to act to shut down all this activity. There would be a lawsuit. The president said if the court action doesn't work, then he would be willing to pursue legislative action and work with Senator McCain on that.

—White House press secretary Scott McClellan

Apparently, that bit about "Congress shall make no law … abridging the freedom of speech…" escaped George Delano. Little wonder, though, considering that the president once declared "How would I know what's unconstitutional?"

And yet the silence from the Republican courtesans in the media is deafening. The Hannitys, Limbaughs, Malkins and the rest of the Republican lapdogs will no doubt soon be rushing to offer their defenses of the ever-innocent president, who just can't seem to stop himself from inadvertantly expanding the power of the central state. Don't listen, don't look, don't think… don't you know there's a war on?

The blind support they offer their beloved Republican president demonstrates an amazing inability to think past the immediate election cycle, as the power that they now cheer will soon be transformed into the power that they fear when the Democrats inevitably take their turn at the wheel.

Even those Republicans troubled by the president's anti-constitutional actions fail to understand the situation. Wes Pruden writes in the *Washington Times*:

> *Republicans don't do politics. It's a game they don't really understand. The soul of the party, such as it is, resides in the corporate boardroom. Republican strategists think like CEOs: When the going gets tough, curtsy and apologize.*

The truth is that it's Wes Pruden, not the Republican leadership, that does not understand the game. Not only does it not matter greatly whether Democrats or Republicans are in control of the federal government, it doesn't matter much to the politicians themselves. For, as the president's actions demonstrate, winning elections is less important than ensuring no cracks appear in the oligarchy that they have established in partnership with the tyrannophilic press.

And this is far from the only example of George Bush's unfaithfulness to the Constitution he swore to defend. He supports the Law of the Sea treaty, a U.S. sovereignty-destroying attempt to provide a permanent tax base for the United Nations, and American submission to almost every supra-national organization. He has led America into an open-ended war, unconstitutionally undeclared, as his own Secretary of Defense has admitted.

George Bush is about as reliable a Defender of the First as Henry VIII was a Defender of the Faith. It is an outrage that Republicans should stand by this treacherous man who has repeatedly betrayed republican ideals, the Bill of Rights, the Constitution and the American people.

Neither George Delano Bush nor Krazy John Kerry respects the Constitution or your liberty. But take heart, they are not your only options! Perhaps
you've never considered voting outside the bi-factional ruling party, but if
you're displeased with the direction of your government, you would do well
to consider the words of Libertarian presidential candidate Michael Badnarik:

*If you continue doing what you've always done, you're going to get what
you've always got.*

No case for internment

September 6, 2004

ICHELLE MALKIN'S *In Defense of Internment* runs to 416 pages. Seldom have so many words been written to such pointless effect. While Ms. Malkin appears to have done copious research with regard to the bureaucratic justifications for the internment, she also reveals her utter ignorance of military history and strategic logistics.

This is a rather serious flaw, as her entire case rests upon the flimsy and ultimately unsupportable notion of the military necessity for the federal government to violate the life, liberty and property rights of 120,000 individuals of Japanese descent, many of them American citizens. She states in the book:

> *The disparate treatment of ethnic Japanese vs. ethnic Germans and ethnic Italians is often assumed to be based on anti-Japanese racism rather than military necessity. Japan, however, was the only Axis country with a proven capability of launching a major attack on the United States.*

Malkin attempts to prove this military necessity by quoting intelligence memos, having neither the background nor the dedication to examine the question of military necessity for herself. Nor, clearly, did she bother to ask anyone who does. Consider the following facts:

The Overlord invasion required 4,600 ships to travel 100 miles under the air cover of 12,000 planes to land 156,000 troops on a French coastline 3,437 miles long. Over the next three weeks, the Allies brought in another 850,000 men, 148,000 vehicles, and 570,000 tons of supplies.

The unopposed landing at Anzio required 369 ships to land 100,000 men. Over the next four months, the Allies brought in another 14,000 men and 450,00 tons of supplies. Despite this, and the fact that the British Eighth Army and U.S. Fifth Corps were only 50 miles away on the other side of the Gustav line, the Sixth Corps remained helplessly trapped in its small beachhead.

In January 1942, prior to both Executive Order 9066 and the battle of Midway, the Imperial Japanese Navy possessed 717 carrier-borne planes and 176 ships, of which 15 were troop transports. The IJN's troop-bearing capacity was about 42,000 men. Reinforcement and resupply required a roundtrip transit of 11,000 miles to a coastline only 1,359 miles long.

None of this is hindsight, as the facts and logistics of the Pacific situation were very well known to American military strategists at the time. So much for the fears of invasion.

Malkin also writes:

The West Coast, where the vast majority of ethnic Japanese were concentrated, was uniquely vulnerable to attack, invasion, spot raids, sabotage and surveillance that could potentially cripple the war effort.

Such blissful ignorance of the realities of World War II military production is sublime. From January 1942 to August 1945, the United States launched 37 fleet carriers, 83 escort carriers and 349 destroyers. The Japanese built three fleet carriers, six small-carrier conversions, and 63 destroyers. Even if those sneaky, treacherous Japs could have destroyed 50 percent of the West Coast production facilities, the war effort would not have been slowed, much less crippled.

There was never a genuine military threat to the West Coast or to the war effort from individuals of Japanese descent on either side of the Pacific Ocean. To argue military necessity in support of the internment requires a complete disregard for the relevant facts.

In the unlikely event that you still believe Michelle Malkin has a shred of credibility left to her with regard to this matter, consider the opinion of a former member of the Joint Chiefs of Staff, a man not entirely unfamiliar with amphibious invasions.

Question: Is it credible to assert that fears of a Japanese invasion of the West Coast were well-founded?

Answer: No. No.

No, as in it was improbable, or no, absolutely not?

Absolutely no. At that time, after Pearl Harbor, the average American was afraid of just about anything. The fear factor was so bad, they had the Japanese storming the Presidio. The reality was that the Japanese did not have any amphibious shipping to speak of, they had no ability to resupply over great distance, they had no ability to manage the umbrella of air. It was not feasible.

Was that known to the military strategists of the time?

Yeah, yeah, it was.

It is fortunate that *In Defense of Internment* has some heft to it. Worthless as a contribution to the historical debate, the reader may find it to have some utility as a doorstop.

Illiterate in L.A.

September 13, 2004

THE LOS ANGELES DAILY NEWS recently lamented the tremendous increase in "functional illiteracy" among the working population of Los Angeles County. In reporting the results of a recent study, it said:

In the Los Angeles region, 53 percent of workers ages 16 and older were deemed functionally illiterate, the study said ... It classified 3.8 million Los Angeles County residents as "low-literate", meaning they could not write a note explaining a billing error, use a bus schedule or locate an intersection on a street map.

While the article took note of the wasted "hundreds of millions of dollars spent in public schools over the past decade", it blamed the terrible results on an influx of non-English speaking immigrants and a 30 percent high-school dropout rate.

But the dropout rate can't possibly explain the low level of literacy, because if the public school system was even remotely competent, the children would be reading adequately long before they ever reached high school.

Long-time readers may recall a column titled, "A Tale of 2 Children", wherein I compared two 3-year old children, one of whom was being taught to read by his parents and one who was destined for public school. The two children are now 5 years old, and I recently examined their progress.

The child in kindergarten is not yet reading, but he has learned his complete alphabet now. The homeschooled child, on the other hand, surprised me by reading at an error-free fifth-grade level on the San Diego Quick Assessment test. I verified his competence by asking him to read selections from C.S. Lewis's *Prince Caspian* to me, a book with which he was previously unfamiliar.

While he occasionally stumbled on words such as versification and centaur, (he pronounced them "versication" and "kentaur"), his comprehension was reasonably good as well.

Suddenly, it was not so hard to understand how homeschooled children, on the average, test four years ahead of their public-schooled counterparts.

The problem with public schools and reading is not hard to grasp. Whole language, the favored method, is a disastrous approach to reading that is destined for failure. Children who learn to read while being taught this method learn to read in spite of it, not because of it. Anyone who speaks Japanese and has learned both kana (phonetic) and kanji (whole language) can testify to the ease of the first and the extreme difficulty of the latter.

It's a pity that the *Daily News* does not have access to studies tracking the reading ability of children who are schooled at home in Los Angeles County. It would be interesting to see how well those children read compared to these illiterate workers, particularly immigrant children taught at home, because as hard as it may be for the *Daily News* to imagine, people who speak other languages, even Spanish, have been known to be able to read. I can't confirm this, but I have even heard rumors that there are reputed to be one or two authors, such as the suspiciously foreign-sounding Arturo Perez Reverte, who actually write in Spanish, if you can believe anything so outlandish.

The truth is that it is extremely simple to teach any normal child to read. All it requires is a consistent 15 minutes a day between the ages of three and five. If a child is capable of rote memorization, he is capable of learning the alphabet and the basic phonics, and reading will follow within months. The fact that the public schools so regularly fail at this simple task is not indicative of anything but the absolute incompetence of the public-school system—an incompetence that is not only designed into the system, but is its very raison d'être.

One need only look at an elementary school's curriculum to realize that the bulk of a child's education necessarily comes from outside the school environment. It may come from parents, peers or the television, but very little of it comes from the free day-care centers that are the public schools.

Fred Reed has a simple answer for America's education problem. It is an inventive, capitalist solution involving the intimate interaction of cement and potassium cyanide with the teaching colleges, and bounties on certified teachers. But, as he has said himself, America isn't interested in solutions that will work—much better to wring our hands, hope for the best and condemn yet another generation to illiteracy, ignorance and idiocy.

A challenge to Michelle Malkin

September 20, 2004

D EAR MRS. MALKIN,
As you may know, I am rather underwhelmed by your defense of Franklin Delano Roosevelt's executive order to intern and re-locate over 100,000 American citizens and resident aliens of Japanese descent. For, as I believe I have demonstrated in this column and on my blog, there was, in fact, no genuine military necessity whatsoever and this was known by the American military authorities at the time.

Two weeks ago, I asked you to admit that your assertion of military ne-cessity was mistaken and to retract the erroneous conclusions of your book, *In Defense of Internment.* You refused and claimed that I was "bitter and uninformed". I then sent you a list of 10 specific and simple questions, to which you declined to respond.

So, you can understand that I was delighted to read your column last week, when you wrote:

> *The wall between the self-anointed press protectorate and the unwashed masses has crumbled.... Rather and his geriatric empire are combating these powerfully persuasive blogs with anemic smears and sneers. And they are losing so very, very badly that they can't keep on top of their own spin.*

I am sure you would agree that Mr. Rather's refusal to answer the specific challenges posed to his specious assertions have badly damaged his credibility and reputation. And, as you so wisely said, with "publishing freedom comes a tall glass of responsibility. For serious blogging pundits and news-gatherers and discussion board operators, cyber-cred is everything."

In the interest of allowing you to maintain your credibility, then, I would like to invite you to defend your case for the military necessity for internment on the Northern Alliance Radio Show in a one-hour debate moderated by the gentlemen from the Fraters Libertas and SCSU Scholars blogs. This is an environment which you know is well-disposed toward you, as you appeared there to talk about your book only last month, on Aug. 21.

I understand that after your unpleasant confrontation with the ill-mannered Chris Matthews you might be reluctant to subject yourself to an acrimonious shoutfest. Therefore, in order to cultivate a more civilized debate, I propose a format wherein each person will make a brief statement, followed by five questions to which the other individual will provide short, specific and unevasive answers. After both parties have had the chance to ask five questions of the other, the moderators will ask three questions of the party of their choice, and then the process will repeat itself. This will allow for a fair and substantive discussion of the relevant issues, unlike those often heard on talk radio and the cable news shows.

The Northern Alliance Radio Show has cleared its schedule for Saturday, Sept. 25, but in the event that you are already committed to previous obligations, they, and I, remain at your disposal and will be happy to reschedule in favor of a date more convenient for you.

If I am as uninformed as you claim, no doubt you will easily be able to explain to both me and the moderators the need to intern the ethnic Japanese in order to prevent the "attack, invasion, spot raids, sabotage and surveillance" that imperiled the United States from 1942 to 1944. Should you be able to so enlighten me, I will not hesitate to publicly retract my statements about the worthless nature of your book and your total ignorance of military history.

If, on the other hand, I am able to demonstrate to the satisfaction of all that your assertions are incorrect and your conclusions are therefore fatally flawed, I am confident you will wish to correct the record as soon as possible, as would any intellectually honest individual with regard for her continuing credibility.

I await your acceptance with great anticipation.

Cordially,

Vox Day

Was Al Franken right?

September 27, 2004

I AM NO FAN OF AL FRANKEN, who likes to play tough guy as long as he's dealing with people who are too civilized or surprised to fight back. I'm very much hoping he will run for the Senate seat in Minnesota, just so I can engage in the *schadenfranken* of watching a car crash of a campaign that would make John Kerry's ongoing debacle look competent.

But since I first expressed my opposition to Michelle Malkin's *In Defense of Internment*, I have been deeply disappointed to discover that Alice was not entirely wrong to cast stones at the right-wing commentariat in *Lies and the Lying Liars Who Tell Them*. The sad fact is that there truly appear to be people on the right who have the same distant relation with the truth as the media whores of the left.

Just to give one of many possible examples, in defense of her assertion that potential espionage by Japanese-American citizens required their internment, Michelle Malkin wrote on her blog:

> *Spies on the West Coast, where the movements of our aircraft carriers could be easily monitored and where the risk of hit-and-run attacks like the one at Pearl Harbor was substantial, posed a greater threat than spies on the East Coast, where there were no aircraft carriers and no risk of a major attack.*

This is wildly untrue. In early 1942, the period with which she is concerned, the aircraft carriers Wasp, Hornet, Ranger, Charger and Long Island were all on the East Coast, operating out of Norfolk, Va. On the West Coast, there was only Saratoga, being repaired while Enterprise, Yorktown and Lexington were out raiding and protecting convoys in Samoa.

John Leo, who ominously salutes Malkin for breaking a taboo and opening a debate on "internments past and present", also delves into historical fantasy by writing:

With most of the U.S. fleet destroyed at Pearl Harbor, the Pacific became a Japanese pond.

Which is true only if you consider five of 17 battleships, zero of 9 aircraft carriers, zero of 18 heavy cruisers, zero of 20 light cruisers and two of 250 destroyers to somehow equal "most".

Most disappointingly, the eminent Dr. Thomas Sowell, who has long been an intellectual hero of mine, defends internment by writing:

No one knew where Japan would strike next.

However, the Blue Flag Messages at the Naval Historical Center record that:

Admiral Ernest J. King, Commander in Chief, U.S. Fleet, insisted on a more aggressive plan of attack during the early months of 1942... He knew that the Japanese had weakened their defenses in the central Pacific by transfers of land-based aircraft from the Mandates to the southwest Pacific, and he knew in detail the whereabouts and often the destinations of each element of the Japanese Combined Fleet.

Now mistakes—even howlers—are made by every columnist from time to time. But when egregious mistakes are compounded by evasive half-truths, it raises real questions about whether they were honest mistakes at all. On WBAL radio last Tuesday, Ron Smith asked Michelle Malkin how she would be responding to my challenge to debate the question of military necessity. She backed down, saying:

I won't be doing that. I have already addressed those questions on my blog.

However, the only posts at michellemalkin.com related to the question of military necessity were made on Aug. 6 and Sept. 6. I did not join the growing number of Mrs. Malkin's critics until Aug. 18, and I did not even send her my list of 10 specific questions until Sept. 8. The truth is that she has never successfully addressed a single point that I have made with regard to her many factual inaccuracies and erroneous assertions, on her blog or anywhere else.

Conservatives, libertarians and Republicans often pride themselves as being more committed to the objective truth than the biased left-wing media. But when confronted with the mistakes and misrepresentations of those who are on "our side", we have two choices. We can reject them, or we can imitate the other side, circle the wagons, and pretend we are all in agreement that black is indeed white.

There is no more to write on this matter. The facts are well-established. I hope, however, that we will prove ourselves to be better and more principled than the Al Frankens of the world say we are.

Homeschool or die!

October 4, 2004

An Iraqi man with suspected links to terrorism had a computer disk con-
taining crisis planning information for San Diego and other school districts
when he was arrested by U.S. authorities in Iraq, 10News *reported. The*
man's intentions were not known, and there was no indication that schools
in San Diego or any other district were targets for terrorism, according to
San Diego law enforcement officials...

"The clear message is that your children are safe and our schools are very well
prepared, as well as our school district," San Diego School District Police
Chief Don Braun said.

O NE CAN ONLY ASSUME that this police chief was educated in the
San Diego public schools himself. To conclude that the clear
message of this news is that the children of the San Diego public
schools are safe brings to mind the thought that you'll probably be able to
score some excellent ganja in the San Diego School District as long as this
cretin is in command.

Now, some might say that this headline is a little... exaggerated. And
perhaps it's not entirely fair to scare parents into pulling their kids right out
of the public schools, as it seems unlikely that Islamic terrorists will be able to
commit massacres at more than two or three schools, probably five at most.
Then again, if one considers how TV shows such as *Law and Order* see fit to
preach that homeschooled children are malnourished and abused little freaks,
it seems only reasonable to point out in like manner that public schooled
children are brainwashed, quasi-illiterate savages, with targets painted on
their chests to boot.

In fact, when one considers the Breslan massacre, the two Israeli children
murdered in Sderot and the 35 Iraqi children killed in South Baghdad last

week, the sad fact is that my sensationalistic characterization is likely more accurate. The terrorists have raised the stakes once again, targeting children to demonstrate how much they envy our freedom or whatever highly implausible motivation the Bush administration is imputing to the enemy today. I have to confess I haven't been keeping up with the president's tiptoeing around the strange and surely coincidental number of co-religionists of Peace who have unaccountably devoted themselves to murdering children.

One disturbingly familiar element to this story is the assertion that parents need not trouble their pretty little heads about Islamic terrorists bent on recreating Breslan in the suburbs.

I've never quite been able to wrap my mind around the notion that parents should not be notified that their children are being taught how to perform oral sex or are seeking to kill off the next generation. But the San Diego Unified School District has lowered the concept of in loco parentis insciens to new depths. I mean, you'd think that even the worst and most indifferent parent in the nation might like to know if his child is being targeted by suicide bombers, if only to take out an insurance policy.

I'm just curious to know what the FBI has concluded that an Iraqi man was doing with the information in the first place, given that it is so sure that the thought of attacking a school had not even begun to consider the merest possibility of thinking about the prospect of crossing the man's mind. Perhaps it was an innocent coincidence, the gentleman simply happens to be in charge of crisis planning for the local madrassah and only wanted to be sure that its emergency plans were up to date and in line with those belonging to schools run by the Great Satan.

In any event, if advanced academic achievement and avoiding social Darwinist socialization isn't enough for you to keep your child off the Yellow Bus of Doom, perhaps the idea of massacre avoidance will hold some appeal. Or perhaps not. After all, it's surely safe to assume that it can't possibly happen here.

Corporations are not capitalism

October 11, 2004

O NE OF THE MOST widely believed myths in America today is the belief that corporations are an inherent part of capitalism. Concomitant with this is the idea that big corporations and big government have an intrinsically hostile relationship and that the stock market is a free market.

Nothing could be further from the truth.

Capitalism was already well entrenched and the Industrial Revolution was complete when the U.S. Supreme Court radically altered the concept of the corporate charter in 1886 by ruling that the Southern Pacific Railroad was a "natural person" under the U.S. Constitution. Prior to this time, corporations were strictly controlled by state law, which is why the word "limited" still occurs in corporate language.

The Supreme Court had tried once before to expand corporate power by stripping sovereignty from the state of New Hampshire in 1819. In response, many states wrote laws to ensure that they would retain their sovereignty— 19 "even amended their constitutions to make corporate charters subject to alteration or revocation by their legislatures."

The 1886 ruling trumped these efforts, fulfilling Thomas Jefferson's prescient fears. In a letter to George Logan written on Nov. 12, 1816, he wrote:

> *I hope we shall take warning from the example and crush in it's birth the aristocracy of our monied corporations which dare already to challenge our government to a trial of strength and bid defiance to the laws our country.*

But these monied corporations did more than challenge our government, they corrupted it entirely and established a symbiotic relationship with it.

This symbiotic relationship is openly anti-capitalistic, as undying corporations take advantage of laws originally written to protect the entrepeneurs who are the genuine engine of technological progress and economic growth, and use them to sustain their unnatural, parasitic life.

For example, Disney successfully lobbied Congress in 1998 to extend the period of copyright law for 20 years, increasing it to the life of the author plus 70 years. This is obviously of no benefit to a deceased author or his children, but it does prevent Mickey Mouse from entering the public domain while remaining technically within the constitutional dictates that copyrights be granted for a "limited time".

Corporations also use the government to protect their pool of investment money in the stock market. Due to the massive regulation of this anti-capitalist and unfree market, entrepreneurs needing to raise large sums of capital to challenge established corporate competitors are forced to submit to the predatory regime of the investment banks. In a genuinely free market, the owners of small, but growing businesses could simply sell their public shares over the Internet to anyone who wished to invest.

Indeed, with today's high-speed communications technology and digital money, there is no more need for Wall Street than there is for Congress. Eliminating both and replacing them with electronic systems—Free and Open Source, of course—would result in the realization of significantly more pure and efficient strains of capitalism and democracy alike.

One need only look at the various socialist and communist states around the world and the friendly relations that giant Western multinationals have with them to realize there is no fundamental link between capitalism and corporations. Gozprom, LUKoil and 400 other Soviet corporations were operating inside and outside the USSR prior to 1989, while Communist China not only permits corporations, but owns several that are listed on the Global Fortune 500. Some of them, such as PetroChina and Sinopec, are even traded on the Hong Kong and New York stock markets.

In fact, it is not the Chinese government, but the People's Liberation Army that owns the International Trust and Investment Corporation, which among other things has more than 200 Canadian corporations and is the largest "private" operator of shipping container terminals.

Not everything to which the idiot Left is hostile is necessarily good. It is impossible to assert that the age of untrammeled corporatism has been friendly to individual liberty or prosperity, especially when real wages have been falling for three decades—they are 14 percent lower than they were in 1972.

The genius of human invention and the undeniable blessings of capitalism do not stem from artificial structures at law, they come only from the mind of the individual. Conservatives would do well to remember that the next time that the corporations go to their comrades in Congress, demanding more violations of human freedom and more restrictions on individual liberty in order to sustain their vampirish unlives.

Slick Willy and Bad Sir Billy

October 18, 2004

WELL, GRAB ME A LOOFAH and toss me the phone! There is a certain irony in how Three Monkey Republicans—most noticeably those inhabiting supposedly conservative bastions such as *Fox News*, *National Review* and assorted cheerleader blogs—are reacting to accusations made recently against their Bill of preference. Whereas they could not get enough of All Monica, All The Time, (or, more recently, RatherGate), they appear to have rather less interest in Miss Andrea Mackris of *Fox News* and her lawsuit against The Freaky Factor, Bill O'Reilly.

And yet, self-destruction by sexual impropriety is hardly uncommon among those who place the pursuit of fame, money and political power ahead of principle. Bill Clinton, Newt Gingrich and Bob Livingston are only three of many examples of men whose personal principles were as weak as their commitment to freedom and human liberty.

Those who hold to no principles with regard to their ideology seldom subscribe to any involving their personal behavior either. Show me a man who prefers to split the difference between right and wrong, and I'll show you a man who won't keep his pants zipped if given the opportunity.

Conservatives may remember this as the "character counts" argument made by many of the very individuals who have been so uncharacteristically silent after the Drudge Report posted one of its biggest headlines since the notorious one about a certain blue dress. Wherefore art thou now, Jonah Goldberg? It took two days before NRO's Corner so much as emitted a peep about what is already a matter of public record!

Still, I find this silence understandable because I have experienced the pressure not to speak poorly of those who can make or break a right-wing pundit's career. The reason that many conservative pundits are not leaping all over this is not because they don't possess the facts—let's face it, when does that stop anyone—but because they fear losing their precious air time should they fall afoul of the powers-that-be at Fox.

For example, I cannot overstate the fear and awe of the Third Triumvirate—which is to say, Rush Limbaugh, Bill O'Reilly and Sean Hannity—that pervades every conservative publishing house, because any one of these three men can make or break a book intended for a conservative audience. As I was told by one publisher: "You may not care about the consequences of taking on O'Reilly or Hannity, but we have to be careful." This is not moral cowardice on the part of the publishers, it is simply the market reality with which they must deal. It is also why most conservative commentators are eventually forced to decide if certain individuals are to be considered off-limits or not.

Only the very few who either don't give a damn about television and radio or are too obtuse to understand what's going on are immune. That's why the lionhearted conservative commentariat will be as reluctant to address the issues raised by Brave Sir Billy's telephone talk as the stalwarts of the mainstream media were to discuss Dan Rather's forgeries and Slick Willy's perjury and peculiar ways with a cigar. They'll do it, eventually, but only if it's proved beyond any shadow of a doubt and continued silence is simply not an option.

Now, as then, it is impossible for anyone not directly involved to ascertain the truth of the matter. Bill O'Reilly may be entirely innocent, or he may be guilty of moral failures far greater than those alleged. Like Bill Clinton before him, Bill O'Reilly is aggressively asserting that he is being falsely accused. And like the former president, he is also failing to deny the very specific charges being made:

> *In a case like this, you have to fight, even at some risk. These people trying to extort this money from us will lob all kinds of charges, knowing that some in the press who don't like me or* Fox News *will gleefully pick the stuff up … Obviously, I can't get into specifics as the litigation is in motion, but I do respect my audience and feel you should know exactly what's going on.*

Unfortunately, it looks as if the conservative media is once again determined to imitate its great nemesis, the mainstream media. But the public abhors a vacuum and no one should know better than the commentators of the right that if they will not hold their own accountable for their failures, moral and intellectual, someone else will be happy to fill in the void.

Fox News is a firebreak

October 25, 2004

LIKE MANY MEN AND WOMEN of the right, I was absolutely delighted when *Fox News* first came on the scene. It was so refreshing to hear someone in front of a camera criticizing Democrats and left-liberal policies that I seldom paid attention to what was actually being said in between all the car chases.

Unfortunately, while *Fox News* is certainly to the right of the *ABCNNBCBS* cabal, this is rather like saying that Sweden is to the right of the People's Republic of China, North Korea and the defunct Democratic Republic of Kampuchea. It may be true, but it's not exactly significant.

Like its mainstream rivals, *Fox News* does its best to avoid overt ideology or other overly intellectual matters. The horserace is all, never mind that regardless of who wins the upcoming election, the governance of the nation will be identical. The Republican argument that John Kerry will not enthusiastically wage war is blown away by 20th-century American military history (World War I, World War II, Korea, Vietnam, Somalia and Yugoslavia = Democrats, Grenada, Kuwait, Afghanistan and Iraq = Republicans.)

Meanwhile, the Democratic case against Bush is characteristically insane. George Delano has governed to the left of Bill Clinton, JFK and Harry Truman, so if Democrats were as interested in their principles as they are in the naked pursuit of power, they'd celebrate the man, not denigrate him. As I've said before, modern American liberalism is nothing but the socialism too stupid to recognize itself in the mirror.

The success of Fox should come as no surprise. When all three traditional networks, plus one public network and two cable networks lean left in a country that is split roughly down the middle into "liberal" and "conservative" camps, logic dictates that any network which so much as throws a bone to the tens of millions of ignored conservatives, Republicans, libertarians and various and sundry other right-leaning individuals will thoroughly trounce the opposition in the ratings. And yet, it is Fox's very success that contains within it the seeds of conservatism's media demise.

As *Fox News* has grown, so too has its appeal to the unprincipled media whores who care nothing for anything but personal fame, money and power. They creep in from *CNN*, from the Columbia School of Journalism and the Ivy League. Even those who found their success in an iconoclastic approach now find themselves under pressure from their newfound friends to abandon their foolish pretensions to ideological purity and be pragmatic about the political realities.

What was a voice of opposition to the ever-expanding federal bureaucracy and moral sewer that was the Clinton administration has become what amounts to a firebreak for the present anti-conservative Republican administration. Even a casual observer can easily see the line that has been drawn between what is considered acceptable opposition to the statist agenda and what is genuinely dangerous to it.

For example, it is acceptable to advocate lower tax rates, but you'll never hear a whisper of the truth that the IRS is an utter fraud and that 667 IRS employees—who are obviously in a position to realize this—were recently investigated and confirmed to be noncompliant by the IRS itself. Those 667 employees equate to 60 PERCENT of the total number of cases successfully prosecuted on an annual basis by the Department of Justice at the recommendation of the IRS. The Government Accountability Office even reports that since 1998 "the number of tax service employees accused of noncompliance with tax filing and reporting laws steadily increased."

And who can forget the image of the unborn Samuel Armas's arm reaching out of his mother's womb, which Matt Drudge wanted to show America to demonstrate the appalling evil of the national atrocity, abortion? But that was an image he was forbidden to show his viewers—forbidden by the supposedly conservative (and, you would think, anti-abortion) management of *Fox News*.

Such a mystery, such an intriguing dichotomy. But the truth is that any time a genuine conservative dares to raise an issue that threatens to strike too hard at the heart of the government and the nation's ongoing centralization, Fox's attack dogs and killer vamps will be there at the command of their masters to belittle, to marginalize and to defang.

Not too terribly long ago, the word "liberal" meant an advocate of individual liberty and human freedom. It is not unthinkable to suggest historians may one day look back to the inception of *Fox News* to mark when the word "conservative" was similarly redefined.

Federal fox and the conservative chickens

November 1, 2004

PITCHFORK PAT has turned in his plowshare for a sword. Joseph Farah has decided that he has a dog in this hunt after all and more than a few chicken-little libertarians have flown the coop for the safety of the federal fox's protection. Such rampant abandonment of principle would be disheartening if I thought that it made any difference at all.

Let's get one thing out of the way first. John Kerry is a bad man. The Democratic candidate is an open advocate of unvarnished evil. He is a liar, he is a tin soldier without honor, he is the all-too-eager tool of those who hope to use him to institute both national and global socialism, and much to the dismay of those who sneer at the president's intelligence, he simply isn't very bright. John Kerry would make a mediocre president and only the combination of Kerry's extreme incompetence and a Republican Congress would prevent him from making a horrible one.

George Bush, unlike John Kerry, is an excellent politician. Unfortunately, he has used his political gifts and his trustworthy persona to betray his base constituency, conservative Republicans, at nearly every turn. Just a week before the election, he again delivered a stunning slap in the face to his core supporters, this time to social conservatives who believe (wrongly, in my opinion) that using the power of the federal government is the best way to protect the institution of marriage.

The battle cry of the current conservative con, "we are at war", is an ancient political device. After more than 400 years of non-contiguous terms for Rome's ruling consuls, an astute politician, Gaius Marius, used the very real threat posed by the Cimbri and the Teutoni to justify his unprecedented re-elections to the consulship. Previously, a few consuls had served more than one term—though almost never twice in a row—but Marius arranged to hold six consulships between 107 and 100 B.C., and in the process instituted the bloody proscriptions that led to Rome's first civil war. Interestingly enough, his first consulship also saw the passage of the Lex Caelia tabellaria, which introduced secret voting in trials for treason.

Shades of the Patriot Act, one might say. Like Marius, George Bush poses as the defender of the nation, although the continuing conflict in Iraq manifestly demonstrates that he is not the martial peer of the great Roman general. He has other poses, too, as imaginative conservatives continue to claim him as one of their own though he is not and has never really claimed to be.

George Bush's most successful pose has been his iconic image as a patriotic, anti-U.N. defender of American national sovereignty. This is wildly off-base, considering that most of the president's statements and actions on the international scene have been inimical to national sovereignty and strongly supportive of the globalist agenda. He ordered the country to rejoin UN-ESCO, supports the Law Of The Sea treaty and in 2002 declared before the U.N. General Assembly "we will show that the promise of the United Nations can be fulfilled in our time." Indeed, he gave defending the legitimacy of the United Nations as one of his primary reasons for invading Iraq.

It is true that everything that can be counted against George Bush can be counted three times over against John Kerry. Nor can it be denied that for advocates of freedom and human liberty, George Bush is still the lesser evil. Many have said that supporting the lesser evil is therefore the good and right thing to do, but I strongly disagree. Those who claim God is dead can do as they see fit, but Christians are not commanded to do the lesser evil, they are told to do what is right in all things, even if that requires them to walk a hard and narrow path alone.

If America is a car headed for a cliff, a vote for John Kerry is like stepping on the gas, while voting for George Bush can be best equated with leaving it on cruise control. However, if you are at all concerned with the long-term direction of this country, I strongly suggest pulling on the emergency brake by voting for one of the two men who are genuinely committed to reclaiming America's stolen birthright, Michael Badnarik of the Libertarian Party or Michael Peroutka of the Constitution Party.

Neither man will win tomorrow's election. But at least you will have the satisfaction of knowing that you are not a willing accomplice in the ongoing bipartisan destruction of your country.

God, George Bush, and war

November 8, 2004

> *Religion makes enemies instead of friends. That one word, "religion", covers all the horizon of memory with visions of war, of outrage, of persecution, of tyranny, and death. That one word brings to the mind every instrument with which man has tortured man. In that one word are all the faggots and flames and dungeons of the past, and in that word is the infinite and eternal hell of the future.*

> —Robert Green Ingersoll, "The Damage Religion Causes"

EVEN AS IT REELS from last week's election returns, the atheist left continues to insist that George Bush has engaged the nation in a modern crusade because of his faith in the Christian God. They believe this in part because their godless relativism somehow does not prevent them from believing that Manichean evil exists in the form of Republican politicians, and partly because they subscribe to the theory that religion is the primary cause of the wars that have plagued human history.

And in this age of jihadist revival, it is easy to see why such a theory of martial causation would hold some appeal to the historically ignorant. The recent conflicts in the Sudan, Nigeria, East Timor, the Philippines, Kashmir and Chechnya certainly have a strong Islamic element, and the thought of an army of the West swooping down on the Middle East cannot help but conjure up images of Raymond, Godfrey and Bohemond before the walls of Jerusalem.

But much time has passed between the taking of Jerusalem in 1099 and the fall of Baghdad in 2003, and very little of it has been peaceful. Furthermore, Islam did not exist prior to the year 610, nor did Christianity prior to A.D. 33. And yet ancient documents such as the Chronicles of the Assyrian Kings are filled with descriptions of what certainly appear to be matters of martial concern. For example, the Black Obelisk of Shalmeneser III records some of the bloody-minded Assyrian king's martial deeds:

> *In my 24th year, the lower Zab I crossed. The land of Khalimmur I passed through. To the land of Zimru I went down. Yan'su King of the Zimri from the face of my mighty weapons fled and to save his life ascended [the mountains]. The cities of 'Sikhisatakh, Bit-Tamul, Bit-Sacci, Bit-Sedi, his strong cities, I captured. His fighting men I slew. His spoil I carried away. The cities I threw down, dug up, [and] with fire burned ... The cities of Cua-cinda, Khazzanabi, Ermul, [and] Cin-ablila with the cities which were dependent on them I captured. Their fighting men I slew. Their spoil I carried away. The cities I threw down, dug up [and] burned with fire. An image of my Majesty in the country of Kharkhara I set up.*

It is true that Shalmaneser gives much credit for his victories to his god, Assur, but not once does the son of Assur-nasir-pal claim that he is waging war in an attempt to perpetrate the worship of his god. For one thing, Shalmaneser does not seem inclined to leave many potential converts alive and one further notes that the statues erected to commemorate his victories are not of Assur, but of Shalmaneser himself.

To cite a more recent example, historians record that all of Europe anticipated that Charles VIII of France, upon coming into his own in 1491, (he had been subject to an 8-year regency upon inheriting the crown at 13), would launch a military campaign because that was what was expected of young, energetic kings with armies. And within three years, Charles had invaded Italy and laid the groundwork for 30 years of war on the Lombard plain.

But this is simply anecdotal evidence. A more systematic review of the 489 wars listed in the Wikipedia's list of military conflicts, ranging from Julius Caesar's Gallic Wars to the 1969 Football War between Honduras and El Salvador, shows that only 53 of these wars—10.8 percent—can reasonably be described as having a religious nature, even if one counts each of the 10 Crusades separately. If there is a god responsible for this ever-present bloodshed, it is Mars, not Jehovah or Jesus Christ.

America does not fight religious wars—it never has, the jihadist aspect of the present conflict notwithstanding. As America's martial involvement in the Middle East broadens in the next four years, disappointed Democrats can at least console themselves with the thought that God is not to blame.

Outside the asylum

November 15, 2004

I T WAS BOTH TRAGIC and metaphorically apropos. Only five days after the Democratic Party committed electoral suicide by casting stones at military veterans and embracing the attempt of various government officials to cram the homosexual parody of matrimony down the throats of an unwilling America, one of its members literally followed suit.

Andrew Veal's death was a dash of cold water in the face of political observers around the world, who have grown accustomed to taking the nonsensical hysteria of the Democrats' public relations with a boulder-sized grain of salt. But it is not so easy for the weak, sick and mentally feeble on whom the Democratic party is reliant to do the same—they simply do not have the facility to understand that the cartoonish hyperbole in which the Democratic Underground, MOVE-ON, ACT-UP and the *New York Times* so often engage is nothing more than propagandistic exercises in political showmanship.

If you truly believe that Bush is Hitler and that his re-election marks the final step into a new Dark Age run by Christian theocrats intent on establishing the American Inquisition, then perhaps suicide is a reasonable solution. True, you'd have to be an idiot to believe that, but then, the Democratic Party is filled with those that the Penguin Dictionary of Psychology defines as being "borderline deficient".

The Democrats' claims to being the party of the more intelligent have been reliably fraudulent, so it should come as no surprise that the national exit polls from the recent election indicate precisely the opposite. The correlation between intelligence and income is widely recognized, so the fact that John Kerry's support was strongest—63 percent—among those earning under $15,000 should give even the most left-inclined Mensan pause.

In fact, as incomes rose, support for Kerry reliably declined, reaching its nadir at 35 percent of the $200,000-plus crowd. And speaking of nadirs, Ralph's 1 percent only began to make an appearance over $100,000, providing support for the theory that if you maleducate an intelligent person over an extended period of time, you can turn them into a high-functioning political simulacrum of an idiot.

John Kerry also had the edge among those who did not complete high school, and, further sustaining the maleducation theory, did not regain the upper hand until the postgraduate crowd was surveyed. George Bush, on the other hand, won among high-school, partial-college and college grads.

Unions these days largely consist of state and federal government employees—union households went heavily for the Democrat, 59 percent to 40 percent. Your mileage may vary, but I, for one, have yet to encounter a government employee that I would consider to be on the north side of the median. Sure, it's possible that the blank stares one so often encounters at the drivers license bureau and similar offices mask minds too busy contemplating last night's Proust reading to summon any interest in the quotidian banalities that surround them at work, but Occam's razor suggests this is an unlikely explanation.

The reality is that the modern Democratic Party can be broadly divided into four basic groups. The maleducated utopians (academics, students and media), the stone cold killers (feminists and global socialists), the cannon fodder (the mentally sub-par dependent class) and the deranged window dressing (the lavender lobby and the eco-freaks). This is a ragtag collection more suited for an asylum than the halls of power, if only to protect them from themselves.

So, forget the division into the United States of Canada and Jesustan that some bloggers have proposed—all this nation truly needs is a Wonko the Sane to erect signs indicating to bewildered Democrats that they have inadvertently wandered into that strange land Outside The Asylum, where people believe in strange things such as God, moral values, personal responsibility and a literal Constitution.

Abusing homeschoolers

November 22, 2004

L AST WEEK, I received an e-mail suggesting that as a champion of home-schooling, I might do well to revisit the matter in light of a series on the subject by the *Akron Beacon Journal*, which raised some questions about the supposed benefits of homeschooling as well as the potential risks. While there is not space to address all of the subjects raised—some are nothing but mudslinging, while others are actually relevant—I thought it most important to examine the idea that homeschooling allows child abusers to act in secret by avoiding the school authorities.

Child abuse, as defined by the Child Maltreatment 2002 report by the U.S. Department of Health and Human services, is defined rather broadly. While the overall statistics legitimately portray parents as the most likely perpetrators, it also includes things such as mental and verbal abuse, which is not what most people are considering with regards to the homeschooling issue.

In keeping with these broad definitions, 58.3 percent of the abusers are women, which should help indicate the definitions are not limited to the extreme abuse about which most people are concerned with regard to the issue at hand. Fortunately, the report breaks the statistics down into highly specific segments which are informative and very useful.

The maltreatment report reveals three problems with the idea that public schooling will help prevent child abuse.

First, the vast majority of child fatalities—82.3 percent—occur before the child has even reached school age, while 40.1 percent of all abuse does. Even if the public schools were made mandatory, no teacher or principal could possibly help a 2-year-old. According to the report, 166 children between the ages of 5 and 17 were victims of lethal child abuse, which is less than one-fifth of the 836 children who died in school-related transportation accidents!

Second, the likelihood that evil pedophile parents will keep their children in order to sexually abuse them seems unlikely considering the following facts. Of the 88,656 cases of confirmed sexual abuse in 2002, 16,210 were committed by parents. Despite having far less time and opportunity than parents, teachers and day-care providers were responsible for 15,098 such cases. In fact, the number of confirmed sexual abuses committed by educational personnel represents almost a quarter of the total cases of all abuses accurately reported by educational personnel.

The third problem is that teachers simply don't make for very reliable reporters. Educational personnel were the single most likely group to make unsubstantiated claims of child abuse. Their 179,098 unsubstantiated claims represented 17.1 percent of all such claims, even higher than the percentage reported by the notoriously inaccurate social services personnel (12.4 percent) and anonymous reporters (11.9 percent.). A case of abuse reported by an educator was 2.83 times more likely to be determined to be unsubstantiated than it was to be found true upon professional investigation, while another 176 abuse claims made by educational personnel were intentionally false.

The reality is that although child abuse is a horrific evil that even moral relativists can find the moral outrage to condemn, there is simply no way to eliminate it completely without eliminating every last vestige of freedom in America. As the sexual-abuse statistics indicate, even permanently removing every child in the country from his parents would not eliminate such abuse, indeed, it might well increase it instead by giving more time and opportunity to the teachers and day-care providers who are molesting children at a greater per-capita rate than parents.

But the real question underneath it all is this: To whom does a child belong? The child either belongs to the state or to the parents. There is no middle ground. And considering the long, lethal history of the relationship between governments and children dating back to King Herod, turning to the state to prevent child abuse would appear to be rather similar to relying on the National Socialists to protect Jews.

Government schooling is not a reliable force for good, it is merely a force to be wielded by whomever holds the whip hand at the moment. Home-schooling is the best way for a parent to control how that force is permitted to mold and manipulate his child.

It is not an accident that public schools were a major component of the Communist, National Socialist and Fascist party programs; conservative parents who believe their neighborhood public school is excellent would do well to examine precisely how excellence in education is defined by the educationist elite.

Movies for the military

November 29, 2004

Greetings from Kuwait. Been over here in the desert with the Army for about 10 months and trying to keep up my sense of humor. Enjoy your Monday commentary on WorldNetDaily. A little intellectual stimulation goes a long way over here... I would love it if you would consider this unusual request:

Everyone has their favorite movie. You know, that special movie you can watch over and over again by yourself or with someone special. I'd like for you to send us your favorite movie on DVD.

But there's a catch. With each movie sent, I want you to attach a note telling us what makes it your favorite movie (i.e., how it touched you, special memories, favorite scenes, why you relate to it, etc). I'm not asking for a lengthy review, just a small note with your personal thoughts.

Write your thoughts on a 3×5 card or sticky note and insert it inside of the DVD case. Please include your e-mail and/or mailing address. I know plenty of soldiers and sailors here who would love to watch them... I'm eager to know what you consider to be your favorite movie.

WHAT IS MY FAVORITE MOVIE? That's a hard one. The *Lord of the Rings* trilogy are certainly the DVD's I treasure most, but that's almost cheating since they're based on the greatest fantasy novel ever. I can't call them my favorite movies because they're not really movies to me, they're visual realizations of my favorite books.

Star Wars was my favorite movie growing up, but its magic began to fade with *Return of the Jedi* and disappeared altogether with the abominable prequels. I don't even like to think about it anymore.

Kenneth Branagh is one of my favorite actors, and I very much enjoyed both *Henry V* and his remake of Hitchcock's *Dead Again*. If only Keanu Reeves didn't poison *Much Ado About Nothing* with his iniquitous inability to out-act his wardrobe, that could be a contender, too. But in all three cases, there is the sans originality factor.

Aliens is my favorite military and sci-fi movie, but it's a downer and doesn't compare well the aforementioned films. For brainless action flicks, it's hard to beat *Con Air*. Forget John Malkovich—Steve Buscemi simply makes that movie. The scene when the mask is removed from the most-dangerous psychopath alive to reveal a weedy little white guy cracks me up every time.

The major added a footnote: "…keep in mind that most of these soldiers and sailors are guys, so go easy on the chick flicks" which knocks what is probably my all-time favorite movie out of contention, *Bridget Jones Diary*. (I'm totally kidding, I'm actually thinking of *A Room with a View*, a chick flick for which I harbor unashamed affection. For some inexplicable reason, I'm a sucker for period romances.)

I have probably seen *Monty Python and the Holy Grail* more times than any other movie. But I can't even see it as a movie anymore—it's more of a cultural artifact and source of communication with my friends. *Being There* has the single funniest scene ever, but it's too low-key throughout. And while I enjoy the silliness of a *Weird Science*, a *This is Spinal Tap* or a *Caddyshack*, they would not qualify as a favorite.

In the end, however, I think it has to boil down to two black comedies. *Heathers* was a brilliant over-the-top explication of how it felt to attend high school in the 1980s. Sure, the beautiful people were never quite as beautiful or as brutal as the *Heathers* clique, and persecuted teenagers didn't actually try to blow up the school until Columbine a decade later. But in my opinion, Christian Slater's lame "no one loves me" defensive soliloquy at the end has to prevent *Heathers* from claiming primacy of position.

That leaves *Grosse Point Blank*, which manages to juggle both darkness and light in a man's belated discovery that he has a soul, and that life cannot simply be reduced to abstract relativism. The combination of brutal humor, intelligent discourse and genuine sweetness makes it my favorite movie. I hope the soldiers in the sand will enjoy it as much as I did.

A militant Merry Christmas

December 6, 2004

I'M NOT SURE WHEN I NOTICED that "Merry Christmas" had been supplanted by "Happy Holidays". I thought this generic term was rather strange, considering that Hannukah is a minor Jewish holiday and Kwanzaa has less of a historic basis than Middle Earth or "Star Trek", but I simply filed it away for future reference.

Two years ago, though, I noticed something that struck me as bordering on the ominous. People I did not know, namely salesclerks, were starting to correct me when I wished them a Merry Christmas. "Don't you mean Happy Holidays?" I was asked. "No, actually, I don't," I replied. "I am buying these gifts and having them wrapped here at your store, which is decorated with an overtly Christmas theme, because Dec. 25 is fast approaching.

"I am not buying them because of oil magically reappearing in a Jewish lamp. I am not buying them because Kwanzaa Timmy is coming to town with his maize and his copy of the 'Communist Manifesto'. I am buying them because it is Christmas time."

Since then, I have become militant about any generic reference to "the holidays" or even worse, "the season". The season of what? "Have a good season" is something you tell an athlete, not a fellow celebrant of Jesus Christ's birth.

Now, I have no quibble with those who harbor doubts that the Prince of Peace was, in fact, laid in a manger 2,000 years ago. Believe or don't believe, that's totally up to you. If God is content to let you decide, then who am I to tell you what to think? But if the fact that Christians celebrate the birth of their savior bothers you so much, then for the love of all that is collectively approved and societally consensual, don't celebrate it! Forget the carols, the gift-giving, the candlelight services. Forget "Silver Bells" and "Silent Night" and the stockings hung with care.

Celebrate your own holiday. Get some woad and paint your butt blue. Burn a druid to death in a wicker basket. Jump over a bonfire and have sex with a stranger at the solstice. Sacrifice a black goat at midnight. I truly don't care and if you'll just let me know which holiday is your big one, I'll be happy to wish you a Blessed Beltane, an Inspired Imbolc or a Serendipitous Samhain.

Christians, it is time to realize that the gloves are off and the gauntlet has been thrown down. The TV shows of our childhood have come to life and the Christmas grinches are real. The separation of Church and State has invaded our department stores and both Santa and the little baby Jesus are under attack. The secular elite seeks to establish its atheist apartheid, and now that Christianity has been eradicated from the government schools, it has the most popular symbol of Western Christianity firmly in its sights.

So, refuse to accept this. Don't go along! Don't buy from a store that is celebrating "the holidays" or "the season". If they're not celebrating Christmas, then why should you buy your family's Christmas presents from them? Give a cheerful "Merry Christmas" back to every "Happy Holidays" you receive. Select a Bible verse for your Christmas cards. Skip the "Festival of Lights" and go see "A Christmas Carol" instead. Invite a stray to your Christmas dinner and a stranger to your midnight mass.

Corporations have no conscience. A season or two of holiday sales sans Christmas shoppers and we'll be seeing verses from Matthew, Mark, Luke and John on every store front, advertisement and Web page. Christmas survived 70 years of communism, it can conquer politically correct capitalism too.

And even if you're not a Christian, even if you don't believe that Christ the Savior is born, do you really want to trade in the happy Christmases of your childhood for a secular smorgasbord of Hanukah, Ramadan, and Kwanzaa? People, if nothing else, there is an aesthetic imperative here. There's a reason, after all, that those evangelical fundamentalists of Band-Aid did not sing "Do they know it's Kwanzaa time at all…"

Merry Christmas.

Abandon truth, all ye who enter

December 13, 2004

A S I APPROACHED the spring of my high-school graduation, with middling grades but stratospheric PSAT and SAT scores, I found myself getting recruited by colleges as if I were a six-four howitzer-armed quarterback. Lesser schools pitched full rides plus book and living expenses, while Ivy League universities beckoned with the opportunity to become a diploma-carrying member of the East Coast elite.

If intelligence is mental firepower, wisdom is knowing where and when to use it. Looking back, it is apparent that at 17, the amount I possessed of the former was in inverse proportion to the latter. Due to various family connections, I was encouraged to attend Harvard, the Naval Academy or Princeton; I favored SMU myself based on its reputation for a) parties, and b) really hot girls. A compromise was reached, and I attended a second-tier Ivy wannabe that knew one brief shining moment as a top-five party school before the administration decided things were getting a little out of hand during my stay there.

In fact, the only time I can recall getting misty-eyed about the old alma mater was a year after graduation, when my best friend called to tell me about the two busloads of police being brought in to control the riot that started when the administration tried to shut down House Party weekend. Our apathetic student body had never gone in for the anti-apartheid shanty towns or other activist fads, but by the sacred Stroh's 30-pack, we were more than willing to fight for our right to party. Hurray for the Orange and the Blue!

As an athlete, I visited a number of other campuses, including Harvard, Princeton, Dartmouth, William and Mary, Georgetown, Syracuse and others I can't remember. Only the Dartmouth campus partied harder, but the basic scene was always the same. I particularly remember one pompous Harvard jerk who was trying to impress a few Harvardettes by implying that he, a hockey player, was a member of the university's top-ranked NCAA Division One squad. Unfortunately for him, I happened to know that Harvard's team was playing the University of Minnesota in Minnesota that night…

Now, it seems my memories have just been sold. Tom Wolfe, America's distinguished Novelist Emeritus, has recently drawn attention to the devolution of the university with his latest masterpiece, "I Am Charlotte Simmons". (I haven't read it yet, as I'm presently enjoying a bilingual literary threesome with Charles Stross and Umberto Eco.) But Wolf's condemnation of the university of a student body far more concerned with matters carnal than academic rings very true. Indeed, my first thought upon reading the various book reviews was that this was a novel someone of my generation could have—should have—written, and in writing it, launched their career into the literary firmament.

The truth is that I learned very little in college, despite graduating with a double-major. Had my father not provided me with a strong background in Austrian economists such as Hayek, Schumpeter and Mises, I might easily have joined my fellows in falling for the neosocialist claptrap spouted by the same professors who had literally written the Econ 101 book we were using. And as bad as the situation is at elite schools, it is even worse at public universities. I once spoke with a graduate of the University of Minnesota who majored in economics—she had never heard of John Maynard Keynes. While one could argue that the nation would be better off if no one had ever heard of the man or his poisonous theories, the question of what on earth that economics department had been doing with its students for four or more years remains a mystery.

Last weekend, two students from Patrick Henry College, a venerable institution founded all of four years ago, defeated Oxford University's moot court team at Balliol Hall. I suspect that the victory of the two former homeschoolers may presage the next step in the ongoing homeschooling revolution, which could eventually engulf the present university system in its rising tide of independent anti-academic intellectualism.

The universities abandoned their Christian roots over a century ago. Beginning in the '60s, they abandoned their commitment to intellectual development as well. Having already purged their collective Borg minds of almost every vestige of religion and non-leftist thought, the tenured faculties that dominate the academic asylums have ensured that the devolution of the academy will continue, until eventually the idea of sending your child to college for intellectual development will seem as absurdly counterproductive as watching *ABCNNBCBS* to learn what's really going on in the world.

The children's crusade

December 20, 2004

I N THE YEAR OF OUR LORD 1212, a few medieval sources have it that two peasant boys, Stephen of Cloyes and Nicholas of Cologne, began to preach that innocence and good intent could achieve what kings and armies could not in recovering the holy city of Jerusalem, lost for the second time in 1187. The "Chronica Regiae Coloniensis Continuatio prima" describes it thusly:

> *About the time of Easter and Pentecost, without anyone having preached or called for it and prompted by I know not what spirit, many thousands of boys, ranging in age from six years to full maturity, left the plows or carts which they were driving, the flocks which they were pasturing, and anything else which they were doing. This they did despite the wishes of their parents, relatives, and friends who sought to make them draw back.*

> *Suddenly one ran after another to take the cross. Thus, by groups of 20, or 50, or a hundred, they put up banners and began to journey to Jerusalem.... Some were turned back at Metz, others at Piacenza, and others even at Rome. Still others got to Marseilles, but whether they crossed to the Holy Land or what their end was is uncertain. One thing is sure: that of the many thousands who rose up, only very few returned.*

As the academic excellence of homeschoolers becomes less and less deniable—the 1.8 percent of children homeschooled now account for 16 percent of the 800 annual National Merit Scholars and 17 percent of the 1,600 National Merit Semifinalists—parents who prefer to keep their children in the public schools are forced to become ever more inventive in producing excuses for doing so.

A favorite excuse of Christian parents is that their children are acting as missionaries to the other children, who will otherwise be deprived of the chance to hear the Gospel. But this makes little sense on several counts. First and foremost, it is questionable to assert that a young child can even be considered a Christian. Many children become "Christians" in order to please their parents only to completely reject this instilled faith by the time they are adults.

And even if they can rightly be considered Christians, the use of children as missionaries directly contradicts the example of Jesus Christ. While he suffered the children to come unto him, he did not choose them as his disciples and send them forth to preach, nor did he begin his own ministry until he was over 30. And if a prophet is sure to be regarded without honor in his home town, how much more contemptuously is a missionary first-grader to be regarded in his local public school?

Furthermore, the hysterical reaction on the part of the educratic bureaucracy to even the most minor potential Christian influence, from Christmas carols to anti-drug Christian rock bands, is significant in light of their open-armed acceptance of schoolchildren from Christian families. Like Vladimir Ilyich, they believe that given "four years to teach the children and the seed I have sown will never be uprooted." If children really were capable of being the positive influence that their Christian parents believe them to be, they too would be banned from setting foot on school property.

The scientific purpose of the public school, as explained by William Torrey Harris, is to subsume the individual, to suppress the child's natural independence and turn him into an obedient cog in the collective. This is known as "socialization" in the vernacular. Christianity—being focused on the individual soul and its sole accountability to God—is inherently inimical to this concept, which is why homeschooled children often appear as different and alien to their government-indoctrinated counterparts as Midwestern Christians appear to atheist New Yorkers.

Now, it is true that the evil seed of socialization does not find fertile soil in every public schoolchild. And while committed parents can help counteract it, the salient question remains: If one would not insert one's children in a meat grinder in the faith that the machine will not function, why would one place them in an intellectual grinder specifically designed to destroy much of what you hope to pass on to them in the hope they will survive it?

As the public schools continue to sink into mindless depravity and Christianity comes under increasing attack, it should be easy to see that the Children's Crusade of the last 50 years is, like its semi-mythical historical predecessor, a disastrous failure.

Sprinting toward Gehenna

December 27, 2004

JEAN-PAUL SARTRE once famously said that "Hell is other people." At this time of year, when we find ourselves in the close company of extended family who may cause that quote to flicker unbidden into our minds, we celebrate the birth of the One who came to save man from himself.

For man is adept at creating hell on Earth. The pattern is inescapable, and no sooner does one man build something up than another man is arrayed against him to tear it down. And it is ironic, too, for the very force that builds is denounced by that which destroys as being the evil that must be eliminated. The darkness looks upon the light and, as always, fails to comprehend it.

Just as the anticlerical French intellectuals failed to recognize that their intellectual tradition depended on the church scholars who kept it alive during the Middle Ages, and so branched off into the destructive orgy of Jacobinism, the nihilist despair of existentialism and the anti-intellectual foolishness of post-modernism, secular America fails to see that even its shabby pretense at a moral tradition depends wholly on Christians past.

The irony is profound. Consider the secular Jewish fascists at the American Civil Liberties Union and the Anti-Defamation League. Even as they attempt to eradicate Jesus Christ from "the holidays" in this nation of Christians, Jews in America remain unbeaten and unharassed, while predictions of Passion-inspired anti-Semitic violence were proven to be nothing but Goebbels-style propaganda. Meanwhile, in gloriously secular Europe, Jews walk the streets in visible fear and are physically attacked on a regular basis in France, Germany and Belgium.

One wonders why so many Jews in the media elite wish to see America move toward a more perfectly secular society, considering that they will doubtless be the first to be victimized should they ever get their wish.

Or consider the abortionettes, who hold sacred a woman's right to murder. (That this goes well beyond a woman's right to her own body can be seen in the feminist support for women who kill sleeping men "in self-defense", murderous mothers and young women committing Singerian infanticide.) Now that sex-selection technology is on the verge of widespread availability, abortionettes are appalled at the notion that a disproportionate number of unborn baby girls will be slaughtered. There is a silver lining in this, though, as we'll likely be inflicted with far fewer abortionettes in the future.

The moral vision of America has always been Christian. It was Christians in the British Navy and the American abolition movement who ended 19th-century slavery, while even a left-liberal *New York Times* columnist admits that today it is the Christian Right that is fighting the battle against genocide in Africa, human-rights violations in Asia and sex slavery around the world. Meanwhile, the European Union and United Nations—those twin temples of secular moral supremacists—are too busy committing atrocities of their own in Bosnia, the Congo and other places to concern themselves with the similar evils of others.

The secular vision is ultimately a collective death cult, lethal on both a personal and a societal level that makes Kali look like a fecund fertility goddess by comparison. One need not look to the most notorious examples of the 20th century to demonstrate this, for it can be seen equally well in examples ranging from the statistically anomalous homosexual predilection for cannibalism to the sub-replacement birth rates of post-Christian Europe.

Against the death cult stands nothing but the tradition of the fairytale, the hope that is brought by a baby lying in a manger. Persecuted by the authorities, hated by kings, the Child nevertheless rose to conquer Death itself. In Him, there is the promise of life, both in this world and in the world to come.

But one need not invoke the afterlife or the immortal soul to see that without Jesus Christ, one is destined for Hell. Jean-Paul had it half-right. History clearly shows that Hell is a place of people who reject the Way, the Truth and the Life.

Anti-Christian America

January 3, 2005

YOUR PAPERS, PLEASE has long been shorthand for the intrusion of the state into private affairs, as historically was most notoriously exemplified by the National Socialists of Germany from 1933 to 1944. Now, in the name of "fighting terrorism", the Republican Congress has, in one fell swoop, managed to eradicate some of the last vestiges of constitutional federalism and exceed the wildest dreams of the most ambitious totalitarian.

In the new Intelligence Reform Bill, S. 2845, Sec. 3064 "Establishment of Electronic Birth and Death Registration Systems" states the following:

In consultation with the Secretary of Health and Human Services and the Commissioner of Social Security, the Secretary shall take the following actions:

1. *Work with the States to establish a common data set and common data exchange protocol for electronic birth registration systems and death registration systems.*

2. *Coordinate requirements for such systems to align with a national model.*

3. *Ensure that fraud prevention is built into the design of electronic vital registration systems in the collection of vital event data, the issuance of birth certificates, and the exchange of data among government agencies.*

4. *Ensure that electronic systems for issuing birth certificates, in the form of printed abstracts of birth records or digitized images, employ a common format of the certified copy, so*

that those requiring such documents can quickly confirm their validity.

5. *Establish uniform field requirements for State birth registries.*

The significance of this small section tucked away within the bill is that it finally completes Social Security's transformation from a pension plan (however fraudulent a Ponzi-scheme) into a de facto national ID program. No longer will Christians who object to the number of the federal beast on religious grounds be able to refuse to have their children assigned a number— it will be interesting to see if the silence that has greeted the passage of this law will be matched by the shouts of outrage once these numbers are to be forcibly implanted, as is foreshadowed by (3)'s requirement to ensure fraud prevention.

It also spells an end to the pretense that America is the most-free nation in the world. In fact, it isn't even close. In most European and Asian countries, one can freely withdraw cash from a bank without a federal report being filed, purchase cars and other expensive material goods with legal tender without coming under suspicion of being a criminal, buy a cell phone without ID and have a child without having an identification number electronically tattooed upon it for life.

Sadly, this is not a development that surprises me in the least. In fact, in my very first political column on WorldNetDaily, published on Sept. 14, 2001, and titled, "Yield No More Freedom", I wrote:

> *It is said that the price of freedom is eternal vigilance, but that vigilance must be applied within as well as without. A thousand suicide bombers could not destroy America, but America is quite capable of destroying itself in the pursuit of any number of false idols, among them wrongheaded and illusory notions of security at any price. Individual privacy, like private property, is one of the foundations of our freedom, and it must not be thrown away out of fear.*

Well, we yielded more nevertheless, thanks to our Republican administration, House and Senate. It is clear that the American people have been betrayed with this so-called reform bill by again having their liberties sacrificed on the altar of homeland security. It stuns me that so many supposed champions of freedom support these abominable actions—I can't even imagine the howls of outrage were it President Hillary Clinton leading the charge for such a step toward 1984-style government.

George Bush may not be Hitler, as the Move-On buffoons insisted, but he is building a monstrous edifice that the late and unlamented National Socialist might well have envied. In a Christmas season where we have just seen an increase in the number of government attacks on Christianity, one does not have to be a paranoid "Left Behind" fan to see where this government appears to be headed.

Women hating women

January 10, 2005

THE COMMUNIST GOVERNMENT of China is the most bloody-minded government in the history of mankind. Long before tanks were mashing bicycles and students into lifeless red pulp at Tiananmen Square, Chairman Mao's left-wing revolutionaries killed an estimated 35 million people in the Great Leap Forward and the Great Proletarian Cultural Revolution.

The Chinese government appears to have adopted as its mantra an epigram composed by Chang Hsien-chung, who had the following words inscribed in stone to commemorate his series of massacres in Chengtu:

Heaven brings forth innumerable things to help man.

Man has nothing with which to recompense Heaven.

Kill. Kill. Kill. Kill. Kill. Kill. Kill.

And yet, even these most merciless of men are beginning to recoil at the murderous extremism of the abortionettes now that the feminist logic has finally reached a long-expected milestone. It is no secret that parents traditionally prefer male babies to female—the availability of pre-natal sex identification technology combined with pro-abortion extremism has resulted in a 16 percent shortfall of baby girls from the natural ratio, which approximates 50–50.

To put it into terms that feminists might understand, a girl baby in China earns only 84 cents on the boy baby's dollar. Except in this case, the dear girl isn't out 16 cents of spending money, she's just dead.

Whereas the abortionettes will not suffer any limits on a woman's right to kill her children—no doubt they are still celebrating the overturning of a famous post-natal water abortionist's murder convictions last week—the

Chinese National Population and Family Planning Commission, not generally considered to be made up of right-wing religious fanatics, announced:

> *As a new measure, the commission will start drafting revisions of the Criminal Law in order to ban foetus gender detection and selective abortion other than for legitimate medical purposes.*

What? No exceptions for rape, incest and the mental health of the mother?

The truth is that with over 45 million American abortions committed since 1973, (and adding another 800,000 to the body count every year), the abortionettes have proven themselves to be the most lethal organization of the 20th century. I have said before that calling a feminist a feminazi is an insult to National Socialism. Now, it is clear that even Mao, Stalin and Pol Pot are second-rate killers in comparison with Ms. Sanger, Ms. Friedan and Ms. Steinem.

The ideology of feminism represents the triumph of death over life. It is a societal suicide pact as Europe, where the birth rate has fallen almost 30 percent below replacement levels, is demonstrating in real-time. It is not so much an abdication of motherhood as a rejection of the concept that women have an integral role to play in the continuance of civilization.

The great contradiction of feminism is that as women attempt to reduce themselves into nothing more than men with chromosome variants, they make themselves increasingly unnecessary. Science-fiction writers and life-partners in lesbianism have suggested that artificial insemination might eliminate the need for men, but once technology allows the replacement of the womb with artificial birth chambers and the science of cloning is sufficiently improved, women will become equally irrelevant to the propagation of the race.

An unconscionably stupid ideology, feminism's only redeeming characteristic is that it will likely eliminate itself before it eliminates society. Forget the Bible, even from a secular scientific perspective, it is an obvious evolutionary cul-de-sac, as delaying reproduction, embracing homosexuality and a harboring a predilection for murdering one's young are not exactly the traits of a Darwinian survivor.

Fortunately, many smart, highly-educated young women are beginning to figure this out. Last week, I received a Christmas card from a high-powered Ivy League MBA turned wife and mother, featuring her firstborn child in a

Santa hat, and I spoke with another Leaders of Tomorrow sort, who told me that since everyone keeps telling her she can be whatever she wants to be, she intends to use her MBA to pursue a career as a wife and mother... just as soon as she can find herself a partner in the joint venture.

American society does not need even one more woman lawyer, professor or junior executive. Frivolous lawsuits will be filed, students will be brainwashed with leftist propaganda, and tedious Powerpoint demonstrations will be assembled with or without female assistance. Instead, what American society needs is women strong enough to be the anchors of their marriages, the foundation of their children's lives and the bedrock of our civilization.

Won the war, lost the peace

January 17, 2005

A MERICA'S MILITARY is the finest in the world. It is very good at its job, which consists of killing people and breaking things. That is why it managed to defeat the Iraqi army in a very short period of time, at an extraordinarily low cost. The Army, Navy, Air Force and Marines accomplished their mission of toppling the Iraqi regime and capturing Saddam Hussein. Unfortunately, instead of being content with achieving the achievable, the Bush administration foolishly embraced the impossible.

The impossible is the plan that was pushed for years by the World Democratic Revolutionists, the Wilsonian crew sometimes known as neocons. The idea was that with the forced installation of a modern two-party system of limited democracy in Iraq, the close exposure to this "freedom" will cause the oppressed people ruled by surrounding Middle Eastern regimes to rise up and overthrow their totalitarian rulers—presumably with a little help from their friends—in pursuit of similar governance for themselves.

In fact, the plan sounds remarkably like the student revolutionaries' gambit in "Les Miserables". And like the administration's echo chamber in the Three Monkey Republican media, Enjolras and company were not inclined to listen to criticism of their sure-fire, guaranteed-to-succeed, most-excellent plan.

Damn their warnings, damn their lies! They shall see the people rise.

You may recall that the students at the lonely barricade waited in vain for the people to rise and were slaughtered almost to a man. You may also note that it's fast approaching two years since April 10, 2003, when American troops took Baghdad and a year since I last called publicly for the return of our troops. Since Baghdad fell, America has lost more than nine times as many troops in the post-war peace as it did in the war itself, with 1,163 post-war KIA compared to 122 wartime fatalities as of Dec. 12, 2004. A few months ago, I wrote that optimistic comparisons to postwar Japan and Germany were foolish and inaccurate—one no longer hears even whispers of them now, only increasingly desperate assertions that Iraq is not Vietnam.

And it isn't. It's arguably worse. Fractured and divisive though it is, the Middle Eastern regimes have recognized the danger that a genuinely democratic Iraq poses to them, although not in the cartoon villain manner ascribed to them by the lapdog conservative media. Just as the militaries of Turkey and Algeria stepped in to prevent the will of the Turkish and Algerian peoples from being realized, the Arab dictators know that a democratic Iraq is not synonymous with a quiescent Iraq and they are willing do almost anything that will stop the proposed transformation.

This means America is now in a situation that approximates trying to build a quasi-democratic system in Saxony-Anhalt while being surrounded on every side by forces of the Third Reich. This is why the World Democratic Revolutionists are still pushing hard for expanding the war into Iran and Syria, because without taking the entire Middle East, America cannot hold Iraq or guarantee the continuance of any government installed there. (The same is not necessarily true of Afghanistan, which is neither Arab nor surrounded by hostile forces.)

George Bush has not made the case for World War III. The American people are already divided on Iraq and will not support an attempt at a complete conquest of the Middle East. Therefore, George Bush must do what he should have done 20 months ago, accept America's victory over the Hussein regime and bring the troops home to be honored for their historic triumph. That this triumph might taste sourly of defeat can be laid squarely at the door of the World Democratic Revolutionists, who were not content with the bird in hand and insisted on grabbing for the 10 in the bush.

And perhaps the president would do well to hear a voice in his ear, whispering, "remember, thou too art mortal." This is not only true of men, but nations, too.

My decision to speak out again on this issue was inspired by conversations with friends returned from Iraq, including one two-tour volunteer and one highly-regarded U.S. Marine Corps shooter. Despite being generally favorable toward the Iraqi freedom effort, the consensus of these combat veterans is that the conflict there has been successfully transformed into a guerilla war by the external enemies and that victory through pacification and democratic transformation is implausible.

I have no doubt that many will complain that I am not "supporting the troops" by pointing out the strategic failures of their commanders. This is utter hogwash. If anyone is not supporting the troops, it is the World Democratic Revolutionists, who would spend the lives of American soldiers in support of an objective, however laudatory, that appears to have increasingly little chance of success.

Sex, the slave girl and national security

January 24, 2005

OVER THE PAST YEAR, I've found myself in the unfamiliar position of coming to admire a *New York Times* columnist. Unlike most of his cowardly, left-liberal ilk, Nicholas Kristoff is not afraid of the truth, regardless of whether it comfortable or not. He has not only called out the sanctimonious would-be moral supremacists on the Left for leaving the battle against the global sex trade to the religious right, but even got his own hands dirty and purchased two Cambodian slaves from their owner a year ago in order to set them free.

This is astonishing proof that there is at least one left-liberal who does not confuse a responsibility to help others with expressing verbal support for the government doing so.

Kristoff is a good writer, and he does not hide the depths of his personal disappointment nor his feelings of helpless failure upon learning that one of the two slave girls he'd freed had voluntarily run away from her village and returned to her former brothel. He does not profess to understand why the girl should prefer her enslavement—Kristoff rather innocently attempts to ascribe this common phenomenon to methamphetamine addiction—but it clearly grieves him:

> *Maybe that's what I find saddest about Srey Mom: She is a wonderful, good-hearted girl who gives money to beggars, who offers Buddhist prayers for redemption—but who is already so broken that she seems unable to escape a world that she hates and knows is killing her.*

But the harsh truth is even sadder. Most individuals, like the unfortunate Srey Mom, do not love freedom. Instead, they fear it to such an extent that they will accept a security that they know full well will eventually prove fatal to them.

This is true of people around the world. But while we Americans have little trouble recognizing the predilection of others for the security of slavery, we do not see it so clearly in ourselves. In our terror of the extremely unlikely event of the black flag of Islam ever waving over the nation's capital, the American people have not hesitated to embrace the most openly anti-American, anti-freedom presidential program in over 60 years. After all, they can't hate our freedom if we throw it all away, can they?

But as the apostle Paul writes, God does not give us a spirit of fear. Decisions that are based on fear rarely, if ever, stem from the font of all that is good—they are rooted, instead, in that which furthers the evil the Bible describes as the prince of this world. The formula is an old, old one: The fear of one evil inspires actions which enable the appearance of an even greater evil.

The gradual encroachment on American liberties by their government is one that is primarily inspired by hypothetical fears. One cannot legally buy an anonymous cell phone because of the possibility that a terrorist might do so. One cannot withdraw more than $3,000.00 from one's bank account without a report being filed because of the possibility that one might choose to spend the money on chemical substances deemed illegal. One cannot even drive an injured woman to the hospital without being repeatedly interrogated because of the possibility that one might be the culprit responsible for those injuries.

Thus fear triumphs over all, ensuring a disastrous end. For whether one seeks security in a brothel or from Congress, the results are likely to be the same. Indeed, there is more honesty to be found in the whorehouse. Consider Chuck Colson's take on the president's inaugural address:

> [T]he president's address focused on liberty and what it means to the world. This was the most idealistic and moralistic presidential message since Franklin Roosevelt summoned us to the heroic task of saving the world from tyranny in World War II.

Although the Three Monkey Republicans never seem to see or hear them, their Dear Leader is never shy about announcing his intentions to those few with the wits to pay attention to the fine print. I have no doubt whatsoever that Chuck Colson is right—I am quite sure that George Delano, like his archetypical predecessor, is committed to idealistically and moralistically saving the world from one form of tyranny while simultaneously delivering another at home.

Democracy in Iraq

January 31, 2005

S UPPORTERS of the Coalition of the Willing's occupation of Iraq postulate that a large voter turnout will demonstrate a strong justification for the administration's decision to attempt nation-building in Iraq. Other supporters, rather less convincingly, argue that a poor turnout will also justify it, since the decision of voters to stay away from the polls would show how strong the anti-democratic opposition is, and since American national security is dependent upon the liberty of others...

It's all irrelevant, of course, because the percentage of Iraqis participating means no more on Jan. 30 than it did in the previous election, when Saddam Hussein won 100 percent of the vote. What truly matters is how the election results are permitted to influence the makeup of the subsequent government.

I was a little surprised when Colin Powell assured the world that the Sunni minority, which may or may not be boycotting the election, would be guaranteed positions of power. If you're not running for office and no one voted for you, then how democratic is a system that grants you electoral office anyhow?

Even more worrisome are the rumors that "A formula is being actively sought to retain him [current Iraqi Prime Minister Allawi] as premier even if his showing is low" despite preliminary indications that his Iraqi National Accord party will receive only 8 percent of the vote and win only 22 seats of the 256 up for grabs in the Iraqi Parliament. In other words, vote for who you like, we'll choose the winner anyhow. One could hardly blame the poor, confused Iraqi who wonders how this Western-style democracy is substantially different from the previous system of pre-determined elections.

But potential Coalition hypocrisies aside, the real problem may be if the will of the Iraqi people is allowed free reign. The party leading in the polls is the Iran-backed Shiite Unified Iraqi Alliance, which DEBKAfile reports is projected by CENTCOM's chief analyst Gregory Hooker to win a near-majority of 120 seats. Its leader, the Grand Ayatollah Ali Sistani, promises that while the Iraqi constitution will be based on Sharia, the government will not be a theocracy.

One can't help but harken back to the last time that the United States sanctioned the removal of a dictator and his replacement with a popular Shiite ayatollah. While the destruction of the Hussein regime is without question a good thing, I am not so certain that his replacement with a potential Khomeini was what Bush and his neoconservative advisers had in mind when they embarked on their Mideast nation-building.

Democracy, even in the corrupted sense of the limited representational form that now passes for the concept proper, has a very troubled history with regard to Islamic parties. Turkey is most often cited as the successful case, but few seem to recall that the Turkish military has directly interfered with the electoral process there four times since 1960, most recently in 1998 when it banned the most popular party in the Turkish parliament after forcing the removal of the nation's first Islamic government the year before. I rather doubt that anyone would consider America to be a healthy democracy if the U.S. Army were called out to cancel election results every time a Republican won the presidency, no matter how much the notion might tickle Hillary Clinton's fancy.

Democracy is not a panacea, which is one reason why America's founding fathers feared it so. There is a reason that Aristotle considered it one of the three evil forms of government, along with tyranny and ochlocracy, after all. It has either brought to power or sanctioned the legitimacy of a number of infamous men including Alcibiades, Daniel arap Moi, Yasser Arafat and Adolf Hitler.

Still, thanks to the U.S. president and soldiers from many countries, in-cluding America, the people of Iraq appear to have a chance to participate for once in determining how their lives are governed. I hope that they will be given permission to do so and that their choice will not only be wise, but honored by outside parties. And I certainly wish them well. But I also know that it is almost certain that the law of unintended consequences has unpleasant surprises in store for those arrogant enough to assume they can order the future to their liking.

Idiots at the chalkboard

February 7, 2005

S OMEONE OUT THERE IS WORRIED. Due to the rapid growth in the popularity of homeschooling and the increasing obviousness of the concept's superiority, the legacy media has all but openly declared war on parents who wish to personally direct their children's education.

If an act of child abuse even tangentially involves children who don't attend a state-approved school, you can be sure that the media will not fail to mention that the children were "homeschooled" regardless of whether the parents were actually schooling them at home or torturing them instead.

So much for accuracy in media. If those now-infamous Florida parents were homeschoolers, then Abu Ghraib was a military academy.

One argument often heard in defense of the public schools is that education is better left to those trained to teach, to the "professionals". Most teachers, after all, are required to have a college degree in education, and in many states they are forced to take tests purported to prove that they are not drooling idiots. Although one has to wonder what exactly is on those tests considering that after 59 percent of prospective teachers failed to pass the Massachusetts Teachers' Test in 1999, the test was assailed by FairTest, a teacher-run organization that opposes tests for teachers, in the following manner:

> *The MTT included many bizarre questions unlike those on any other state's teacher licensing exams. On one, candidates were asked to transcribe a portion of 'The Federalist Papers' as dictated from a low quality tape-recorder. Other items asked for dictionary definitions of words with questions such as "What is a preposition?" and "What is an adjective?"*

Clearly, it is outrageous to expect public school teachers to know elementary grammar or be able to perform tasks that entry-level secretaries with two-year vo-tech degrees handle with ease. If the MTT is considered to feature bizarre and difficult questions, one can only imagine that tests in more teacher-friendly states such as Minnesota and New York must run something like this:

What is your favorite color?

a) red

b) green

c) blue

d) purply-pink

The immortal PJ O'Rourke once declared: "Anybody who doesn't know what's wrong with America's educational system never screwed an el-ed major." And while one has no doubt that he is correct, it turns out that there is more empirical evidence for the dismal state of teacher intelligence than Mr. O'Rourke's sexual history or the fear and loathing with which the teachers' unions regard competency testing.

In 2001, the National Center for Education Statistics reported the average SAT score for intended education majors to be 481 math and 483 verbal. Only those interested in vocational school, home economics and public affairs scored lower.

But while the SAT is considered to be a generally reliable intelligence test, the 2001 SAT is not the same SAT that many of us took prior to attending university. Those 2001 scores on the 1996 SAT, which was replaced this year by the New SAT 2005, are equivalent to pre-1996 SAT scores of 451 math and 403 verbal. In case any education majors are reading this, 451 plus 403 equals a cumulative score of 854.

Examining an SAT-to-IQ conversion chart calculated from Mensa entrance criteria, a combined 854 indicates that the average IQ of those pursuing an education major is 91, nine points lower than the average IQ of 100. In other words, those who can't read teach whole language.

Now, not every would-be education major goes on to complete her degree—77.4 percent of those who do are women—nor does every college graduate with an education major go on to teach in the public schools. But since teaching's best and brightest are frequently quit upon exposure to the labyrinthine public school system and since most teachers who fail their competency tests are still allowed to teach—in Illinois, 7.8 percent of the teachers who have taken these extraordinarily easy tests since 1988 have failed them—it is not logical to conclude that the average teacher's IQ is any higher than the average would-be education major.

Many a parent has wondered aloud what sort of idiots were teaching the anti-intellectual poison that currently passes for a modern public school curriculum, but I doubt that most ever considered that the pejorative might be more literal than metaphorical. Instead of wondering if they are sufficiently qualified to homeschool their children, parents would do well to instead ponder the wisdom of turning over their offspring to demonstrably sub-optimal morons for daily indoctrination in the name of education.

The gatekeepers crumble

February 14, 2005

FIRST, DAN RATHER WAS EXPOSED as a liar and a fraud by the men at *Powerline* and *Little Green Footballs*. Now, *CNN*'s chief news executive, Eason Jordan, has been forced to resign over his infamous comments that American troops have intentionally targeted journalists in Iraq for murder.

Of course, Jordan's accusation made no sense at all. Because if American troops were going to target journalists, those topping the list would almost surely be the left-liberal elites working in New York City and Washington, D.C. The legacy media has hated the American soldier since Vietnam—I may be an opponent of George Delano's nation-building exercises myself, but even I can see that the glee with which military casualties are reported in papers like the *New York Times* and by the *ABCNNBCBS* cabal don't stem from mere partisan opposition, but sheer anti-American vitriol.

This can hardly come as a surprise. The Left has never had any regard for the individual, no respect for his rights or his life. The supremacy of the collective is the heart of their creed, so what are the lives of a thousand soldiers, of their 10,000 grief-stricken friends and families, except cannon fodder in the Left's long march toward lethal socialist utopia?

The difference between the legacy reporting on military casualties—where it's little more than a numbers game—and the milblogs is significant. Whereas the legacy stories almost always attempt to spin the families' grief into a political weapon, those recounted at sites like Blackfive's focus on the individual himself, his life and what he meant to those who loved him. And the loss of these fine young men is all the more heart-breaking when you see the pictures of them with their little boys and girls.

Unlike the legacy media, the milblogs also regularly devote time and space to the casualties who are not fatalities, chronicling the painful recoveries of those who have survived but suffer from what are all-too-often permanent injuries. They don't just wallow in the pathos either, but they encourage their readers to act and ensure that these wounded warriors are not forgotten in their convalescence.

To be sure, one need only visit a milblog to see that much of their material is derived from the small local papers that still take note of the soldiers in their midst. But those humble purveyors of community news are not the journalistic elite that considers itself more loyal to the United Nations than to America and regard America's defenders as the enemy.

So, two down, only a few hundred more to go. Not bad work for a mere six months. I imagine that Sun Tzu or Clausewitz would probably recommend focusing on the center of gravity and launching surgical strikes on the Columbia School of Journalism and its sister schools, but that may prove to be unnecessary as time and technology appear to be on our side.

The blogosphere is still unlikely to completely replace the legacy media as a primary producer of news, although a grass-roots replacement of the AP is neither unthinkable nor technologically impossible. After all, television did not eliminate radio, nor did radio eliminate print. But the blogs do appear to be supplanting the op-ed pages and cable TV commentariat as opinion leaders.

When five blogs—Blackfive, Blue State Conservatives, The Adventures of Chester, Bill Roggio and The Gogblog—can force papers such as the *Los Angeles Times* and the *Wall Street Journal* to cover a story they had hitherto been ignoring, it is clear that the torch of opinion leadership is passing.

The failure of the legacy media to hide the story of the swiftboat veterans could have been dismissed as an anomaly had it been a unique event, but the subsequent exposures of Eason Jordan and Dan Rather indicates a trend. An extremely healthy trend, I might add.

A few weeks ago, I was informed by Universal Press Syndicate that since they had been unable to sell my column to a single newspaper over the course of a year, they were dropping it from syndication. I was not the least bit upset by this, nor did they expect me to be, for we are both aware that the time of the legacy gatekeepers is coming to a close.

This is only the first chapter and these are only the first of many legacy scalps that will be claimed. Already Creative Labs, the computer hardware giant and maker of Web cams, is beginning to eye the blog phenomenon with interest... and it will not be long before the video blogs begin their assault on the cable news channels.

The barbarians are within the gates... let the pillaging begin!

Why women can't think

February 21, 2005

S USAN ESTRICH, the University of Southern California professor whose chief claim to fame is her failed management of an American presidential campaign—she was able to help Michael Dukakis turn a 17-point lead into a historic election debacle—last week offered the world ironic proof of Charlotte Allen's thesis that feminism destroys female intellects.

In a remarkably vicious hissy fit, Estrich argued that *Los Angeles Times* editor Michael Kinsley's disinclination to print her criticism of Allen's article was due to the decline of his brain, his judgment and his ability to do his job because of his Parkinson's disease. She also announced in a Feb. 18 article that both Kinsley's and Harvard President Larry Summers's days "were numbered" because both had provoked her by insulting women.

Her dedication to freedom of speech and diversity of opinion is remarkable, isn't it? And while her shrewish pettiness does bring a great thinker to mind, it is only because one finds oneself lamenting the fact that Shakespeare did not have Estrich to serve as a model, for she would have no doubt inspired the playwright to heights of insight that would have made Katherine Baptista's shrewish barbs look downright simpatici in comparison.

It should come as no surprise that I strongly support Allen's contention, for as I wrote in a 2003 column titled, "Gynomythology":

> *But the most damning argument against this myth [of male oppression] is the appalling behavior of the leading female pseudo-intellectuals over the past 30 years. Instead of taking advantage of their intellectual freedom and unprecedented access to education, the feminist vanguard has embraced an anti-intellectual dogmatism that imprisons the current generation of young women in the academic convent of Women's Studies, robbing them of both*

foundational knowledge and the capacity for rational linear thought, thus ensuring that this generation, like its foremothers, will also fail to accomplish anything worthy of historical regard.

Estrich clearly subscribes to this gynomyth herself—she explicitly blames the three men who run the editorial page of the *Los Angeles Times* for lack of intellectual regard in which she and her 50 co-signers are held by the world. The fact that she has a third-rate mind and a reputation for failure so total that it borders on proverbial apparently doesn't factor into the equation as far as she's concerned.

As everyone who's ever attended an elite university knows, a shocking number of women there are academically cauterized into intellectual brain death. While men are listening to professors lecture on history, economics and engineering, far too many women are yammering on and on about their feelings in Women's Study classes. The less academically rigorous a subject, the more women you'll find in it—there were 20 times as many women in my political geography class (40) as my computer science engineering class (2). But on the bright side, at least they know where the Soviet Union was…

The mental pollution of feminism extends well beyond the question of great thinkers. Women do not write hard science fiction today because so few can hack the physics, so they either write romance novels in space about strong, beautiful, independent and intelligent but lonely women who finally fall in love with rugged men who love them just as they are, or stick to fantasy where they can make things up without getting hammered by critics holding triple Ph.D.s in molecular engineering, astrophysics and Chaucer.

And in the world of female political non-fiction, the situation is arguably worse. Only Ann Coulter even tries to write serious books, as the rest are ghostwritten autobiographies (which is to say literally more talking about feelings); a collection of complaints about Daddy (the Left sees the nation's president as a father figure, so all those anti-Bush books are best understood as the Daddy Dearest genre); complaints that there is no one to date them; and vapid ex post facto attempts to justify Granddaddy's hatred for those dirty Japs who raped Manila.

There is only one way to receive intellectual respect, and that is to earn it. A degree doesn't mean anything, as there are too many maleducated morons running around with them to impress anyone. Nor does a resume.

Because no matter what sex you are, if you can't defend your assertions, if you can't fight on an equal playing field and if you won't engage in open intellectual battle with anyone who challenges your opinion, then you deserve the contempt in which you will be held.

Stock market suckers

February 28, 2005

MANY CONSERVATIVES are aquiver with excitement that George Delano is daring to brave the third rail of American politics, the much-beloved welfare program set up by his philosophical predecessor, FDR. It is true, of course, that Social Security is nothing but a government-run Ponzi scheme, that there is no trust fund, that as an investment it is a complete rip-off, that it rewards white women at the expense of black men and that it is an outrageous violation of the Constitution of the United States of America.

But this does not mean that the Bush administration's plan to allow a modicum of private investment in the stock market is necessarily a winner or even an expansion of individual freedom in America. A single column is not sufficient to address a subject this complex, so I shall simply focus on one erroneous argument that is often used to support the administration's plan, namely, the notion that stock prices inevitably move up over time.

Superficially, this appears to be a most persuasive argument. If one looks back to 1965, which is when 65-year-olds retiring now were first entering the job market en masse, the Dow was around 900. Last Friday, the Dow closed at 10,800, a 12x gain. There can be little question that no Social Security recipient is getting back $12 for every dollar he put into the system, and yet, we must consider the first of several flaws in this crude analysis, namely, inflation.

Of that $12, almost half was nothing but inflation. One 1965 dollar is worth $5.81 now. That phenomenal gain doesn't looks so great now, given that one could do better than half as well just collecting compound interest, even at the miserable interest rates offered in basic savings accounts. But that's not all—it gets much worse.

One of the many dirty little secrets of Wall Street is that the Dow of 1965 is not the Dow of today. In fact, the Dow of 1995 is not the Dow of today, nor is that of 2003, for that matter. This is due to "rebalancing", which is a reconstitution of the index to get rid of companies that are underperforming or disappearing altogether. It is vital to understand this, because no investments are made in indices and relatively few are made in index-matching funds. Most investments are made in the stocks of individual companies and, due to this "rebalancing", the return on the dogs and the bankrupted dead are not reflected in these historical comparisons. Since 1999, seven corporations representing almost one-quarter of the Dow have been dropped and replaced.

The situation is significantly worse with regard to the NASDAQ-100 (NDX), which flip-flops more often than John Kerry running for office. Last year alone, eight companies were kicked out of the showcase technology index—Cephalon, Compuware, First Health Group, Gentex, Henry Schein, NVIDIA, Patterson-UTI Energy and Ryanair. Some of these corporations had been added only recently, and it is even possible for companies to bounce in and out of the NDX as their stock price alternately soars and sinks. For example, Synopsys and Symantec both rejoined the index in 2001 after being previously dropped.

In the last four years, there have been 44 changes to the 100 companies making up the NDX—1999 was a banner year for such beauty-enhancing alterations, as the addition of 30 new companies helped drive the index to its all-time high of 4,816.35 on March 24, 2000. Despite the rebound year of 2003, and the aforementioned attempts to pretty up the index, the NDX is still down 68 percent since that 2000 high.

And if you'd been unfortunate enough to invest in some of those 30 corporations added in 1999, you'd have done even worse. You'd likely have nothing at all. Global Crossing (GX) was one of those high-flying newcomers—it was dropped by December of the following year and an attempt to see how it's doing on today an online financial site will reveal the following result: "Symbol(s) do not exist: GX."

Yes, and neither does your retirement fund…

A legitimate historical analysis of any index must account for all of this rebalancing turnover. Unfortunately, the market masters do not make this easy. The NASDAQ even claims not to keep track of this information—it's much more interested in explaining how it is the stock market for the next

100 years, even if its annual rate of 11 percent turnover means it will have fewer original pieces left to it than Cher in a decade, let alone a century.

The ancient Roman saying caveat emptor is applicable to every proposed transaction, but never more so than with regard to the stock markets, where history is rewritten on an annual basis. The Bush administration's plan features a number of questionable assumptions, but its biggest flaw is that its logic is based on a foundation of historical fiction.

Burning down the housing market

March 7, 2005

CONTRARIAN INVESTING is the key to consistently making money. This should be obvious, as everyone knows that the basic goal is to buy low and sell high. For some reason, however, human psychology makes this very difficult, as emotion makes it much easier to go with the flow despite what one can see on any market chart.

What investors failed to realize back in 1999 is that the all-time record highs that the stock market indices were hitting were not cause for celebration, but concern. And what even more investors, homeowners, real-estate agents and mortgage sellers fail to realize today is that the all-time record highs being registered by home prices in 2004 should be a similar cause for concern.

Notice that I said concern, not panic. Even in a crash, markets almost never liquidate value overnight. What looks dramatic on a 50-year chart might have actually been all-but unnoticeable to those who lived through it. For example, how many people even now realize that the U.S. dollar lost 40 percent of its value in the last four years? Perhaps those few who were investing in gold or the euro, but almost surely no one else.

Furthermore, real estate is less vulnerable than many other investments. Even the painful long-term 22-year decline of the Japanese real estate market has only reduced residential housing values by 32 percent. That might seem appalling, but it is markedly better than the NASDAQ, which is still down more than 50 percent five years into its bear market. This does not mean, of course, that it is wise to ignore the signs, especially if one has followed the example of many American homeowners in trading in their increased home equity for debt.

While the latest numbers from the National Association of Realtors don't look particularly ominous at first glance, two things stand out right away. First, the monthly number of existing home sales has stayed essentially flat for nine months, around 6,800,000 since April 2004. Second, average home prices peaked in June at $245,000 and have likewise remained flat. The 10.6 percent year-on-year gain trumpeted in NAR's press release was all made between February and June.

The reason this may serve to demand some attention is that as Elliott Wave International points out in its March Global Market Perspective, a reversal happens when demand wavers and supply begins to increase as sellers hold out, until eventually a few sellers give in and sell at lower prices, kicking off a wave of decline. In the stock market, this wavering demand can play out in a matter of minutes, but the longer time frame of real estate transactions requires a period of months.

The mitigating factor would appear to be that the NAR data shows a declining inventory, thus negating one factor typically required for a reversal. The problem is that NAR happened to choose precisely this time to "rebalance" its data, which otherwise would have shown a steep decline in the number of monthly home sales due to a 9.2 percent drop in the sales of new homes. This decline was accompanied by a corresponding fall in new home prices of 13 percent, to $199,400.

One is always suspicious of methodology changes, especially because they show an uncanny ability to accompany significant market points. A large decline followed the Dow's 1999 rebalancing; the 2004 repetition has thus far proved harmless. (The NASDAQ-100, being rebalanced annually, is practically useless for even short-term historical analysis).

Other potential red flags are the percentage of homeowners, at an all-time high of 69 percent, as well as the increasing willingness of state governments to get involved in helping first-time homebuyers enter the market for the first time. As the Prophet of the Waves, Bob Prechter, teaches, when the slow boat of government is finally pulling into port, it's time to ship out yourself.

It's also important to remember that an inflated home price does not mean that your wealth has increased—not if you intend to buy another house after selling your own. After all, the house you'll be buying will most likely have increased in price too. Fortunately, a real estate crash is easy to ride out as long as you keep your level of debt from exceeding the value of your house. If you're considering a home sale anyhow, this might be the right time to do it.

The saintly sinners

March 14, 2005

I N HIS RECENT CRITIQUE of libertarianism, "Marxism of the Right", published in the March American Conservative, Robert Locke immediately sets an erroneous tone by lumping ex-socialists in with the "free spirits, the ambitious ... drug users and sexual eccentrics" to whom libertarianism actually appeals. Actually, those ex-socialists now call themselves neoconservatives, not libertarians, and they not only belong to the Republican Party, they are currently running it.

One might not quibble with Locke—a good conservative name if there ever was one—if he were content to assert that libertarianism is a purer form of conservatism in the same way that Marxism is a more refined form of the democratic socialism that is now dominant in the Democratic Party and the "strong government" branch of the Republican Party. But Locke instead asserts that libertarians are not mirror-images of Marxists in a metaphorical manner, but in a very real and legally binding sense.

> *Like Marxism, libertarianism offers the fraudulent intellectual security of a complete a priori account of the political good without the effort of empirical investigation. Like Marxism, it aspires, overtly or covertly, to reduce social life to economics.*

This is simply untrue. First, it reveals Locke's misunderstanding of Marxism. Marxism does not aspire to reduce social life to economics, it aspires to reduce it to religion. Friedrich von Hayek demonstrated its "economics" to be nothing but distribution-side mythopoesis in his famous demonstration of the impossibility of socialist calculation, while Joseph Schumpeter, in "Capitalism, Socialism And Democracy", showed how Marxism is a religion, complete with a deity (History), a prophet (Marx), a priesthood (the

Vanguard) and a Heaven (the Withering Away), masquerading as a political science.

Locke's failure to understand Marxism is compounded by his failure to even begin to grasp the pessimistic heart of libertarian philosophy. He writes:

> *Libertarian naivete extends to politics … Libertarians are also naive about the range and perversity of human desires they propose to unleash. They can imagine nothing more threatening than a bit of Sunday-afternoon sado-masochism, followed by some recreational drug use and work on Monday.*

This is wildly off base. Following a century in which hundreds of millions of people were legally slain by their own governments, libertarianism is the only political philosophy which identifies and attempts to address the problem of government democide. Libertarians are deeply aware of the human propensity for evil, which is why their entire focus is reducing the state to a position where it is too weak, vis-a-vis its citizens, to even attempt to liquidate them en masse Mr. Locke has it exactly backward, for where is the harm in an individual's drug addiction or predilection for spanking in comparison with the guillotine, the gas chamber and the gulag?

Unlike today's conservatives and liberals, libertarians remember George Washington's admonition that government is force, "a dangerous servant and a fearful master." Unlike every other group in the political spectrum, they possess a memory which lasts more than four years, knowing that every expansion of central power is inherently dangerous, even in trustworthy hands, because each contemplative Aurelian philosopher-king is succeeded, sooner or later, by a Commodus.

Locke's article reaches its nadir with the following statement:

> *Libertarians in real life rarely live up to their own theory but tend to indulge in the pleasant parts while declining to live up to the difficult portions.*

It is surely true that the behavior of every individual libertarian does not hew strictly to the ideological lines. But as a party, the Libertarians are ideologically pristine. The party does not accept the federal matching funds that are its legal due and despite its paltry support in the 2004 election, it accepted no taxpayer money to fund its convention, something that neither the Republicans nor the Democrats were willing to do.

This charge of hypocrisy is little more than the massive, coal-filled, tar-covered pot calling the sparkly little kettle black, considering that conservatism's Dear Leader, George Delano Bush, has simultaneously managed to follow in the domestic footsteps of FDR while enforcing a Wilsonian foreign policy abroad. Politicians are proverbially dishonest, of course, but one need only glance at *National Review*, the Washington Times or Townhall.com to find a so-called conservative championing yet another aspect of central government expansion.

Locke's essay boils down to the distaste of the sinner for the saint. Since libertarians have become the conscience of American conservativism, it should come as no surprise that a conservative movement lost in the passionate throes of a fling with ascendant central power should show little inclination to listen to those still small voices advocating a return to reason and restrained government.

Adios, America

March 21, 2005

ANTI-IMMIGRANT SENTIMENT appears to be growing in the United States, Mexican President Vicente Fox said Wednesday, and he urged U.S. officials to act quickly to control movements such as the 950-member-strong Minuteman Project on the Mexico-Arizona border.

> *We will use the law, international law and even U.S. law to make sure that these types of groups, which are a minority ... will not have any opportunity to progress.*

Fox said he plans to push for U.S. immigration reform during a meeting with President Bush in Texas next week. He also said the two leaders, along with Canadian Prime Minister Paul Martin, likely will announce a plan to expand the scope of the North American Free Trade Agreement.

In the spring of 1950, the foreign minister of France, Robert Schuman, proposed that France and Germany collectivize their coal and steel resources. On June 3 of that year, Belgium, France, Luxembourg, Italy the Netherlands and Germany subscribed to what became known as the Schuman Declaration, which in 1951 led to the Treaty of Paris establishing the European Coal and Steel Community.

Fifty-one years later, the sale of national sovereignty was completed when most of the governments across Europe abandoned their national currencies in favor of the euro and accepted that the dictates of the unelected 17-man European Commission would thenceforth supersede national legislatures.

Two score and 11 years was all it took to transform a diverse community of sovereign nations into a single oligarchic dictatorship, beginning with nothing more than the humble coordination of mining activities. The European Union is far more civilized than its Soviet namesake, for it uses banks instead of tanks to enforce its will, but the absence of a body count does not mean that the institution respects individual liberties or suffers any limits upon its power. Still, if the Europeans are shortsighted enough to allow their governments to sign them up for the de facto Fourth Reich, it's hard to find much sympathy for them—particularly when the same process has already begun here at home.

Like the European Common Market, NAFTA was billed to an unsuspecting public in 1992 as a free-trade agreement, when in fact it was simply the first step toward the supra-national pan-American political entity that will be called the American Union. Or perhaps, as the current parlance has it, the Union of the Americas.

This is why George Bush and the Republican leadership so freely—and otherwise inexplicably—ignore the will of the Republican Party membership, which is strongly in favor of enforcing the immigration laws, if not tightening them. There is no point in attempting to prevent Mexican citizens from entering the United States when citizens of Mexico, the USA and Canada will soon enjoy a shared national identity.

This is also why grass-roots efforts to change the status quo of de facto open borders are doomed to failure, as any attempt by state and local politicians to enforce the law in border states will be quickly shut down by federal organizations and the judiciary, and as President Fox helpfully points out, private attempts will be prosecuted in any court likely to find them illegal.

Since the U.S. Constitution no longer exists as a definitive legal document, but has instead been transformed into an occasional inspiration for the pronouncements of the unelected nine-man American Commission (also known as the Supreme Court), there is no longer anything to prevent the delivery of the rough hydra-headed beast slouching toward Washington, waiting to be born. Voters can't prevent it, since both the present administration and its Democratic opposition support pan-American amalgamation, nor can state or local officials since the concept of a right to secession was settled by military force in 1865.

The patterns of history are clear. The political pendulum is swinging heavily toward increased centralization, and in American terms, that spells the end of the nation as a unique proposition dedicated to individual freedom, unalienable rights derived from God and limited government. The only question that remains is if the nation's weakening economic foundation will speed or slow this process, or if it will end the project altogether.

So, my fellow Americans, enjoy your national sovereignty while it lasts. I estimate you've got about 38 more years to do so.

Schiavo solves Social Security

March 28, 2005

B Y THE TIME YOU READ THIS, Terri Schiavo may well be dead, and America will have taken the next step down the road to democide. While the brothers Bush may not have found it within their executive powers to prevent a woman from being legally starved to death, they did manage to con an entire nation into thinking that they did not act because they could not.

This is most unfortunate, because it is quite clear that neither George Bush nor his brother Jeb ever had any intention of saving Mrs. Schiavo from death by starvation. Like Pontius Pilate, they engaged in meaningless political machinations intended to deflect the blame from themselves while pretending that they were helpless to act. A simple executive order from either man would have sufficed to see the woman fed; the notion that the president has too much respect for either the 10th Amendment or the separation of powers doctrine to act is simply laughable.

For you see, George Bush has yet to veto a single law on the grounds that it requires exercising a power not specifically granted to the United States by the Constitution; instead, he has lobbied hard for many such unconstitutional laws. The Constitution gives the federal government no power with regards to children being left behind, for example. And every IRS tax court, every Justice Department immigration court, is a far greater violation of the separation of powers than the insertion of a feeding tube into a starving woman's stomach.

As for Jeb Bush, it's hard to know precisely what his position is since he's been hiding out ever since the Florida Legislature decided that it's down with offing the disabled. Considering the number of elderly concentrated in the Sunshine State, you'd think the Florida voting public would be paranoid about anything that might conceivably lead toward eradicating the useless eaters of society, but then, I suppose someone's got to play on all those golf courses.

Which leads us to what this affair is really all about. This is not a Democrat or Republican thing—many of the pro-starvation judges have been Republican appointees—it is a demographic thing. Already, the elderly soak up a staggering amount of national resources, as the blessings of technology allow them to live longer while turning them into wrinkled chemical cyborgs. This would be unobjectionable to anyone, except for the fact that the elderly are not paying for most of the expense of their much-needed medical treatments, and they are collecting Social Security for many more years than anyone previously envisioned.

The move to health maintenance organizations 20 years ago essentially sealed the doom of the elderly. It is already a well-established fact that when the health of an individual is at odds with the profitability of these government-mandated corporations, the individual is out of luck. This trade-off, writ large, serves as an example of what we can expect to see over the next 30 years when the "right to die" will become the "responsibility to die" and quality of life becomes a legal question to be determined by Department of Health bureaucrats instead of a pallid excuse to justify high taxes in certain locales.

It won't happen overnight. Schiavo simply represents the first nibbling about the margins. But soon will come the *Fox News* debates about the terminally ill and the mentally disabled—if an Alzheimer's patient can't even recognize his own daughter, is he really there anymore? It's customary to dismiss slippery slopes as a false form of hypothesis, but when there's both historical and international models that are obviously being followed, we're no longer talking about possibilities, we're looking at time frames.

And eventually they'll get around to the cripples and the Jews. This is an inspired evil that stems from a supernatural source whose inhuman goals are always the same: death, division and destruction. If you don't see how these things connect, recall that it was Jesus Christ who said: "I tell you the truth, whatever you did not do for one of the least of these, you did not do for me."

Keep that in mind the next time you're trying to decide if your government is on the side of the angels or not.

The dangerous death penalty

April 4, 2005

T HE RECENT MURDER by judiciary of Theresa Schiavo marked an ominous new turn in the movement toward the next great wave of democidal mania. And there can be no doubt that this was murder, for while the mere removal of a feeding tube was arguably nothing more than the cessation of extraordinary measures, no such defense can possibly apply to the Florida government forcibly preventing anyone from providing the late Mrs. Schiavo with food and water, however useless such offerings might have been.

And yet, despite the great alarm of many conservatives and more than a few liberals, the Schiavo murder does not convey any new power to the state or federal governments. It is simply an expansion of an existing power, the power of the United States' government to legally kill its own citizens. As the definition of humanity is increasingly restricted, we can expect this power to be exercised more often and on a wider basis.

Engaging in arguments over redefining humanity is a fool's game, for it is engaging the Culture of Death on its chosen battleground. Simply opening the matter for discussion is a victory for these Ahrimaniacs, as it represents the second of the three stages of their modus operandi:

- **Declare:** Assert X, a concept which is completely at odds with mainstream thinking.

- **Debate:** Insert X into the daily media flow in order to desensitize the mainstream.

- **Destroy:** Attack opponents of X in the courts, in the legislatures, in the media and, above all, in the court of public opinion.

These modern-day devotees of Kali-Durga seek to engage the nation in an ongoing discussion of matters relating to the quality of life, the economics of health care for the elderly and the responsibility of the individual to the collective. They know that what is horrific in the eyes of the mainstream today may well be accepted as normal, even natural, tomorrow. Slippery slope argumentation is much maligned, but critics of it find it hard to otherwise explain the evolution of everything from smoking bans in bars to homosexual marriages in Massachusetts.

But stopping the Culture of Death before it builds up steam will require that conservatives give up their irrational love for their favored form of government killing: capital punishment. This affection is sadly misplaced, for even the most powerful arguments in favor of the death penalty can be refuted with ease. For example, which has more likely led to the drop in violent crime over the past four decades, 70 annual executions or the fact that 192 million Americans now live in Right To Carry states? And given Dun and Bradstreet's 1999 estimate that 1,100 Chinese laogai produce annual revenues of $9.36 billion, it is impossible to argue that housing prisoners for life must necessarily be an economic burden for society.

In embracing the death penalty and attempting to defend it on biblical principles, conservatives are again confusing legality with morality, mistaking human legislation for God's Law. This confusion was highlighted by the angry conservative response to the Schiavo murder, which was, from start to finish, manifestly legal. But the death penalty sanctioned by Mosaic Law had no connection to any government, and from a Christian perspective, Jesus Christ's only encounter with the death penalty was to interfere with its operation and spare the intended victim.

Against this, pro-death penalty Christians will naturally turn to Romans 13. But this verse is a double-edged sword, for such an interpretation not only requires acceptance of the American death penalty, but also the Communist Chinese government's forced abortions, the Soviet Union's mass starvations and the National Socialists' gas chambers, among many other lethal historical events—all of which were legal actions of the legitimate authorities. It would also require the repudiation of America's own Founding Fathers, who were unquestionably in rebellion against the well-established authority of King George III.

The inescapable truth is that people have far more to fear from their own government than they do from violent criminals living in their midst. In the 20th century, national governments killed an estimated 185 million people—far more than the 8.4 million murders estimated to have been committed by criminals. These murderous governments represent more than 30 percent of the current United Nations' member states, and in addition to the usual suspects include Mexico, Poland, Spain and even the modern, democratically elected French Fifth Republic.

The great lesson of government is that its power, once possessed, will eventually be used. One cannot give a government the ability to kill the worst of its citizens without also giving it the power to kill the rest. The tombstone of Theresa Schiavo bears mute witness to that deadly fact.

Stay single, young man!

April 11, 2005

ARRIAGE, AS CONCEIVED BY GOD, is a good and fruitful thing. Marriage, as conceived by the state, is an evil man-trap designed to deprive men of their property and their children. For as the Ohio State Bar Association helpfully explains, the marriage license is:

> *...a legal contract. There are three parties to that contract. 1. You; 2. Your husband or wife, as the case may be; and 3. the State of Ohio.*

This contract grants the third party jurisdiction over all the property owned by the first two, as well as anything produced by the other parties, including children. And it is this marriage license which gives the state legal power to dictate who gets what in the case of a divorce.

The explosion of divorce in the latter half of the 20th century and the commonplace abuse of men in the family "courts" (which are actually fraudulent executive-branch entities that operate in total violation of the constitutional law's separation of powers) is bad enough. But since feminists have discovered how the power of government can be used to forcibly transform civil society to their liking, they have been emboldened to make even more creative use of the state's power over marriage.

In Spain, for example, a law is being passed to force men to do more housework. Since the vast majority of Spanish men—81 percent—are traditionalists who believe that women with school-age children should stay at home and not work full-time jobs, Spanish feminists are waging war against them through the national legislature.

As the law's sponsor, Margarita Uria, helpfully explains:

> *The idea of equality within marriage always stumbles over the problem of work in the house and caring for dependent people. This will be a good way*

of reminding people what their duties are. It is something feminists have been wanting for a long time.

No doubt they have. Because, according to Marian Salzman, described by the U.K. Observer as a "trend-spotter extraordinaire", women are

...rejecting equality in the workplace and prefer the idea of becoming full-time housewives—but not ones who actually do housework ... women are happy to abandon the workplace, but not if it means spending all day at home cooking, cleaning and looking after children. Instead, they want to play the 'role' of housewife with a little help from, for instance, a nanny, and someone who does the ironing.

Her warning should sober even the most infatuated man.

Women think: 'What's mine is mine, and what's his is mine.'

Since the U.S. Supreme Court now sees fit to take international law into account when deciding what is and is not constitutional, it can only be a matter of time before a woman's right to force her husband to do the ironing or breast-feed the baby is discovered in an emanation or a penumbra. After all, someone has to do the housework when mommy is busy sitting on a corporate board, which she'll be doing as soon as the Norwegian concept of sex-based affirmative action for company directors crosses the Atlantic.

Young men are already responding to the increasingly odious burden of marriage by delaying it or avoiding it altogether, but for the most part, they are doing so without conscious design. It is time for men to become aware that as the more economically productive class, they are the natural prey of the government and its family-control machinery. The courts have already demonstrated that a man—any man—will do for their purposes when child support is required, even if that man can be proved to have no relationship to the child.

For non-Christian men, the answer is easy: Avoid marriage at all costs. Marriage only weakens your legal and emotional positions vis-a-vis a woman, and since American women will freely provide companionship, sex and children upon request, to marry is to give up a great deal for what is literally less than nothing.

A Christian man, on other hand, cannot freely engage in non-committal sexual relationships, and so must marry. He can improve his odds, however, by marrying a Christian woman who is not on the career track. This will significantly increase the chances that he will not find himself at the legal mercy of a sociopath obsessed with momentary happiness über alles, but blessed by a traditional wife committed to building a family and a life together with him instead.

But is it possible for a Christian couple to avoid the state's machinery of control and still marry before God? Yes, according to pastor Matt Trewhella.

What's recorded in a family Bible will stand up as legal evidence in any court of law in America. Early Americans were married without a marriage license. They simply recorded their marriages in their family Bibles. So should we.

What would John Wayne do?

April 18, 2005

AFTER ALMOST EVERY column or blogpost I've written about the various idiosyncracies of women, some woman writes to complain that I never criticize men. Of course, there's not exactly a shortage of male-bashing in the mainstream media today, to say nothing of chick rags like *Cosmopolitan*, *Ms.*, *Self* and other variants on the Me, Myself and I theme so popular with women.

And while there is something about the modern American man that is absolutely worthy of criticism, I don't think it's exactly what these feminists had in mind. For you see, the main problem with men today is that they are not men, but frightened little boys—afraid of their bosses, their wives, their girlfriends and their government. They are afraid of their employees, their children and their children's teachers.

They are not men because the hallmark of a real man is one who is not ruled by fear. Consider the real men of history, the immortals whose names we still honor today. Leonidas and his Three Hundred did not run before the Persian army at Thermopylae even though they knew they would fall before the host of Xerxes. Winston Churchill, a military and political failure, did not quail before the might of Nazi Germany, but inspired the nation of Britain to stand with him. And not even years in the Soviet gulags could silence the brave voice of Aleksandr Solzhenitsyn, whose iron will enabled him to outlast the very government that imprisoned him.

Can you imagine one of these men meekly submitting to the harsh words of a boss? Can you imagine Cicero cowering before the sharp tongue of a nagging wife, who did not cower before an emperor? Or the Apostle Paul remaining silent for fear someone might take offense to his words?

What men lack today is a defining point separating boyhood from man-hood. The mere accumulation of years is not enough, for as the saying goes, a woman is, but a man must become. It is interesting to see the difference between one's friends who enter the Marine Corps and those who enter college—four years later, there is seldom a question that the Marine is indeed a man, but far more often than not, the college graduate is simply a post-adolescent version of what he was before.

For the knowledge of manhood is the assurance that one has faced the test and passed. This is not a test of what one knows, but the test of character that only comes from facing your fears. As society has become safer, and in many ways better thanks to technology, it has also eliminated many of the tests that boys of previous generations were forced to face in becoming men.

In my boyhood, I envied my uncle and my grandfather. They were men. The much-decorated Marine veterans of five wars between them, they both survived everything the Japanese, Chinese, Vietnamese and Iraqis could throw at them and no longer feared anything but God. When at 71, my grandfather broke his hand on the jaw of a carjacker who foolishly thought a .38 revolver and a six-inch height advantage should suffice to cow an old man, I asked him if he hadn't been afraid.

He shrugged and said that he figured if Guadacanal and Tarawa didn't kill him, no young buck with a popgun stood a chance.

But too many young men today lack such role models. And yet, they seek to find their manhood as if by instinct, all too often making do with inadequate substitutes such as fraternities and gangs. At the time, I did not know I was looking to test myself when my best friend and I joined our martial-arts dojo after being informed by the Marine recruiter that the Gulf War would be over before we finished basic training and our assistance, while appreciated, was surplus to requirements. In retrospect, however, that's precisely what we were doing.

It isn't until he faces the test that a boy begins to understand that it isn't the absence of fear that's the issue, it's how you accept that fear and face it. It is the boy who gets knocked down… it is the man who rises again in the full knowledge of what's coming next.

Women are not to blame for the demasculization of the American man. It is men who have allowed this to happen, it is the fathers who shirk their responsibility to their sons and the young men who choose the soft and easy way of leisure over the less comfortable path of discipline who are to blame.

So, young man, if you harbor any doubts in your head about your manhood, let me assure you they are correct. The question is, what are you going to do about it?

The National Democrats

April 25, 2005

AS I HAVE REPEATEDLY WRITTEN, despite the desperate and semi-successful propaganda engineered by leftist academics to convince the historically ignorant masses that the National Socialist German Worker's Party and the Italian Fascist Party were extreme right-wing groups, both parties were founded by socialist activists, guided by socialist principles and governed largely according to left-wing ideals.

Only those who know so little leftist ideology that they do not realize that Marxism is merely a subset of socialism can fail to understand that while both the National Socialists and Fascists rejected Marxian socialism, they remained hard-core socialists. For if rejecting Marx is the ideological definitive, then every socialist from Francois Babeuf and Charles Fourier to Sidney Webb and Edward Bernstein must be likewise characterized as right-wing thinkers.

This is, of course, absurd.

If one examines both the political programs and subsequent governance in Germany and Italy, it is easy to see that both National Socialism and Fascism offered nothing but socialism with a nationalist spin. Hence, in the case of the German party, the name. For example, the following elements of Karl Marx's 10-point Communist program were adopted, more or less, by the National Socialists:

- State control and regulation of private property

- Progressive income tax

- Abolition of inheritance

- Confiscation of the property of all emigrants and rebels

- A central bank

- Centralization of the means of communication and transport

- Extension of factories and instruments of production owned by the state

- Free education for all children in public schools

The two points of the Communist plan explicitly rejected by the National Socialists were:

- Equal obligation of all to work. Being influenced by the Kaiser-Kirche-Kinder-Kuche slogan of imperial Prussia, the National Socialists preferred women to stay home and breed the next generation of Aryan ubermensch.

- Combination of agriculture with manufacturing industries; gradual abolition of all the distinction between town and country by a more equable distribution of the populace over the country. While the National Socialists insisted on the state's right to seize property without compensation, they were rather more Green than their Communist kin; their concept of Lebensraum did not encompass the amalgamation of town and country.

As with Lenin and Stalin, the most significant area where the National Socialists and Fascists departed from Marx—and his true successor, Leon Trotsky—was not in their dismissal of class consciousness, but in their nationalist approach to socialism. What Stalin called "socialism in one country" is essentially the same concept that Hitler dubbed National Socialism. In fact, one would not be amiss to label Stalin a National Communist.

Today, when one surveys the American political landscape, one sees much the same uniformity of opinion that existed in early 20th-century Europe. There are few—very few—who question the superiority of the State's demands over the individual's rights. And despite clear majorities opposed to unlimited immigration, open borders, abortion on demand and political integration with Mexico and Canada, the Republican and Democratic parties are either pushing remorselessly ahead or maintaining the unpopular status quo.

The primary difference, now as then, revolves around the question of nationalism, and, to a lesser extent, militarism. George Bush and his cadre of Strong Government Republicans are not so much neoconservatives as neoliberals of the decidedly non-classic variety, combining the domestic program of Franklin Delano Roosevelt with the foreign policy of Woodrow Wilson.

The American Left's hatred for George Bush is not because they are ideologically opposed to the spirit of his governance, but because he has co-opted them. By moving consistently leftward, he has marginalized them and seized the reins of central power that the Democratic Party considers to be rightfully its own. After all, it does seem a little unfair that after 70 years of steady centralization, they should be forced to hand over the massive federal machine they have constructed to a heretic.

At this point, it is primarily the nominal Republican opposition to the United Nations and an openness to the use of military force in what can at least theoretically pass for being in America's national interest that really separates the two parties. The Democrats have been roundly defeated at the polls, only to be replaced by George Bush and what should more rightly be termed his party of National Democrats.

But the successful heist of central power on the part of these National Democrats no more represents a move toward genuine freedom and a return to constitutional republicanism than the National Socialists' 1933 electoral defeat of the previously dominant socialists was a move toward restoring the Kaiser. And as history teaches, socialism with a nationalist face is little more palatable than the pure strain of the disease.

Flattered to deceive

May 2, 2005

I T'S NO SURPRISE that the less intelligent and the less informed you are, the more likely you are to get your news from local television. After all, you're not likely to learn much about the world from the constant repetition of crime, weather, sports and human interest.

Network TV news is a little better, although you can't expect to learn very much from a 10-second soundbite from a senator, much less the minute-long rebuttal cum explanation helpfully provided by the Capitol Hill correspondent.

At first glance, the 24-hour news offered by *CNN*, *Fox News*, *MSNBC* and *CNBC* theoretically provide the opportunity for genuine, in-depth coverage of events. Unfortunately, this opportunity has been as badly squandered as those originally offered by television itself, which was once seriously viewed by some early optimists as an educationally beneficial medium.

While I have no doubt that there are plenty of children learning new things every week from watching *Desperate Housewives*, I don't think this was exactly what those academics had in mind.

Fox News is rightly the king of the cable news hill, as basic division predicted from the start. A product designed to present monopoly appeal to the more conservative 50 percent of the population is obviously going to outperform those products designed to split the more liberal 50 percent among *PBS* and the *ABCNNBCBS* cabal. Unfortunately, this worldview monopoly was not enough for *Fox News* producers, as the siren song of live-car chases, missing white women and celebrity trials proved impossible for them to resist.

For all their popularity, the editorial shows are not much better. Ann Coulter could be a guest on both the *O'Reilly Factor* and *Hannity & Colmes* every night for a year and one would not learn one-fourth as much from the experience as one would from reading one of her books. It is quite common, of course, for TV talking heads to write books these days, since publishers have discovered the concept of transmedia synergy, although this merely conceals the fact that very few of these TV pseudo-intellectuals have either expertise to share or anything significant to say.

This is why the Rush Limbaughs, Bill O'Reillys and Al Frankens, unlike the polemicists of yore, only write two or three books—often with a ghost writer—before discovering that they have run out of steam. While the TV audience never seems to tire of hearing variants on the "liberals bad, conservatives good" or the "conservatives bad, liberals good" theme, readers tend to be a bit more discerning. Or at least more easily bored.

There are a few exceptions, of course. Ann Coulter's books are not merely controversial, they are also substantive, even if her critics found it difficult to find the endnotes. I have been a steadfast critic of Michelle Malkin's book on internment, and yet I must give her credit for at least attempting to write a substantive work. It would have been much easier, after all, for a media personality of her appeal to simply hurl a random collection of polemical red meat to the carnivores. And Paul Krugman's pop econ books do educate the reader, even if the education is in an outdated and increasingly inaccurate theoretical model.

But I do not know if there has ever been a time when so many people have known so little while considering themselves so well-informed. Most people would agree, I think, that newspapers offer a generally more substantive medium than television, and yet on Saturday, Maureen Dowd of the *New York Times* complained that the new Iraqi government was being "ruled by men rooted in the sort of conservative Shiite religious politics that will not produce a new dawn of equality for Iraqi women."

In an effort to sound intellectual, she instead provided inadvertent hilarity:

The bad news: This is not an Iraqi government that will practice Athenian democracy...

Apparently it was unknown to Ms. Dowd that women were not permitted to vote or hold office in Athens, and I rather doubt she would be terribly upset should Iraqi democrats fail to pass death sentences on dangerous philosophers as did their Athenian forebears. Then again, one should probably not assume that Ms. Dowd is capable of distinguishing Socrates from Michael Stipe.

Journalists have a very dangerous tendency to assume that if one has heard about something, one knows and understands it. It seems to me that the second great evil of cable news—after the Cryptkeeper, formerly known as Larry King—is the transference of this illusion from the TV commentator to the viewer.

750 words such as these can't teach you anything of substance, but 750 pages can. And only after building a solid base of knowledge can one begin to make sense of the bits of information floating in the media stream around you. Tonight, why not consider turning off the low-wattage cable dialectic, and, in the words of Flavor Flav, read a book and learn your culture.

Only then can you begin to wake up.

The Devil's own?

May 9, 2005

I T IS MORE THAN A LITTLE IRONIC, I think, that the North Carolina minister forced almost 50 people to leave his church for the newly discovered sin of failing to support George Bush.

As one former member of East Waynesville Baptist Church was reported as saying:

> *…if we didn't support George Bush, we needed to resign our position and get out, or go to the altar and repent, and support George Bush.*

The minister, Chan Chandler, insists that he is acting according to God's Word. However, despite searching the King James, the New International Version and the American Standard Bibles—not to mention running various letter sequences through the Bible Code—I was unable to find the verse that said "That if thou shalt confess with thy mouth the President George Bush, and shalt believe in thine heart that God hath raised him from the dead, thou shalt be saved."

I did, however, run across Jesus Christ's parable of the tree and its fruit in the book of Matthew, warning of false prophets, wolves dressed as sheep. And I wondered: Who might these false prophets be? Who are the false Christs working evil, deceiving even the elect as they bring about the dominion of the last and greatest antichrist?

Then I considered the following description of the RealID plan:

> *Starting three years from now, if you live or work in the United States, you'll need a federally approved ID card to travel on an airplane, open a bank account, collect Social Security payments, or take advantage of nearly any government service.*

This sounds more than a little remniscent of words written on the isle of Patmos almost 2,000 years ago:

He also forced everyone, small and great, rich and poor, free and slave, to receive a mark on his right hand or on his forehead, so that no one could buy or sell unless he had the mark…

That's a rather impressive forecast, especially if you consider how far off the best science fiction writers of the Golden Age were from accurately portraying a reality only 50 years after their time. But then, I suppose one could argue that divine inspiration is a form of cheating.

It is true that even in latter-day America, which is already 40 percent government-owned, it will still be theoretically possible to do some buying or selling after our Republican House, Senate and president impose this RealID monstrosity on us. After all, who has a bank account, travels on airplanes or pays income taxes, right? And no doubt some bright Three Monkey Republican will be quick to point out that an ID card containing digital information is not the same thing as a mark on your body.

Not yet, anyway.

It will be a delicious surprise to almost everyone except me, I think, when the Department of Vaterland Security informs a surprised American people in a few years that due to the theft of RealID cards by suspected Islamic terrorists, it has determined that the most effective way to ensure security of the RealID system is to implant miniaturized RealIDs into the card-owner's body. This will be mandatory, of course, because otherwise it will be impossible to protect America from the imminent threat of destruction by people paying cash for their Cheerios at the supermarket.

I realize that many Christians believe George Bush is a godly man, that he has been selected by a higher power for a special mission at a critical time in this country's history. Nor do I deny that this may well be so. But the vital question is to discover which god he serves—God, the Father of Jesus Christ, or the god that Jesus Christ described as the prince of this world.

For it is written that many will be deceived, and it is impossible to argue against the fact that this president, like his father before him, is dedicated to expanding the size and scope of government, to sustaining and supporting the legitimacy of the United Nations, and to building a new world order on the ashes of American sovereignty.

No man can judge another man's heart or his soul. That is for God alone. But we can, as Jesus Christ told us, know the tree from its fruit. And while I did not believe the president's qualified claims to being a conservative during his 2000 campaign, I saw no reason to doubt his religious faith.

Now, after five years of a presidency that has conclusively proven George Bush is no conservative, I am beginning to wonder if his claims of sharing a faith with the Christians of America might not be dubious as well.

Here we go again!

May 16, 2005

E VEN THE MOST CURSORY examination of any commodity, currency or equity market makes it very clear that prices seldom go
straight up or straight down, and yet most financial analysis ignores
this simple and undeniable fact. Worse, financial journalists have shorter
memories than their front-page colleagues—it seems only sports reporters
have any interest in what happened five years ago, much less 50.

In early 2000, tech stocks were a sure thing. I knew many people who had
never invested in the stock market before and were taking flyers they could
not afford—up to 80 percent of their savings—on profitless companies and
stocks with price-earning ratios of 100 or more. This behavior is characteristic
of a mania, and indeed, the enthusiastic involvement of investment rookies
is an inevitable sign of a market in its final stage.

When the Federal Reserve slashed interest rates to prevent the economy
from absorbing the full impact of the March 2000 to October 2002 equity
meltdown, the hot money was given an incentive to move from the stock
market to the real-estate market. A 40 percent reduction in mortgage rates
since 2000 has resulted in a 34 percent increase in the number of new houses
sold annually, and I have read that 36 percent of all residential home sales
in 2004 were not primary residences, but were intended as investment or
vacation properties. Nationwide, home prices have increased 50 percent in
the last five years.

I find it an ominous sign to hear real-estate agents now echoing the same
assertions of a "new economy" that stockbrokers and financial market cheerleaders were making in 1999. But their self-interested arguments in favor of a
permanent real-estate bull are nonsensical, as market movements demonstrably driven by low-interest debt financing are not going to be supported in the

long term by a limited housing supply. People in Japan need housing every bit as badly as Americans, their residential property stock is much smaller and yet these factors have not prevented their residential real-estate prices from declining more than 40 percent in 14 years.

As a wise financial sage once said, the trick to making money is determining which argument is based on false assumptions and betting against it. While the newcomers to the real-estate market will almost surely get burned in the same way their stock-market counterparts were five years ago, the real-estate permabull is only one of the more significant false assumptions currently operative.

Less noticeable to most, but perhaps equally important is one at work in the currency markets. I, too, have been guilty of subscribing to it in the past, assuming that because it is worthless paper debt being created at historically high rates on a daily basis, the dollar is doomed to fall inexorably over the next few years, thus driving up the price of commodities such as oil and gold. The fact that this perspective worked very well for the last five years, plus the comments of Fed governor Ben Bernanke, widely considered a possible successor to Alan Greenspan, about how the digital printing press is powerful enough to overcome any potential price deflation, only made the long-term hyperinflation scenario look more credible.

But I was forced to recall my 2004 interview with Robert Prechter, who has been insisting that the dollar will rise into the 94–99 range since it was down around 80, (it's now at 86.10), after receiving the following spam a few months ago:

> *The U.S. dollar has fallen to an all-time low against the euro. The euro hit a new high of U.S. $1.3646, exceeding the record U.S. $1.3643 set in European trading. Now is the time for you to take advantage of the opportunities the Euro has to offer.*

The subsequent 6 percent fall in the euro against the dollar suggests we should consider adding a spam corollary to the contrarian magazine cover theory, which states that the appearance of an investment trend on the cover of a mainstream magazine is a strong indication that the trend is at an end.

In closing, I leave you with the words of a man who has forgotten far more about investing than I will ever know, Richard Russell:

Look, we don't have to get into the theory of why deflation can or cannot occur. I go by what I see in the markets and in chart action. The fact is that the stock market has been deflating all year. Now the stock market has been joined by oil, commodity prices, copper, steel, aluminum, gold, Goldman Sachs Natural Resources Index, materials in general…

All debt must be paid off, some debt paid off in a hurry and some paid off over time. But you pay off debt with dollars, and if there's too much debt outstanding and there's pressure to pay off that debt—that's going to create a demand for dollars. The greater the debt, the greater the potential demand for dollars to pay off that debt.

Choosing evil

May 23, 2005

ONE OF THE COMMON REASONS given for rejecting the Christian God is the idea that the ability to choose between Heaven and Hell is not a real choice, but more of a semantic trick or even a con game on the part of the Divine. After all, given the choice between paradise and eternal torment, who in their right mind would choose the latter?

This presumes a rational ability on the part of Man that nearly all the evidence suggests does not exist. For example, one might as easily apply this sophisticated analysis to obesity. Given the choice between being slender and attractive and being fat and less desirable, it is obvious that no one in their right mind would choose the latter. Therefore, there are no fat people and anyone you happen to see that appears to be overweight is merely a visual hallucination or a construct of your imagination. Q.E.D.

The fact of the matter is that if there truly is a God, one's opinion of the cosmic fairness of any such choice is completely irrelevant with regard to the fact that one has made one's choice. Given that the Bible predicts negative material consequences to such an extent that martyrdom is a distinct possibility, it seems doubtful that an opinion of the overly obvious nature of the choice will be considered an acceptable excuse for making the wrong one.

A similar logic holds true for individuals in modern society, and, for that matter, societies themselves. How many people opposed to the coming system of total financial tracking from cradle to grave nevertheless sign their children up for a Social Security number because it saves them a bit of money on their taxes every year? Implanted digital currency is less than 10 years away—I used to wonder how it would ever be possible for St. John's bad guys to get people to go along with something as monstrous as the Mark of the Beast.

Now, I know. Governments will offer a $1,500 credit for paying your taxes that way and so-called Christians around the globe will sign up in droves.

The saving grace of evil is that it appears to have a compulsion of some sort to announce itself. No one who read *Mein Kampf* or "What is to be Done" could have been truly surprised by the subsequent actions of either Adolf Hitler or Vladimir Lenin. George W. Bush campaigned as an anti-conservative, openly rejecting individualism, while echoing rhetoric from the likes of LBJ and FDR, then to the apparent surprise of nearly everyone in the Republican Party, began governing in a manner nearly indistinguishable from the two archliberals.

Nor should anyone be taken unaware when Hillary Clinton picks up precisely where she left off in 1994, for just the other day she was quoted by the Nation as saying:

You may remember that when my husband was president, I tried to do something about health care. Well, I still have the scars to show for it. But I haven't given up.

No doubt she hasn't, and yet there will be millions of Americans who will vote for her, then be shocked—truly shocked and appalled—when the transition of our mixed health-care system to a socialist one is made complete under her aegis.

The decision to choose evil is always easy, usually much easier than one would ever imagine. This is because it's the popular choice—the one that will allow you to fit in, the one that will prevent people from pointing fingers at you and describing you in unflattering terms. But perhaps it will help some of you to keep in mind that the urge to submit to the temptation of the hive mind and go along with the herd is the very same one that once led a crowd to shout "Crucify Him!"

There is a reason the right path is described as being the difficult one. One should not be depressed when the way seems difficult—indeed, it is only when everything seems obvious, easy and socially acceptable that we should begin to question the rightness of our chosen direction.

Heil to the victor

May 30, 2005

THE EXPECTED TRANSFORMATION has begun. The Long March from Goldwater Republican to radical Wellesley socialist to reasonable and moderate centrist is nearing its end. As with Mao's dream of conquering the vast and populous land of China, the goal appears utterly unthinkable, and yet, is this not the woman who once declared "The challenge now is to practice politics as the art of making what appears to be impossible, possible"?

The bars to a second Clinton presidency seem, a priori, insurmountable. She is a Democrat in a country where the Democratic Party is not only in national decline, but burdened with a low-watt lunatic at the helm of the Democratic National Committee. She is a U.S. senator—a position which rarely serves as a stepping stone to the top. She is the most widely recognized liberal symbol in the world, at a time when even the most liberal politicians attempt to evade the title. Even with her Arkansas connections, she is a Northeasterner in spirit, breeding, education and demeanor, and politicians from the Northeast do not win national elections anymore.

Above all, she has the handicap of her sex, and many men and women will vote against her on that basis alone.

How, then, is it possible that a recent *USA Today* poll conducted by Gallup could report that Hillary Clinton has as much support as Texas Gov. George W. Bush and Vice-President Al Gore had at a similarly early stage prior to the 2000 election?

There are several possible explanations. The least convincing is that her travails were simply the result of Clinton Fatigue, which is now wearing off after six years of the second Bush presidency. Such fatigue is more journalistic ennui in writing about the same subject for an extended period of time than anything else—no one else really cares about such things. "ER" and "CSI" have both been around for an apparent eternity, after all, and millions of Americans still watch them.

A second explanation is that celebrity trumps all other considerations in American politics. One could make a reasonable case that Paris Hilton would command the support of at least 25 percent of the American electorate were she to run for national office tomorrow. Consider, if you will, the genuine excitement expressed by the John Stewart crowd about one of the most shockingly uncharismatic men to have ever run for president, John Kerry. Hillary Clinton is a bona fide celebrity candidate, her icily sexless public persona makes her a feminist icon, and still she is the femme de la crème for the editorial spinstresses at *Vogue*, *Vanity Fair* and *Cosmpolitan*.

The fawning media coverage she is guaranteed to receive from them and the more activist elements of the legacy media cannot yet be fully counteracted by talk radio and the blogosphere, barring the appearance of a sex tape starring Hillary and the aforementioned Miss Hilton.

The chief reason, however, for the likelihood of her ascendancy in 2008 is that the omens point to it being her time. Bill Clinton's mentor at Georgetown, Professor Carroll Quigley, once wrote of the 1896 U.S. presidential election:

> *The inability of plutocracy to control the Democratic Party as it had demonstrated it could control the Republican Party, made it advisable for them to adopt a one-party outlook on political affairs, although they continued to contribute to some extent to both parties and did not cease their efforts to control both.*

In the process of moving her political persona to the center, I suspect that Hillary Clinton has sufficiently demonstrated to many important people who have been skeptical of her in the past that she is willing to temper her national socialist instincts in favor of continuing George W. Bush's international program. As is the case with Europe, a "no" vote is not permissible, and who better to oversee the transformation of the United States of America into a transcontinental entity than the woman who does not know the meaning of the word? Just as there were signs that George W. Bush was the Chosen One prior to 2000, this push to reinvent the former co-president appears designed to set the stage for her rise to power.

These are early days, of course, but look for the Republicans to nominate an unelectable candidate in the Dole mode to serve as a sacrificial lamb. Jeb Bush would be ideal, although Rudy Giuliani might be even better as a candidate who looks credible on the surface, but who will suppress the turnout of the Republican base.

But there is a silver lining: At least health care will be free.

2 to the tushy

June 6, 2005

FROM THE WAILING AND GNASHING of teeth in Brussels, one would think the two failed referendums on the so-called constitution of the European Union were two stakes through the vampire's chest. But as the Danish vote on Maastricht and the Irish vote on Nice previously demonstrated, European voters can stab it with their steely knives but they just can't kill the beast.

Born in shadow, nurtured in deception, the European Union has been a pack of lies from the very start. Intentions of a monetary union were denied when it was nothing but a free-trade zone. Once that was accomplished, the Europhile political elite swore up and down that the slightest inkling of a notion of political union had not even dreamed of crossing their collectivist mind.

But soon enough, it became clear that this, too, was a lie. It's hard to say when Europeans—always slow to recognize tyrants—began to realize this. It might have been when it was reported that 80 percent of the United Kingdom's new laws were being dictated to the British Parliament by the unelected European Commission. Or perhaps it was when the citizens of Lithuania, Hungary, Slovenia, Slovakia, Austria, Latvia, Greece, Italy and Germany learned that they would have no say in accepting the complete surrender of their national sovereignty, except through those trustworthy voices of their national legislatures.

Nor has the fact that the euro—far from aiding Europe's competitiveness as advertised, has proven downright detrimental to nearly every European country that adopted it—convinced anyone of Brussels' trustworthiness.

The American media has made much of the supposed irony that the French rejection of the E.U. constitution was due to its failure to provide enough socialism, as if the matter at hand was one of free trade and French disdain for unfettered capitalism. But this is a profoundly misguided analysis, as even a brief perusal of the treaty suffices to demonstrate that it has next to nothing to do with economic philosophies of any kind and everything to do with the structure of political power.

The central point of the two referendums did not revolve around how the French and the Dutch wish to order their societies, but whether they wished to continue governing themselves in the Western democratic tradition or if they were ready to abandon it in favor of an unelected external oligarchy. The answer, as it will be understood by the governing elite is this: Not yet.

As everyone who has ever voted against a school levy knows, the nature of government at all levels is to continuously expand. As long as passing new laws is viewed as productivity by politicians, as "getting things done", there will be a natural impetus for government to expand. The problem for Europe's politicians is that their governments have already intruded into the national economies about as far as they can without engendering a collapse. After all, with only 24 hours in the day, there is a finite limit to the amount of activity one can dictate.

The European Union, with its higher level of centralization, offered a rare growth opportunity to the political class and it should surprise no one that they rushed to sell out their countries in order to grasp it. When a man is drowning, he will clutch at anything thrown to him, even an anchor that will sink him faster than before. But it is this very desperation that will compel the national politicians to return again and again to the question of continued European integration—by force, if necessary.

It is a pity that the two referendums are unlikely to prove sufficient to end the monstrous experiment. A unified Europe was not desirable under Philip II of Spain, Napoleon Bonaparte or Adolf Hitler. It is no more desirable today, for all that the would-be rulers are wise enough to use central banks instead of tanks.

But the politicians have learned. It may take years, even decades, to return to the subject, but the next time it is broached, I rather expect that the people of France and the Netherlands will not be permitted to crassly interfere with the grand schemes of their masters.

End the charade

June 13, 2005

THE COGNITIVE DISSONANCE required to believe the Bush administration is approaching critical mass. Some semblance of victory in the War on Method has been declared at least four times that I recall, and yet American troops are still being murdered on a weekly basis in free and democratic Iraq.

The armed forces are now reduced to lying about who killed its poster boys, putting its own troops on trial and revising its recruitment targets to disguise the fact that no amount of media triumphalism suffices to convince most young Americans that extending the Pax Americana to the Middle East is worth death by improvised explosive device.

Bear in mind that I am not an opponent of the American military—I know too many good men serving in its various branches to view it in a negative light. To hold our men and women in uniform responsible for the manifest failures of their commander in chief and his administration would be tantamount to blaming the car for crashing when its intoxicated driver failed to see a red light and ended up driving through a store window.

And it is easy to demonstrate that one can criticize the Iraqi Occupation without criticizing America's armed forces. The Marines are not particularly keen on the 20,000 mercenaries—they prefer to be called "military contractors"—who represent almost 18 percent of the USA's military strength now in Iraq.

It will take years, perhaps a decade or more, before it is possible to determine ultimate success or failure in Iraq. But by some measures, the dual invasions of Afghanistan and Iraq have certainly served their purpose. The Taliban and Saddam Hussein have been driven from power and they have been replaced by elected governments that are no less legitimate than our own Washington plutocracy. What, then, prevents the president from declaring victory and bringing our soldiers home? Why was it necessary for 266 Americans to die after the Jan. 31 election of a free Iraqi government?

And finally, if free elections are not enough to assert victory, what is the definition of success? Does one even exist? The metrics, nebulous as they are, appear to keep changing.

The danger is that the conspiracy theorists were right and that this was nothing but a steppingstone to a Middle East empire from the start. Michael Ledeen, the brilliant neoconservative, has been pleading for an expansion of the war to include Iran from the very start—the drums beginning to beat slowly in the media deep would appear to suggest that he's finally going to get his wish. "Faster, please"? I don't think so.

One of the great mysteries of World War II was how Germany did not go on an industrial war footing until long after the die had been cast. Ironically, although the War on Method has now lasted longer than the War in Europe, the United States has not only refused to go on a war footing, but disdains to even bother declaring war, while maintaining almost completely open borders, the better to serve enemy combatants.

Let's face it: If carrying a bloody chainsaw is not enough to deny a foreigner entrance to the United States, there is no border control. Indeed, the president has made it clear he's more concerned about preventing private citizens from doing the job that his administration is neglecting than he is about enemy aliens armed with suitcase nukes entering the country.

As long as immigration remains open, the administration's position is obviously nonsensical. The push for Patriot II combined with the president's antipathy for the Minuteman movement clearly demonstrates that he is more concerned about ending the potential threat to Washington from American civil liberties than he is with the danger to America from alien terrorists.

It is time to end this charade. The troops have won the war, history proves they cannot impose a nonexistent peace. Bring them home.

Sun Tzu and the Art of Chicanery

June 20, 2005

USINESS BOOKS usually sell very well, usually because they represent the near-perfect harmony of buyer's greed and seller's greed. There's nothing wrong with this in a capitalist society, even if it's difficult to resist the urge to weep at the pathetic sight of an overweight 40-something middle manager wearing a bad suit and reading a copy of *Who Moved My Cheese?* so intently that one would think it contained The Ultimate Question. (The answer, of course, is 42.)

I found myself in an airport of late, and eschewing the usual titles by familiar names such Grisham, King and the author du jour, Brown, I elected to peruse the business section, which was located next to what appeared, judging by the book titles, to be the orgasm section. (One imagines that the scientific news that there may be a genetic component to the likelihood of female pleasure will likely lead to a reshuffling of the literary sections, as well as reduce the number of articles in *Cosmopolitan* by one-third.)

There seem to be four primary schools of thought when it comes to business management. One is the whimsical approach, as epitomized by the *Cheese* book. This generally involves some sort of unpleasant metaphor, in this case likening corporate employees to rats in mazes. The second school involves an aphoristic approach, featuring a pithy sentence that is explicated over the following two pages. The third school is autobiographical, although what one has to learn from Messrs. Trump and Zigler, et al., is of dubious utility to the average assistant account executive.

P.J. O'Rourke once wrote a hilarious review of Lee Iacocca's contribution to this literary sub-genre, wherein he likened the value of the book for would-be future executives to the author's feelings during a certain period, i.e., lower than cetacean excrement.

The fourth school could be characterized as the pseudo-historical approach. There are a number of variants, usually incorporating the sayings of a historical figure so famous for his intellectual firepower that even business majors have heard of him, such as Niccolo Machiavelli. But this school might best be characterized as the school of Sun Tzu, as there are more business-related books attempting to ride the silken coattails of the ancient Chinese general than all the others combined. A few of the books devoted to Sun Tzu and his seminal work on martial strategy include:

- *Sun Tzu for Success: How to Use the Art of War to Master Challenges and Accomplish the Important Goals in Your Life*

- *Sun Tzu Was a Sissy : Conquer Your Enemies, Promote Your Friends, and Wage the Real Art of War*

- *Sun Tzu's Art of War for Traders and Investors*

- *Sun Tzu and the Art of Business: Six Strategic Principles for Managers*

- *The Art of War for Executives*

- *Sun Tzu: The Art of War for Managers; 50 Strategic Rules*

- *Sun Tzu Strategies for Winning the Marketing War: 12 Essential Principles for Winning the War for Customers*

- *Sun Tzu Strategies for Selling: How to Use The Art of War to Build Lifelong Customer Relationships*

- *Sun Tzu: War and Management : Application to Strategic Management and Thinking*

This is ironic for two reasons. The first should be eminently obvious. Business is not war. Furthermore, there is a very poor metaphorical relationship between the two concepts, as business is inherently constructive, ideally involving transactions that benefit both parties involved, whereas war is inherently destructive. Even if an impudent whippersnapper were to take semantic liberties and attempt to link Schumpeter's concept of Creative Destruction and build off a theory of entrepreneurship to strengthen the metaphor, more precise minds would point out that even this semantic gamesmanship requires a shift from business to economics, and the metaphor therefore fails.

The second is that despite Sun Tzu's status as a legendary Chinese general from the Chunqiu Shidai, the state of Wu he is supposed to have served was not a significant success militarily or economically. Instead, it lasted little more than a century before being conquered by the state of Yue in 473 B.C. The notion that the intellectual heirs of Aristotle, Smith, Rothschild and Drucker have anything important to learn from the semi-mythological military leader of a failed, half-barbarian Chinese kingdom is questionable at best.

And yet, if one examines Sun Tzu's text, one may ascertain part of the ethical problem inflicting American business today. For the general once wrote:

All warfare is based on deception.

If the arrests of men such as Dennis Kozlowski, formerly chief executive officer of Tyco, and Kenneth Lay, once CEO of Enron, are any guide, it would seem that many American business leaders have learned their Sun Tzu all too well.

The great leap backward

June 27, 2005

I T IS TIME TO CHANGE the national anthem. The land is no longer free. Last week, in an appalling decision that will prove to be every bit as infamous as the Dred Scott and Roe v. Wade decisions, the Supreme Court eliminated the American right to property and in one fell swoop, converted the country into the legal equivalent of a Third World society.

This is not a minor matter, it is a calculated provocation, an insult to the American people and their rights which makes a mockery of them as well as the current administration and its obsession with external terrorists and exogenous threats to liberty. The White House is chasing phantoms of democracy in the Middle East, pretending to bring freedom there even as the most basic freedoms are being methodically destroyed within America itself.

No 9-11 attack, no suitcase nuke exploding in Manhattan or Los Angeles, could injure the nation one-tenth as much as the Supreme Court harmed America in its totalitarian Kelo decision, wherein a majority of the ironically named "justices" declared that a government may forcibly take property from one party and give it to another party, at its sole discretion.

This is a major expansion of the eminent domain concept, and I can confidently predict that the redefinition of the constitutional term "public use" will soon be as stretched beyond recognition as the now-meaningless phrase "interstate commerce", the Orwellian term that now covers things that do not cross state lines (and thus are not interstate) and have not been sold or exchanged for other goods (and thus are not commerce).

The poisonous and contorted logic used by the judicial fascists is childlike, only no parent with detectable brainwave activity would accept it from his child. Consider the paper-thin veil of words with which Stephen Breyer attempted to cover his tortured reasoning:

> *[T]here is no taking for private use that you could imagine in reality that wouldn't also have a public benefit of some kind, whether it's increasing jobs or increasing taxes, etc. That's a fact of the world. And so given that fact of the world, that is law, why shouldn't the law say, OK, virtually every taking is all right, as long as there is some public benefit which there always is…*

So therefore, public is private, black is white, war is peace and Kelo is constitutional. Q.E.D.

Clearly, Joe McCarthy didn't know the half of it. Seizing property from one party and giving it to another is a hallmark of communism (as well as other left-wing variants on socialism such as Maoism, Nazism and fascism); the fact that the Supreme Court did not follow its decision by bursting into song with a lusty chorus of "The International" should not cause anyone to miss the significance of this latest step toward the United Socialist States of America.

Although perhaps the court's actions would be better viewed as a great leap backward. For the Left has always been a fraud, and certainly Kelo serves to shine a bright light on the myth that the liberals on the court actually give a damn about the little guy and the less-fortunate.

Merely substitute a few terms in describing the system and it becomes clear that the Supreme Court has established a neofeudal oligarchy, where all land is held in the name of the federal government-king, governed by his local government-nobles and worked by taxpayer-serfs. Should one serf fail to produce a satisfactory harvest of crops-tax revenues, the noble can take the land from one serf and give it to another who promises to produce a more abundant harvest.

61 years ago, F.A. von Hayek warned of *The Road to Serfdom*. We have reached our destination and it is time now for Americans to decide if we are still the Sons of Liberty or if we are merely modern-day serfs. Some will argue that we have no choice but to submit to the judicial tyranny of our five would-be masters—Sam Adams and Ebenezer McIntosh, among others, would never have agreed.

The first widely known acts of the Sons took place on Aug. 14, 1765, when an effigy of Andrew Oliver (who was to be commissioned Distributor of Stamps for Massachusetts) was found hanging in a tree on Newbury Street, along with a large boot with a devil climbing out of it. The boot was a play on the name of the Earl of Bute and the whole display was intended to establish an evil connection between Oliver and the Stamp Act.

The sheriffs were told to remove the display, but protested in fear of their lives, for a large crowd had formed at the scene. Before the evening, a mob burned Oliver's property on Kilby Street, then moved on to his house. There they beheaded the effigy and stoned the house as its occupants looked out in horror. They then moved to nearby Fort Hill were they built a large fire and burned what was left of the effigy. Most of the crowd dissipated at that point, however McIntosh and crew, then under cover of darkness, ransacked Oliver's abandoned home until midnight.

What independence?

July 4, 2005

Accoording to the Columbia professor being interviewed on National Public Radio this weekend, freedom is an amorphous concept that is primarily a state of mind. This would appear to be at significant odds with the principle of unalienable rights to life, liberty and the pursuit of happiness envisioned by Thomas Jefferson in the Declaration of Independence, as well as the list of specific freedoms delineated in the Bill of Rights.

The right to life has long been under assault, as the culture of death has successfully placed the aged, the helpless and the unborn on the list of those defined as inhuman and therefore legal to kill. The last vestiges of a right to private property have been eliminated, as the recent Kelo decision makes all property officially communal, held only at the seigniorial whim of the local council. The right to bear arms has been limited, too—while it has not yet been destroyed completely, it is obvious that an attack on it will soon be forthcoming.

White House spokesman Scott McClellan's statement that Americans "obviously have to respect the decisions of the Supreme Court" are downright Toryish. After all, the founders of this country rejected the notion that they had to respect the decisions of the English Parliament and King George's ministers, for they had decided that they were going to be a free people. But considering that President Bush, as an owner of Major League Baseball's Texas Rangers, was the beneficiary of a pre-Kelo land seizure himself, what other position could his spokesman possibly take? As McClellan said, "the president has made his views clear when it comes to private property rights."

There is always an inherent conflict between government and freedom. Nearly every act of government, almost every law and regulation that is imposed from above, is intended to limit freedom. What conservatives must understand is that it is not always possible to be a fine, upstanding, law-abiding citizen and be a free man at the same time. In fact, for most of human history, it has been impossible. The American revolutionaries were lawbreakers of the worst kind, for they were directly challenging those who were their rightful masters in the eyes of the law. And yet even today, few would argue that their disobedience was both just and right.

The question of justice turns on the point of whether government—on all levels—has overstepped its lawful bounds. For if the laws of government have passed those limits, they are not law, but mere dictatorial assertions, with no more force than that which the government can muster. And while it is wise to obey under the threat of force, one has no moral obligation to do so, and as the recent history of Eastern Europe shows, once the people become aware that the threat of force is empty, they will begin to ignore both the government and its illegitimate laws with alacrity.

It is impossible to know what the future holds for the United States, but one thing is sure. All governments fall in time. Ironically, governments that rely on force are more fragile than most and tend to fall even faster. The merciless totalitarians of the Soviet Union lasted a mere 72 years, a historical blip when compared with the lifespan of the British monarchy, the Roman Empire or even the neo-democratic oligarchy of the United States of America.

The genius of America was its independence. As that independence has been systematically reduced over the years, so too has its competitive advantage over other, less free, nations declined. The best and brightest have been leaving the country for years, and the American brain drain is accelerating as the Internet has made it possible to run a software company from the Bahamas or an import-export operation from Ireland, where the taxes are lower and there's no danger of losing your home to a Wal-Mart.

In summary, this is not a day to celebrate American independence. It is, instead, a day to mourn America's passing and pray for its eventual rebirth.

Dumbfounded Democrats

July 11, 2005

L IKE MILLIONS OF AMERICANS, I spent a fair amount of time on the highways over the last week or two. Thus, I spent more time listening to the radio than usual and in between frequent repetitions of Disturbed's new single and System of a Down's "B.Y.O.B.", I caught an amusing snippet on Minnesota Public Radio, NPR's regional soviet.

It seems that the Minnesota Legislature, in its infinite wisdom, modified the state tax laws last year and reduced the value which individuals donating cars to charity can place on their vehicles and deduct from their state income taxes. Although the law has been in effect for only a short time, the 60 charities which run vehicle donation programs have already been hard hit, as the number of cars being donated has fallen from 25 to 50 percent, depending on the charity.

The gentleman speaking with the MPR reporter seemed resigned to the likelihood that many of these charities were likely to abandon their vehicle donation programs, as spending more money to raise awareness of programs bringing in markedly fewer cars simply wouldn't make sense for them.

This was amusing, because liberal dogma insists that the public always has a static response to modifications in tax law and asserts that individuals simply do not change their behavior in reaction to changes in their taxes even if those changes will affect their economic well-being. This is why the liberal-dominated legacy media is always taken by surprise when tax increases fail to bring in the expected amount of revenue, as their faith in static tax models inevitably outweighs their willingness to remember what happened the last 10 times that taxes were increased.

For example, two years ago, the *St. Paul Pioneer Press* ran a massive multi-day investigative reporting story on attempting to explain why the dot-com boom had missed Minnesota and why no new technology companies were growing up to replace old-school giants such as Honeywell, Medtronic and Control Data. A panoply of reasons were suggested, ranging from the weather to a failure to spend sufficient money on the University of Minnesota.

Not once did the writers see fit to mention the fact that Minnesota's state-local tax burden was 10.8 percent in 2003, almost a full percent higher than the national average. Nor did they note the 7.85 percent state income tax or that Naples, Fla., is known as Edina South to the many snowbirds who have made Florida their permanent domicile. In 1998, I was a member of a corporate board where nine of the 13 board members—all of whom had been Minnesota residents at one time—were making their homes in Florida. And that didn't include the guy who had moved to the Bahamas.

When I called the business editor and asked him why taxes had not been mentioned in the article, he said his reporters simply didn't believe people would move simply to avoid paying income taxes. He said he'd raised the subject with them, but it was pointed out that since Silicon Valley and the 101 Corridor in Massachusetts were both located in high-tax locales, taxes couldn't possibly be an issue.

Apparently no one stopped to consider the fact that while it's probable that the presence of Caltech, Stanford and the Massachusetts Institute of Technology might outweigh the tax issue, none of these elite entrepreneur-producing universities happen to be located in Minnesota. On the other hand, it is really freaking cold in the wintertime, so at least the state has that going for it.

Another mystery befuddling believers in paradise by politicians is the methamphetamine explosion. Why, one might ask, are drug users today so interested in smoking home-cooked battery acid that will rot their teeth faster than hot sauce from Taco Bell soaked in Pepsi when previous generations of druggies were content with natural opium and coca derivatives?

The answer, of course, lies in the application of the dynamic reaction, in this case to the federal government's War on Drugs. You may not be able to buy a tin of Guatemalan Snoose at Walgreen's these days, but no one's going to ask any questions about what you're doing with a jug of antifreeze in the trunk of your car.

While the Law of Unintended Consequences eventually bites everyone in the backside from time to time, one has to be either foolishly stubborn, brain-damaged or a liberal Democrat to repeatedly find oneself victimized by it.

How to save society

July 18, 2005

O NE OF THE GREAT MYSTERIES of modern faith is knowing how and when to act. Unfortunately, God seldom appears as a burning bush, and when He speaks to us, we hear him with our hearts, not our ears. Regardless of whether one believes in an omniderigent Divine or a God who has created us in His image with genuinely free will, it can be difficult to know whether we are acting in accordance with His will or simply following the capricious whims of our own.

Sometimes the path seems obvious, or as is perhaps more commonly the case, obviously wrong. But I have noticed that when God speaks to an individual, He seldom tells him to maintain the status quo. Noah was told to build an ark. Moses was told to go to the Promised Land. Jonah was told to go to Nineveh. David was told to abandon his flocks and take up the mantle of kingship. Saul was told to stop persecuting Jesus and to go to the Gentiles and preach the Gospel.

What are the chances God's will for you is to sit numbly in your cubicle and mindlessly pay your taxes and your mortgage while you wait for the sweet release of death?

The liberal theologians are correct in one regard: Jesus Christ was a revolutionary. He overthrew a tyrant worse than Nero, King George and Stalin combined when he defeated the prince of this world by means of his death on the cross.

And yet, in America, Christians have somehow become the de facto guardians of the middle-class taxpayer's dream. Cleanliness, an adjustable-rate mortgage and a three-car garage are not next to godliness, they are considered to be rather more important. There is, I submit, more faith in George W. Bush than Jesus Christ in the evangelical wing of the Republican party; one imagines that Karl Rove will soon prophesy of the Third Coming of The Bush, a King of the South of pure blue blood who will save America from the Scarlet Woman of Arkansas.

But the world is fallen, damned. Salvation comes through grace alone, not through politicians.

This is not to say that Christians should sit idly by, watching in mute dismay as their rights to speech and property are systematically dismantled, as their pastors' sermons are monitored and as their children are indoctrinated by left-wing pedophile propagandists masquerading as public school teachers. Action is required, but it is important to understand that only action on an individual level is capable of transforming hearts, and only when hearts are transformed can society be reformed.

Change is atomic. Transformation ordered from on high can only go so far, as the Communist leadership in country after country has discovered to their displeasure. Bill Gates and Steve Jobs did not change the world by passing laws and dictating how people would use computers; they realized their visions by transforming it one desktop at a time.

So, I encourage those Americans who are dismayed by what they see around them to abandon their trust in the saving power of party and politicians and to rely instead on God guiding their own actions. There are a multitude of small steps that will bring about that atomic change that will leave an indelible mark on those around you. Homeschool your children, or if you already do, learn to encourage other parents who are open to the concept. Take your neighbor to the gun range; it may sound strange, men, but you'll be surprised to discover how many women enjoy target shooting once they give it a shot.

Start a Bible study, but invite at least one or two nominal Christians so that the focus is on learning God's Word, not wallowing in everyone's feelings about it. Determine to be bold about admitting your belief in Jesus Christ when asked and refuse to hide your faith simply because someone might think less of you for it. And most of all, remember that you are not given a spirit of fear, but of victory.

The law is nothing before God's Law. Christians would, I think, do very well to remember that the apostle Paul was a serial lawbreaker who would have certainly fallen afoul of a three-strikes law, and that like his Lord and Savior, he was executed by the authority of the state.

If the Almighty God can use liars, adulterers, cowards and killers to further His will, He can certainly use you too. You have only but to let Him.

Let's get naked!

July 25, 2005

WHEREAS the wearing of unseasonal or inappropriate clothing can be reasonably expected to have lethal consequences in light of the London subway bombings;

And whereas the federal government authorities have deemed it necessary to the security of the national air transport system to thoroughly scan, search and even strip-search passengers prior to airplane embarkation;

And whereas metropolitan officials have decided that the safety of major municipalities is dependent upon the ability of the police to randomly search persons who offer their consent;

And whereas failing to offer consent to be searched is tantamount to providing reasonable suspicion requiring an invasive personal search;

And whereas the pending renewal of the Patriot Act provisions originally intended to expire indicates that individual privacy is not only no longer a natural right, but a serious threat to the continued existence of the nation;

And whereas many state governments have already been deprived of taxes on certain items that are commonly designated tax-free;

And whereas it is unusually hot this summer;

And whereas the general consensus of scientists quoted in the mainstream media is that the global warming phenomenon is unlikely to stop anytime soon;

And whereas modern plastic surgery allows for the ready modification of the insufficiently attractive;

And whereas the entire pool of international fashion designers have clearly and collectively gone off the deep end;

And whereas the massive financial success of the porn industry indicates that we the people enjoy few things as much as looking at massive quantities of uncovered flesh;

Let it be proposed, therefore, that the citizens of this great nation return to their natural state. That is to say, eliminate the business suit in favor of the birthday suit. Nude in the air is tough on terror. Ask not what your country can do for you, ask what you can take off for your country. We have nothing to fear, but modesty itself.

For it seems eminently clear that what is required to end this lengthy War on Terror is a constitutional amendment banning all clothing in public places. Think of the immeasurable benefits! No terrorist will ever conceal a box-cutter, much less a suicide bomb vest, ever again. Families will reduce their household spending by the average of 5 percent that is currently wasted on clothing. Massive amounts of energy now wasted on air conditioning will be saved. Best of all, no man will ever be forced to undress another woman with his eyes again.

True, this natural step toward national nudism will not come without a serious cost. Seeing Ted Kennedy or Hillary Clinton standing naked on the floor of the Senate will be hard on everyone. But at least the 61 percent of the adult populace who is overweight will be given additional motivation to lose weight, and I am certain that the American people, in their infinite wisdom, will soon see fit to elect better-looking representatives with more attractive bodies.

As the Patriot Act pushers repeatedly tell us, if you're not doing anything wrong, you don't have anything to hide. So, get naked for your country, now!

We are not at war

August 1, 2005

F OR NEARLY FOUR YEARS NOW, Americans have been subjected to histrionic news pundits puffing pompously about how "we are at war". The absence of a war footing or a declaration of war, not to mention the significantly unwarlike presence of wide-open borders has not slowed them down a bit, as they have used their favorite martial mantra to support evils ranging from the Patriot Act to the designated hitter.

Now, this is not to say that American warriors are not risking their lives and exhibiting excellence in their craft in Iraq, Afghanistan and other places around the world. But the nation is not at war and it has not been at war these past four years even though the violent forces of expansionist Islam have declared war on America at every opportunity.

I will admit that this is not a very popular view on the right-wing of the national commentariat, Pat Buchanan and a few fellow libertarians notwithstanding. On this very page, only five days ago, my WND colleague Ben Shapiro asserted that "this is a war, blockhead" in supporting "temporary safety measures" to suspend those pesky civil liberties that are so endangering the citizenry.

Why it is necessary to suspend the rights and liberties of American citizens, but it is not necessary to return millions of illegal aliens and non-citizen residents to their homelands or respond in kind to those organizations, institutions and individuals that have declared war on the United States of America and its inhabitants remains a mystery.

For despite the feverish assertions of neoconservatives and those few conservatives who still believe the president is one of them that the congressional authorization for the use of force in Iraq was tantamount to a declaration of war, it has become ever more clear that this is demonstrably not the case. As the Bush administration has proven remarkably wont to do, it stabbed more of its most fervent supporters in the back on July 25 when it introduced a new nomenclature in an attempt to freshen up a product grown increasingly stale.

> *The Bush administration is retooling its slogan for the fight against al-Qaida and other terrorist groups, pushing the idea that the long-term struggle is as much an ideological battle as a military mission, senior administration and military officials said Monday…*
>
> *The shifting language is one of the most public changes in the administration's strategy to battle al-Qaida and its affiliates, and it tracks closely with Mr. Bush's recent speeches emphasizing freedom, democracy and the worldwide clash of ideas.*
>
> *"It is more than just a military war on terror," Steven J. Hadley, the national security adviser, said in a telephone interview. "It's broader than that. It's a global struggle against extremism. We need to dispute both the gloomy vision and offer a positive alternative."*
>
> —"U.S. Officials Retool Slogan for Terror War", *New York Times*,
> July 26, 2005

We are at struggle, blockhead! And who is we? Why, none other than the global community! "They Blew Up Bus No. 30" is a peculiar battle cry for an automotive American public, after all. Nor does "Remember Madrid" quite rank up there with "Remember the Maine!" And with whom are we at struggle? Violent extremists, clearly, which is why we must be prepared for Romanian special forces infiltrating the forests of Oregon, hunting down Earth Liberation Front treehuggers while the Sri Lankan navy shells evangelical anti-abortion fortresses on the South Carolina coast.

But the administration cannot let a cat out of a bag that it was never actually in. It turns out that the truth about the current state of non-war can be best seen in a simple example of federal bureaucracy. In the July 9 New Scientist story, titled "Patents gagged in the name of national security", Don Hajec, a director at the U.S. Patent and Trademark office, stated:

> *When the U.S. is not in a state of war, the secrecy order is imposed for one year. But we almost always renew those every year. In a state of war, the*

order is permanent. Congress advises us when we are at war. We are not at war.

William of Ockham is famous for writing "Pluralitas non est ponenda sine necessitat."—"Plurality should not be considered without necessity." Applying this principle, famously known as Occam's Razor, suggests that the reason American rights and freedoms are under widespread assault is not because we are at struggle, but because they do not serve the long-term interests of those currently roosting on the three branches of the American government.

Why women's rights are wrong

August 8, 2005

THE GREATEST MEDIA SCRIBE of these latter days, Bill Simmons, is known for a certain pithy mantra. "The lesson, as always: Women ruin everything." While one does not usually expect to find deep sociological truths in the sports pages, so great has been the degradation of the acerbic art once known as the editorial, so filled with fear are the vanilla-minded commentators, that one finds more veracity on a single page of *ESPN* than in opinion pages of the *New York Times*, the *Washington Post* and the *Wall Street Journal* combined.

Now, at this point, it is customary for women to immediately reject any assertion that women's rights are wrong as the Talibanistic ranting of an embittered man who has been denied ready access to attractive women's bodies. In the interest of dismissing this red herring, I merely note that few men fortunate enough to possess a turbo Porsche and a record contract at 23 have any reason to be bitter about the hand that life has dealt them.

In fact, I very much like women and wish them well, which is precisely why I consider women's rights to be a disease that should be eradicated. For what is rather more difficult to dismiss are the simple and easily verifiable facts that indicate women have seldom been less able to pursue their dreams and less able to achieve their desires than today, the Golden Age of Feminism.

Consider the two great laments of the modern American woman. For the unmarried woman, it is the reality that she must marry later in life than ever before, if she is able to marry at all. For the married woman, it is that unlike generations of women before her, she cannot afford to stay home with her children unless she is fortunate enough to have married to a man of the financial elite.

Both of these developments can be traced directly to women's rights. Men's increasing unwillingness to marry stems primarily from two causes — the feminized family court system that transformed marriage from a mutually beneficial contract into a financial and emotional liability, and the removal of paternal responsibility for the sexual behavior of young women. Ergo, the need for marriage has been eliminated while its liabilities have increased. As Blue America and de-Christianizing Europe increasingly show, in the absence of religion there is now very little impetus for marriage.

And few indeed are the women who understand that their present need to work is inextricably tied to the societal expectation that they will do so. When women began to enter the work force en masse in the latter half of the 20th century, the overall supply of labor increased, obviously. As per the iron law of supply and demand, over the last 60 years, this increase in supply has somewhat outstripped the growth in the economy and the attendant demand for labor, which is why real wages are still lower in 2005 than in 1973. Combined with the ever-increasing tax burden, this decline in real wages is why both husband and wife must now work when previously the husband's labor alone would have sufficed.

(The decline in wages would be much more obvious to the casual observer if men had not begun retiring earlier at the same time women entered the work force. To state that young women are working today so their grandfathers can play golf is reasonable shorthand for what happened.)

But the greatest evil of women's rights is demographic. Europe's demise is all but assured, thanks to them, as women's individual choices taken in the collective have stricken European society and brought on successive waves of feminist-friendly Islamic immigration by reducing Europe's birth rates far below replacement levels. And women's-rights advocates are now finding themselves in an ironic intellectual bind, as the onset of sex selection technology has them arguing that while a woman has a right to choose abortion, she can only do so for approved reasons.

This is because scientists are estimating that there are 100 million women missing from India and China and as the technology becomes cheaper and more widespread, this rate of loss is increasing. A U.N. official named Khalid Malik has warned that at present birth rates, with only 826 girls born per 1,000 boys, China will be missing 60 million more women within a decade. And in India, when a family already has two girls, a third pregnancy results in 78 percent of unborn girl babies being aborted.

The women of America would do well to consider whether their much-cherished gains of the right to vote, work, murder and freely fornicate are worth destroying marriage, children, civilized Western society and little girls. They can at least console themselves with the thought that, in the long run, it doesn't matter what they do, because the women's-rights ideology is an evolutionary dead end, and it is increasingly apparent that societies embracing it will not survive.

In the end, it's not that hard to understand. A little girl who is not born will never vote, work or raise a little girl of her own.

Girls just want to have fun

August 15, 2005

I WASN'T TERRIBLY SHOCKED to learn that there were quite a few women who were less than entirely enthusiastic about my description of women's rights as a disease that society would do well to eradicate. I was surprised, however, to learn how many women agreed with my position and were delighted to see a man take on the Sisterhood and its dogma.

But the criticisms were particularly interesting for what they revealed of the fruit of 35 years of education and liberation. Below are selections from five of the more coherent critics of last week's column:

> *Yes. It's defintely the influx of WOMEN into the workforce that caused this low 'real wage.' It's not:*
>
> *a) the exponential increase in child births.*
>
> *b) the exponential influx of immigrants (both legal and illegal)*
>
> *c) the increase in the retirement age, thus putting exponential increases of people working later in life in the work force*
>
> *d) the exponential growth of corporations in this country*
>
> *e) drops in economy because of exponential offshoring of jobs*
>
> *Jesus… for a woman… I just made this guy look like an idiot. I better get back in the kitchen.*

This was an interesting—and all too typical—response, notable primarily for its tangential relationship to the world we currently inhabit. In response:

- American childbirths have dropped from 18.4 to 13.9 per thousand

- 34 million women entered the labor force between 1970 and 2000; 2 million more than all legal and illegal immigration into the U.S.A. during the same period

- fewer people are working past the age of 55 than ever before

- more corporations would increase the demand for labor, not reduce it

- The economy has not dropped but grown from 5.03 trillion in 1970 to 11.75 trillion in 2004 as measured in 2005 dollars.

Oh yes, because my only, most important goal in life is to get married to some guy like you who'd keep me pregnant and in the kitchen and stupid until I either died in childbirth or just got too old. Because honestly, I can't even IMAGINE a better, more fulfilling life than that. Please…

FYI, my dream is to be an archaeologist. Now tell me, would it really have been easier for me to become one 50 years ago than it is today? I don't think so… As for kids, I really don't want any. If every woman did, we'd be way more overpopulated than we already are. I don't want to be tied down for 18-plus years and it sounds too painful to be worth it.

For every five women who don't have children, another five must have 21 in order for the population to remain stable. Perhaps in studying the dead societies of the past, this critic will begin to realize why her own is reaching a terminal stage.

And as for population decline… the answer, as I see it, is adoption… Why should I sacrifice my goals and dreams because someone who doesn't even have to worry about giving birth thinks it's my responsibility to do so?

The reason that this sacrifice is worth considering is because those adopted children are already being counted in the birth rates. From the demographic point of view, it doesn't matter by whom they are being raised, there still aren't enough of them in any Western country even with current levels of immigration.

I must point out one profound flaw in your reasoning below, one which seriously calls [into question] your intellectual credibility. To call 'liberated secular society' only 30 years old is to ignore thousands of years of Western intellectual and cultural tradition, going all the way back to the Greeks, through the Enlightenment, right up to the founding of our own nation and into the present… What changed so profoundly in 1975 that our very existence as a nation is now under threat? I'll answer you: nothing.

Nothing besides adding 34 million more women into the labor force, the birth rate falling by nearly 25 percent to sub-replacement levels, a 5-year increase in women's median marriage age and 36 million abortions. That's all.

Man, that was an awesome fake article you wrote for the Onion. What a brilliant parody of the conservative patriarchal mindset... Oh, wait—you were actually serious with that article, weren't you? Well, all I can say is thank god your breed is dying out. Keep it up, dude, you give us something to laugh about.

Ironically, right-leaning Christians are one of the few groups in American society that are still successfully replacing themselves. It is the secular left which has become as sterile reproductively as it always was intellectually and threatens to destroy not only America, but the entire West. For not all societies are so foolishly short-sighted, and it seems at least possible that the patriarchal society that is projected to have 160 million expendable men in the next 10 years will be able to find a way to keep them occupied by transforming them into someone else's problem.

Throw the Jew down the well

August 22, 2005

Throw the Jew down the well
So my country can be free
You must grab him by his horns
Then we have a big party

—Borat the Kazakh

THE PEOPLE OF ISRAEL were cursed by foolish and evil rulers long before Shimon Peres and Yitzhak Rabin shared a Nobel Peace Prize in 1994 with that late, great man of peace, Yasser Arafat. Time and time again, the Old Testament pronounces judgment on the kings of Israel with words that rumble like an ominous drumbeat: "He did evil in the eyes of the Lord and did not turn away from any of the sins of Jeroboam son of Nebat, which he had caused Israel to commit."

Imagine, if you will, that George Bush were to follow Ariel Sharon's lead. While anathema to most Americans, many Europeans and the vast majority of Arabs accept the idea that America has been attacked by Islamic terrorists due to its financial support for Israel. And it is even more widely accepted that the primary reason for this material American support is that quiet, but effective alliance of Christian evangelicals with wealthy American Jews who wield significant power and influence in Washington.

By this logic, no doubt Prime Minister Sharon would agree that an excellent way for the president to protect American cities would be to issue an executive order sending every Jew in Washington and New York City to Israel, where they would receive $350,000 in compensation for the loss of their Manhattan apartments and Georgetown brownstones. Any Jews who did not obey the president's order to evacuate would be forcibly removed by the New York Police Department and the district police in order to expedite their involuntary aliyah.

Can you imagine the utter firestorm of furious indignation and outrage that would instantly engulf the national media? The *New York Times* would be shrieking at such a fever pitch that dogs would be bleeding from their ears in Los Angeles. The *ABCNNBCBS* cabal would be howling for George Bush's impeachment and execution while the Fox brigade would be calling for the castration of the entire Bush line unto the fourth generation down from Poppy. Within hours, Abe Foxman, Jesse Jackson and James Dobson would be leading a march together that would dwarf the Million Man March, the Promise Keepers and the WTO protests combined.

"We are down with Hymietown," one can almost hear the Reverend Jackson chanting. The ADL's Abe Foxman would accuse the president of the most virulent anti-Semitism since Mel Gibson filmed the "Passion", while a weeping James Dobson would remind the assembled masses that America is not mentioned in the book of Revelations, then lead them in a heartfelt prayer, pleading with the Lord God of Israel to refrain from destroying America for its sin against His chosen people.

This scenario is, of course, utterly absurd. The president knows very well that the violent practitioners of the religion of peace don't hate us because we send money to Jews, they hate us for our freedom. (Yes, I am rolling my eyes here. I don't believe the jihadists particularly hate America, it's just that as the preeminent world power, the USA is the primary obstacle to their dream of global sharia. America is in their way, as the current occupations of Iraq and Afghanistan should suffice to demonstrate.)

And even if it could be proven that support for Israel was the cause of three decades of Arab anti-Americanism, no decent citizen would cravenly betray his fellow Americans simply because they happened to be Jewish.

But apparently ethnic cleansing, so appalling in Finland and Pakistan, so outrageous when performed in Yemen, Yugoslavia and Turkey, is perfectly acceptable, even lauded, when Jews are being ethnically cleansed by Israeli forces. Even if removing Jews from the Holy Land is not an offense to God, the removal of the Jewish settlers from Gaza is a violation of their rights to liberty and property, it is a foolish incitement to Hamas and it sets a horrific precedent in a fallen world that has never been overfriendly to the Jewish people

Sharon's decision can only be defended on the basis of short-term security. But it fails in military, political, ethical and spiritual terms. It will not be long before Hamas will transform Gaza into a base for operations into Israel and the Israeli Defense Forces will be forced to return there. Sharon is an old man and has no political future, but the president's support for the prime minister's action will be rightly seen as yet another Republican dagger in the Christian right's back.

As for the spiritual aspect, if, as I and many other evangelical Christians believe, the Lord God Almighty intends for His people to return to the Promised Land, then the will of no prime minister or president will ultimately prevail. Israel has been led into disaster after disaster by leaders who did not fear God and it seems likely that Ariel Sharon will prove to be yet another curse on the Jewish people.

Is throwing the Jew down the well OK when it is an Israeli who does the throwing?

The chickenhawk clucks

August 29, 2005

I T IS ENTIRELY POSSIBLE that my WND colleague has a perfectly good reason for not serving his country in its moment of need. For all I know, he may have a weak heart, a wooden leg, a predilection for San Francisco bathhouse sex or some other condition that prevents him from joining the military. But devoting two columns to criticizing a single word strikes me as a lady protesting a bit too much.

Mr. Shapiro's first argument against the appellation is that it is nothing more than a leftist attempt to silence debate. This is partially true, but the argument is deceptive because it is incomplete. It is not leftists but the military that has long despised civilians who clamor for war from the safety of their homes. In 1879, Gen. William Sherman said: "It is only those who have neither fired a shot nor heard the shrieks and groans of the wounded who cry aloud for blood, more vengeance, more desolation."

His second and third arguments are that the insult is dishonest and "explicitly rejects the Constitution." But there is nothing dishonest about calling into question the credibility of one who does not practice what he preaches. If a *CNBC* analyst urges viewers to buy a stock he is secretly shorting, he will rightly be dismissed as a hypocrite unworthy of further regard. The unconstitutional argument is spectacularly silly, since no one in Congress has proposed a federal law barring such hypocrites from office. One can only assume that Mr. Shapiro's first Constitutional Law class lies ahead of him.

His fourth argument, which asserts that use of the term is somehow "un-American", reveals a similar failure to understand the First Amendment and American history. Mr. Shapiro might wish the Constitution prevented people from calling him names, but it actually protects their right to do so and American political history is littered with an abundance of inventive insults.

As for the reference to the Bush daughters, hiding behind the skirts of young women is no way to prove you're not a coward.

His fifth and final argument—that use of the term "chickenhawk" is an attempt to avoid substantive debate—is easily disproved. I have repeatedly criticized numerous aspects of this global struggle, have openly opposed both the Iraqi and Afghani occupations, and am quite willing to debate Mr. Shapiro or anyone else on the issue in the forum of their preference. Yet I—like 62 percent of the soldiers and veterans who frequent Vox Popoli and Blackfive—am in accord with the notion that "chickenhawk" is an appropriate label for a warmongering young columnist who urges others to make sacrifices he has no intention of making himself.

I would be remiss if I did not note that many of these military men and women favored a different 11-letter word that also begins with "chicken."

The genuine flaw in the use of the "chickenhawk" label is that in most cases it is being applied years, even decades, after the fact, and inherently attempts to equate two different historical situations. However, due to Mr. Shapiro's precocious position in the national media, this common flaw does not apply. While his peers are dodging sniper bullets and IEDs in Afghanistan and Iraq, Mr. Shapiro is bravely urging them to invade five more countries in the establishment of global empire from the safety of his Harvard dorm room.

The America Bar Association already boasts more than 896,000 lawyers, America has no desperate need for another one. The U.S. Army, on the other hand, is currently 8,000 men short of its 2005 recruiting goals. I am only one of many non-pacifist, non-leftist Americans who believe that Mr. Shapiro would do well to heed his own words of Aug. 26, 2004. "Now's the time: Either put up, or shut the hell up."

The folly of empire

September 5, 2005

Neocons do not feel that kind of alarm or anxiety about the growth of the state in the past century, seeing it as natural, indeed inevitable ... People have always preferred strong government to weak government, although they certainly have no liking for anything that smacks of overly intrusive government.

—Irving Kristol, "The Neoconservative Persuasion"

I T IS SAID that in every cloud, there is a silver lining. And if there is one to be found in the recent debacle in New Orleans following the hurricane, it is that the president and his neoconservative advisers have received a salient reminder of the limits of government power.

The swift conquests of Afghanistan and Iraq were heady wine to the neocons, who in their exuberant triumphalism soon began arguing that terms such as "imperial decline" and "imperial overstretch" were outmoded, historical artifacts holding no validity for a singular global superpower. In their enthusiastic cheerleading for continued military interventions—ranging from Pakistan to Iran—they have clearly followed the lead of their intellectual godfather, Irving Kristol, who holds that "the 'national interest' is not a geographical term" for a great power and that the mere possession of power dictates its use:

With power come responsibilities, whether sought or not, whether welcome or not. And it is a fact that if you have the kind of power we now have, either you will find opportunities to use it, or the world will discover them for you.

—Irving Kristol, "The Neoconservative Persuasion"

And indeed, the neoconservatives within the administration have been kind enough to find these opportunities for their fellow Americans. And if the people of Louisiana might prefer to have had the 256th Mechanized Infantry Brigade and other elements of their National Guard at their disposal in New Orleans instead of Baghdad, well, that is simply one of the many sacrifices that Americans will have to make in the exercise of their neonational interest.

Furthermore, there are serious practical, ethical and moral problems with the establishment of an American global empire. First and most obvious, we lack an emperor... or an empress. This quandary is easily resolved, however, and no doubt Hillary Clinton will be pleased to bring an end to the quadrennial turmoil of national elections once she slithers to the Cherry Blossom Throne in 2008.

The practical problem is numbers. America already has over 240,000 soldiers stationed in Afghanistan, Iraq, Kuwait, Germany, Iceland, Panama, Italy, Spain, Japan, Bosnia-Herzegovina, Turkey, Hungary, Kyrgyzstan, Qatar, Uzbekistan and Korea—an estimated 702 bases in 130 countries in all. And yet, U.S. generals have complained from the very start that they did not have enough troops for a proper pacification and occupation of Iraq.

Neocons dreaming of a global Pax Americana have apparently forgotten that when Rome secured a new province, it did so by enslaving a significant portion of the inhabitants and distributing them about the empire, then granting its retired legionaries vast quantities of land and establishing Roman colonies. Somehow, I don't envision thousands of Manhattanites clamoring for 40 acres of Iraqi real estate, even if it comes with a killer view of the Tigris.

A few advocates of empire cite oil as a justification for establishing a new world order, but the very argument is a monstrous ethical transgression. The oil of the Middle East does not belong to us and no matter how much we might like to believe that cheap gasoline is a national birthright, it is not. Nor is a stable and growing economy a natural right—launching a direct assault on private property rights, even property owned by foreigners in foreign lands, is no basis for a capitalist system that wishes to remain free in the long term. And as for morals, historians are well aware that empire and moral degradation of the people have a tendency to coincide. Empire will not arrest the American decline into immorality, it will only exacerbate it.

Ultimately, the idea of establishing an imperial order is a futile, short-term solution that merely sweeps intransigent problems under the jackboot and postpones them for the future. Moreover, the sacrifice of American liberties that is required for such an establishment is not worth the temporary installation of their watered-down imitations around the world. I close with a note from Umberto Eco, the Italian medievalist, who noted in his 1992 essay "Quanto costa il crollo di un impero?":

An empire is always coercive and autocratic: It is like a cover that presses on a boiling cauldron. At a certain point, the internal pressure is too strong, the cover is blown off and there is a sort of volcanic eruption.

The water-soluble Constitution

September 12, 2005

F OR 216 YEARS, the Roman Republic adhered to a custom that eventually became a law. No senator was permitted to serve as consul
twice in succession because extended command over the legions
might cause the soldiers' loyalties to shift from Rome to their general—a shift
that might well tempt an overly ambitious man. (M. Claudius Marcellus was
elected to a third consular term in 214 B.C. immediately following his second
term, but that second term he had only served as a suffect consul, selected to
replace a predecessor who had died in office.)

In 152 B.C., this custom was made explicit, as ex-consuls were required to
wait 10 years before running again for election to their former office.

And yet, less than 50 years later, in 103 B.C., the Roman Senate elected
Gaius Marius consul for the third time, the second time in succession. The
reason, of course, was a national emergency. This emergency was not the
flooding of a small town representing less than one-fifth of 1 percent of the
Roman population, but the emergence of two powerful German tribes that
had invaded the Roman province of Spain and were threatening to invade
Italy proper after defeating no less than three Roman armies and slaughtering
more than 80,000 Roman soldiers.

Although he was a demagogue, Marius was also a military genius who
ended the 5-year Jugurthan war in 18 months and is credited with making
the Roman legions more effective by organizing them into cohorts. He soon
had occasion to put that genius to the test, as the situation became even more
dire when the Teutoni and the Cimbri allied with the Tigurini, a Celtic tribe
that had defeated a Roman army four years before, and began a three-headed
invasion of Italy.

Gaius Marius was elected consul four more times, and deservedly so. He
defeated both the Teutoni and the Cimbri, killing some 165,000 Germans,

and in doing so intimidated their Celtic allies into retreating from Cisalpine Gaul. Rome was saved, but at the price of its liberties. Within 20 years, Rome fought a civil war, was invaded twice by its own legions and endured two reigns of terror at the hands of its purported leaders. And 59 years later, Gaius Julius Caesar was not only elected consul for the fifth time, but dictator-for-life, effectively bringing an end to the Roman Republic after 466 years.

Americans have been told that the Constitution which guarantees their unalienable rights is a living document, which changes over time depending on the current meanings of the words it contains. Recently, we have also learned that it is a water-soluble document, which dissolves any time a federal or state official declares a national emergency or even a hypothetical threat to your life. These officials are, of course, interested in nothing but helping you. The mere notion of the concept that such Constitution-overriding declarations might happen to increase their own power has never even begun thinking about entering their petty, bureaucratic little minds.

Now that the floodwaters are being drained from New Orleans, we have learned that it is not only water, but its potentially maleficent aftereffects that trump one's rights (which would seem to be alienable after all) to liberty, property and bearing arms.

I have no doubt that many optimistic—and historically ignorant—fools will continue to buy into the idea that these "temporary" intrusions on liberty are justified on the basis of saving lives, winning wars and various other good things. They find it very difficult to believe that any elected official could possibly have anything but their best interests in mind, forgetting that many of the leaders responsible for destroying their nation's liberties have not only been elected, but were wildly popular with the people as well.

Gaius Marius, Alcibiades, Adolf Hitler and Margaret Thatcher ("We had to learn the hard way that by agreement to what were apparently empty generalizations or vague aspirations we were later held to have committed ourselves to political structures which were contrary to our interests."—Lady Margaret Thatcher, *The Downing Street Years*) were all freely elected individuals who nevertheless betrayed their countrymen.

Lest anyone should find the "temporary emergency" argument for disregarding the Constitution and American civil liberties to be compelling, let me hasten to remind them that FEMA's declaration of a disaster in Louisiana is only one of 43 such declarations this year alone, and that there are 13 or more national emergencies declared by executive order which are still active today.

What is truly remarkable is the way in which the federal government's solution for everything from terrorism to drugs to war in the Middle East to natural disaster is the same—eliminating American liberties. Why, if one didn't know better, one would almost think that it is the elimination of those liberties, not solving the purported problems, that is the genuine goal!

Now tell me, again, why it is that we know better?

The coming conservative collapse

September 19, 2005

T HE TURN OF THE CENTURY was supposed to be the triumph of the conservatives. From the dark era of the Democrat-dominated '60s and '70s, conservatives began their protracted march toward electoral power, culminating finally in the long-awaited capture of all three branches of the federal government. The Reagan Revolution was finally to be realized in earnest!

But just as most Republican Supreme Court nominees have turned out to be treacherous supporters of big government—activist liberals in disguise—their legislative- and executive-branch colleagues likewise revealed themselves to be every bit as unfaithful to conservative principles of small government and individual freedom. As is all too often the case, conservative success carried within it the seeds of its own demise.

President Bush's recent speech on his administration's planned long-term response to Hurricane Katrina marked an interesting point in the continued devolution of American conservatism. Whereas his first five years had previously been a strange combination of strategic Wilsonian foreign policy and tactical Keynesian domestic policy, the president managed to make it abundantly clear that in domestic terms, his presidential guiding light is Lyndon Baines Johnson, not Ronald Wilson Reagan.

Real conservatives now understand they have been betrayed—badly—by this fraudulent man. Compassionate conservatism, as it turns out, is simply another name for Great Society liberalism, and not even the Texas swagger is original. Genuinely conservative Republicans are dismayed by the president's unveiling of his core liberalism and rightly fear for the future of a party which has likely seen its high-water mark already.

But nothing dissuades the Three Monkeys from screeching and howling their enthusiasm for their Dear Leader's every action. They have redefined conservatism to be the actions of one known as a conservative, so the individual is no longer defined by his ideology, the ideology is defined by the individual.

Consider radio host and former WND columnist Hugh Hewitt's take on the president's speech:

> *Perfect pitch returned tonight, and the president's looks backward and forward were on target. As Chris Matthews observed, it sounded a little LBJ-FDR-like in its vows about the underclass of the recovery region, but that is exactly why it worked so well.*

My acquaintances at the nation's leading "conservative" blog, Powerline, agreed:

> *The president was at his best tonight. Hugh Hewitt's take is on the money. And speaking of money, it's going to be pouring into the Gulf region to the tune of at least $200 billion, I imagine. You can call it FDR-LBJ liberalism, big-government conservatism, or compassionate conservatism. I call it American-style pragmatism.*

Unfortunately, celebrating the realization of that which one opposes is the predictable end result of pragmatism, which is nothing more than a euphemism for the slow sacrifice of one's principles. Longtime readers may recall that I wrote the following in 2003:

> *The Bush administration is demonstrating this truth in real-time, as its compassionate big-government neo-conservatism expands the federal leviathan at a pace faster than anyone since FDR. Would President Gore have been worse? Perhaps—but then there would be an opportunity to elect a man who actually opposed the rising tide of government in 2004 instead of surfing it like a cattle rancher gone beach-boy stoner.*

As I feared, that tide has continued to rise under the aegis of a Republican House, Senate, presidency and Supreme Court. So, are there truly no conservatives left in the Republican Party today? Or is the determination to see, hear and speak no evil about the present gang of Republican charlatans in office based on a fear of giving aid and comfort to Hillary Clinton in 2008?

In either case, it is apparent that mainstream politics in America has been reduced to a Seinfeldian sport wherein voters are simply rooting for laundry.

Since the Republican Party has dedicated itself to racing its Democratic rivals in offering more bread and circuses to the underprivileged masses, there is no longer any reason for conservatives to support it. Disenchanted and dismayed Republicans will do well to remember these pragmatic betrayals of conservative principle when The Most Important Election of Our Lifetime rolls around again three years from now.

How democracy feeds terror

September 26, 2005

OST OF THE DEBATE surrounding the Iraqi occupation concerns tactical questions. How many soldiers are needed, how many schools have opened, how many terrorists have been killed? In Donald Rumsfeld's famous formula, American success is ultimately to be determined by the ratio of terrorists killed over terrorists created remaining above one.

Even the critics of the war, both left and right, tend to frame their criticisms around the rightness or wrongness of the administration's philosophy, not the basic viability of its strategy. This is a pity, because it is on the question of strategic viability that the neoconservative warmongers are at their most vulnerable.

It is strange, but few have questioned the core neoconservative justification of the war, which is that if the Coalition of the Willing is capable of installing Western-style quasi-democracies in Iraq and the rest of the Middle East, the Global Struggle Against Violent Extremism will be won and terrorism will finally come to an end. Perhaps this is because most observers don't realize that leading neocons such as Michael Ledeen and Bill Kristol are entirely serious when they champion the notion of repeating our democratic successes in Iraq and Afghanistan in Iran and Syria.

Mr. Ledeen closes every column he writes for National Review Online with the words "faster, please." What he means is actually *Iran delenda est*.

And while it is entirely possible that he is right about the danger posed by nuclear-armed Iranian mullahs, this does not change the fact that the neoconservative prescription for ending terrorism is hopelessly flawed and doomed to failure. The reason is democracy cannot possibly be a cure for terrorism, as several surveys of the history of terrorism have indicated that democracy actually fosters the promulgation of terrorism.

There was a time when the popular theory was that poverty caused terrorism. But that theory had to be abandoned when it became obvious to everyone that the leading terrorist in the world, Yasser Arafat, was a very rich man. Nor was he an anomaly, as the terrorists of the Red Brigades, the Baader Meinhof gang and the Japanese Red Army were mostly college-educated children of the upper-middle class. And, as everyone knows now, the most famous terrorist in the world, Osama bin Laden, is an extremely wealthy Saudi.

The neocons filled this explanatory vaccuum with the self-serving argument that the true root cause of terrorism was a lack of democracy, and they were just the very people to solve the problem with their concept of world democratic revolution.

In an article in *Foreign Affairs* entitled "Can Democracy Stop Terrorism?", University of Vermont professor F. Gregory Gause III calls this myth into question, citing a number of different studies before concluding: "There is, in other words, no solid empirical evidence for a strong link between democracy, or any other regime type, and terrorism, in either a positive or a negative direction."

Gause also happens to mention some problems that I have previously noted, namely, that there is no evidence that democratic Islamic societies will be any friendlier to the United States or less disposed to subsidize terror directed against U.S. interests, while there is no shortage of evidence suggesting they will not. While Turkey is oft cited as a positive example of Islamic democracy, its government is only secular because of three anti-democratic military coups, and the vicious Algerian civil war is still raging 13 years after the military refused to accept the Islamic Salvation Front's electoral victory.

But the real reason democracy cannot end terrorism is that terrorism is ideally suited for influencing democratic results. Terrorism is violence by and for the people, which is to say, it is expressly designed to speak through the mass media in order to influence the masses. As every successful politician knows, fear is an excellent means of manipulating the minds of the voting populace, and so terrorism has a utility in democratic societies that it does not have in autocracies.

The political effect of this can be seen in Israel and Spain, where terrorism has effected genuine policy change, and the reality of its democratic utility can be seen in Iraq and India, where there is far more terrorism than in autocracies like China and pre-invasion Iraq. Thus, it is increasingly clear that the administration's strategy of ending terrorism sponsored in the Middle East by effecting regime change in favor of democratically elected governments will fail, indeed, that it never had a chance of success in the first place.

A clampdown cometh

October 3, 2005

I TEM:

The government will grant increased powers to law enforcement and security agencies to enhance their capacity to prevent attacks. Importantly, control orders will be available to our law enforcement agencies in circumstances where a person might pose a risk to the community but cannot be contained or detained under existing legislation.

—John Howard, prime minister of Australia, Sept. 7, 2005.

Item:

I think when people say this is an abrogation of our traditional civil liberties, I think it is possible to exaggerate that. I mean, as far as I know people have always accepted that with rights come responsibilities.

—Tony Blair, prime minister of the United Kingdom,
Sept. 16, 2005.

Item:

The system itself is the problem. We are trying to fight 21st-century crime—ASB, drug-dealing, binge-drinking, organized crime—with 19th century methods, as if we still lived in the time of Dickens. The whole of our system starts from the proposition that its duty is to protect the innocent from being wrongly convicted. Don't misunderstand me. That must be the duty of any criminal justice system. But surely our primary duty should be to allow law-abiding people to live in safety. It means a complete change of thinking.

—Tony Blair, prime minister of the United Kingdom,
Sept. 27, 2005.

Item:

Clearly, in the case of a terrorist attack, that would be the case, but is there a natural disaster—of a certain size—that would then enable the Defense Department to become the lead agency in coordinating and leading the response effort? That's going to be a very important consideration for Congress to think about.

—George Bush, president of the United States of America,
Sept. 25, 2005.

Item:

President Bush yesterday sought to federalize hurricane-relief efforts, removing governors from the decision-making process. "It wouldn't be necessary to get a request from the governor or take other action," White House press secretary Scott McClellan said yesterday. "This would be," he added, "more of an automatic trigger." Mr. McClellan was referring to a new, direct line of authority that would allow the president to place the Pentagon in charge of responding to natural disasters, terrorist attacks and outbreaks of disease.

—*Washington Times*, Sept. 26, 2005.

Item:

Bird flu "could kill 150 million people" A flu pandemic could happen at any time and kill between five to 150 million people, a U.N. health official has warned.

—*BBC News*, Sept. 30, 2005.

Despite wide-open borders and a consistent federal refusal to enforce national immigration laws, there have been no terrorist attacks in the United States for more than four years. Despite decades of warnings about AIDS, Ebola, SARS, West Nile, Anthrax and now Bird Flu, there have been no mass outbreaks of disease in the United States for more than eight decades.

At a certain point, one is forced to wonder. Are these top government officials primarily concerned with preventing potential dangers to the public, are they primarily concerned with covering their political posteriors in the event of failing to prevent such dangers that actually come to pass or are they primarily concerned with using the perception of potential danger to destroy the liberties of their nations' citizenries?

It seems most strange that three of the most powerful leaders in the once-free West should simultaneously choose the very same moment to call for drastic changes in their respective legal systems. Coincidentally, all three leaders happen to be arguing for the elimination of individual liberties and centuries-old legal protections by dangling the fabulous carrot of increased safety and security before the public.

Since the passage of the Patriot Act—which conservatives who should have known better argued themselves blue in the face in trying to convince everyone of its innocuous nature—the Bush administration has steadily continued its ominous drumbeat for an ever-increasing expansion of central government power. Now, it is daring to openly argue that a single attack, natural disaster or outbreak of disease should grant the executive branch the power to shred the Constitution and declare martial law at will.

This is freedom-hating idiocy of the highest order. Even if the current president has the purest and most angelic of intentions, as well as Christ in his heart, such legislation is akin to placing the collective neck of the American public in the guillotine for the remainder of the Republic's doomed existence. For sooner or later, there will be other presidents who are not so virtuous. If the American people are so foolish as to grant the present administration its wish for this anti-constitutional abomination, they will richly deserve the servitude to which they will inevitably be reduced.

Women! Someday is today

October 10, 2005

I S MOTHERHOOD INSTINCTIVE or learned behavior? Both religion and science tell us that it is instinctive, much to the distaste of the feminist ideologists, who have never been overburdened by a solid grasp on either. But one need only watch the way in which a young girl mothers her stuffed animals to see the maternal instinct at work.

This is not to say behavior that contradicts these instincts cannot be learned, only that the individual will always possess a certain level of instinct—and, for the purposes of this discussion, it does not matter if those instincts are instilled by evolution or a Creator God—that must be overcome by years of propaganda and social pressure.

Although the Equalitarian Society is now, by most statistical measures, structured so as to favor its female members, it nevertheless poses a cruel choice to those women cursed by its costly blessings. Consider the words of Melissa Cole Essig, who writes in *Newsweek* of her difficulty in getting pregnant at 39:

> *As certain as I am that now is the right time for me to have my children, it's hard not to blame myself for how difficult it's turning out to be.*

Nature, it seems, would disagree. And a woman foolish enough to wait more than two decades before attempting to have children has no one to blame but herself. As for the likelihood that the technological future will eventually solve such problems, it is worth noting that no society that possesses artificial wombs, robot sex dolls, multiplayer video games and 24-hour sports networks is one in which men are likely to show a tremendous amount of interest in relationships or the opposite sex.

Fortunately, as we have not yet reached Nerdvana, there are a number of steps that a woman whose priority remains marriage and children can take in order to happily achieve those goals:

- Don't engage in casual dating relationships after 18. They're fun, and they'll also prevent you from pursuing more fruitful relationships.

- Make those potential long-term relationships your top priority. If you put college or your job first, there's a reasonable chance that a job is all you'll have at 40... and 60. Consider the president's new Supreme Court nominee. The unmarried and childless Creepy McCrypto is on the verge of becoming one of the two most powerful professional women in the country—does she really represent the ideal American woman?

- Settle earlier rather than later. I can't tell you how many women I know who blew off good men in their late teens and early 20s who now regret doing so. Those who are not still single at 35 are now married to men generally considered to be of lower quality than the men they spurned before. Remember, your choices narrow as you get older, while men's choices broaden.

- Let everyone know that marriage and children is your ultimate goal. Too many women, fearing the wrath of the Sisterhood, secretly wish for them while publicly and piously professing feminist-approved cant to the contrary.

- Bait-and-switch doesn't work. Unlike their female counterparts, men who say they don't want to get married or have kids usually mean it. Play that game and he'll be perfectly justified in dumping your dishonest posterior despite your time-investment in him.

- Don't hesitate to end relationships that aren't leading toward marriage, or with men who are less than completely positive about the near-term prospect of children. If he hasn't proposed in 18 months, he has no intention of doing so. Cut your losses. Most men know how to string women along and know they'll have no problem replacing you when you finally call their bluff. Never confuse the masculine desire for conflict avoidance with malleability.

- Shed your man-hating friends, as well as those who buy seriously into the Equalitarian dogma. Misery loves company and miserable women like nothing better than to make everyone within a five-mile radius miserable, too.

- Be brutal when assessing the men who are interested in you. Too many women make the mistake of looking only at a man's desirable traits and ignoring his weaknesses early on. But it's not the first kiss that matters—it's the happily-ever-after part. The way he treats others is the way he will eventually treat you.

- If you want the odds of easily bearing healthy children to be in your favor, set a goal of marrying by 25. You can always go back to school, you can't go back in time.

- Remember that love is a choice, an action and a commitment, it is not a feeling.

The Polygamous Paradox

October 17, 2005

T HE SPAN OF A MAN is three score and 10, or thereabouts. As most Americans are not especially keen on availing themselves of the lessons contained in 6,000 years of recorded history, we have a tendency to believe that the current status quo is pretty much how the world has been and how it will always be.

And yet, the concept of marriage as an exclusive, state-licensed, unilaterally annullable relationship between one man and one woman is, in fact, a relatively new concept. As I wrote previously in a column entitled "Divorcing the state", government-licensed marriage was implemented as recently as 47 years ago in some American states and no-fault divorce hasn't even been around that long. Thus, the institution many conservatives rightly wish to defend as a necessary pillar of a free Western society is not the same institution today that it was for many centuries prior.

One theme I noted during the heated public discussions of the homospousal issue 18 months ago was how opponents feared that the state legitimizing gay "marriage" would inevitably lead to polygamy as well. In this, they are correct, because if the state possesses the power to redefine the nominal terms of a relationship previously characterized as "one man and one woman", it can—and probably will—redefine the numerical adjective, as well.

Nor were the opponents alone in noting this. Eugene Volokh of the Volokh Conspiracy, a UCLA law professor who describes himself as a tentative supporter of homospousy, wrote the following during the mainstream media-manufactured Rick Santorum controversy:

> *Santorum's point is that if the Constitution is interpreted to secure a constitutional right to consensual gay sex, then it would be likely to be inter-*

preted to secure a constitutional right to (presumably consensual on all sides) bigamy, polygamy, incest and adultery. This is actually quite a plausible prediction....

Leaving aside the very significant question of the ability and propriety of the state defining what has long been a religious sacrament in the West, I think it is worth considering if the knee-jerk conservative and Christian opposition to polygamy makes any sense. And contrary to what some might assume, I have concluded that it does not.

From the religious perspective, it must first be remembered that legality is not morality. Only three of the Ten Commandments are enshrined into our legal system, and the Bible is rife with examples of men who God considered to be righteous and worthy of favor that were married to more than one woman. And in his letters to Timothy and Titus, the Apostle Paul writes that church overseers and deacons "must be the husband of but one wife." The clear indication is that while monogamy is desirable for the Christian, it is about as important as being "temperate, self-controlled, respectable, hospitable, able to teach, not given to drunkenness, not violent but gentle, not quarrelsome, not a lover of money", and is in no way a required element of a Christian's faith.

As for the conservative perspective, I find it difficult to understand how polygamy, an institution seldom associated with historical societal instability, should be considered inherently dangerous to human liberty. No one is arguing that women—or men—should ever be forced into any multi-party relationships. The ability to enter voluntarily into a contractual relationship is virtually the opposite of being legal chattel, and it is hard to argue that easy divorce, unmarried cohabitation and the resultant serial polyamory practiced by Americans today are better for the children produced by such unstable relationships.

Indeed, polygamy certainly offers the obvious solution to the child versus career conundrum so many women have pondered over the last 35 years and in doing so might offer the demographically declining West an opportunity for survival.

But there are at least two genuine problems with legalized polygamy. The first is that it violates the Western romantic tradition of two hearts meeting as one as well as the Sisterhood's equalitarian agenda, which means that women across the political spectrum will almost certainly oppose it, regardless of whether they are pro-traditional marriage or contra. However, because laws governing social behavior are no longer legislated, but are instead imposed by the U.S. Supreme Court, opposition on this basis will likely prove futile.

The second problem is not an objection, but a practical observation. Polygamy tends to render low-status men completely unmarriageable, and their access to women is usually restricted, if not eliminated altogether. It is difficult to say what precise effect this would have in a modern, Western culture, but while it could have some positive effects with regards to crime and other ills, it is also theoretically capable of creating a persistent underclass even more prone to destabilizing behavior than before.

Nevertheless, in the larger scheme of things, it should be clear that Christians and conservatives have, in this particular case, rather less to fear from the Supreme Court's ongoing social experimentation than is probably assumed. After all, the Law of Unintended Consequences applies to liberals, too, and in a fallen world where the rise and fall of numerous societies has been well-chronicled, it strikes me as profoundly silly to assert that the momentary status quo in modern America is mandated by the Almighty God.

Flirting with fascism

October 24, 2005

FASCISM, David Ramsey Steele writes:

> *...was an attempt to pluck the material fruits of liberal economics while abolishing liberal culture. The attempt was entirely quixotic: There is no such thing as economic development without free-market capitalism and there is no such thing as free-market capitalism without the recognition of individual rights.*

One of the great imponderables is the question of which is more ironic: the American left's feverish denial of its ideological kinship with the historical Fascist and National Socialist parties, or the Republican Party's continued leftward drift toward what both Benito Mussolini and Tony Blair described as the third way between capitalism and socialism.

Since the term "fascism" is so often misunderstood thanks to five decades of European academics desperately trying to scrub the history books clean, let us put it aside for the nonce. Perhaps a more useful term capable of accommodating honest individuals on both sides of the political spectrum is "corporatism", which refers to a political ideology which gives primacy to the marriage of state and big business.

Even this term is imperfect, as it is not uncommon to confuse corporatism for capitalism. But this can hardly be the case, as the modern concept of the corporation as an artificial person with legal standing only dates back to 1886, a scant two years before Karl Marx was scientifically predicting capitalism's certain demise. And while the marriage of corporation and state is indubitably more civilized and less lethally inclined than socialism—after all, someone has to buy those products that generate the profits that are the lifeblood of the corporation—it is nevertheless inimical to human liberty.

There are four obvious dangers of the corporatist Third Way:

1. Corporations have no loyalties. A government that is beholden to corporations is one that will not defend its citizens' rights or its own national sovereignty.

2. Corporatism represents a constant and growing government interference with the capitalist operation of the free market, usually at the behest of the established players. This produces the same sort of wealth-inhibiting technological and entrepreneurial sclerosis that plagues socialist systems, albeit to a lesser extent.

3. Corporations perpetuate the continuation of government power without limitation, because they can so easily become direct extensions of it should the government choose to acquire them.

4. Because they are artificial persons, they have no direct stake in individual freedom and have no inherent reason to oppose intrusions upon it.

For example, the Electronic Freedom Foundation has discovered that the Brother, Canon, Dell, Epson, Hewlett Packard, Konica, Kyocera, Lanier, Lexmark, Ricoh, Savin and Xerox corporations all appear to have quietly added secret codes to the output of the color laser printers in order to facilitate the federal government's ability to track printed material. This is nominally conceived to interfere with monetary counterfeiting operations, but could easily be used for a whole host of liberty-reducing actions.

Now, there is nothing illegal about the government requesting such codes, nor is there anything inherently wrong with the corporations acceding to the government's request. But, by the same token, consumers have a right to know what they are buying, so that if they would prefer to instead buy a printer that allows them to print an anonymous document, they have the ability to do so. This is only one of many ways in which corporatism sacrifices the interests of individuals for the benefit of both corporations and the government.

While the Third Way may look somewhat reasonable to both liberals and conservatives, it is actually in the interests of no one but the professional bureaucratic class that runs both sides of the corporatist equation. Liberals who oppose big business need to recognize that it is big government which enables and protects the very big business policies that they despise, and conservatives who prioritize economic growth must likewise understand that big business does not provide it, but instead are feeding and growing fatter upon the small businesses that actually provide the impetus for such growth.

Despite themselves, the wild-eyed liberal lunatics are not entirely incorrect. The Bush administration does harbor an identifiably fascist ideological strain, but the salient fact that liberals fail to recognize is that the Democratic Party happens to share it. A Rodham administration in 2008 will not represent an ideological change from the present domestic regime, but rather a continuation of the Third Way openly declared by President Clinton in 1992.

Making more Americans

October 31, 2005

F OR ALL THAT they are ignored by 40-something American academics and callow college students convinced that marriage and children are nothing more than one of many potential lifestyle choices, the demographic threats to Western Civilization described by Pat Buchanan in "The Death of the West" are being taken very seriously by European governments.

In Switzerland, for example, monthly payments of up $265 per child are made, depending on the canton, irrespective of family income and with the amount increasing with each additional child beyond two. In both England and Italy, on the other hand the direct child benefit is wage-related, but runs around $200 and $120 per month, respectively.

Unfortunately for these increasingly demographically challenged countries, these generous child benefits have had the perverse affect of making immigration more attractive to impoverished Third World families, while failing to increase the birth rates of their citizenries. Though $12,720 may not seem like much to an American family with four children, it is obviously of great interest to individuals hailing from countries where the average income per capita is less than one-third that amount.

The reason that demographic decline is not yet on American radar is that the importation of 21 million legal immigrants who are demonstrably more fecund than native Americans over the last 30 years has kept the United States fairly close to the 2.1 child per woman replacement level. This strategy has also been successfully implemented by France, which alone among European nations has avoided a plunge in its birth rates, although the French have recently begun to reconsider the wisdom of embracing an Islamic majority in a nominal democracy.

But being a nation of immigrants, most Americans are more than a little uncomfortable with the idea that immigration can be a bad thing, or that there can be too much immigration. Libertarians cling to the romantic notion of open borders while Democrats scent a whiff of racism in the notion, and establishment Republicans are petrified at the notion that wages might increase if their supply of low-wage workers is curtailed. Only the conservative wing of the Republican Party seems to grasp the basic concept that too much of an otherwise good thing can be fatal.

The problem with population growth by immigration is that it is, at best, unproven and, at worst, insane to assert that families consisting of illiterate peasants from Guatemala and Somalia, murderous thugs from Rwanda and Liberia, and communist-educated professionals from China and Vietnam can be seamlessly incorporated into American society and its tradition of constitutionally limited government without irrevocably changing it.

This has nothing to do with race—it is an obvious question of cultural tradition. The national myth of the melting pot necessitates melting, after all, and it should be obvious that the embrace of diversity amounts to precisely the opposite. The problems certain to result from welcoming immigrants—who possess cultural consciousnesses steeped in centuries of totalitarian rule—might be a little less obvious than importing millions of headhunters from Papua New Guinea and celebrating the diversity of their cultural tradition. But while these problems might also take longer to manifest, manifest they most definitely will.

So, if economically productive Americans cannot manage to replace themselves on their own, if direct financial incentives have proven ineffective, and if immigration poses a threat to the continuation of Western cultural traditions, is there anything that can be done?

The answer is yes, but what is required is a means of providing an incentive that is of appeal to the economically productive classes in the West that simultaneously harbors no appeal to immigrants and the economically unproductive.

One major reason the educated middle classes do not have more children today is their fear of being unable to provide their children with a middle-class lifestyle in a time when their major expenses—housing, health insurance, education and taxes—are increasing dramatically. An easy means of reducing their family expenses is to delay having children and to reduce the number they have, which the statistics clearly demonstrate middle-class Americans have done.

While the federal government can and should reduce the costs of housing, health insurance and education by ending its policies and regulations which have an inflationary effect on those industries, the easiest and most effective means of encouraging families to have more children is to eliminate all federal taxes on families with more than three dependent children. This incentive would be meaningless to the economically unproductive classes that pay no taxes, but would become increasingly appealing as a family's income rose.

Since wealth and the number of children now tend to negatively correlate, this policy would serve to counteract that correlation, as well as providing a powerful incentive for married couples with children to avoid divorce.

While such a policy would doubtless provoke howls of outrage from the childless, there is no logical reason why a government that already regulates social behavior in a myriad of ways should not act to materially incentivize the only group within American society that is acting to perpetuate it.

How to argue like a conservative

November 7, 2005

ONSERVATIVES like to think that they are more solidly grounded in reality than their liberal counterparts. And they have good reason to do so—conservative philosophy seldom depends on wholly fictitious definitions of value, a short-term event horizon or every human on the planet inexplicably deciding to play nice for the first time in recorded history.

However, after observing how conservatives argue in the blogosphere, both among themselves and with liberals, I have decided that some of them might find a few suggestions to be helpful in honing their debating skills. I hope they will be received in the humble manner in which they are respectfully offered.

- Turn the debate toward biblical theology at the first opportunity. It's always tremendously effective to base your entire argument on something the other party believes is the equivalent of the collected wit and wisdom of the Tooth Fairy.

- When expressing outrage, do so in the apparent belief that your venting is somehow equivalent to actually doing something. The vehemence with which you communicate is vital, because it magically transforms your feelings into an aetheric meme capable of significantly modifying the thought processes of individuals on the other side of the country.

- Cling to the notion that there is a silent majority out there who believe what you believe, all evidence to the contrary notwithstanding. This eliminates the need to persuade anyone who openly disagrees with you of anything, because they can be safely dismissed as the vocal and visible minority whose eventual comeuppance is inevitable.

- Place irrevocable trust in everyone who has ever claimed to be conservative or a Christian at any point in their lives. Judge them by their words—or, if necessary, what you believe their words would be— instead of their actions. After all, only liberals, deviants and atheists have ever been known to shade the truth on occasion. That Peter guy who followed Jesus Christ around probably had long hair, belonged to the fisherman's union and would have voted for John Kerry if given half a chance.

- Assume that history started in 1776 with the signing of the Declaration of Independence. It is also helpful to assume that there is no data produced outside the borders of the United States that could possibly be of any use in considering the wisdom and probable result of policies enacted within said borders.

- Accept the notion that an accusation of racism, sexism or National Socialism automatically grants the victory to the person with whom you are arguing. It can be especially effective to visibly panic and begin frantically reciting examples of ways in which you have personally refrained from offering open hostility to blacks, women and Jews. An in-depth discussion of your personal preferences is always the final stage prior to winning an argument about politics.

- Don't bother to read any of the foundational works of the Left. After all, almost no self-professed leftists do, so why should you bother? There's no point in spending any time learning exactly what is contained in the writings of Marx, Lenin, Trotsky, Hitler, Veblen, Gentile and Gramsci, because what are the chances that you're going to recognize any similarities in the sound bites you hear from Clinton, Rodham, Pelosi and company?

- Always try to debate people who aren't interested in politics. Arguing with someone who doesn't know anything and won't argue back really improves your ability to debate, in much the same way that melted butter sharpens steel.

- Fall back on arguing what is and is not natural as often as possible, especially if you don't have a degree in biology, have never read Thomas

Aquinas and are under the impression that positive law refers to a law that is good.

- Rest secure in the knowledge that if you ever change your mind about something, God will change His, too.

Feeding the fires of Moloch

November 14, 2005

NOT LONG AGO, I bore witness to a small thing that many would consider sweet, and others would regard as ominous, even sinister. It was a Sunday, I was attending a small evangelical church, and the 50 or so people there were singing an upbeat contemporary Christian song accompanied by a decent electronic sampler with a built-in drum machine.

Having been raised amidst scathes of Scandinavians, I've never been inclined toward the demonstrative customs of Southern Baptists and other evangelicals, to say nothing of the rump-shaking ebullience of the Brazilian contingent at this particular church. But their enthusiasm is contagious, and it does not take many cheerful cries of "Oh gloria!" before one finds one's lips beginning to curl, not in contempt, but in appreciation for an expression of defiant joy piercing the darkness of a fallen world.

The small, sweet thing I saw that morning was a pair of little hands belonging to a young girl, lifted up in praise in the unconscious imitation of the adults and older children around her. She was beautiful, only 2- or 3-years old, her eyes were closed and she swayed to the music as she sat in her seat. She was too young to understand the significance of her gesture, just as she was too young to understand how unusual it was to see people from at least five different cultures worshipping together, or to know how seldom one sees a black man embracing a white man and greeting him as his brother.

She was not, however, too young for the gesture to be without meaning.

Lean's "Collectanea", a 19th-century collection of Elizabethan proverbs, contains a maxim it ascribes to the Jesuits: "Give me a child for the first seven years, and you may do what you like with him afterwards." In like manner, Vladimir Lenin said: "Give me four years to teach the children and the seed I have sown will never be uprooted."

All around the world, parents are stunned and dismayed by the actions of the educational bureaucracy. Germans are again fleeing from their government into France and Switzerland as officials announce they will take children away from parents who refuse to turn them over to the state-mandated schools. California parents are reeling from the recent decision by a three-judge panel of the 9th U.S. Circuit Court of Appeals which asserts that parents' have no right to control how the public schools educate their children. In Texas, parents are angrily protesting their children being medicated by school personnel against their wishes.

However, these despicable actions should come as a surprise only to the ignorant—who are clearly the great majority—since only an ignoramus or a fool would voluntarily pass his children through the pagan fires of the public schools.

The Association of California School Administrators is reported to have issued the following statement:

> *"Parent choice" proceeds from the belief that the purpose of education is to provide individual students with an education. In fact, educating the individual is but a means to the true end of education, which is to create a viable social order to which individuals contribute and by which they are sustained.*

It is perhaps apocryphal—I could not find an original publication to cite here—but in it one hears a distinct echo of the man who established the first public kindergarten and was the U.S. Commissioner of Education from 1899 to 1906. In "The Philosophy of Education", William Torcy Harris let the cat out of the bag by asserting that the entire point of public education is "the subsumption of the individual."

This is why Marx, Lenin and Hitler were all supporters of public schooling in their attempts to permanently secure the individual's services for the State. The standing in line, the bullying, the drudgery and boredom of the mind-numbing daily school routine is not incidental to the education of the schoolchild, it is the education. Contrary to what most parents believe, It is actually reading, writing and arithmerk that are entirely incidental to the true purpose of public school—subservience is the "socialization" of which educationists correctly complain that homeschooled children lack.

The homeschooling movement was inevitable, as it is only a symptom of the fundamental conflict between Christianity and the utilitarian collectivism that lies below the surface of the public-school system. The little girl who raises her hands to praise the Son of God who loved her enough to die for her will never buy into the lie that she is nothing more than an insignificant and eminently replaceable cog in the great machine of the collective. She is an immortal soul, a creature of eternity who cannot be subsumed.

The latest battle for the minds of the next generation's schoolchildren has barely begun, but the result is already certain. Nero failed. Lenin failed. Hitler failed, and so, too, will the American educationists and their evil school system. If the gates of Hell will not triumph against the Church, then what chance do the NEA minions infesting your local Molochian altar have?

The irony of the intelligent believer

November 21, 2005

L ET ME BEGIN by assuring the reader that I am no genius, except by some outmoded and ill-chosen intelligence classifications. Genius is a word best reserved for the supremely gifted, great and original minds such as Mozart, Shakespeare and Babbage, not third-rate novelists with a prediliction for techo-dilettantism and blogosphere debate.

And yet, I am perhaps reasonably well-suited to answer the question that has been asked many times of every intelligent and educated Christian by incredulous atheists. How can you—an intelligent individual with an expensive education—possibly take seriously what is at best archaic mythology? How can someone who is otherwise considered to be smart subscribe to what amounts to nothing more than fairytales dressed up as history? And how can anyone who is clearly cognizant of Science ever declare allegiance to its great antithesis, Superstition?

I take no offense at these questions, for if they are meant to ridicule, they nevertheless reveal that the questioner has perceived that vital dichotomy which so often precedes a major transformation in one's thinking. It is all too easy for the highly intelligent to dismiss the convictions of the average individual, after all, especially when one's IQ is as far from the norm as the norm is from those unfortunates who were once considered imbeciles.

It is not so easy, however, to dismiss the beliefs and thought processes of those one otherwise considers one's intellectual peers.

The first, and most obvious, answer is that one obviously can because others of historically remarkable intelligence have. There is no shortage of devout Christians on the list of mankind's most legendary geniuses—many of whom are still rightly revered by atheists and agnostics today. From Galileo and Newton to Doestoevsky and Tolkien, men of outstanding intellect and achievement have placed their trust in the Resurrection of the Lord Jesus Christ. However, it is all too easy to dismiss many of these men as having lived in the pre-Enlightened era and it can always be argued, however disingenuously, that if those now dead had only been privy to the latest developments in modern science, they, too, would have turned their backs on the faith of their fathers.

The second answer is a utilitarian one. Science is a whore. Her very essence precludes certainty, which is both a genuine strength and a grave weakness. It is a strength because the scientific method of testing hypotheses encourages a continual seeking after the truth, to which no one who lives by a book that declares "seek and ye shall find" should object. It is a weakness because the inherent mutability of science is at odds with the human desire for objective guidelines by which to live. This conflict tends to repeatedly create faux-sciences, which, however outmoded, are clung to with all the diehard fervor of the religious fanatic.

For example, the field of psychoanalysis and the scientific disciplines of psychology and psychiatry are still heavily influenced by the theories of Sigmund Freud, who asserted that religion was an illusionary means of avoiding anxiety from which an individual must be freed in order to mature and reach full mental health. However, genuinely scientific studies have tended to demonstrate precisely the opposite, that at least in the Christian West, religion is a positive predictor of longevity and social maturity, as well as physical and mental health.

Being trilingual, I do not subscribe to the literal 100 percent Word of God theory of the Bible. Nor do I understand how anyone who has read more than one English translation of the Bible can hold to it. (My own theory is that the Bible is the perfect and inspired Word of God revealed through imperfect men; while there are likely flaws created by that process, it is unwise to introduce more errors by attempting to further filter it through our own logic and one does well to accept John's admonition to neither add nor take anything away.)

And yet, I find it remarkable how often the wise men of the world, despite the advantage of two millennia's history on which to draw, are repeatedly confounded by an ancient and static text. The archeologists and historians who cited the mythical Assyrians and Hittites as proof of the Bible's inaccuracy have already been proven wrong, and soon those who doubt the historical existence of a rich and powerful Davidic kingdom of Israel will be embarrassed as well.

Psychologists, psychiatrists and child-care experts have led parents to turn millions of American children into drugged-out zombies because the sum total of their expertise doesn't function half as well as the book of Proverbs. Physicists and cosmologists are proposing imaginative theories of strings and multiple universes—which suggest some interesting supernatural possibilities to me, by the way—primarily in response to the way in which the anthropic principle threatens to render their disciplines mere tautological explanation.

As for the secular humanists who are second to none in waving the black-and-white flag of Science, the ongoing demographic collapse of their cherished equalitarian societies in every Western nation is proving their theory of religion's deleterious effect on society to be as errant and intellectually bankrupt as Freud's is with regard to the individual. Theirs is a rotten fruit indeed.

From a utilitarian perspective, then, it makes a tremendous amount of sense for an individual or a society to live by the precepts of the Bible, even if one does so sans belief. This is, I would argue, the most purely rational position, and indeed, famous non-believers such as Voltaire and the 18th-century deists so beloved by modern atheists—as long as they stay safely buried in the 1700s—would agree.

Economists will tell you that the value of any model is its predictive ability. This is why I reject Keynesian macroeconomics—which are wildly unreliable—in favor of the Austrian school and wave theory, both of which actually work on occasion. And while there is no shortage of prophetic charlatans today, it is interesting to note how those who interpret world events through a biblical lens have proven to be more reliable than political scientists.

Every dispensationalist believed the United States of Europe was an inevitability back in the late 1970s, while the poly-sci professors and politicians were still insisting that the Common Market was nothing more than a free-trade area as late as 1994. The establishment of Israel came as a surprise to almost everyone but the wild-eyed watchers of the end times in 1948. Today, who believes that the United States will surrender its national sovereignty to the United Nations and force implantable currency on its citizens except the most literally minded Christians? ADSX and DOC are both selling near all-time lows—an interesting empirical test might be to pick up 100 shares and see what happens over the next 10 years.

The fourth answer is reciprocal action. Newton's third law states that all forces occur in pairs, and that paired forces are equal in magnitude and opposite in direction. Even when I was an agnostic, I marveled at the hatred and energy expended on Christians by non-Christians. I could not understand the cognitive dissonance demonstrated by the so-called experts in their rabid attempts to discredit all things even nominally related to Christianity—the nominally Jewish Anti-Defamation League's attack on the Ten Commandments being only the most ironic example of late—as well as their ready willingness to distort and even fabricate history.

Who has not heard the Catholic Spanish Inquisition, (2,000 death sentences passed on to the Spanish Crown over 349 years) conflated with the pagan Holocaust (12 million murders in five years), and the atheist slaughters of the Great Terror, the Great Leap Forward and the Killing Fields. (4 million murders in 20 years, 30 million murders in 3 years and 2 million murders in four years, respectively.) And it is commonly asserted that religion is a major cause of war, although, as I have previously demonstrated, religion has only played a role in about 10 percent of all the wars in recorded history.

As Jesus Christ declared it would, the world has hated those who followed Him from the moment it became aware of them—from Nero to Kim Jong Il's North Korea. While American atheists attempt to stamp out all public and private expression Christianity for fear of being wished a Merry Christmas at Wal-Mart, Christians are being murdered for their faith in Indonesia, Iraq, Nigeria and the Sudan, and are being imprisoned for their beliefs in Iran, China, Vietnam and Canada. This virulent and near-universal reaction to a religion that is more peaceful than Islam, more intellectual than Hinduism, more inclusive than Judaism and more historically beneficial to human society than Humanism makes little rational sense, and can be seen as evidence of an important element of the Christian worldview, namely, a fallen world ruled by an evil god in opposition to the Creator.

Now, this is not a Christian apology and these are not reasons meant to convince one to accept the fundamental truth of Christianity. I trust, however, that it will help those who disdain religion to understand how it is at least possible to believe such things while also being in possession of an education and a functioning brain.

C.S. Lewis vs. today's literature

November 28, 2005

This is a selection from an essay published in the anthology Revisiting Narnia, *from BenBella Books.*

IN THE CENTER OF OXFORD, there is a brass sign indicating the proximity of The Eagle and Child, the pub in which the informal group known as the Inklings used to gather on Thursdays. Three of these Inklings eventually became fantasy writers of some reknown, one of them, J.R.R. Tolkien, stamped an image on the genre which, 60 years and three movies later, is arguably more powerful than ever.

These three writers, Tolkien, Lewis and Charles Williams, were not only Oxford men—Tolkien and Lewis were dons while Williams was an editor at the university press—but also devout Christians. Ironically, while Lewis is now considered to be the more recognizably Christian figure thanks to works of Christian apologetics such as *Mere Christianity* and *Miracles*, it was the Catholic Tolkien who played a major role in the atheist Lewis's conversion to Christianity in 1931.

The Christian themes in both Lewis's fantasy and science fiction are undeniable. Even a child conversant with both *The Chronicles of Narnia* and the Bible will readily recognize that the lion Aslan, who voluntarily lays down his life in exchange for the life of a criminal condemned to death in *The Lion, The Witch and the Wardrobe*, is a barely disguised metaphor for Jesus Christ. And this diaphanous veil disappears entirely six books later when the link between Aslan's country and Heaven is disclosed upon the death of the Pevensey family at a railway station in *The Last Battle*.

The religious themes are even more overt in Lewis's Space Trilogy. From the name of the protagonist—Ransom—to the replay of the Edenic temptation in Perelandra, Lewis consciously provides a fictional retelling of vignettes straight from the Bible. Indeed, the very title of the first volume, *Out of the Silent Planet*, refers directly to Lewis's concept of God's divine invasion of nature, which he lays out explicitly in *Mere Christianity*.

The Christian foundation of the other famous Inkling's work is less blatant, yet almost as obvious to all but the most willfully blind. While there have been a few brave souls foolhardy enough to attempt to deny the self-evident, even those with no discernible Christian agenda freely acknowledge the powerful religious elements integral to *The Lord of the Rings*. For the Secret Fire of which Gandalf is a servant, as Tolkien explained for the benefit of those too unfamiliar of the book of Acts to recognize the symbolism, is nothing less than the Holy Spirit whose flames were first seen at Pentecost, and in case things were not perfectly clear, the author once described his landmark trilogy as "a fundamentally religious and Catholic work."

Thus, it is not the fantasy elements—which are actually not very similar in the particulars—but the Christian themes running through both that tie Lewis's and Tolkien's works together in our minds. Nor are these themes the only relationship. Tolkien, Lewis and Williams were all influenced to varying degrees by the same literary and spiritual mentor, a Scottish minister and prolific author by the name of George MacDonald. MacDonald is largely forgotten now, but he was a well-known author of the late 19th century— among other things, he corresponded regularly with a certain American writer he had befriended by the name of Samuel Clemens. In one letter, Clemens even mentioned to MacDonald how his daughter Susy had worn out her copy of MacDonald's *At the Back of the North Wind* and requested that MacDonald send her a replacement.

It is interesting to note that while Jules Verne and H.G. Wells are generally considered to be the fathers of science fiction, as far as the literary historians are concerned, modern fantasy is imagined to have leaped like Athena, fully accoutered, into the pulp magazines of the 1920s. And yet, George Mac-Donald's claim to paternity is difficult to dismiss. His first work of fantasy fiction, the aptly named *Phantastes*, was published in 1858, six years before Jules Verne published *Journey to the Center of the Earth*, seven years before Lewis Carroll published *Alice in Wonderland* and before H.G. Wells, H.P. Lovecraft or Lord Dunsany were born.

This failure to recognize MacDonald's influence on the genre appears to stem primarily from the radical secularization of the science-fiction and fantasy genres dating from science fiction's Golden Age. While the short stories and novels of the Golden Age are fondly recalled by many, and are rightly known for many good things, one must admit that character development was not among them. This is unfortunate, because the Golden Age preference for plot over personalities and for ideas over individuals played a significant role in the relegation of science fiction to a literary ghetto disdained by the *New York Times Review of Books* and others too self-consciously erudite to take seriously what is still too-often dismissed as juvenile space opera and futuristic twiddle-twaddle. While character development in science fiction has improved dramatically of late, it is still only the exceptional work that manages to transcend the genre and break out of the ghetto.

This disdain for character left a mark on the genre which lasts to this day. Almost to a man, the writers of the Golden Age were secular humanists, and they felt as strongly about the deleterious effects of religion on collective human development as did Sigmund Freud with regards to the individual. Their antipathy toward all forms of traditional religion in favor of a dogmatic faith in the scientific method cast science fiction into an artistic ghetto from which it has not yet even begun to escape.

Fortunately, science and religion need no longer be at war, as developments in modern physics have shown, (especially those relating to the significance of the fundamental constants), which may indicate that the time for hostilities may finally be over. It is interesting to note that the "multiple universes" concept which has inspired so many short stories in the past decade is a purely hypothetical theory developed without any experimental basis in an attempt to answer the "anthropic principle", which not only has a solid foundation in current scientific method, but threatens to demolish the entire notion of a random, mechanistic universe. The concept does not, of course, provide the least bit of evidence for the legitimacy of the prophet's revelation, the infallibility of the pope, or the likelihood of the Second Coming. What it does demonstrate is that what has been long considered an antagonistic dichotomy between science and religion may not actually exist at all.

Still, this distaste for all things religious has been a costly one, both in artistic and financial terms. While sufficient evidence exists to reject the idea that only a true believer is capable of writing accurately about his faith, it is true that presenting a reasonable and believable image of a religious individual presents a greater challenge to one who has no experience of such strange beings and therefore lacks even the most basic information about them. One would not expect one who knows nothing of math beyond addition and subtraction to write a convincing portrayal of calculus, after all. And while one may no more believe in aliens than in Jesus Christ, a survey of the current literature suggests that far more thought typically goes into depictions of the former than into those who profess to believe in the latter.

Compare the vast difference between the guilt-racked seducer of Hawthorne's *The Scarlet Letter* and the foam-flecked fundamentalists who haunt mediocre short stories in *Asimov's Science Fiction Magazine* like clockwork cartoon bogeymen. Is it any wonder that the science-fiction and fantasy writer's pretense to literary status is scoffed at by those familiar with Dostoevsky, Goethe, and Tolstoy?

The morality of rape

December 5, 2005

E THICAL MEN have always been opposed to rape," declares Camille
Paglia, the brilliant iconoclast who has herself been accused of being
a rape apologist, in "Sex, Art and American Culture." But on
what grounds have they done so, if this is indeed the case? I found myself
considering this question after inadvertently sparking a minor eruption in
the blogosphere with a post reflecting on what I consider to be the dubious
nature of "date rape."

It is, I have been reliably informed, nauseating, vile and hateful to assert
that women are capable of bearing responsibility for their actions—there are
many individuals who sincerely believe that a woman must be allowed to
behave however she likes without being forced to endure a word of criticism.
This is called "blaming the victim" even when the woman has not yet managed to be victimized.

And yet, despite reading hundreds of missives featuring varying degrees of
hysterics, it remains a mystery as to what grounds these rape mythomoralists
have for objecting to rape in the first place.

The criminality of rape in this country is beyond question, but as I have
pointed out with regard to other matters, legality is not morality. It is
illegal to walk across the street when a specific light is red, but this is not
an immoral act. It is immoral to seduce your friend's wife, but it is not illegal.
Furthermore, there are no shortage of countries where rape is not only legal,
but an established policy of the government authority, so the criminal aspect
is obviously irrelevant with regard to questioning the fundamental morality
or immorality of the act.

But which morality? The Judeo-Christian moral ethic is clear—rape is
a sin, a willful pollution of a temple that rightly belongs to God. Neither
the Jew nor the Christian need hesitate before asserting the act of rape to be

evil and justly holding the rapist accountable. But this ethic does not offer a blanket excuse to victims, near victims and would-be victims either, since the element of consent—which today draws the dividing line between sex and rape—can also provide a contrarian condemnation of the woman's own actions.

(Here one must note the intellectual poverty of the rape mythologists. If rape concerns power, not sex, then how is it possible for the simple absence, or worse, withdrawal, of consent to immediately transform a "date rape" situation from an inherently sexual one to one where sex plays no role at all?)

To put it more clearly, if a woman consents to extramarital sex, she is committing a moral offense which is equal to that committed by the man who engages in consensual sex with her, or by the man who, in the absence of such consent, rapes her. Christianity knows no hierarchy of sins. Since only the woman who is not entertaining the possibility of sex with a man and is subsequently raped can truly be considered a wholly innocent victim under this ethic, it is no wonder that women who insist that internal consent is the sole determining factor of a woman's victimization find traditional Western morality to be inherently distasteful.

But what of the other moralities that one could insist are equally applicable? And what of other religions? The Quran does not mention rape per se, and while the hadith of Wa'il ibn Hujr appears to be even stricter than the Old Testament in relating the account of a death sentence passed upon a man who admitted to attacking his accuser, I suspect few mythomoralists would draw upon Islam for intellectual support. Nor upon Hinduism, as the Brhadaranyaka Upanishad eerily prefigures Nietzsche:

> Surely, a woman who has changed her clothes at the end of her menstrual period is the most auspicious of women. When she has changed her clothes at the end of her menstrual period, therefore, one should approach that splendid woman and invite her to have sex. Should she refuse to consent, he should bribe her. If she still refuses, he should beat her with a stick or with his fists and overpower her, saying: "I take away the splendor from you with my virility and splendor" (6.4.9,21).

While they might find genuine solace in the wisdom of the Buddha, where rape, the rapist and the victim alike are naught but Mara, it leaves no material grounds for condemning the perpetrator. And the Taoist slogan might well be: If rape is inevitable, relax and accept it.

Drought burns basins to dust,
Light rain is a dew of mockery.
Receive without complaint,
Work with fate.

—Deng Ming-Dao

It is ironic that mythomoralists show a predilection for paganism, given the historical pagan approach to rape. For example, one of Rome's most important founding legends was the Rape of the Sabine Women, which one can see celebrated in stone by Giovanni Bologna in Florence. Ovid, too, commemorated the event, albeit in verse:

The ravished girls were led away to marriage;
Their very shame made them more beautiful.
And when one struggled hard against her captor,
He carried her away in eager arms,
And said: "Why spoil your pretty eyes by weeping?
Your father took your mother, I take you!"

As for Greece, the Greeks not only worshipped gods given to rapine, but as Nancy Baker Worman points out in her review of *Rape and the Politics of Consent in Classical Athens*:

Omitowoju focuses primarily on the issue of consent, a central concern of modern discussions. She demonstrates that this concern is largely absent from the ancient discourse...

Not only were the pagan Vikings notoriously enthusiastic about the concept of rape as sport—the historical account of a Viking chieftan's funeral makes for truly appalling reading—but a study of their increasingly post-Christian descendants offers some interesting points of analysis for anyone questioning mythomoralist rape dogma.

Despite being acknowledged as the most pro-feminist country in the world today, during the 50 years from 1950 to 2000, the rate of reported rapes in

Sweden rose 356 percent. While the mythomoralist would assert that this is due to empowered women being increasingly willing to come forward and make complaints they previously failed to make out of shame, this baseless assertion is eviscerated by the fact that reports for all criminal offenses rose 424 percent over the same period and the increase in reported rapes is dwarfed by the concomitant increase in robberies reported, 3,604 percent.

As I have previously asserted, most atheist and agnostic morality is parasitical, the cultural residue of previous generations. Witnessing atheist mythomoralists attempt to articulate a reason for their nominal opposition to rape during the recent discussion was particularly amusing—while the more philosophically inclined appealed to basic utilitarianism or Kant's Categorical Imperative, one frustrated fellow finally threw up his hands and declared:

> I swear to God, if you use the phrase "moral relativist" one more time, I'm gonna crush your teeth with a hammer.

And while "might makes right" is the true essence of atheist amorality, it is not exactly the most convincing means of attempting to assert the moral evil of the rapist. As for Utilitarians in a demographically declining West, it is quite easy to make numerous cases for the inherent common good of rape on societal and social Darwinist grounds that are more powerful than the comparatively nebulous cases to the contrary.

There may be a genuine moral argument against rape to be made outside of the Judeo-Christian ethic, but I have yet to hear it. And, more significantly, much finer minds than mine have reached similar conclusions in a broader sense, which nevertheless encompasses the moral question of rape considered here. In an article that recently appeared in the *Telegraph*, Umberto Eco quoted another lapsed Catholic, James Joyce, in condemning the moral and spiritual bankruptcy that pervades the West today:

> What kind of liberation would that be to forsake an absurdity which is logical and coherent and to embrace one which is illogical and incoherent?

When each does what is right in his own eyes, all distinctions between right and wrong become meaningless. Regardless of whether one believes in God or celebrates Christmas as the birth of one's Risen Lord and Savior, one would do well to seriously consider the likely implications of a world that rejects both.

Myth of the electable moderate

December 12, 2005

D URING THE CALIFORNIA RECALL election, when my then-WND colleague Hugh Hewitt was in the forefront of leading a merry band of Republican optimists to reject Tom McClintock—a genuine conservative—in favor of a man much esteemed by the Kennedy family, I wrote a column titled "Satanic Schwarzeneggerians", in which I encouraged eschewing the sacrifice of principle in favor of the "pragmatic" pursuit of power.

Now, I quite like Arnold as an action hero, and would consider it an honor to lift weights with the legendary body builder. But there are decent and even delightful individuals in every party across the political spectrum and personality is no sign of worthiness to hold political office. I have known and liked a number of individuals who would nevertheless be of more benefit to humanity dead than in power.

The idea behind the Schwarzenegger gubernatorial candidacy was that his popularity and sheer manly presence would cause the Democrat-controlled legislature to genuflect in humble awe before him, thus allowing the state Republicans to return California to some semblance of fiscal and operational sanity. The subsequent prosperity would naturally lead to a revival of Republican fortunes in the state, repeating in miniature what the Reagan revolution wrought on a national scale beginning in 1980.

The backup plan, in the event that the state Democratic leadership proved more recalcitrant than expected, was that the Great Man would simply bypass the Assembly and Senate and go over their heads in an appeal to the people of California. This was a reasonable idea, as California's system allows for a limited form of direct democracy through referendums, and indeed, this backup plan was put into effect earlier this year.

Unfortunately for California's Republicans, Gov. Schwarzenegger went zero for four in the November elections. And even more ominously, the governor is showing that he has no interest in sacrificing his political career at the behest of the conservative movement or the Republican Party, two things toward which the strength of the strong man's loyalty has always been dubious. His recent appointment of Democrat Susan Kennedy, a liberal lesbian enforcer and former executive director of the California Democratic Party, as his new chief of staff, is a strong indication of his intention to tack left for the remainder of his term—look for a major compromise initiative supported by the government unions and state Democrats designed to jump-start his popularity in the run-up to the next election.

Even more disquieting are rumors that Schwarzenegger may opt to wash the political detritus of the last two years from his record with a shrewdly tactical announcement of a newfound political independence. Doing so would allow him to free himself of any blame for his recent failures, tossing it aside along with the Republican Party.

This would be a masterstroke, as the *Los Angeles Times* and other Democrat-leaning media would spare no effort in selling Schwarzenegger's version of events to saddle California Republicans with the political liabilities success-fully sloughed off by the governor, while they are still reeling in disarray from the loss of their so-called leader.

In Schwarzenegger's action movies, he often left his opponents bloodied and burned. It is not difficult to imagine that California Republicans will soon be wondering if Arnold is planning to leave them the same way.

As I am neither Californian nor Republican, this scenario troubles me not. And since Republicans have been chasing the myth of the electable moderate for most of my adult life, it wouldn't surprise me either, although I do marvel at those who managed to forget the Machiavellian history of elected Austrian imports. Beware of Greeks bearing gifts and Austrians running for office. In conclusion, I offer the following words, written in September 2003—I see no need to revise them now:

> *Schwarzenegger, far from representing the salvation of California's Republi-can Party, stands for its complete immolation.... Pragmatism in politics is self-defeating in the long run. It is a euphemism for the slow sacrifice of one's*

principles. The constant substitution of "electable" moderates for principled conservatives is what repeatedly kills the Republican Party and prevents it from ever realizing even a small part of its platform when it is in power.

The anti-American president

December 19, 2005

S EPTEMBER 11 CHANGED EVERYTHING has been the mantra of
the strong government conservative, the pragmatic dialectoids who
are flexible enough to justify any expansion of central government
power in the name of the very conservatism that opposes it. Since "we are
at war", Republican media whores have repeatedly claimed that because of
an attack that killed the same number of people who die on American roads
every 26 days, the following actions are therefore justified:

- An undeclared war of indefinite end against an undefined enemy.

- Invading two sovereign nations without a congressional declaration of
  war.

- The anti-American Patriot Acts I and II.

- The suspension of habeus corpus.

- Torture.

These acts have all been justified under the guise of imminent national
peril, despite the fact that the peril is so non-perilous that it has not been
deemed necessary to expel foreign nationals, let alone enforce the wide-open
national borders or existing immigration laws. If federal agents were to begin
shooting innocent and unarmed civilians on the street, would that too be
justified?

Unfortunately, we already received the answer to that question in Miami
last week when federal agents murdered Rigoberto Alpizar, with the post-
facto support of the White House.

The frustrating truth is, no matter what happens, Three Monkey Republicans around the country will nod their heads and intone mindlessly: "It

was necessary, it was unfortunate, it was an accident." They will cling to the official story no matter how absurd or overtly biased—if an air marshal heard a bomb threat, then a bomb threat there must have been, even if none of the dozens of other witnesses will corroborate the claim. At this point, it's not hard to imagine supporters of the administration defending an executive order sending B-2 bombers to carpet-bomb the Cotton Bowl. In this, they echo the Clintonistas in their unthinking and furious defenses of all acts Clintonian.

America was founded on the principle that it is right to sacrifice blood for liberty. It is telling that the Bush defenders make precisely the opposite argument, that it is right to sacrifice liberty in order to avoid the shedding of American blood. In this they are, like the Dear Leader, avowedly anti-American.

That George Bush is in open and repeated violation of his oath to uphold and defend the Constitution is no longer debatable. In keeping with his many anti-constitutional actions, he has publicly declared that he has no way of knowing what is, and what is not constitutional.

This attitude, while hardly unique in Washington, should be absolutely anathema to every American of all political stripes. And it appears that Americans are increasingly turning away from the president in rightful disgust. A recent poll here on WorldNetDaily showed that 45 percent of WND readers—who tend to lean strongly Republican—believe that George Bush deserves to be impeached.

I find it interesting to note that a 2003 Elliott Wave report predicted that if George Bush was re-elected, his second term would likely follow the pattern of Richard Nixon's. Given the recent reports of George Bush's personal authorization of domestic spying and more revelations yet to come, this seems entirely possible. After all, Richard Nixon merely spied on his political opponents, while George Bush is spying on the American people.

For this and other crimes against the American people and their Constitution, George Bush must resign. Failing that, he should be impeached.

I have little doubt that this column will infuriate many Republicans and conservatives, millions of whom twice voted enthusiastically for George Bush. It is always painful to realize that one has been betrayed, and even more painful to discover that one has been made a willing accomplice in the destruction of that which one cherishes. You can continue to believe that

George Bush is a patriotic American, though he is not. You can dismiss me as a liberal, a left-winger or a lunatic, though I am not.

But as you do so, try to keep in mind that railing against the messenger does not make the message any less valid.

Empire and unexpected consequences

December 26, 2005

Men do not rest content with parrying the attacks of a superior, but often strike the first blow to prevent the attack being made. And we cannot fix the exact point at which our empire shall stop; we have reached a position in which we must not be content with retaining but must scheme to extend it, for, if we cease to rule others, we are in danger of being ruled ourselves. Nor can you look at inaction from the same point of view as others, unless you are prepared to change your habits and make them like theirs.

—Alcibiades before the Athenian Assembly, 416 B.C.

IT IS WRITTEN that there is nothing new under the sun. Some 2,421 years ago, a politician convinced a powerful democracy that in order to defend itself from an enemy that had attacked it, it was necessary to attack an enemy that had not attacked it. In the event that the analogy I am drawing here is not immediately apparent to the reader, the relevant comparisons are Athens to America, al Qaida plus Saudi Arabia plus Iran to Sparta, and Iraq to Syracuse.

Like Alcibiades before him, George Bush has staked his entire strategy on the idea that Sunni, Shiite and Kurdish Iraqis are all burning to breathe free, assuming that breathing free is equivalent to a strictly limited democracy subject to constitutional power-sharing enforced by foreign arms. That the current situation is vastly preferable to living under a murderous dictatorship is undeniable, however, this is not to say that any of the so-called Iraqis who identify with one of the three major factions—or others, such as the various nomadic tribes and so forth—will be content with the new order established by America and her willing coalition.

For ingratitude tends to be the order of the day when it comes to geopolitics. Neoconservatives dreaming of a grateful Iraqi people would do well to heed the words of Felix Furst zu Schwarzenberg, subsequent to receiving Russian aid in putting down a Hungarian rebellion: "Austria will astound the world with the magnitude of her ingratitude."

Unfortunately, the force of sweet reason is not always as great as we heirs of the Enlightenment might like to believe. Alcibiades subsequent words sound eerily familiar—one can easily discern an expectation of the sort of purple fingerism to which the supporters of the administration's global democratic revolution ascribe such significance.

> *[Don't] rescind your resolution to sail to Sicily, on the ground that you would be going to attack a great power. The cities in Sicily are peopled by motley rabbles, and easily change their institutions and adopt new ones in their stead…*

But institutions are seldom changed so easily as those who would change them like to believe. And democracy is one of the most short-lived and notoriously mutable political systems of all, which is why the administration has worked so hard to fetter it in Iraq. Being susceptible to demagogues, dependent upon the ever-changing emotions of the majority and inherently unstable, the true test of the administration's success is not the body count suggested by the secretary of defense, nor the various events and elections hailed by so many neoconservative writers, but how long it survives the departure of American troops.

The occupation and nation-building cannot continue much longer. Never popular with the American people, it will become increasingly unpopular as the administration's mendacity and fundamental unsoundness become more apparent with each new revelation of its misdeeds; it is striking how the administration's attempts to explain the previous revelation are invariably dishonest and lead, inevitably, to the next exposure of its deceit.

Given these ongoing revelations, it is considerably illuminating to read the words of Victor Davis Hanson, ironically, a supporter of both the Iraqi occupation and the Global Struggle Against Violent Extremism, in his excellent new history of the Peloponnesian War, *A War Like No Other*:

> *A central theme [of Thucydides' narrative] is the use and abuse of power, and how it lurks behind men's professions of idealism and purported ideology. What men say, the speeches diplomats give, the reasons states go to war, all*

this "in word" (logos) is as likely to cloak rather than to elucidate what they will do "in deed" (ergon). Thucydides teaches us to embrace skepticism, expecting to look to rational self-interest, not publicized grievances, when wars of our own age inevitably break out.

Skepticism, I submit, is the very least that is merited by what passes for American leadership today. Especially when one recalls that only 10 years after Athenian forces embarked for Syracuse, a young Syracusan democracy collapsed into tyranny. A year later, defeated, weakened and impoverished, once-mighty Athens herself fell to Sparta.

Appendix A: Unabomber

Unabomber misses how technology aids freedom

St. Paul Pioneer Press
October 4, 1995

While the *Washington Post*'s publication of the Unabomber's treatise, "Industrial Society and its Future," has attracted much attention and commentary, it is unfortunate that most of the discussion has revolved around the question of publication rather than the manifesto itself.

The publication issue is not only of little interest to anyone outside the newsrooms, but also will resolve itself soon, as Unabomber imitators will either begin to crawl out from under their rocks, or they will not.

But the treatise is not worthy of attention so much for the macabre means through which it reached the mainstream media as for the concepts it contains. The Unabomber's discussion of modern leftist psychology is not only thought-provoking but insightful, while his indictment of the evils brought about by industrial society carry more weight than the critiques put forth by latter-day Marxists. Nevertheless, when it comes to the issue of technology and human freedom, the Unabomber goes astray.

The manifesto traces many of the psycho-social problems of modern society to the Industrial Revolution. Since technology has made it unnecessary or impossible for humans to support themselves independently, it prevents them from exercising the natural Power Process of goal setting and attainment. (The "Power Process" is a concept that psychologists say is necessary for human mental health; it is the natural need of humans to exert some degree of control over their own destiny.) This inability to exercise the Power Process leads inevitably to the loss of dignity and human autonomy. The central point of the treatise thus revolves around the inherent conflict between technological development and individual freedom.

The Unabomber sees the seductive nature of technology as a more powerful social force than the aspiration for freedom. While each new technology appears desirable by itself, the totality of societal-technological advance slowly envelops us, whether we actively choose to accept it or not. As we become dependent on the new technologies, government steps in and regulates access to them, removing even limited opportunity to exercise the Power Process and eventually resulting in the reduction of human beings to engineered products and mere cogs in the social machine.

What this theory ignores is that technology is a double-edged sword. Far from being the inevitable tool of government repression, technology has historically shown itself to be a primary force in providing freedom and power to the people. The monopolistic power of the medieval Catholic Church could not have been broken without the printing press, just as the omnipresent television cameras recently helped Boris Yeltsin and the infant Russian democracy movement survive the last reaction of the Soviet hardliners.

Governments and other would-be oppressors may use technology, but they are also afraid of it in the people's hands. Witness our own government's fear of high-level encryption software and its tawdry attempts to force the Clipper encryption chip on us. The Clipper chip would have allowed the FBI and other government agencies to read any data supposedly encrypted by the public. God forbid that we should send e-mail without the FBI being able to read it!

And the Chinese government has a tiger by the tail as it learns how difficult it is to allow free technological development and still keep the masses under control. The point is that technology can be a force for freedom as well as a weapon against it.

To prevent us from being turned into cogs in the techno-industrial machine, the Unabomber's manifesto prescribes a return to a more natural state where our time would be spent exercising the Power Process by surviving via primitive methods, so we would no longer need to find surrogate means of exercising the Process. By "surrogate means," he meant art, science, sports and anything not immediately related to survival. One wonders where the dignity and autonomy are to be found in the primitive life that Hobbes once characterized as nasty, brutish and short.

This regressive longing for a return to the natural state is nothing new. At the very least it echoes back 200 years to Rousseau. But human nature is very much a part of nature too, and like the Left he disdains, the Unabomber argues his way into the totalitarian corner of making choices for people in order to preserve their freedom to choose. George Orwell would have been proud.

But truly autonomous freedom, the freedom to choose and to exercise the Power Process also means the freedom to choose poorly. If Americans are working harder and longer than before, it is not because technology forces them to do so, but because many of us have decided to work more in order to pursue the larger TV, the BMW or the second home. These decisions to pursue things we do not need may well be foolish, but they are not the Unabomber's to make. They are ours.

Appendix B: Counterpoint

Empowering the people means allowing them to carry guns

Minneapolis Star Tribune

Tourists gunned down in Florida. Train commuters blown away by an embittered madman in Long Island. And before the Brady Bill even takes effect, calls go out for another dose of the statists' favorite panacea: gun control. No one would be so foolish as to deny that violent crime is a terrible problem in this country. But to try solve this problem by attempting to remove firearms from the general populace opens the door to a deeper and far more deadly evil.

It is easy to forget that our country was founded by men who were deeply distrustful of central governments, and that the Second Amendment's purpose was to ensure that the people would have the means to defend themselves against a central government. Advocates of gun control should remember that the men who penned the Constitution had very recently been engaged in armed rebellion against their own government.

Keep in mind too that centralized government has been the greatest malevolent force of this century. Recently, Professor Rudolph J. Rummel at University of Hawaii published research analyzing lethal violence committed in the 20th century. By 1985, governments around the world had deliberately murdered 119,394,000 of their own citizens. Contrast with this the 35,654,000 slain in the many international and civil wars during the same period. (Note that the former number does not include the latter.) But that can't happen here, you protest. Not in a democracy! Then perhaps you should remember that one of the most well-educated and enlightened peoples in Europe voted the National Socialists into power in 1933. Totalitarians seldom advertise their intentions, and it is not always easy to see the iron fist inside the velvet glove, or the grinning skull behind the smiling face.

I find it horrifying that such totalitarian measures as "assault-rifle bans" and "stop-and-frisks" are now being proposed in legislation as newspapers like the Star Tribune watch and applaud. The idea that the widespread availability of firearms causes violent crime would be laughable—if only so many people did not take it seriously. Guns have been widely available since the foundation of the republic, but the rampant increase in violent crime has taken place in the last 25 years. One example of where the "guns equal crime" theory breaks down is the nation of Switzerland. Every Swiss household containing an adult male is required to possess an automatic assault rifle, yet violent crime is not a problem there.

Clearly we must look elsewhere to determine the cause of violence in America. My money is on the entertainment industry. Hollywood mandarins assert that millions of viewers' lives will be saved by the example of some macho star buckling his seat belt or strapping on a condom and yet somehow remain untouched by watching said macho star massacring dozens of men and women. Of course the images are not real, but the negative influence is there. As a member of a popular rock band, I've discovered that entertainment can make a mighty impact on people.

Robert Heinlein once pointed out that a well-armed society is also a polite society. Such a society is also very difficult to rule over in totalitarian fashion. If you would empower the people, then arm them all. Twenty-three people would not have been shot on that Long Island train had even one armed citizen been present.

But I rather doubt our so-called leaders really want a citizenry that is not helplessly dependent on the protection of the state. Instead, in the expansion of centralized power at the expense of individual liberty, in the growing calls for the disarming of the people, I see the crimson spectre of Mankind's most insidious evil rising again. I can only hope I am wrong.

closing time

CASTALIA HOUSE

Non-Fiction

Clio & Me: An Intellectual Autobiography by Martin van Creveld
Equality: The Impossible Quest by Martin van Creveld
A History of Strategy: From Sun Tzu to William S. Lind by Martin van Creveld
4th Generation Warfare Handbook by William S. Lind and Gregory A. Thiele
Do We Need God To Be Good? by C.R. Hallpike
Appendix N: A Literary History of Dungeons & Dragons by Jeffro Johnson
The Nine Laws by Ivan Throne
MAGA Mindset: Making YOU and America Great Again by Mike Cernovich
Compost Everything: Extreme Composting by David the Good
Grow or Die: Survival Gardening by David the Good
Push the Zone: Growing Tropical Plants Beyond the Tropics by David the Good
Astronomy and Astrophysics by Dr. Sarah Salviander

Fiction

An Equation of Almost Infinite Complexity by J. Mulrooney
Brings the Lightning by Peter Grant
Loki's Child by Fenris Wulf
Six Expressions of Death by Mojo Mori
The Missionaries by Owen Stanley

Military Science Fiction

The Eden Plague by David VanDyke
Reaper's Run by David VanDyke
Skull's Shadows by David VanDyke
There Will Be War Volumes I and II ed. Jerry Pournelle
Riding the Red Horse Volume 1 ed. Tom Kratman and Vox Day

Science Fiction

The End of the World as We Knew It by Nick Cole
CTRL-ALT REVOLT! by Nick Cole
Somewhither by John C. Wright
City Beyond Time by John C. Wright
Awake in the Night Land by John C. Wright
Back From the Dead by Rolf Nelson
Mutiny in Space by Rod Walker
Alien Game by Rod Walker
Victoria: A Novel of Fourth Generation War by Thomas Hobbes

Fantasy

Iron Chamber of Memory by John C. Wright
The Green Knight's Squire by John C. Wright
The Book of Feasts & Seasons by John C. Wright